Also by Michael Stewart Foley

Confronting the War Machine:
Draft Resistance During the Vietnam War

Dear Dr. Spock: Letters About the Vietnam War
to America's Favorite Baby Doctor (editor)

Home Fronts: A Wartime American Reader (coeditor)

Witness Against Torture:
The Campaign to Shut Down Guantánamo (coeditor)

FRONT PORCH POLITICS

FRONT PORCH POLITICS

The Forgotten Heyday of American Activism
in the 1970s and 1980s

•

MICHAEL STEWART FOLEY

HILL AND WANG A division of Farrar, Straus and Giroux / New York

Hill and Wang
A division of Farrar, Straus and Giroux
18 West 18th Street, New York 10011

Library of Congress Cataloging-in-Publication Data

Foley, Michael S.
  Front porch politics : the forgotten heyday of American activism in the
1970s and 1980s / Michael Stewart Foley. — First edition.
    pages cm
  ISBN 978-0-8090-5482-4 (hardback)
  1. Political participation—United States—History—20th century.
2. Protest movements—United States—History—20th century. 3. Political
activists—United States—History—20th century. 4. United States—Social
conditions—1945- 5. United States—Economic conditions—1945-
6. United States—Politics and government—1945-1989. I. Title.

JK1764 .F65 2013
322.40973'09046—dc23
                                                          2013014769

Designed by Abby Kagan

Hill and Wang books may be purchased for educational, business, or promotional use.
For information on bulk purchases, please contact the Macmillan Corporate and
Premium Sales Department at 1-800-221-7945, extension 5442, or write to
specialmarkets@macmillan.com.

www.fsgbooks.com
www.twitter.com/fsgbooks • www.facebook.com/fsgbooks

1 3 5 7 9 10 8 6 4 2

Arts & Humanities
Research Council

For Kathy

The first duty of an American citizen, then, is that he shall work in politics; his second duty is that he shall do that work in a practical manner; and his third is that it shall be done in accord with the highest principles of honor and justice.

—**Theodore Roosevelt**

Contents

A photographic insert follows page 178.

FRONT PORCH POLITICS

Introduction: The Rise of Front Porch Politics in America

●

Maybe you have seen it on America's highways, a bumper sticker designed to prick your conscience: IF YOU'RE NOT OUTRAGED, YOU'RE NOT PAYING ATTENTION. A few years ago, that slogan most often appeared alongside an image of George W. Bush inside a circle with a line running through his face; these days, the face might be Barack Obama's. It is an amazingly versatile phrase, equally at home on bumpers sporting Tea Party or Occupy Wall Street slogans. Over the years, it has been marshaled in the service of many political causes, but it originated in the 1970s and 1980s, when Americans were notably outraged about a wide range of issues.

At the risk of overthinking mass-manufactured protest items, I begin with the bumper sticker because it expresses a very particular and personal kind of passion and anger over the state of the union. "You're not paying attention" means that you, individually, are ignoring things that *should* preoccupy, rankle, and motivate you. The driver in front of you hopes to leave you thinking about who you are as an American, what you expect from your country and fellow citizens, and what you are prepared to do to get it. The point is to shake you from your reckless complacency.

This book is an on-the-ground history of countless Americans who followed their concern, their anger, their outrage into the streets in the 1970s and 1980s. It is a history that has largely been buried under the many books that recount one or both of two now-tired tales about those years. In the first tale, the decades after the 1960s mark a national shift toward conservatism and the final undoing of the midcentury liberal consensus. This is, in most tellings, a story of a rout, of conservatism triumphant and liberalism vanquished, signaled by such events as President

Ronald Reagan's sacking of unionized air traffic controllers in 1981 or his landslide reelection in 1984.[1]

In the second tale, the 1970s and 1980s are understood as years of disengagement that saw a retreat from civic life of all kinds, whether political organizing, Parent Teacher Associations (PTAs), or bowling leagues.[2] Although these two story lines have been modestly revised in recent years, they continue to have a strong hold on the national memory.[3] Taken together, the prevailing interpretation of the 1970s and 1980s is that the great bulk of Americans, sometimes dubbed the "anxious class," experienced a crisis of civic membership. Beaten down by economic decline, failed by government, or burned out from years at the barricades of the "turbulent Sixties," they hunkered down, turned inward, and either retreated from politics or came out only to support politicians who promised to get government off their backs.[4] Free markets and individualism overcame ideals of community mobilization and activist government. By the 1990s, political participation, we are told, involved—for all but some—little more than writing checks and maybe going to the polls.

But these generalizations hold true only if we examine America in the 1970s and 1980s through a wide-angle lens, looking for trends primarily in the arena of national electoral politics. If we vary our scope—zoom in on the highly local, and pull back out to view the broader landscape—we see that Americans in fact experienced politics in multiple ways. On the one hand, most Americans followed national politics the way they did sporting events, consuming news accounts in print and on television and radio; the terms of debate were set by political and media elites. National political discourse, such as it existed, became grist for spectatorial conversation around the watercooler, at the dinner table, or after church. That version of politics may have been significant in determining the way a person voted for a congressional representative or president, and it may have guided citizens as they labeled themselves conservative, moderate, or liberal, Democrat, Republican, or Independent, but it did not often move Americans to sustained political activism.

In contrast, another kind of political experience proved much more likely to propel Americans into action. This is a politics that begins closer to home and, as the historian Robin Kelley once defined it, "comprises the many battles to roll back constraints and exercise some power over, or create some space within, the institutions and social relationships that dominate our lives."[5] Collectively, the grassroots campaigns chronicled in this book demolish the myth that Americans retreated from activism after the Sixties; they also demonstrate how little it matters whether Americans identify as conservative or liberal when the question before them is the safety and security of their families, their homes, and their dreams.

In approaching political questions, Americans in the 1970s and 1980s were often less motivated by predetermined ideological positions than by the promptings of their own experience. They relied not only on the rhetoric of freedom and equality, enduring staples of American political life, but also on a primal concern with *fairness*—particularly as it related to an individual, his family, her community.

This book reorients our approach to recent American history by recovering the perspective of what I call "front porch politics." Rather than follow politics through elections and public opinion polls, the book explores what moved Americans to work in politics—to initiate and join political campaigns. As the dozens of fights chronicled here make clear, citizens' engagement originated at their front door—on their porch, stoop, or landing—where they could see one or more ominous forces encroaching. In many of the struggles recounted in this book, the front porch perspective is obvious: homeowners faced with burdensome taxes, unfair government decisions, or toxic waste; tenants crushed by high rents; farmers fighting off foreclosure. All of these Americans were moved to defend their home, hearth, and livelihood in circumstances where government had failed to do so. But I also use "front porch" as a metaphor to describe the politics of those—such as migrant farmworkers, squatters, or the homeless—who, in fact, had no front porch at all. For them, a home was a slice of the American dream they hoped one day to claim. And in other cases—for feminists, gays and lesbians, pro-family activists—the locus of struggle was actually within the home, behind the front porch. Here, too, politics was existential and emotional. The common denominator was an immediate sense of threat—from government, corporations, the law, or other citizens with opposing interests—that required something more than a vote. It required action.

The power of the front porch perspective became apparent to me not only through reading the sources, but also through my own experience as an organizer. At the same time that I was writing about the grassroots campaigns of the 1970s and 1980s, I was working on Witness Against Torture's campaign to shut down the U.S. military prison at Guantánamo

Bay and end torture. Although large numbers of Americans opposed the war in Iraq and the War on Terror's excesses—sometimes turning out for international days of protest by the millions—the antitorture movement rarely broadened beyond a small circle of lawyers, professional human rights activists, and little groups of grassroots campaigners like ours. Many Americans were disgusted by their government's endorsement of torture and indefinite detention, but the vast majority of them stayed home even as we staged one direct action after another. Therefore, at the same time that I was investigating how and why Americans had left their front porches for the streets in the 1970s and 1980s, I was puzzling over why Americans did not rise up and join the antitorture movement in any significant numbers. The missing ingredient, I concluded, was the front porch perception of threat. Unlike the accidental activists I write about in this book—who, through personal experience and perception of danger, felt that they had no choice but to start a host of protest movements—the American people could have no experience of the war crimes being committed at Guantánamo. Any potential threat posed by Guantánamo to their sense of themselves as Americans, to their sense of personal security, remained too distant for them to notice—or it was offset by the perceived threat of additional terrorist attacks. Either way, for most Americans, Guantánamo was not their problem.

In contrast, the front porch ethos that flourished in the 1970s and 1980s relied on self-help. The disastrous war in Vietnam, urban unrest, economic stagnation, and the Watergate scandal led Americans to think that government, at all levels, was failing to offer remedies or effective leadership on the issues that mattered most. As economic conditions deteriorated and life became tougher and less predictable, government seemed unable to solve a host of crises, either because it was incompetent or because it was itself the source of the crises.

The main mistake scholars have made in evaluating this period has been to conflate a rising skepticism of government with the rise of the right. The right may have benefited electorally, but when Americans mobilized, they did so because they were searching for solutions—and often they looked to government itself to provide those solutions.

Indeed, from the perspective of the American front porch, there really never was a rise of the right. Americans may have increasingly identified with candidates who seemed to share their frustrations with government's failings, but they did so not out of partisan ideological convictions so much as practical ones. In fact, political scientists have shown that although Americans began more frequently labeling themselves as either "conservative" or "liberal" in the 1980s (primarily in response to the national punditocracy's frequent use of such terms), they did so in spite of "a lack of attitudinal change" on the pressing political, social, and cultural issues of the time.[6] The GOP racked up a string of national electoral victories during this period, and succeeded in introducing conservative approaches to economic and social policy; however, most of the core problems Americans faced in their homes and in their communities persisted, and sparked public responses. As this book shows, grassroots activism across the political spectrum was as robust in the 1980s as in the 1970s. Life in the Reagan era remained tough and unpredictable. One could even make the case that Ronald Reagan's first term as president was most notable for the rise of community service organizations dedicated to helping Americans of all kinds—families in farm country, urban groups in the midst of the AIDS epidemic, suburbanites living on toxic waste dumps—weather the hardest hard times since the Depression.

Clinging to the rise-of-the-right narrative obscures what mattered to most Americans: addressing the central issues—economic, legal, environmental, medical, cultural—affecting them and their families. Americans sometimes mobilized to defend what they saw as hard-won ways of life—as when suburban homeowners or family farmers or workers displaced by a factory shutdown saw their American dream lost or threatened. Other times, they mobilized around a visceral commitment to fairness and civil liberties, as in women's rights and gay rights campaigns, where "the personal is political" (a phrase first coined by feminists) became the foundation for activism. Sometimes, protecting one's family from environmental damage (as in mobilizations against toxic waste and nuclear power plants) or from other Americans (such as the pro-family movement mobilizing against feminists and gay rights advocates) drove grassroots campaigns. At still other times, battles raged against being marginalized or discarded, as in the case of tenants, the homeless, and people with AIDS.[7] The front porch perspective, the perception of crisis fueling an emotional response, and the primacy of practical solutions are what tied all of these disparate campaigns together.[8]

The expectation that government could and should provide remedies did not recede all at once or completely. When confronted with a crisis, individuals and groups reached for any tool at hand, including government, or at least some government mechanism (regulation, legislation, court ruling), to right perceived wrongs. That is, even as Americans became palpably disenchanted with government, seeing deceit and incompetence where once they saw expertise serving the public interest, many still regarded government as the unique or sole protector of notions of the common good against caprice or organized threat. The stories told here show time and again that the usual generalizations of our Sunday morning talk shows—conservatives want less government, liberals want more—hide a much more complicated reality of American ambivalence toward government.[9]

A budget crisis brought on by economic stagnation leads your city to close your local firehouse: What do you do? Think about whom to vote for, or grab your neighbors and organize a campaign to save the firehouse? You realize your dream of home ownership in a sylvan neighborhood, only to find out that it is built on a toxic waste dump: What do you do? Write a letter? Okay, but you almost certainly follow the letter with action. You buy a house in a suburban neighborhood with good schools, only to have a judge order your kids sent to an inner-city school as a way of compelling equality of education. Or you see your kids finally getting a crack at an equal education thanks to that court order, only to see a grassroots campaign try to undermine it. What are you prepared to do for your children? You are a factory worker in a company town that the company announces it will abandon; maybe your father worked there, too, and you raised your family in this community, but now it faces a death sentence: What choice do you have but to fight the shutdown? Or you face persistent discrimination because of your sex or sexuality: Do you stand in the shadow of the civil rights movement and do nothing? Or, as a Christian traditionalist, you see the family under assault by feminists and gays and lesbians who want to teach in the public schools, keep abortion legal, and let kids with AIDS sit in the same classroom with your children. Maybe you call your congressman or city councillor. But then what?[10]

In such conditions, a great many Americans felt that they could not count on their elected representatives or anyone else to solve these problems for them, even as they often appealed for government intervention. Not only had Americans' faith in government collapsed, but so, too, had national confidence in business, trade unions, the media, higher education, lawyers, doctors, and pretty much any other institution or supposed authority.[11]

Coming out of the "long 1960s," a period marked by powerful social movements, the United States had effectively become a nation of activists-in-waiting. Americans of all political views had absorbed the lessons of Sixties movements, breathing in the language and tactics of politics and activism even if they had not participated in those movements. In the same way that an adult with little interest in baseball somehow understands the basic rules of the game thanks to years of indirect exposure, Americans with little or no activist experience or training were, in the 1970s and 1980s, just as likely to mobilize and organize as any Sixties veteran. Indeed, as this book shows, in many ways the 1970s and 1980s turned out to be more like the "Sixties" than were the 1960s themselves.

The American front porch perspective and culture of self-reliance should not be mistaken for selfish individualism, an engagement not truly civic, or a politically sophisticated version of that old saw, the "Me Decade." Nor should it be equated only with NIMBYism (for Not in My Back Yard), a term that first came into use (and abuse) in the 1970s and 1980s, describing, in most cases, local opposition to hosting toxic waste incinerators, low-income housing, or other perceived threats to a neighborhood.[12] In fact, this book reveals how the self-reliance impulse almost always turned into an activism defined by collective reliance that often went beyond the most parochial concerns. Even if you at first sensed danger in isolation, the first steps off your front porch led to others who, like neighbors gathered on a street corner in the event of fire, took stock of where they were and made a plan to act. "To be encouraged to surmount rigid cultural inheritances and to act with autonomy and self-confidence, individual people need the psychological support of other people," the historian Lawrence Goodwyn once wrote of the Populists in the 1890s. "The people need to 'see themselves' experimenting in new democratic forms."[13] The same could be said of nearly every activist described in this book, regardless of the issue they were concerned with or whether they called themselves conservative or liberal. Americans increasingly came to see themselves experimenting in grassroots organizing, an old democratic form but one that seemed, in the wake of the Sixties, newly available to everyone and, amid the widely held perception of a damaged American dream, newly necessary.

Although historians seem to have mostly neglected the front porch experience, scholars and activists in the 1980s knew well the importance of self-reliance and adherence to the community ideal.[14] Important research on neighborhood organizing, in particular, appeared at the time, and the still-influential *Habits of the Heart*, a study of American values by a team of sociologists led by Robert Bellah, noted the importance of communitarian commitments to Americans. Bellah and his team found that most Americans defined happiness not only by success at work but through service to their community, and many looked on the public-spiritedness of the small town "not only as an ideal but as a solution to our present political difficulties." Although the long hours of labor and commuting required to pursue professional success were difficult to balance with the "kind of concern required to gain the joys of community and public involvement," Bellah wrote, Americans still sought those joys. Of course, it is easier to do so when one's way of life is under threat and self-interest and community service intersect.[15]

If we have often missed the full extent of grassroots politics in the 1970s and 1980s, it may be due to a certain skepticism about its motives and consequences. As group demands for freedom, equality, and justice escalated, Bellah and colleagues noted in 1980, they were "not readily accepted as matters of justice. They began to be treated instead as simply competing wants."[16] And just as it is easy to caricature committed activists as parochial Not in My Back Yard agitators, so, too, is it easy to mistake relatively spontaneous grassroots movements for the more organized, ideologically inflected efforts that followed. As varied battles stretched into the 1980s, more prominent ideologues, particularly on the right, saw the power of framing national causes in front porch terms. Leaders in the STOP ERA and tax revolt campaigns, for example, successfully "front-porched" their respective issues by emphasizing the acute threat that equal rights for women or property taxes (and, by extension, too much government) posed to the American household. These appeals were often successful, in large part because the front porch ethos and the defensive stand it prompted came naturally in a time of social stress.

Without a proper accounting of the era's grassroots politics, we have misunderstood the 1970s and 1980s, the seedbed for our own times. By seeing modern American political history almost exclusively in terms of right and left, liberals and conservatives, red states and blue states, scholars have failed to fully appreciate how Americans experienced life and politics in a time of rampant conflict in the 1970s and 1980s.[17] The starting point for this book is the premise that electoral politics, particularly as interpreted by pundits and journalists and party operatives, is explained in a language that is spoken *at* Americans, telling them who they are and what they think, without dovetailing with what is actually happening in their lives. Of course, my emphasis on front porch political mobilizations is not intended to diminish the importance of electoral politics or large-scale social structures. Indeed, despite some significant victories, the accidental activists who mobilized around front porch issues often could not overcome the larger structural forces at work in the nation's political economy: campaigns to save jobs, farms, and homes usually came up short, not because they were defeated by organized opposition but because they could not hold back the tide of capital—aided by both Republicans and Democrats in Washington—chasing low-cost labor around the world, importing cheap agricultural produce, and fueling suburbanization or urban gentrification. Many of these activists were beaten before they started, but that is obvious to us only now.[18] At the time, a faith in citizen action still animated the American body politic, and from the front porch perspective, Americans believed they could organize in pursuit of a fair and reasonable solution to their problems—and win.

By the 1990s, the limits of that front porch political model were becoming evident. It seemed increasingly obvious that front porch politics did not always work. This book records a number of modest victories, but there are plenty of defeats, too. For all their practicality, front porch activists were also driven by emotion and did not want partial accomplishments or solutions, but that was usually the best they could get. As a result, the front porch political ethos reached a point of exhaustion in the century's last decade. Despite occasional flare-ups of political mobilization, recent years have seen a political landscape in which faith in both government and front porch politics is weak. Instead, as recent studies show, we tend to see political issues through rigid, ideologically informed worldviews and to let them be fought over by surrogate talking heads on twenty-four-hour news channels.[19] With some notable exceptions, the front porch impulse to mobilize has largely faded even as Americans feel beset by tough and unpredictable circumstances all over again.

PART 1

Laying the Foundation

• • • • • • • • • • • • • • • • • • • •

To recover the early 1970s is to recover a time of fear. If the 1960s arrived accompanied by the youthful optimism of John F. Kennedy's America, the 1970s dawned with anxiety and dread, Vietnam and Attica. In the early 1970s, many Americans awoke to find that the economy had begun to falter, with unemployment and inflation rising sharply. Meanwhile, race relations seemed to be dominated by militants and a government bent on repressing them, and the Vietnam War ground on and continued to tear the country apart; in response, both the government and small numbers of committed activists had turned the country into a battlefield. "Middle America" looked on in shock.

This surge in violence from Vietnam to the United States coincided with a rise in terrorism around the world. By the time Palestinian terrorists attacked Israeli athletes at the Munich Summer Olympics in 1972, the enduring image of the masked terrorist standing on a balcony in the Olympic Village looked familiar to most Americans. Indeed, when a botched rescue attempt by German authorities left both terrorists and hostages dead at an airfield days later, the scene resembled the aftermath of a recent American prison riot. The American people had elected Richard Nixon president in part because he promised to restore law and order in America; instead, lawlessness and disorder only grew—even within the government itself.

It has become conventional wisdom to blame Americans' loss of faith in government on the Vietnam War and the Watergate scandal, but there is more to it than that. Certainly, a paranoid president and an active protest movement impressed on a majority of Americans an appropriate mistrust of their government; most Americans harbored little love for the antiwar movement, but they also did not tolerate governmental deceit and illegality. Add to that a growing perception of White House incompetence in economic matters (and, in fact, a growing sense that Americans were now at the mercy of corporate interests), and the widely held midcentury trust in government and experts washed away. In its place, Americans adopted a more primal concern with protecting themselves, their families, and their communities, and in the process they concluded that they had to count on themselves to effect change.

Indeed, the seeds of the self-reliant front porch politics perspective were scattered, in fact, by the right, by Nixon. If building the front porch politics perspective first required that Americans lose faith in their governing institutions, Nixon's catalog of sins provided it. More than that, the president weakened government's standing, too, when, in attacking welfare programs, he expressed his own thinly veiled antigovernment views. American alienation from government was both the intended and the unintended consequence of Nixon's actions.

Faced with a failure of leadership in government and business, and unable to count on a growing labor movement as Americans in the 1930s had, more and more people took matters into their own hands and joined a growing citizen movement. Confronted with cuts in public services, city dwellers mobilized along the lines first modeled by leading organizers and advocates such as Saul Alinsky and Ralph Nader. But for a nation of citizens losing faith in government, people sure had a funny way of showing it. In fact, as many of the struggles chronicled in this first section of the book show, activists of all kinds demonstrated deeply ambivalent attitudes about the role of government. Many of them—whether faced with a contraction in municipal services, a court's busing order, or a newly passed gay rights ordinance—protested the actions of federal or local authorities. Yet many of them also looked to government bodies or branches for remedies. As much as they disdained the officials making policies they found to be profoundly unfair, they looked to city councils, state legislatures, the courts, and Congress to erase the injustice. Sometimes they lobbied, other times they marched on City Hall, but in choosing strategies and tactics to effect change, Americans proved willing to use any available tool.

These first few chapters show that, regardless of the tactics chosen, more and more Americans—in cities, suburbs, and rural areas—laid the foundation on which the front porch political ethos was built, taking to community organizing because they felt they had no choice but to re-spond themselves to a host of perceived dangers. That impulse toward self-reliance arose as much from a fading faith in government as from a growing understanding that one's personal experience could be political. Americans therefore mobilized in defense of communities under siege in a new age of austerity, but also in defense of their children and families in new campaigns on nagging older questions of equality. In contests over saving city firehouses, court-ordered busing, women's health and physical safety, the Equal Rights Amendment, and homosexuals teach-ing in schools, Americans became activists because they experienced these issues personally. They stepped off their front porches into the streets because, on some level, they were *moved* to; they simply could not sit still when they felt so strongly about the politics in question.

1

This Is the Dawning of the Age of Self-Reliance

•

The volatile political and economic conditions of the 1970s profoundly affected the way ordinary Americans thought of themselves and their country. A great many felt betrayed and forgotten. The country they were raised to believe in as the land of opportunity seemed to have dissolved into the land of dead ends. Worse, there was no familiar remedy. The government, exposed by Watergate and other scandals as corrupt, seemed to pursue policies more out of political expediency than out of concern for the average man or woman. As business exerted new influence, and as American cities catered more to investors than their own residents, many Americans with no prior activist experience instinctively turned to community organizing and to consumer and public interest advocacy—if only to try to regain control over their lives. On the national level, it was a lost opportunity for the two major parties. As Michael Kazin noted, the political allegiance of the "upset and forgotten" workingman "seemed up for grabs" in the 1970s. A candidate or party sounding like the movie *Nashville*'s Hal Phillip Walker or like Ralph Nader might have been able to form a New Majority that would have made Richard Nixon envious. But maybe it was not possible. More important, maybe it did not matter so much. What mattered was that Americans now felt that they were on their own, pushed out of their midcentury comfort and confidence to a new, unsparing frontier. Looking across the plains of American experience from the vantage point of their own front porches, they could see a variety of social, political, cultural, and environmental threats encroaching from different directions. They reacted passionately—sometimes out of outrage, or fear, or despair—and channeled that passion into the only avenue for redress that seemed promising: grassroots organizing.

Much of what one expert called the "government versus the people" culture of the 1970s was cultivated by Richard Nixon's political operation. Certainly, Nixon's handling of the war, of protesters, and of political opponents betrayed the public trust. After 1968, most Americans wanted the Vietnam War just to end, and Nixon won the presidency in part by pledging "peace with honor." Instead, in his first year in office, he willfully deceived the public by creating the appearance of extricating the United States from Vietnam—via a policy of "Vietnamizing" (or de-Americanizing) the ground war and bringing GIs home—while secretly escalating the air war, expanding it beyond Vietnam into Cambodia. Not until the spring of 1970 did it emerge that American B-52s had dropped more than 108,000 tons of bombs on Cambodia over fourteen months, a campaign coordinated in the White House and with the knowledge of only a handful of National Security Council staff members, a few military commanders, and the pilots themselves. And then, of course, Nixon seemed to subvert his own carefully crafted de-escalation narrative by sending ground forces from South Vietnam into Cambodia. The nation erupted in fury, and not only on college campuses.

Just as important as Nixon's secrecy and deception—at least in terms of the public's trust in government—was the president's treatment of his critics. In the same way that candidate Nixon had made political hay out of disparaging protesters of all types during the 1968 campaign, President Nixon wasted no time attacking anyone who dared to challenge his war policies, either by ridiculing them publicly or by spying on them illegally. As early as May 1969, when *The New York Times* reported that American planes were bombing targets in Cambodia, the White House used both the FBI and its own private surveillance team—the first "plumbers" hired to plug leaks—to place illegal wiretaps on the telephones of National Security Council staffers and several journalists. Five months later, following the October 15, 1969, Moratorium protest, when millions of Americans in at least two hundred cities across the country skipped work and school to participate in a wide variety of demonstrations against the war, Nixon famously dismissed them as a "vocal minority" whom he would ignore. Calling instead for "the great silent majority" of Americans to support his plans for winning the peace, the president questioned the patriotism of the Moratorium participants. "North Vietnam cannot defeat or humiliate the United States," he said. "Only Americans can do that."[1] And in the wake of the Cambodian invasion, when a student strike spread to hundreds of colleges and universities across the country, Nixon again denounced the protesters, saying that even if he ended the war, these campus "bums" would find another issue to protest violently. Even after National Guard troops opened fire on unarmed Kent State University protesters, killing four and wounding fourteen, the White House blamed the protesters, sternly warning that "this should remind us all once again that when dissent turns to violence, it invites tragedy."[2]

In 1971, Nixon's assaults on the antiwar movement escalated. After a cascade of rallies and peaceful demonstrations brought hundreds of thousands of protesters to Washington in late April, the White House mobilized a joint military and D.C. police response to organizers' threat to block streets and bridges all over Washington and prevent government employees from getting to work.

As the sun came up on May 3, 1971, military jeeps and other transports swarmed through Washington, tear gas greeted protesters and residents alike, and six Chinook helicopters landed on the Washington Monument grounds, dispatching 198 soldiers in what looked like a massive search and destroy mission. By 8:00 a.m., D.C. police had arrested two thousand protesters, and by noon they had rounded up seventy-five hundred. Police detained thousands in a fortified football field near RFK Stadium, where they "languished without benefit of arraignment." Such tactics may have been illegal, but they helped keep Washington from being shut down.[3] For mainstream America, however, the seemingly constant conflict grew tiring. The news never seemed good. The war labored on, and so did the division in the country.

Six weeks later, the leaking of the Pentagon Papers sparked another high-profile suppression of dissent. Officially known as the "History of U.S. Decision Making Process on Vietnam Policy," the forty-seven-volume "Top Secret" report had been commissioned by Defense Secretary Robert McNamara in 1967 and completed in January 1969, as the Johnson administration left office. One of the report's authors was Daniel Ellsberg, a former Marine and Pentagon staffer under McNamara and an ex-student of Henry Kissinger's. After the Cambodia invasion, he turned unequivocally against the war and made multiple copies of the report in hopes that he could convince certain congressional officials to hold hearings. When Ellsberg found little interest in Congress, he turned to the reporter Neil Sheehan and *The New York Times*, which began publishing revelatory excerpts beginning on June 13. Over the next couple of weeks, the public watched a back-and-forth battle between a Nixon administration that seemed determined to hide something and the press. The White House turned to the courts to try to stop the *Times* (and later other newspapers) from publishing the Pentagon Papers, but the Supreme Court, on June 30, ruled six to three against the president.

Although the Pentagon Papers did not cover a single day's history of Nixon's handling of the war, the administration's attempts to keep them secret only made many Americans think the president was continuing previous administrations' deception. In the wake of the spring protests and Pentagon Papers revelations, one June public opinion poll showed that 61 percent of Americans now regarded the war as a mistake, and in July, 65 percent wanted the administration to withdraw "even if the government of South Vietnam collapsed."[4] So much for a silent majority of supporters.

By the time Americans learned that Nixon had directed that "plumbers" be sent into Daniel Ellsberg's psychiatrist's office—to find any dirt they could on Ellsberg—the president had bigger problems.[5] The plumbers' arrest during the June 17, 1972, break-in at the Democratic National Headquarters in the Watergate Hotel and Office Complex in Washington began a process that ultimately ended Nixon's presidency. Not only did the Senate Watergate hearings (and the investigative journalism of *The Washington Post*'s Bob Woodward and Carl Bernstein) reveal the Committee to Re-Elect the President's campaign of dirty tricks aimed at political opponents, as well as the administration's illegal wiretapping of journalists and NSC staffers, but it made the president of the United States look, once again, as though he had something serious to hide. At the end of October 1973, following the "Saturday Night Massacre," when Nixon's order to fire Watergate special prosecutor Archibald Cox led the attorney general and his deputy to resign (only to see Cox fired, in any case, by Solicitor General Robert Bork), the president's approval rating had plummeted to 23 percent. He never recovered. On August 8, 1974, soon after subpoenaed Oval Office tapes revealed Nixon's participation in the Watergate cover-up—ordering obstruction of the FBI investigation of the burglary and discussing hush money payments to the burglars—he resigned.

In the aftermath of Nixon's fall from power, it became common to blame Watergate for the collapse of belief in government. Stanley Kutler, the dean of Watergate historians, writes that "Watergate transformed and reshaped American attitudes toward government, and especially the presidency, more than any single event since the Great Depression of the 1930s, when Americans looked to the President as a Moses to lead them out of the economic wilderness." When President Gerald Ford gave Nixon a full and complete pardon a month after his resignation, it "added a new element of cynicism."[6] Maybe so, but to view Watergate in isolation is to miss a much bigger picture. Watergate, like the proverbial tip of the iceberg, only hinted at the widespread abuse of power that permeated public "service" by the early 1970s.

Nixon's resignation was followed, in the public's consciousness, by wave after wave of revelations about the illegal spying on American citizens by the CIA, FBI, NSA, IRS, and local police in cities across the country. To civil rights and antiwar activists, the exposure of domestic spying proved what they had suspected all along. To most Americans, however, the truth was shocking. In the two years after Nixon's resignation, congressional investigations led by Senator Frank Church (D-ID) and Congressman Otis Pike (D-NY) revealed a long list of stunning CIA and NSA abuses, including opening hundreds of thousands of pieces of domestic mail since 1956, listening in on thousands of overseas phone calls, and acquiring copies of millions of international cables—to and from ordinary Americans, and all without court-authorized warrants.[7] The FBI was no better, but since it had previously enjoyed tremendous popularity in Middle America, news of its COINTELPRO (counterintelligence program) operations hit hard. COINTELPRO resonated with the public in large part because the FBI seemed to employ so many of the same tactics used against Ellsberg and the Democratic Party by the Nixon White House, but used them against American citizens in the civil rights, New Left, and antiwar movements. And particularly because the antiwar movement eventually attracted the participation of many Middle Americans, most Americans found COINTELPRO abhorrent. What most infuriated so many citizens was not only that the FBI had abused its public trust, but that six presidents had known about it. Thus, the Church and Pike Committees went beyond making the connections in the public's mind between Watergate and the FBI's abuses; Americans now knew that from Franklin Roosevelt to Richard Nixon, the FBI consistently forwarded political intelligence to the White House, and no president had ever asked the Bureau to stop.[8]

To make matters worse, a series of revelations also demonstrated that the abuse of power extended to police departments across the country. In particular, police "red squads," special police divisions that targeted political dissidents, had engaged in widespread illegal behavior. At the most extreme, COINTELPRO documents confirmed that the FBI's campaign against the Black Panther Party included facilitating the Chicago Police Department's assassination of the twenty-one-year-old party leader Fred Hampton in 1969.[9] Other newly exposed police misdeeds shocked Americans because they were evidently so routine. New York City police officers had files on 1.2 million people and 125,000 organizations, including on Mayor John Lindsay; Representatives Charles Rangel, Herman Badillo, and Shirley Chisholm; actor Dustin Hoffman; and women's rights activists Gloria Steinem and Betty Friedan—hardly threats to American national security; under pressure, the department cut the files back to 240,000 people and 25,000 organizations. A year later, in 1974, as Nixon's presidency collapsed under the weight of Watergate, the Chicago Police Department admitted that public pressure had led it to destroy files on 105,000 individuals and 1,300 organizations. In 1975, Los Angeles followed suit, planning to destroy more than 2 million files on 55,000 people dating back to the 1920s.[10]

The government's betrayal of the American people seemed to know no bounds. Americans saw deceit and illegal behavior at every level of government—from Nixon to the FBI to the local police force—and many suddenly found themselves feeling alienated from mainstream party politics.

Watergate, COINTELPRO, and the fall of Saigon in 1975 may have left Americans wondering what had happened to their country, but these high-profile news stories did not, on their own, affect most people's sense of personal security. It took their inability to pay the bills to do that. In the early 1970s, the two conditions—shocking news of abuse of (and disrespect for) authority and economic decline—existed side by side and sometimes intertwined. While intelligence agencies and red squads battled radicals, and an administration unraveled, and the Vietnam War came to an ignoble end, the economy—for a generation, a steady source of confidence—imploded. And a government that seemed no longer trustworthy appeared incapable of curing the nation's economic woes.

Prevailing Keynesian economic thinking suggested that unemployment and inflation would never rise simultaneously, but in the early 1970s they did, and a new phenomenon—"stagflation"—appeared. American production dropped, foreign competition swelled, companies laid off workers and closed or moved operations, and the prices of goods and services climbed and climbed.

All of this caught President Nixon and the nation off guard. Nixon had entered the White House in 1969 interested far more in foreign policy than in domestic issues or the economy and, like most Americans, he expected the economy to continue to thrive. In a Gallup poll taken shortly after his inauguration, 40 percent of Americans listed the war as the "most important problem facing the country," while only 9 percent identified it as inflation and the high cost of living.

But the country's economic picture turned much gloomier in 1970, and critics blamed Nixon. At first, the president responded by attributing the economic deterioration to his predecessors—the excesses of funding the war and Great Society programs—and tried to use his position as president to persuade industry to voluntarily curb prices while expressing confidence in the economy to the public. But just as Herbert Hoover found in the early years of the Great Depression, it did not work. Congress, in its own smoke-and-mirrors game, passed the Economic Stabilization Act of 1970, authorizing the president to freeze prices, rents, wages, and salaries—though, as the historian Melvin Small notes, it never expected a Republican president to use such power.[11] By the fall of 1971, only 25 percent of Americans answering the same Gallup poll question about the "most important problem facing the country" said the war; now, 45 percent said "economic problems."

Over time, the Nixon administration adopted a series of price and wage freezes that, despite their initial popularity, ultimately made the president look as though he was careening from one unsuccessful policy to another. It did not help that the terminology was confusing (Freeze II, for example, was also referred to as Phase IV), but mostly, Americans grew frustrated that nothing the president did seemed to stop prices from actually going up. *Time* reported that "in the first full week" of a sixty-day freeze on the price of everything except agricultural products (the main inflationary culprit at the time)—and in the same month in which White House counsel John Dean testified about Watergate before the Senate—"each costly ring of the check-out cash register seemed to eat away at public patience with the Administration far more than the revelations of the Watergate scandal."[12]

It only got worse as Nixon wrestled with responding to Egypt's and Syria's surprise attack on Israel during Yom Kippur. At first, Nixon held back, aware that openly aiding Israel would draw the ire of the Arab states on whom America relied so much for its oil. But when it became clear that without American aid, Israel might suffer complete destruction, the administration authorized a major airlift of war matériel that ultimately helped Israel prevail. As Nixon feared, America's support came with a heavy price. The Organization of Petroleum Exporting Countries (OPEC), dominated by Arab states, quickly announced an oil embargo against the United States, Japan, the Netherlands, and other Western European nations. The oil embargo immediately prompted panic buying across the country and, perhaps more directly than anything else, confronted anxious Americans with the grim realities of the nation's economic slide.

Nixon responded to the embargo in ways that may have made sense but that, to the American people, seemed like a Band-Aid approach. He ordered that thermostats be lowered to 68 degrees and speed limits to 55 miles per hour, that air travel be cut 10 percent, and that gas stations close on Sundays. In addition, he urged Americans to limit ornamental lighting for their homes during the upcoming holiday season and to use minimal lighting in commercial businesses. In spite of all of this, the image of huge lines forming at gas stations all over the country—with motorists sometimes waiting hours to buy a half tank of gas—endured as a testament of America's weakened and vulnerable state. Only the American oil companies weathered the crisis well, with Exxon's profits increasing 59 percent, Texaco's 70 percent, and Mobil's 68 percent. This news deflected conspiracy theorists toward the oil companies, leading Senator Henry Jackson to question if the oil shortage was even real. "The American people want to know whether oil tankers are anchored offshore waiting for a price increase or available storage before they unload. The American people want to know whether major oil companies are sitting on shut-in wells and hoarding production in hidden tanks and at abandoned service stations. The American people want to know why oil companies are making soaring profits." In the end, OPEC lifted the embargo in April 1974 and the gas lines receded, but prices never recovered.[13]

Given the prevailing state of economic thinking, no president could have forestalled the slide, but that did not stop the public from expecting a competent response. According to one scholar, Nixon "tried and then discarded all the fashionable economic remedies of his time, unintentionally exposing the poverty of economic theory." As Herbert Stein, chairman of the Council of Economic Advisers, said years later, "our experience really confirmed how little economists know." Politically, however, this failure of economic theory mattered to the American people only insofar as they were coming to know their president not only as a crook but as a poor manager of the economy to boot.[14]

Nixon's successor, Gerald Ford, arrived in office with no magic wand with which to wave away the nation's economic woes. By the end of 1974, the unemployment rate had jumped from 5.4 percent in August, when Ford assumed the presidency, to 7 percent in December. Inflation stood at almost 14 percent and the Gross National Product (GNP) had fallen 9 percent. Not since the Great Depression had the economic indicators looked so grave. In January 1975, Ford proposed attacking the recession with a 12 percent tax cut for businesses and individuals on their 1974 income. Such a policy, the president thought, would put money in American pockets, increase the GNP, and put people back to work—though it ran the risk of generating higher inflation, too. The Democrats in Congress, operating with a significant majority thanks to the 1974 midterm elections that followed Nixon's resignation and pardon, countered by advocating New Deal–like government spending as a way to lift the nation out of the recession. But Ford balked, and over his two-and-a-half-year presidency, he vetoed sixty-six bills. In fact, in his 1976 State of the Union address, the president blamed government spending for bringing on the recession in the first place, though mostly he made it clear how much he disliked federal social programs.[15]

Even though unemployment and inflation dropped for a time in 1976, the term "gridlock" dominated public discourse; for much of the public, the veto battles between Congress and the president only further confirmed that they could no longer count on government. Already, citizens were organizing on a number of fronts—some more prominent than others—and battles raged between labor and management, consumers and big business, and neighborhood groups and city hall. In the immediate post-Sixties period, when activism supposedly took a holiday, a new era of economic and civic engagement was born.

• • •

If most activists of the 1970s and 1980s learned strategies and tactics from the civil rights movement, those in the emerging "citizen movement" also took inspiration from Ralph Nader, a kind of nerdy superhero in a rumpled suit. Although Nader became a much more controversial leader—arguably a presidential election spoiler—in later years, he first rose to prominence as a consumer advocate in 1965, when he published the muckraking book *Unsafe at Any Speed: The Designed-in Dangers of the American Automobile.* Indicting the entire auto industry for institutional malfeasance in manufacturing automobiles that endangered the public, the book, and public reaction to it, led Congress to pass both the National Traffic and Motor Vehicle Safety Act and the National Highway Safety Act. In the meantime, General Motors helped elevate Nader's status to folk hero proportions when the company hired private investigators to, as one GM handler was caught on tape instructing a detective to "get something on him . . . shut him up" and find out "who he is laying." Nader sued the corporate giant for invasion of privacy and settled out of court for $425,000 and a public apology—in embarrassing testimony before a Senate subcommittee—from GM president James Roche.[16]

Nader soon expanded his consumer advocacy by attracting hundreds of college interns each summer—dubbed "Nader's Raiders"—to investigate and uncover corporate irresponsibility, often prompting continued citizen organizing at the local level. Through the newly founded Center for the Study of Responsive Law (roughly modeled on the NAACP Legal Defense Fund), the Raiders then pressured government authorities to pass appropriate legislation. When the GM suit was settled, Nader used the proceeds to start a law firm, the Public Interest Research Group, expanding his mission beyond consumer advocacy to investigating anything that might damage the public interest. That meant that even the government that he expected to respond to his corporate exposés could also be the subject of investigations. Moreover, Nader effectively spread the Raiders concept nationwide when he moved to set up student PIRG chapters on college campuses all over the country to target local business and government.[17]

Perhaps because critics have usually directed their ire at Nader himself, the public interest advocate's image has always been—in spite of the publicity surrounding the Raiders—that of a lone crusading maverick.

But frequently, Nader and his colleagues would uncover a problem and, to their delight, see local organizations rise up spontaneously to tackle the issue. Following the passage of the Occupational Safety and Health Act, a health condition called "brown lung" (byssinosis)—caused by the breathing of cotton dust—became an issue thanks in part to Nader. Although the industry had been aware of brown lung since the 1940s, companies like J. P. Stevens had never warned their workers of the potential harm. When a North Carolina doctor working for the North Carolina Board of Health tried to study the illness in 1966, owners did not let him near their mills and later used their political influence to get him fired. In the 1970s, more than a hundred thousand current and retired textile workers suffered from brown lung, but as one woman said, the first time she learned about it was when she heard Ralph Nader describe it on television. Soon locals formed the Carolina Brown Lung Association to provide health screenings for workers and retirees while also lobbying the state legislature for workplace legislation that would reduce dust levels.[18]

Grassroots consumer organizations—often inspired by Nader's Raiders, but operating independently—likewise agitated at the state and local levels nationwide. The groups turned their attention not on how Americans worked but on how they shopped. "There is a quiet revolt in this country," Utah senator Frank Moss noted at the time. "It is a revolt of people who are not violent, but who are angry—at incredibly shrinking packages and expanding prices and preposterous advertising. We in Congress, and they in the administration, ignore this revolt at our peril." When President Nixon instituted his Phase III price controls and meat prices soared, consumers organized a nationwide boycott. Groups such as Operation Pocketbook, Fight Inflation Together, and Housewives Expect Lower Prices (HELP) launched their own price controls through a one-week nationwide meat boycott in which 25 percent of American consumers participated; prices on meat dropped 80 percent.[19] The boycott, wrote a *New York Times* reporter, "is made up mainly of groups of tenants in apartment buildings, neighbors who shop at the same markets in small towns, block associations, and—perhaps most typical—groups of women who meet every morning over coffee." Conveying the grassroots nature of the boycott, one historian notes that "more than 500,000 consumers from New York, New Jersey, Connecticut, and Pennsylvania sent cash register tapes to President Nixon." Nixon responded with price caps, but more important, such grassroots power led state governments to establish offices of consumer protection and public advocacy agencies to handle consumer complaints. This was a hint of things to come.[20]

In 1974, *U.S. News & World Report* named Ralph Nader the fourth most influential person in the country. And the vast proliferation of public interest groups his work spawned guaranteed what one expert called "an expansion in the scope of political conflict." Nader called for an "initiatory democracy," in which the people could "initiate actions to make sure public officials were acting responsibly," he said. "I'm talking about rights plus remedies plus legal responsibilities so it can be a citizen versus the ICC or the FDA." In his view, "a civil servant should be forced to make the law work, and if he won't do it he should be censured or expelled from the Government." To Americans living in economically desperate communities, struggling to survive, it sounded like a winning formula.[21]

In fact, Nader and those he influenced were just one component of a complex nationwide phenomenon. In the 1970s, by one expert's estimate, some 20 million Americans got involved in some form of "citizen advocacy"—whether in unions, consumer activism, or community or neighborhood organizing. But this was no centralized movement. Advocacy groups sprang up in response to local conditions and evolved in response to both national trends and hometown idiosyncracies. This sometimes made the activism difficult for pundits to see, appearing, as it did to the national media, as a "crazy-quilt array of protests, without apparent themes in common."[22]

With elected officials seemingly overmatched by persistent economic decline, Americans began to organize, particularly at the local level. Such organizing would have been impossible, however, if not for the earlier example of the civil rights, peace, and women's movements, as well as earlier experiments in community organizing. Harry Boyte, an activist and one of the most insightful writers on the citizen movement—what he called the "backyard revolution"[23]—argues that the citizen revolt originated with "an old American practice of cooperative group action by ordinary citizens motivated both by civic idealism and by specific grievances." Like Nader, each group appealed to "some implicit popular conviction that there is a broad public good—a long term interest of the society as a whole which the contemporary generation is charged with guarding and preserving."[24]

American cities, in particular, seemed in need of such attention in the mid-1970s. Urban America had fallen into such disrepair that Travis Bickle's characterization of New York as "an open sewer" in *Taxi Driver* rang true to audiences everywhere. Like *Nashville* and *Network*, two other 1976 films offering astute commentaries on the national temper, director Martin Scorsese's *Taxi Driver* captures the desperate political mood afflicting America at the time.[25] For Americans living outside the nation's cities, Scorsese's depiction of a deranged vigilante may have confirmed a growing sentiment that fixing America's cities was hopeless in an era of government abandonment and social dislocation. By the mid-1970s, with American cities starved of revenue thanks to residents moving to the suburbs, industry following them out and beyond—to havens of cheap labor and lower taxes—and the dramatically increased cost of services, city dwellers could not count on government to help them unless, as Ralph Nader suggested, they took matters into their own hands. Whereas cities had once been sites of wonder and centers of commerce, one commentator noted, "financiers and federal officials" now saw cities "as mismanaged, overly generous, unwieldy bureaucratic messes which needed to be taught the lessons of fiscal responsibility." Banks thus began withholding funding until cities got their finances in order. City administrators were left alone to come up with solutions. Indirectly, poor and working-class residents were left to fend for themselves, too.[26]

By and large, city administrations initiated an array of measures designed to lure business and investment back, and in so doing telegraphed their willingness to cut back on services. During the recession, cities offered businesses massive tax breaks even though that cut some of the revenue that funded schools, police, fire, transportation, and sanitation. In the 1970s, urban "revitalization" focused on corporate development, tourism, and the drawing of entertainment attractions to newly built civic centers and arenas. The gentrification process, in which improvements drove up the prices of rental property—and drove out the poor and minorities (who were replaced by middle- and upper-class home buyers)—was aided significantly by a process called "redlining." Banks "redlined" whole neighborhoods in the 1960s and 1970s, freezing loans to working-class neighborhoods, which sent those neighborhoods into decline and thus precipitated the suspension of city services. In 1976, Roger Starr, the New York City housing and development administrator, actually proposed closing schools and police and fire stations in "slum areas" as a way to speed up "population decline." To do so would not only cut costs, but clear the way for new investment. But as one community organizer later commented, "faced with an eroding tax base, local governments initiated service cutbacks that detrimentally affected disparate elements in the urban core and made them ripe for organizing." City residents prepared to fight.[27]

In 1975, as New York City faced bankruptcy and saw its appeals for federal help go unanswered, only a combination of creative borrowing from municipal union pension funds and service cuts finally earned some short-term loans from Washington and kept the city afloat. Although the city averted a possible revolution in its streets, the results of these drastic measures, one observer wrote, "could be seen on every street and in every institution of working-class New York."[28]

The wealthy streets, naturally, did not have it as bad as the working-class and impoverished streets. People of means could afford private schools, colleges, and hospitals and transit fare hikes (or cars), and they were less likely to see a firehouse closed in their neighborhood. The vast majority of New Yorkers, however, could claim no such immunity from the city's deteriorating physical and psychological state. Many of them promptly gathered together, with no help from activists or outsiders, into neighborhood and community groups to launch rearguard campaigns—"holding actions" in one scholar's words—to get those in power to act on their behalf, regardless of what investors thought.[29]

Thanks to the flight of industry, population decline fueled by suburbanization, and redlining, huge swaths of New York fell into disrepair. Many landlords, unable to attract enough tenants and facing mounting costs, simply abandoned their buildings. In the mid-1970s, the city estimated the abandonment rate at twenty thousand to sixty thousand housing units a year. City banks all but stopped lending money to landlords and building owners in more and more city neighborhoods, and, thanks to recent deregulation, chose instead to invest money outside the city. Landlords were caught setting fire to their buildings (so they could collect insurance) or hiring kids to do it. Daily perils increased still further as economic austerity measures prevented the city from providing adequate safety and fire protection measures.[30]

In a white ethnic community like Greenpoint (in northern Brooklyn), working-class residents formed block associations and otherwise mobilized to protect their neighborhoods. As one scholar studying such communities noted, block associations led "persistent efforts to control the environment" and were a "significant feature of low-income life." Not only did the Norman Street block association in Greenpoint serve as the locus of neighborhood socializing, but it also ran a summer lunch program for kids, built a children's park, and pressed city officials on addressing unsafe, abandoned, and burned-out buildings in the neighborhood.[31]

Two interrelated problems, both stemming from the city's 1975 fiscal crisis, made this kind of neighborhood advocacy necessary. First, in contrast to the 1960s, when the city had built thirteen new firehouses, between 1972 and 1975 it had closed seventeen and relocated seven others. In addition, in 1975 it capped the number of firefighters at 1939 levels (about ten thousand) even though the number of alarms sounded each year had increased tenfold (from about forty thousand in 1939 to four hundred thousand in 1975). Second, for most of 1975 and 1976, the city said it did not have the financial resources to seal abandoned buildings—the most frequent targets of arson. A Housing and Development Administration staffer told Greenpoint residents that instead of sealing buildings, it could demolish them "in an emergency"—which meant the building had to be collapsing before the agency would act. When a Greenpoint resident pointed out that "a building which is a fire hazard right next to our homes is just as much of an emergency," the staff member said, "We agree, but if you're talking about all the four thousand unsafe buildings, we haven't got the money." Eventually, the city cut services to deteriorating neighborhoods, so fewer subway trains and buses ran there; libraries and schools closed, and police precincts and firehouses, too.

When, in November 1975, the city announced the closure of eight engine companies and four firehouses—including one in Greenpoint—two hundred residents of that neighborhood, mostly Polish American, turned out and surrounded the firehouse before the firemen could remove the engine. Following a twenty-hour standoff, the residents finally agreed to let the firemen go, but the city left the engine. Protesters christened the building "People's Firehouse No. 1" and occupied it in a sustained demonstration for the next eighteen months.

Most of the neighborhood's protesters were white ethnics, the very people usually associated with the working-class "backlash" against liberalism, but to see them, one would more likely think of the brash Sixties activists who protested on behalf of civil rights and peace. Indeed, the Greenpointers did not limit their protest to the sit-in at the firehouse; they organized targeted protests in other parts of the city, too, including picketing the fire commissioner's house and a mayor's dinner at one of the city's Hilton hotels. And they seemed downright radical when they blocked traffic on the Brooklyn–Queens Expressway during morning rush hour. Such tactics eventually achieved victory when the firehouse was reopened in March 1977—though, as the rest of the nation would see a few months later, following burning and looting during the city's blackout, life in New York still looked like life in a combat zone.[32]

Another form of urban neighborhood group—the community development organization—gained considerable currency in the mid-1970s, too. Like the activists in Greenpoint, these organizations were neither left-wing insurgencies nor examples of right-wing backlash. Writing after several years of reflection, the sociologist Robert Fisher observed that community development organizations could typically be found in blue-collar, white ethnic neighborhoods where "the emphasis is on maintaining and strengthening neighborhood networks and organizations, not creating social change or a new political movement. They see neighborhood decline, especially physical deterioration, fostered by working-class powerlessness, as the problem."[33]

In Southeast Baltimore, a working-class neighborhood of approximately ninety-five thousand second- and third-generation descendants of Eastern European immigrants, residents founded the Southeast Council Against the Road (SCAR) to prevent the demolition of hundreds of homes to make way for a six-lane highway. In the process, they realized that the city government, in tandem with its financial sector, had broader urban renewal plans about which they knew little, and that banks had already been redlining the neighborhood in hopes of fueling its deterioration and subsequent renewal. As a result, SCAR transformed itself into the Southeast Baltimore Community Organization (SECO), a coalition of more than ninety neighborhood groups that not only put a stop to bank redlining by shaming government officials into investigating it, but also succeeded, in a period of recession, in keeping a nursing home and a library open, obtaining two new schools, organizing a Youth Diversion Project, and, through a direct action protest featuring mothers with baby carriages filling the streets, stopping truck traffic through residential neighborhoods. Maybe most impressive, SECO established Neighborhood Housing Services as a community corporation—presided over by a board of residents and bankers—that helped 245 families become homeowners. Admirers attributed SECO's success to its mainstream approach to political protest. "We knew we had to be tough and militant," said Barbara Mi-kulski, the "godmother of SECO," who later went on to Congress and the United States Senate. "But the 'issue' was always the enemy. And we knew the very institutions that we challenged were the ones we would have to work with when peace broke out." In a time of severe economic anxiety, SECO spared Southeast Baltimore from the wrecking ball.[34]

Meanwhile, advocates of the poor lamented that blue-collar and middle-class organizing in American cities often happened at the expense of the most deprived. The National Welfare Rights Organization (NWRO) and regional welfare rights groups tried to fill the void left by Nixon's dismantling of War on Poverty Programs. In fact, the NWRO had been active in assailing welfare bureaucracy in American cities since its founding in 1966—at the height of the War on Poverty. In many cities, the duplication of bureaucratic effort—with payments coming from multiple agencies—created a jungle of exhausting hoops and red tape. Following a scheme first articulated by the sociologists Frances Fox Piven and Richard Cloward, the NWRO did its best to swamp the system in cities like New York by organizing the poor to join urban welfare rolls, thus adding to the city's accumulating financial woes and moving it toward a crisis. In time, such tactics succeeded in leading the state legislature to move to a system of single payments (which the NWRO nevertheless protested as wildly inadequate).[35]

The NWRO spawned one of the most important advocacy organizations at work in the 1970s and 1980s: the Association of Community Organizations for Reform Now (ACORN). Founded in 1970 by NWRO veterans Walter and Lee Rathke in Little Rock, Arkansas (when the *A* in ACORN stood for the state's name), the association focused on organizing the poor in what it called a "majoritarian" strategy. "If you can fashion a program that will attract people who earn, say, $8,000 or less [a year]," Walter Rathke said, "then you're appealing (in Arkansas) to a very large majority. You can develop an organization with real power." ACORN estimated that low- and moderate-income people might amount to 85 percent of the American population. Rathke took inspiration from the legendary organizer Saul Alinsky, who had pioneered tactics for drawing citizens into political action aimed at gaining power in their own communities. In Little Rock, ACORN started mostly as an organization of welfare mothers. Rathke and another organizer, Gary Delgado, found, with a lawyer's help, a little-known "minimum standard of need" regulation that said welfare recipients were entitled to furniture. Following a strategy that both Alinsky and NWRO would have recognized, Delgado and a group of local volunteers knocked on doors for weeks and spoke to church groups, ultimately bringing out hundreds of welfare recipients in waves of demonstrations demanding furniture from the county Welfare Department. Led by a twenty-three-year-old African American welfare mother named Gloria Wilson, ACORN took the fight to Governor Winthrop Rockefeller, holding demonstrations at his mansion. When the governor agreed to negotiate, Wilson attended the first meeting and, in a moment of frustration, lost her temper. "We have to choose between feeding our kids or buying a decent bed," she said. She then removed her wig to reveal that the stress of life on welfare was causing her hair to fall out. "Something has to be done!" she shouted at the governor and his aides. Spontaneous outbursts like Wilson's showed the power of emotion, both to mobilize Americans around a variety of issues and to move one's political opponents. In part because he had been shaken by Wilson's desperate plea, Governor Rockefeller soon agreed to provide a furniture warehouse where donations could be made and furniture acquired (this later led to a new state agency, Furniture for Families, responsible for collecting and distributing used furniture). This victory led to more campaigns in Arkansas—focused on housing, schools, traffic lights, public transportation, electricity rates, consumer issues, environmental issues, property taxes—and eventually to the proliferation of ACORN chapters in twenty-six states; by 1982, the organization claimed more than fifty thousand dues-paying members waging multistate campaigns on the same issues.[36]

The idea of "building the majority's power"—power for a true silent majority made up of poor, working-class, and middle-class Americans who shared a sense of powerlessness in the face of government and business might—seemed to offer a concrete plan that fictional populist heroes such as *Network*'s Howard Beale and *Nashville*'s Hal Phillip Walker did not. Beyond any particular issues, an organizing manual claimed, ACORN was concerned with a more fundamental problem: the distribution of power in America. "When ACORN attacks a public utility for raising rates, the attack is not based on an analysis which holds that ACORN members, and other low to moderate Arkansans (or Texans or

South Dakotans) are, as consumers, getting nailed by high electric rates," the manual stated. "Undoubtedly they *are* getting nailed . . . but even more important . . . they are getting boxed because . . . a bunch of corporate directors and New York bankers have the power to unilaterally make decisions that affect the lives of ACORN members."[37]

Critics pointed out that professional staffers did the lion's share of the organizing for ACORN and many of the "citizen action" groups that had sprung up like flowers around the country in the late 1960s and early 1970s. In fact, in Chicago, Heather Booth, a veteran of the antiwar, student, and women's movements, founded the Midwest Academy in 1972 as a training institute for organizers. The need for an institution that could both teach the difficult, detailed work of organizing and also "serve as a link between different groups—between community organizers, labor unionists, environmentalists, feminists," and other activists— seemed apparent to Booth and others. By that time, the "citizen revolt" included not only ACORN but organizations such as the Citizens Action Program (CAP) in Chicago, Communities Organized for Public Service (COPS) in San Antonio, the United Neighborhoods Organization (UNO) in East Los Angeles, the Oakland Community Organization (OCO), Massachusetts Fair Share, the Ohio Public Interest Campaign, Oregon Fair Share, the Illinois Public Action Council, and the Connecticut Citizen Action Group. In most of these organizations, professional activists charted strategy, but, as Booth taught at the Midwest Academy, community organizing could not be considered completely successful even if it won clear victories on issues that improved people's lives. Community organizers also had to build organizations "through which people can gain a sense of their own power . . . and which contribute to the general change in power relations, democratizing the broader society."[38] It did not always work out as planned, but whether the front porch activists who mobilized across so many issues in the 1970s and 1980s knew it or not, the mostly local organizing model that they followed was pioneered by the Alinsky-inspired organizers of "citizen action" groups.

Of course, even when an organization did succeed in bringing together many rank-and-file community participants, the results could be uneven. Massachusetts Fair Share, for example, started in working-class Chelsea and East Boston in the early 1970s and won victories involving housing, playgrounds, and street repair. "Perhaps most remarkable," Fair Share had, in one scholar's view, "begun to forge alliances among blacks and working-class whites on issues that transcended race" despite working in a tense racial climate. But then it took on the utilities. In Massachusetts, as in the rest of the country, citizens had seen their utility rates driven up by inflation and the oil crisis. Fair Share, in a major referendum campaign against the utility companies, advocated uniform rates for residential users and the big industrial users, who were then paying much lower rates. Business did its own organizing, taking tips from Business Roundtable strategists, and even enlisting the support of Democratic governor Michael Dukakis and key unions. It also funded an Associated Industries of Massachusetts campaign that warned of a mass exodus of business and investment from the state if business had to pay the same rates as homeowners. Companies enclosed warnings in employees' pay envelopes, and colleges did the same with tuition bills sent to parents. Fair Share had no chance; when voters went to the polls in 1976, the referendum lost two to one.[39]

In other locales, the business lobby's attempts to defeat reform by stressing the need for a business-friendly environment backfired. In San Antonio, Communities Organized for Public Service (COPS) grew by 1976 to a convention of six thousand delegates from the city and surrounding areas, making it the largest urban community organization in the country. Its primary political objective was to challenge San Antonio's long-range development plan, which, COPS believed, privileged suburban development and the real estate and construction contractors pushing it "while neglecting the city neighborhoods and the needs of the majority of its citizens." So COPS moved into electoral politics by interviewing and analyzing city council candidates and choosing which ones to endorse; all of the COPS-endorsed candidates won. After the 1977 election, COPS, with advocates on the city council, mounted a campaign to change the city's approach to recruiting industry. Instead of emphasizing cheap labor as San Antonio's main attraction for industry—as a report commissioned by a Chamber of Commerce research group had done—COPS argued that the city should encourage only businesses prepared to pay employees a living wage (Harry Boyte said "it mentioned $15,000 as a reasonable figure"). As in the Massachusetts utility rate campaign, the Texas Industrial Commission predicted that business would be "scared off." Others in the business lobby threatened a corporate boycott. This time, though, it did not work. The city went with the COPS proposal, and the Chamber of Commerce was shamed into admitting that its "cheap labor appeal was wrong."[40]

In many ways, the United Neighborhoods Organization (UNO) of East Los Angeles grew from the same fertile soil that produced COPS in San Antonio: East L.A. was home to an immense illegal Mexican immigrant population. The area's Catholic parishes became important organizing centers for residents who felt the city and state catered to business and developers to the detriment of their neighborhoods. Certainly, anti-poverty efforts had been tried, but it seemed most government officials saw East L.A. as hopeless. Under UNO, however, priests and nuns (who had been trained by Ernie Cortes, a Mexican American organizer from San Antonio) conducted ten thousand interviews to gauge the most pressing issues facing residents and their families. One frequent response was "skyrocketing insurance rates," which, UNO researchers found, stemmed from auto insurance company redlining practices that charged rates not by how well a customer drove but by where he or she lived. UNO brazenly demanded a meeting with the state Insurance Board chairman, Wesley Kinder, who was stunned when three thousand East L.A. residents showed up, prepared to argue forcefully, if politely. As one priest said of the residents after the meeting, "They're changing, you know, you should see the people talk. Sweet old ladies. It's tremendous. There's dignity in the determination of their lives."[41]

Despite major obstacles, the rural poor also joined the citizens' revolt. As the late Senator Paul Wellstone pointed out, in the mid-1970s, more poverty existed in rural America, proportionately, than in urban America. "While less than one-third of the nation's population reside in rural, small-town communities, 40% of the nation's poor, 9.2 million rural people, live in poverty," he wrote in 1975. Likewise, almost 40 percent of the total rural population had incomes below the poverty level. Wellstone, then a political science professor, saw much of this poverty near his place of employment, Carleton College in Minnesota. In the late 1970s, he became involved with the Organization for a Better Rice County (OBRC).

In Wellstone's experience, rural people seemed more difficult to organize. That was in part because they were isolated, living farther apart than city dwellers and harboring "no expectation for social change." In addition, the power brokers in Faribault, a town of sixteen thousand and the Rice County seat, were the business owners and the local newspaper that "religiously attack[ed] welfare programs . . . and almost all social programs." It seemed an unlikely place for a poor people's movement, and at first, OBRC made little headway.[42]

OBRC had more success, however, when it set out to reform the county food assistance program, attracting not only welfare recipients but working poor and senior citizens to its banner. OBRC's research showed that many people who were eligible for the program did not know it; for those who did know, the process of receiving assistance discouraged participation (it could be an arduous, daylong undertaking that involved not only arranging transportation into Faribault, but often waiting hours in a room with no chairs for the elderly or infirm before receiving any food). Using census figures, OBRC showed that 4,300 people were eligible for food assistance, but only 1,500 participated in the program. The organization demanded a hearing with the county board of commissioners, and dozens of poor people attended. Like the UNO activists meeting with the state insurance commissioner, OBRC members demanded to be treated with dignity. They asked for another distribution center, more staff to speed distribution, chairs for those who needed them, and outreach to inform eligible families about the program. The commissioners agreed to all but the last demand. Charles Liverseed, a seventy-two-year-old handyman with a seventh-grade education who was so poor that Wellstone once observed only "some turtle meat and a little cheese" in his old refrigerator, acted as OBRC spokesman that day. He seemed to understand the gist of Ralph Nader's "initiatory democracy" idea when he said at the meeting's end, "We here at the OBRC have just made a contract with you the commissioners about improving the [food] commodities program. If you don't live up to your word, we're going to come back and make you live up to your promises."[43]

With that victory behind them, poor people became much more active in running the OBRC, but they also became targets of retaliation. The *Faribault Daily News* routinely described poor people as lazy welfare cheats and attacked OBRC for grandstanding. Meanwhile, the state welfare department suspended benefits to the OBRC president, a married woman with eleven children to support who worked a farm that made roughly $1,500 a year. The department argued that the farm's value had increased, making the family ineligible for benefits. The department then violated its own due process regulations in responding to her request for an appeal and sparked a welfare rights movement in the process.

The larger problem was that even as food prices kept going up and up, the welfare department made no adjustments to payments, so Minnesota's poor could buy less and less. The OBRC appealed to the county welfare official for support, but he consistently ignored its request for a meeting—until twenty-five women showed up with their thirty-six children at the Rice County courthouse. "The children were running all over the place," Wellstone recalled, "and the noise level was unbearable." They got their meeting and the simple letter of support they had been seeking, and that led to benefits being raised from $105 to $118 a month. More important than the modest increase, the women gained a sense of their collective strength in taking on the system. As one later said, the one good thing about being poor is that "you can't be sued—so you might as well speak up."[44]

You can't be sued, but you can be intimidated. Once again, OBRC suffered retaliation from the welfare department. Without any prior warning, it obtained a court order and sent a social worker and police to the home of Artis Fleischfresser, an outspoken welfare mother. The officials took her four children into custody as she and the kids begged and screamed in protest. The children returned home a few days later after a county attorney, suspecting a political vendetta, did not hold the scheduled hearing to determine if Fleischfresser was a suitable mother. But even so, Fleischfresser ceased all activism. Thanks to the chilling effect this episode had on other welfare mothers, the OBRC nearly collapsed.[45]

OBRC did eventually close its doors, though not until a few years later, and not because of retaliation but because of organizational inefficiencies. In the meantime, it managed to win other significant victories: it secured from the county a share of federal block grant funds for a much-needed day care center for poor people; after a year of organizing, it launched a senior citizen "dial-a-bus" transit system after the county suspended public bus service; and when the state introduced food stamps to replace the inadequate food assistance program, OBRC played a part in determining that the distribution system was set up fairly and treated recipients with dignity. The most significant OBRC accomplishment, Wellstone said, came in the "dramatic change in the political consciousness among the poor." Even after OBRC folded, plans quickly came together to start a new organization from scratch. At the first steering committee meeting, one woman said, "I still have that damn OBRC consciousness!"[46]

All over the United States, citizens faced with a new economic reality, notable for its effect on local services, saw their own collective consciousness raised. In turn, they channeled their emotional response into action. Perhaps without realizing it, they were both following earlier examples of grassroots organizing and modeling new ones. By the middle of the 1970s, these new forms of collective citizen action could be seen everywhere, from rural areas to cities and suburbs—and not only in response to questions arising from desperate new circumstances. In fact, at times the front porch impulse to mobilize came in response to familiar nagging issues.

2

The Long Shadow of Segregation

•

When Lyndon Johnson, the president who ushered through Congress the most sweeping civil rights laws in American history, looked at black America in 1967, he saw cities on fire. Riots in urban ghettos dominated the news in the mid- and late 1960s, and many liberal whites—supporters of Martin Luther King Jr. and the civil rights movement's quest to end Southern segregation—were bewildered. Why this, why now?

In the declension narrative that still dominates American memory of the civil rights movement, the riots in Watts, Detroit, Newark, and countless other northern and western cities triggered the civil rights movement's terrible decline from the peaceful nobility of the Martin Luther King Jr. era to chaos and violence. White backlash followed and racial liberalism died a relatively sudden death, enabling the triumph of Reagan-style conservatism.

It was hardly so simple. Scholars have been showing for years that the "backlash" began in the 1940s, in the wake of the Great Migration of southern blacks to northern cities—not in the late 1960s and early 1970s in reaction to black power and affirmative action. For anyone willing to listen in 1968, the National Commission on Civil Disorders (also known as the Kerner Commission) predicted the coming battles over race that defined life in urban and suburban America in the 1970s: "What white Americans have never fully understood—but what the Negro can never forget—is that white society is deeply implicated in the ghetto. White institutions created it, white institutions maintain it, and white society condones it. To continue present policies is to make permanent the division of our country into two societies: one, largely Negro and poor, located in the central cities; the other, predominantly white and affluent, located in the suburbs and outlying areas."[1]

The racial conflicts of the 1970s and 1980s over schools and residential space had many causes. First, the Supreme Court's *Brown v. Board of Education* decision affected a much larger swath of Americans than anyone could have predicted when it was handed down in 1954. Initially aimed at rolling back de jure school segregation in the Jim Crow South, *Brown* provided the basis, in the late 1960s, for civil rights lawyers to win de facto school desegregation court decisions in both the South and North. Second, a variety of postwar government programs helped facilitate white middle-class migration to the suburbs. The burden of desegregating urban schools fell mostly on the city dwellers who remained, who were mostly poor and working-class blacks and whites. Third, in the 1970s, as in the 1950s, the White House equivocated. Although Richard Nixon rhetorically advocated racial equality and seemed to support fair housing and fair hiring measures, political considerations tempered any real enthusiasm he may have had for pressing equality.

From the vantage point of residents' front porches and stoops in the affected communities, the president's policies satisfied few and ultimately led to massive grassroots organizing efforts across the political spectrum and all over the country. The abdication of leadership by the White House and Congress meant that state and federal judges filled the vacuum, sparking both fury and applause. Activists who modeled themselves on the civil rights movement pitted themselves not only against government (as neighborhood groups did in demanding vital services), but against one another. Cities and suburbs served as battlefields, and armies of activists clashed over whose version of the American dream would prevail.[2]

In retrospect, it is easy to see that high-profile debates over affirmative action and the "backlash" against civil rights obscured other key changes in the 1970s. Much more important—but poorly understood at the time— was suburban development and its effect on the mind-sets of blacks and whites.

The biggest battles over race in post-1960s America were (and remain) rooted in spatial segregation. Nothing Richard Nixon (or his predecessors) did altered the fundamental reality of blacks and whites moving apart from each other and experiencing different versions of modern America. According to the historian Robert Self, "the most significant political, economic, and spatial transformation in the postwar United States was the overdevelopment of suburbs and the underdevelopment of cities." Until recently, these two phenomena have often been explained as the result of "white flight"—economically mobile whites fleeing the cities—leading to "urban decline" as capital followed those whites out to the suburbs. This is too simplistic. Rather than fleeing, middle- and upper-class whites followed the imperatives of federal and local planning that made moving to the suburbs attractive—and attainable— for them. The federal government subsidized suburban housing development and new highways, and local government promised low taxes to both businesses and individuals. While middle-class whites qualified for federally subsidized low-interest mortgages through the Federal Housing Administration (FHA, which made no such financing available for what it regarded as higher-risk black and minority communities), federal urban renewal policies often cleared black populations from a city's center, removing them from jobs, services, and decent homes and schools. At the same time, suburban communities passed zoning laws prohibiting the construction of multifamily dwellings (i.e., apartment buildings) that might attract lower-income residents.[3]

More important is that this hardening of residential segregation in America—the result of deliberate policies—came without anyone's taking responsibility for it. Although the FHA's *Underwriting Manual* encouraged covenants, from the 1930s to the 1960s, that would defend against mixing "inharmonious racial groups" by restricting the transfer (sale) of properties to members of "the same social and racial groups," white beneficiaries of government planning attributed their ability to move to the suburbs to their hard work and diligent pursuit of the American dream. The urban poor and working-class blacks and whites, by implication, had only themselves to blame for their lot. Government officials in Washington and in suburban town halls across America named this segregation "de facto" and threw up their hands as though helpless. In effect, they left the problem of residential inequality and related issues— such as unequal education—on the courthouse steps.[4]

Thus were drawn the lines of race and class conflict in the 1970s. As urban blacks and whites challenged, from their gritty stoops, the funneling of capital and other resources out of the cities to the suburbs and won the support of key advocates and courts, the suburbanites who had "made it" organized from their front porches as a "tax-conscious voting bloc" to defend the material rewards of their hard work. In the process of mustering this defense, a "color-blind" form of plausible deniability developed: the state established fundamentally racist structures to the advantage of middle- and upper-class whites, who later claimed convincingly that they were not themselves racist but merely the beneficiaries of their own rugged individualism. Oblivious to structural racism and prone to understanding their success in strictly meritocratic terms, suburbanites saw their place as the result of a kind of Darwinian bootstrapping, their hard work rewarded with a home in the suburbs.[5]

Ironically, when the urban poor came and demanded redress— frequently backed by a court order—suburban defenders of home and school claimed to be victims of an oppressive state, not beneficiaries of a generous one. As one Charlotte suburbanite declared, "I think it is time the law-abiding, taxpaying white middle class started looking to the federal government for something besides oppression." This was 1970, after thirty years of social engineering had made the suburban American dream a reality for that same "taxpaying white middle class." The historian Matthew Lassiter tells us that when the social engineering continued, in the form of a low-income housing plan or a school busing plan, those earlier beneficiaries rejected the whole project as "an unconstitutional exercise . . . and an unprecedented violation of free-market meritocracy." And then they circled their station wagons in defense of home and family.[6]

It is impossible to understand the most intense racial conflicts in the 1970s without first grasping the origins of suburban victimization and its corollary—the populist belief in bootstrapping. Long before the tumultuous Sixties ended, even those who supported the civil rights agenda in the South largely presumed that the trappings of postwar American success—a home in the suburbs—were earned through individual hard work alone. As soon as less privileged Americans began to challenge that idea, all hell broke loose.

No case better represents the nation's front porch battles over continuing segregation than the thirty-year contest started in Mount Laurel, New Jersey. Today it is one of Philadelphia's signature suburbs, but up until the 1960s, it was a small rural community. African Americans had lived in Mount Laurel since the days when New Jersey laws allowed slavery. Black residents, including free blacks in the antebellum period, lived alongside white residents through the middle of the twentieth century. But highway development in the early 1950s displaced black families, most of whom worked as tenant farmers on white-owned land. The growing network of highways that came through Mount Laurel—particularly the New Jersey Turnpike—had made developers think about Mount Laurel as a potential haven for Philadelphia commuters. When farmers got so much more for their land than their crops could ever bring them—in 1963, one farm sold for nearly $2 million—they did not hesitate to sell. In the process, tenant farmers were cast off, leaving many of the town's black residents corralled in a kind of shantytown called Springville. Meanwhile, Mount Laurel became New Jersey's fastest-growing community. In 1950, it had fewer than three thousand residents; in 1970, more than ten thousand; and by 1990, thirty-four thousand.

As builders constructed new homes, office parks, and schools (given the biracial nature of the rural community, the schools were integrated), the town's poorer residents started to get priced out. In the spirit of the Great Society Sixties, a group of them secured a small grant from the state to begin planning a low-income housing project on thirty-two acres in Springville. But existing zoning laws allowed the construction only of single-family homes. In order to build the low-income housing, the Mount Laurel township council would have to revise the zoning ordinances. It refused. "If you people can't afford to live in our town," said one town committeeman, "then you'll just have to leave."[7]

The line had been drawn between older poor minority residents and new wealthier suburban residents. Zoning decisions belonged to the township council and, by extension, the township's residents. The council liked the idea of building an "executive-type town" and got excited about plans to build ten thousand units of middle-class housing. No mainstream officials or residents—Democrat or Republican—rose to the poor people's defense. As nearby Camden and Philadelphia lost countless manufacturing jobs in the 1970s, town officials feared the precedent of a housing project would lead to an influx of urban poor into Mount Laurel.

But the township's poor fought back. Led by Mount Laurel resident Ethel Lawrence and the local NAACP, they sued Mount Laurel in a case,

Southern Burlington County NAACP et al. v. Township of Mount Laurel,
ultimately best known as *Mount Laurel I.* Scholars have likened it to
Brown v. Board of Education and *Roe v. Wade,* and they describe Ethel
Lawrence as the Rosa Parks of the fair housing movement. Born in 1926,
Lawrence grew up tenant-farming in Mount Laurel. A mother of eight
children, a Girl Scout leader and church pianist, she made the ideal focal
point for the case.[8]

During the four-day trial in March 1972, township lawyers acknowledged that a "pattern of economic and social segregation" existed in
Mount Laurel, but they denied that town officials had anything to do
with it. The racial separation occurred, they implied, as a result of market forces. The township, they said, had "no legal duty to house the poor."
The judge disagreed. In particular, he expressed shock that the plaintiffs
had been forced to leave their homes, even though some had lived in
them for fifty years. "Nobody came to their rescue," he said. Therefore,
he ruled for the plaintiffs and ordered town officials to work with Ethel
Lawrence and others to come up with an "affirmative program."[9]

Mount Laurel mayor Joe Massari responded with outrage. "Bullshit!"
he shouted. "We're not going to give an inch on this thing. We are going
to fight it all the way." The town's suburban residents were similarly un-
sympathetic to the plaintiffs. The township's lawyer later offered a bootstrapping analysis, explaining that residents feared "somebody getting a
free house next to their own house for which they had worked and slaved,
to get out to their paradise, which was a one-hundred-foot by one-hundred-
foot lot in Mount Laurel." Nevertheless, in March 1975 the New Jersey
Supreme Court unanimously upheld the lower court's decision, and then
it went even further by demanding that all of the state's developing towns
rewrite their zoning laws so that developers could provide a "fair share"
of the state's poor and moderate-income citizens with housing.[10]

It was a stunning victory for the poor African American plaintiffs
in Mount Laurel—far more than they had dreamed of achieving—but it
prompted a fierce reaction (marked at times by barely disguised racism).
One resident said to a reporter: "Nobody has a right to say anybody owes
them anything. They have the option of moving out of Mount Laurel if
they don't like their housing here. Springville is a pigsty, but they wouldn't
live any differently if they moved to Laurel Knoll. You are what you are."
The township responded by stalling, by advancing ridiculously token or
unworkable plans, and by demonizing the court. As the new mayor, Joe

Alvarez, later said, "We were going to do the absolute minimum we could get by with."[11]

As a result, in 1983, the state supreme court once again ruled—in a case known as *Mount Laurel II*—that Mount Laurel and other municipalities must "in *fact* provide a realistic opportunity for the construction of [each community's] fair share of low and moderate income housing," and must prove they were doing so. Under the new court order, in all their long-term planning provisions for developers, towns had to set aside 20 percent of new construction as low- and moderate-income units. Another wave of hostile reaction swept the state as mayors and legislators raised the possibility of writing constitutional amendments to overturn the court's decisions. Governor Thomas Kean called *Mount Laurel II* "communistic." "I don't believe that every municipality has got to be a carbon copy of another," said Kean; "that's a socialistic country, a Communist country, a dictatorship." He called the "fair share" order "social engineering on a scale never imagined by Marx or Engels." In 1985, 221 townships and 5 counties in New Jersey held a referendum—which passed in every locale by an average of 2 to 1—to demand a constitutional amendment "limiting the power of the courts, so that the courts cannot force municipalities to change their zoning laws to accommodate *Mount Laurel* housing."[12]

Eventually, in New Jersey's Fair Housing Act of 1985, the two sides hammered out what appeared to be a middle ground that both validated the fair-share ideal and provided mechanisms for suburbs to, in the words of one team of analysts, "buy their way out of much of their fair-share obligation" with only "a modest cash outlay." Under "regional contribution agreements" supervised by a new agency—not judges—called the Council on Affordable Housing, suburbs paid to trade away as much as half of their fair-share obligation to urban areas. In practical terms, the suburbanites had won: the new law privileged protection of the suburbs over equality of opportunity.[13]

Mount Laurel was just one prominent example of how, across the 1970s and 1980s, the "crabgrass frontier" of American suburbia, from New Jersey to California, proved to be an archetypal front porch politics battleground. For some citizens, suburbia's promise turned on questions of race and equality, but for others what mattered most was the perception of merit, of who had worked how hard to get where. It was as if each group spoke a different language; unable to understand each other, and holding little confidence in their elected officials, Americans on both sides of these familiar battles took to grassroots organizing, from direct action to lawsuits.

When such contests involved schools and education, they inevitably came to concern not only the suburbs but the cities they surrounded.

It has often been said that whereas the 1960s had the Vietnam War, the 1970s had busing. Southern resistance to school desegregation finally broke down fifteen years after the *Brown* decision when the Supreme Court, in *Alexander v. Holmes County* (1969), ordered southern school districts to "terminate dual school systems at once and to operate now and hereafter only unitary schools." President Nixon, bound by the strict requirement of the decision, had no choice but to enforce its mandate, and by September 1970, only 14 percent of southern black students attended all-black schools. Privately he said, "We ought not go one step beyond what the Court absolutely requires," and publicly he criticized the Court by pointing out that 78 percent of Los Angeles's black students attended all-black schools. In Chicago the number jumped to 85 percent, but the Court ruling did nothing about this "de facto" segregation. America, Nixon said, is the "land of opportunity, not the land of quotas and restrictions."[14]

By the early 1970s, the dividing lines in the school desegregation fights had been drawn. There were bootstrappers who might have favored the ideal of integration, but not if it meant shipping their kids away from the neighborhood schools they worked so hard to live near; and there were integrationists like the NAACP or white liberals who were prepared to work through the long, complicated process of ensuring that every child in a school district got an equal opportunity for a quality education. Finally, there were black power advocates who were doubtful of the value of integrating children into a white school system and called for "community control" of the schools. At stake was what it meant to be an American parent in a post-civil-rights-movement United States. Some parents insisted that racial equality fulfilled the American promise. Other parents saw local control of their community institutions as a value dating to the Revolution. Others viewed both racial equality and local control as American ideals.

In Charlotte, North Carolina, grassroots political fights over busing lasted longer than anywhere else in the country. Along the way, political alliances formed, dissolved, and expanded in surprising ways. As a result, simple generalizations do not do justice to a city where hard-line antibusing activists were pushed aside, politically, by a coalition made up of the city's black residents as well as working-class and suburban whites. Charlotte also distinguished itself because its school district included neighboring suburbs; consequently, it was possible to reach a metropolitan solution that did not let the suburbs escape responsibility for the city's educational system.

The school desegregation challenge in Charlotte started with a 1965 case brought by Darius Swann, who had applied to transfer his son to a white school nearer to his home. Swann, an African American college professor, believed "an integrated school will best prepare young people for responsibility in an integrated society." When the school board denied his request, Swann sued. The case came before a new federal judge, James B. McMillan, whose willingness to understand school segregation as an outgrowth of deliberate residential segregation became the key to the case's success. McMillan had grown up in rural North Carolina and therefore had himself been bused to school twenty-six miles round-trip each day. In the new judge's court, the NAACP systematically demonstrated that residential segregation in Charlotte developed thanks to deliberate policies, that the residential segregation perpetuated school segregation, and that the ongoing school segregation was therefore unconstitutional. The city responded by saying, "We have not built schools to perpetuate segregation. We have built them to serve neighborhoods."[15]

The first round of Charlotte's school integration bout—the courtroom clash—went to Swann and the NAACP and laid the foundation for five more years of fighting. In his May 1969 ruling, Judge McMillan found that the Charlotte system of assigning students to neighborhood schools effectively segregated black students in the northwest part of the city and was therefore "racially discriminatory." Remarkably, the judge described the key "facts" of deliberate residential segregation that anchored his ruling. "The quality of public education," he wrote, "should not depend on the economic or racial accident of the neighborhood in which a child's parents have chosen to live—or find they must live—nor on the color of his skin." Consequently, McMillan issued a sweeping integration order, suggesting that the best solution would apply the district-wide ratio of 71 percent white and 29 percent black to the enrollment levels of each school in the district. Only one remedy could achieve such a balance: busing.[16]

Stunned Charlotte officials—city and school board leaders—pursued a formal appeal, but in the meantime, the Concerned Parents Association (CPA), led by Thomas Harris, an insurance executive from the exclusive island suburb of Myers Park, brought out two thousand people to its very tense first meeting. Harris and others like him claimed not to oppose integration per se, but they bristled at losing one of the essential trappings of suburban respectability: the right to send one's kids to the neighborhood school. "I am not opposed to integration in any way," Harris said. "But I was affluent enough to buy a home near the school where I wanted my children to go. And I pay taxes to pay for it. They can bring anybody they like into that school, but I don't want my children taken away from there." Another father, Augustus Green, put it a little more directly: "To expect me to put my children on buses and send them across town to a school located in a predominantly black area for the sole purpose of fulfilling a mathematical equation is both ridiculous and unreasonable." Most CPA members—young white professionals, a lot of first-time homeowners—agreed to one-way busing of black pupils to schools in their communities, but they would not suffer two-way busing.[17]

Here, they co-opted Richard Nixon's "forgotten Americans" rhetoric of victimization, insisting that their civil rights be respected, too. In short, CPA members regarded their geographic location as their due reward. Never, in this emotionally charged climate, did CPA members mention the city's history of purposeful residential segregation (even though the judge had spelled it out in his decision), nor did they acknowledge that the residents of the sixteen census tracts from which the CPA drew almost all of its membership were beneficiaries of that segregation. Just as most Americans do not carefully study their nation's history, suburbanites invested little energy in investigating the historical forces that— along with their own industriousness—might have brought them to that place at that time.

On the other side of the tracks, though, black parents viewed the historical and political landscape more clearly and accused white parents of "contradictory double-talk" for saying they believed in integration but not busing. When the CPA mounted a petition drive that netted twenty thousand signatures, black parents matched it and also began boycotting downtown stores.[18]

At first, however, the CPA seemed on its way to a rout. At one point in 1970, the organization held seven major rallies in a week, and it planned a boycott of all public schools as soon as a two-way busing order was carried out. Bumper stickers, lawn signs, and buttons carrying antibusing slogans flooded the city, and protesters regularly picketed the judge's house. Suburbanites used a rhetoric of victimization and suggested that integration measures destroyed freedom. "It creates dictatorial power and undermines the American Constitution," read one flyer. "It destroys individual liberty in an area that is close to the hearts of us all." At the same time, but more quietly, the League of Women Voters and local religious leaders held discussion forums in churches and elsewhere with the goal of "get[ting] the facts about urban problems to our friends in middle class suburbia."[19]

The unfolding conflict over busing and the power of the federal courts attracted Richard Nixon's attention in March 1970. The president strictly interpreted the *Brown* decision as a mandate to eliminate de jure dual school systems, but nothing more. He criticized the court for trying to use mandatory busing to eliminate de facto segregation. Here Nixon, too, ignored the evidence cited by Judge McMillan that showed that de facto residential segregation was in reality a more shadowy form of de jure segregation. Like the antibusing activists, Nixon held the belief that residential segregation occurred naturally.

In May 1970, the Fourth Circuit Court of Appeals finally issued a cryptic ruling. "Busing is a permissible tool for achieving integration," it ruled, "but it is not a panacea." Such equivocation fueled suburban outrage in the weeks leading up to the new school year. Nightly rallies attracted thousands of parents, and the CPA collected more than a hundred thousand signatures for their protest petition. A small number of parents began enrolling their children in private schools. Still, some volunteered to try to ensure a smooth and safe transition, riding as bus chaperones, painting classrooms, or helping out around the schools.[20]

On September 9, two-way busing finally began. More than thirty thousand students rode buses (or were driven by their parents) to new schools. About 20 percent of the enrolled student body did not go to school that day, "with the boycott most evident in the suburban neighborhoods reassigned to formerly all-black schools." But the boycott fizzled. Within two weeks, districtwide attendance rose to 92 percent. It went unnoticed at the time, but the failure of the boycott represented the emergence of a moderate middle that may have opposed busing but did not want to sacrifice their kids' education over it.[21]

In April 1971, the United States Supreme Court at last ruled in the *Swann* case, upholding McMillan's initial ruling and driving a stake through the heart of the Concerned Parents Association. The battle did not end there, however; henceforth, integration via busing would be a reality, but the central question became whether the burden would be borne equally.

The next stage of Charlotte's integration wars sprang from a history of activism in working-class neighborhoods. Owing to the city's at-large electoral system—which consistently produced a disproportionate number of representatives from the elite communities of southeast Charlotte—working-class activists had developed a wariness of city government. Fortunately for them, as it happened, a city effort to consolidate with the Mecklenburg county government led to a charter reform in which district representation replaced at-large representation; now, the city council served all neighborhoods.

Over the next few years, one coalition of parents formed after another, each reacting to circumstances and each seeking a solution that would garner widespread support. First, a new coalition of activists from white neighborhoods in northwest and northeast Charlotte—Citizens United for Fairness (CUFF)—grew out of the charter battles and mobilized when the latest busing plans, designed to accommodate parents in affluent areas like Myers Park, allowed some children to stay in their neighborhood schools while busing working-class white and black students between north and west Charlotte (Judge McMillan admitted that the plan was based on "class discrimination" but tolerated it as better than racial discrimination). CUFF included a lot of white parents who had been active in CPA but who now led the way in 1971 in calling for "equalization." "Until all of the community is involved in busing, there will be no stability in our school system," one spokesman said in 1973. Suddenly, neighborhoods that had supported CPA now pushed for integration—*fair* integration—and in partnership with parents from black neighborhoods.[22]

Finally, a new group, the Citizens Advisory Group (CAG), managed to hammer out a long-term solution that most residents agreed was fair. Led by Maggie Ray, a former schoolteacher and mother (and friend of

Judge McMillan) from Myers Park, the CAG was broadly representative of the entire district. Negotiations within CAG were complicated, but the group eventually came up with a "proximity plan" in which students would, "for as many years as possible," be assigned to nearby schools, and that included "a fairness recommendation of busing equalization and an affirmative commitment to guard against resegregation." Since the plan included southeast Charlotte, it effectively limited "the overall amount of busing across the school district" without insulating any single area of the district from busing altogether. In short, every neighborhood in the district would experience busing equally.[23]

Ten years after Darius Swann first brought suit against the Charlotte-Mecklenburg school board, the CAG plan, widely regarded as fair and reasonable, won public support and led Judge McMillan to end the court's oversight. Although this came about not because of consensus on the historical forces that created residential segregation, but rather because, for many, it was the only way to "satisfy the judge," the school integration settlement became a point of pride for Charlotte. City and business leaders boasted of the moderate, progressive urban culture that had led to this uncommon resolution. The populist silent-majority rhetoric that neglected deep social divisions and emphasized what scholars call suburban middle-class "meritocratic individualism" could not, in the end, prevail; at the local level, fissures of class and race could not be erased. But thanks to the urban-suburban school district, a broad-based coalition of moderates, and a judge who would not buckle, Charlotte-Mecklenburg turned out to be that rare case in which the remedy for racial inequality also, in some ways, addressed problems of class.[24]

The Charlotte model did not easily apply elsewhere in the nation. Compared to northern cities already experiencing sharp economic decline in the early 1970s, Charlotte seemed a thriving metropolis. Detroit and Boston hemorrhaged capital to the suburbs and far, far beyond. Detroit, especially, suffered from the effects of deindustrialization. As manufacturing jobs left the Motor City—195,000 jobs vanished between 1967 and 1985—so, too, did the middle class and their tax payments. Between 1960 and 1980, Detroit's population dropped by more than 25 percent. As a result, the African American proportion of the city's total population grew from 29 percent in 1960 to 63 percent by 1980; with jobs scarce, the city's remaining population was largely poor. When stagflation hit in the early 1970s, it only made matters worse. Unemployment among the city's black population reached nearly 50 percent. While property values in the suburbs (where blacks made up 4 percent of the population) soared, Detroit's property values plummeted to pre-1960 levels. As in so many American cities, faced with more poor people than at any time since the Great Depression, Detroit struggled to pay for a rapidly ballooning social services budget.[25]

Detroit's school integration fight unfolded in the face of these over-whelming obstacles. Throughout the 1960s, declining property values and the attendant drop in property tax revenue combined with rising school enrollments and a well-organized teacher's union calling for higher pay and better working conditions to create a financial nightmare for the city. Even with a Democratic majority in Lansing voting for increases in state funding of Detroit's schools, by 1968 the city received from the state only $193 per pupil—$32 below the state average.[26]

Beyond the financial struggles, additional factors—mostly cultural—led to growing tensions over the state of the schools and, ultimately, to a showdown among several factions over their future. At the time, increasing numbers of black parents were calling for community control of city schools—putting parents in charge of personnel and curriculum decisions. Many black leaders blamed white administrators for poor student performance. As one claimed, schools in black neighborhoods had become "'colonial outposts' manned to a great extent by 'white suburbanite mercenaries' who come into the ghetto at dawn and flee well before dusk." Students and parents called for a complete reorientation of the educational program to emphasize a black studies curriculum that taught the black experience and black history, and they petitioned to rename schools in the district after black nationalists such as Malcolm X and H. Rap Brown. In addition, by 1970, Detroit's schools were unsafe. Taken together, these issues and causes led many in the black community to call for local control of the schools. In their view, the seven-member city school board had failed miserably, and the only way to ensure a good education for one's children would be for the community to assume control of the school they attended.[27]

As in Charlotte, a major court case played a determinative role in Detroit's busing battles, but with a different result.[28] In September 1971, in the *Milliken v. Bradley* case, Judge Stephen Roth ruled that the Detroit school board and the state had been guilty of segregation and ordered the state board of education to come up with a desegregation plan for the city and, most notably, the surrounding suburbs. The decision to include the suburbs arose from evidence presented during the trial showing that communities just outside Detroit had deliberately crafted policies and local ordinances to keep out African Americans. In June 1972, Roth himself issued the most ambitious busing order to come from any court in the country. Roth's plan affected three counties and more than 780,000 students (300,000 of whom would be bused daily) in Detroit and fifty-two other suburban school districts. One year later, the Sixth Circuit Court of Appeals upheld Roth's decision.

In July 1974, however, the Supreme Court, in a 5–4 decision, struck down Judge Roth's decision and desegregation order. Justice Potter Stewart, writing for the majority, stated that the suburbs had not played any role in causing segregation in the city schools. The segregation present in Detroit, Stewart asserted, had been "caused by unknown and perhaps unknowable factors such as immigration, birthrates, economic changes, or cumulative acts of private racial fears." As in Mount Laurel, such a declaration flew in the face of the evidence presented in the case. As one academic expert later said, while some things are "unknown and perhaps unknowable," the "tight, unremitting containment of urban blacks over the past half-century within the bowels of American cities is not one of them." The Court put defense of the suburbs ahead of equal opportunity in the cities. Eighteen months later, the city began busing twenty-two thousand students within the city. As Supreme Court Justice Thurgood Marshall presciently predicted in his *Milliken* dissent, with suburbs effectively exempted from metropolitan desegregation plans, the burden of addressing segregation in Detroit fell on the poor of both races.[29]

In popular memory, busing is most closely associated with Boston. It is the violence we remember, the firebombings, the riots, the school corridor stabbings, and an attack—immortalized in a prizewinning photograph—on a black lawyer by a mob of whites wielding a flagpole. In short, we remember mostly the ugliness. The actual history, in all its complexity, is harder to recall.

There is no question that, compared to Charlotte's relatively peaceful negotiation of its school desegregation crisis, Boston's three years of resistance to "forced busing" made the "cradle of liberty" look more like the last outpost of Jim Crow. At least that is what it looked like on television. In fact, the use of busing as a solution to long-standing inequalities in Boston schools came only after decades of civil rights organizing, and though it sparked multiple antibusing movements, it was welcomed by no small number of Bostonians. A majority fell somewhere beyond easy categorization, perhaps favoring integration but not busing, or opposing both busing and the antibusing movements—just as so many Americans hated both the Vietnam War and its protesters.

As in Charlotte and Detroit, postwar urban and suburban development in the greater Boston area did much to shape the ensuing battles over school integration. In the 1950s and 1960s, a ring of suburbs sprouted like mushrooms in the shade of the fast-growing electronics and defense industries along the Route 128 beltway. Subsidized by federal and local government, these companies brought more than 66,000 new jobs to the 128 corridor between 1958 and 1967; in turn, thousands of jobs left Boston, followed by members of the white middle class. At exactly the same time, the city saw its largest in-migration of African Americans, as jobs and homes around 128 were beyond the reach of Boston's poor and minority population; Route 128 became "Boston's Road to Segregation."[30]

Within Boston city limits, residential neighborhoods had clear racial and ethnic identities. Working-class Irish dominated Charlestown, South Boston, and Dorchester, while the Italians filled East Boston and the North End. Thanks to the same kind of bank redlining seen all over urban America, the city's African American population was contained primarily in Roxbury and Mattapan. Hyde Park and West Roxbury were basically suburbs within city limits, populated by a white, upwardly mobile middle class. Strong cultural ties bound working-class whites to their neighborhoods and encouraged this balkanization of Boston. In this context, neighborhood schools were what the historian Ronald Formisano calls "community socializing agents"; locals felt a deep connection to their schools not because of their quality, but because "high school days were often the best times of their lives."[31]

Suffering like Detroit from steady deindustrialization, Boston lost working-class jobs rapidly as the city tipped toward its new identity as a haven for financial and service industries. When the 1973 recession and the oil crisis hit, many of the city's workers felt their world caving in;

competition for construction and civil service jobs aggravated racial tensions. One of the city's civil rights advocacy groups called for a 50 percent minority quota in construction industry hiring; picketing at job sites led to several scuffles. With the city's unemployment rate at 12 percent, activists demanded "Boston jobs for Boston people" and pointed out that many of the white construction workers lived in the suburbs, while out-of-work black tradesmen lived in the city. At the same time, a federal court found the police department—long an epicenter of political patronage—guilty of discriminating against minorities.[32]

Boston was a tinderbox, waiting for the fuse to be lit. Busing was the match.

Since the early 1950s, the NAACP, working on behalf of black parents, had called for the desegregation of city schools only to be met with prevarication and defiance by the Boston School Committee. Led by South Boston's Louise Day Hicks, the committee for years simply denied that segregation existed. Civil rights veteran James Farmer once called Hicks "the Bull Connor of Boston," but Hicks presented herself as a spokeswoman for, and defender of, the "little people." A woman with mayoral aspirations, she succeeded for a long time in invoking the populist lingo of Richard Nixon and George Wallace, defining Bostonians as "the workingman and woman, the rent payer, the home owner, the law abiding, tax-paying, decent-living, hard-working, forgotten American." When the Massachusetts legislature passed the Racial Imbalance Act of 1965, calling on the city to integrate its schools, Hicks and the school committee followed a strategy of endless delaying tactics, discussing and debating various desegregation plans while committing to none.[33]

In response, the Parent Association, an organization of African American parents, created a model of self-reliance by forming their own busing organizations. They thought they could shame the school committee into acknowledging the inequities in education by launching a parent-run, privately funded program—Operation Exodus—to shuttle black children to better city schools with "open seats" that could, under a 1961 policy, be filled by any Boston child, no matter where she lived. Similarly, the Parent Association joined with suburban school districts to form the Metropolitan Council for Educational Opportunity (METCO), which in 1967, started busing kids from poor black neighborhoods in Boston to schools in surrounding towns; by the mid-1970s, thanks to additional support from the federal government and state legislature, METCO expanded to include thirty-eight suburbs. Ultimately, in a city where the school committee had long asserted that there were "no inferior schools, just inferior students" with parents uninterested in education, Operation Exodus and METCO showed just how much parents were willing to do for their children (who thrived in better schools). Even so, these programs did nothing to move the Boston School Committee to equalize the quality of education for the overwhelming majority of black students (who, in 1971, made up more than 50 percent of the population in sixty-seven different schools) in Boston.[34] Finally, in March 1972, fifty-three plaintiffs sued the school committee in a case that became known as *Morgan v. Hennigan.*

While federal judge W. Arthur Garrity considered the case, the Supreme Court ruled against a Colorado school district in *Keyes v. School District No. 1, Denver* (1973) because it found "segregative intent" in the district's policies. This gave Garrity a precedent. Citing a vast paper trail, Garrity wrote in his June 1974 ruling: "The court concludes that the defendants have knowingly carried out a systematic program of segregation affecting all of the city's students, teachers and school facilities and have intentionally brought about and maintained a dual school system. Therefore, the entire school system of Boston is unconstitutionally segregated." Six months later, the appellate court agreed. The Supreme Court let the ruling stand without hearing the case.[35]

Garrity's ruling was often portrayed—and is still often remembered—as the solitary act of a liberal and overreaching judge, but in fact it represented a major victory for an organized constituency—an early front porch example of Americans mobilizing to protect and advocate for their children. At the same time, the ruling became the catalyst for a countermovement of parents mobilized to protect *their* children.

Having found the school committee guilty of willfully maintaining a segregated school system, Garrity began working on a remedy. Only a month after Garrity decided the Boston case, the Supreme Court handed down its *Milliken* opinion, exempting suburbs from desegregation plans; and since, unlike in Detroit, few plaintiffs had an appetite for community control in a city where the white-controlled school committee could not be trusted to delegate authority, Garrity issued an order that called for approximately fifteen thousand students to be bused primarily between South Boston and Roxbury, beginning with the new school year.

Thousands of soon-to-be antibusing activists prepared for massive protests, believing that grassroots pressure, rooted in tactics co-opted from the civil rights movement, could change policy. The impulse to resist the judge's order had many origins, not least of which was a sense of class bias. As Thurgood Marshall had predicted in his *Milliken* dissent, the desegregation of Boston schools would take place on the backs of the poor and the working class. The New York journalist Jimmy Breslin described the Boston busing crisis as a fight between "two groups of people who are poor and doomed and who have been thrown in the ring with each other." In fact, scholars argue that Bostonians fought busing for a variety of reasons; their children were being shipped "to areas they regarded as dangerous"; the court order had taken away from them "the decent schools that they had worked hard to live near"; "they knew their cousins in the suburbs were wholly exempt from 'the law.'" And, according to the city's African Americans, it was racism, pure and simple.[36]

Most of all, many Bostonians regarded Garrity's decision as unfair, unreasonable, and disproportionate in its application of the busing remedy. In the front porch ethos that defined both the black and white experience of desegregation in Boston, having a say in the decisions that affect a person's everyday life—or that of his family—was an essential demand.

In South Boston, a grassroots organization, Restore Our Alienated Rights (ROAR), established itself as the main antibusing organization even before Garrity's ruling and specialized in marshaling and channeling emotion in service of its cause. Over the summer of 1974, it grew quickly and became especially strong in Southie, Hyde Park, and Charlestown (which was not subject to the court order in the first year); the "Townies" of Charlestown named their ROAR branch "Powder Keg" because, as one activist said, "we have a short fuse." Just as the CPA in Charlotte had done, ROAR called for a boycott at the start of the school year; over the next nine months, citywide attendance rarely rose above 75 percent. It is clear, however, that violence in the schools also led parents to keep their kids home.[37]

On the Monday before the school year started, public officials got a little taste of the fury to come. Following a demonstration on Boston Common, ROAR led a march to City Hall, where the day's theme emphasized the politics of motherly love. "We're doing God's work today," the activist Rita Graul told the crowd. "We're protecting our children." Senator Ted Kennedy, an outspoken integration advocate, impulsively went to the rally to speak in support of the court order. As Kennedy began to speak, some heckled, and most turned their backs on him. The senator gave up and began walking across the windswept City Hall Plaza toward the federal building named for his brother John, but hecklers followed him; one woman kicked him and others threw debris at him. Someone suggested that he, like his brothers, should be shot. After the shaken senator slipped into the building, the crush of demonstrators pressed up against the glass doors until they shattered. "It's about time the politicians felt the anger of the people," shouted one demonstrator. South Boston mother Jane DuWors later recalled thinking of the women who stalked Kennedy to the federal building as "scorned"—not in love but "in the most important thing in their lives, their children," she said. "Their children were being scorned," and they were acting to protect them.[38]

The anger of "the people" made its next appearance on the first morning the buses rolled. South Boston High School soon looked like a war zone. Racist graffiti, including at least one KKK, marked the walls. Some Southie residents threw rocks, bottles, and anything else they could lay their hands on at the buses carrying the African American students arriving from Roxbury. The scene reminded a Swedish journalist of Belfast. The notion that the protests were primarily about parental control of their children's education seemed spurious amid reports of protesters shouting "Niggers go home!" and "Monkeys get out!"[39]

Mayor Kevin White, who had tried to walk a tightrope of neutrality while criticizing the court in general terms, responded by sending huge numbers of police. South Boston residents reacted like Belfast Catholics facing an invading British army; they hurled rocks, built barricades, and set fires. When members of the elite Tactical Patrol Force failed to apprehend some stone throwers because patrons of a local bar, the Rabbit Inn, helped them escape, a few of the TPF returned to the pub the next day to deliver beatings to anyone they could find.

As the violence spread, President Gerald Ford offered his assessment of the judge's order. Busing is "not the best solution to quality education in Boston," he said. "I have consistently opposed forced busing to achieve racial balance . . . and therefore, I respectfully disagree with the judge's order." Few things could have made the members of ROAR happier. The president of the United States, it seemed, stood by them.[40]

Although police arrested some kids carrying Molotov cocktails in Hyde Park following a stabbing there in October, by Thanksgiving districtwide attendance rose above 70 percent for the first time since the school year began. State troopers ultimately stayed at South Boston High for three years, but they were helped immeasurably by Peggy Coughlin, a Southie mother who, though opposed to busing, organized a volunteer corps of a hundred parents who took shifts patrolling the school's corridors in order to keep the school safe and open.

The violence ebbed and flowed, but the anger toward the judge and the suburban liberals who supported him never subsided. ROAR's activists sometimes traveled out to Wellesley, an upscale suburb west of the city, to picket Garrity's house. "If the suburbs are honestly interested in solving the problems of the Negro, why don't they build subsidized housing for them?" asked Louise Day Hicks.[41] As one Charlestown mother put it in a letter to Garrity, "How can it be the law of the land when you can move less than one mile away and be out from under this law?"[42]

In particular, antibusing activists seethed at the liberal *Boston Globe*, which most in the antibusing ranks perceived as the condescending voice box of suburban editors and reporters. Although the paper later won a Pulitzer Prize for its busing coverage, militants fired shots through the windows of its Dorchester plant several times, made frequent bomb threats, and slashed the tires on delivery trucks. More theatrically, some of the *Globe*'s opponents stole copies from all over the city and dumped them, like tea, into Boston Harbor.

Ultimately, as in Charlotte, the moderates who opposed both busing and breaking the law did their best to "make the best of a bad situation." In the second year, Judge Garrity implemented Phase II of his plan, designed to enforce "a more uniform racial ration on the entire city." Under Phase II, the city bused up to twenty-five thousand students each day and, in an effort to elicit more parental participation in the desegregation process, established Racial-Ethnic Parent Councils in each school and a citywide parents' advisory board. Particularly in the first year, many of those who joined the REPCs, like Peggy Coughlin, opposed busing but seemed to have concluded that they were not going to make it go away. "I disapprove of the law, but I felt that I'd be teaching the child to break the law if [we] boycotted," said a Hyde Park mother. "Also, I would not want [them] to form prejudices. Keeping them home would do more harm than good."[43]

In the second year, with Charlestown getting its first taste of busing, the Powder Keg chapter of ROAR initiated massive protests, including a prayer march led by mothers who dramatically confronted police in the shadow of the Bunker Hill Monument. More notoriously, at a City Hall protest in April 1976, teens carrying an American flag attacked an African American lawyer, Ted Landsmark, who had inadvertently walked into the protest. In the award-winning photograph that seared the moment into the city's memory, Landsmark looks to be pirouetting in a desperate effort to avoid being impaled. Boston, it seemed, had renounced its progressive past.

Overlooked, however, were the many Bostonians who supported integration. Although the media gave priority to coverage of antibusing demonstrations, on any number of occasions these were matched by marches and rallies in support of the court order—including one in May 1975 that drew forty thousand marchers. But more important, parents had taken matters into their own hands and founded a handful of independent, experimental public schools—"wrenched," as J. Anthony Lukas described it, "from a skeptical school system" by groups of determined parents and teachers—even before Judge Garrity ordered redistricting of Boston's schools and the busing of children: the Highland Park Free School educated black students, while the Roxbury Community School and the New School attracted middle-class students, black and white, from all over the city and, as one scholar noted, "modeled what a quality interracial education could look like." Similarly, the George Bancroft School in the city's South End neighborhood succeeded in providing a nontraditional educational program to an integrated student population. For six years, teachers and parents joined together in offering a course of instruction at Bancroft that taught not only reading, writing, and arithmetic but also weaving, pottery, poetry, philosophy, and bicycle repair. As word spread of this experimental school, parents in and beyond the neighborhood, black and white, clamored to get their children admitted. In the early 1970s, families began moving to the neighborhood because they wanted their children educated in an integrated school.[44]

But Garrity's desegregation plan designated all Boston schools—no exceptions—either as district schools, to which students would be assigned only from within a newly drawn racially balanced district, or as magnet schools, to which students from all over the city could apply, with only one-fourth of its seats allocated for children within its district. Parents of Bancroft's students bristled. After all, they had already achieved desegregation. In the end, the majority of parents voted for Bancroft to become a district school; they hoped that most of the children currently attending would thereby be able to continue. When Garrity's office assigned students to Bancroft in 1975, however, many of the white students fell within the new district, but most of the black students did not; new students from other black neighborhoods were assigned to the school. Predictably, parents reacted angrily.

The Bancroft school story reveals the complex motives and values that underpinned challenges to northern desegregation. The battle for equal educational opportunities was not fought simply between liberal courts and reactionary citizens' groups. Indeed, even as the most outrageous antibusing activists were often driven by racism and parochialism, other Boston parents who had joined community groups to press for integration protested against the court-ordered desegregation plans, too. The common complaint was of alienation, of having one's children's futures arbitrarily administered by a technocrat in an ivory tower.

In the end, by 1977, the Boston school system lost nearly twenty thousand white students, out of its 1972 total population of ninety thousand. Pundits blamed white flight, though white middle-class residents had been leaving the city for more than ten years prior to Garrity's busing order. Nevertheless, the contrast between suburb and city remained an all-important factor. Even the Divers, the idealistic young South End couple whose son attended the Bancroft school—captured so vividly in J. Anthony Lukas's *Common Ground*—eventually abandoned the city for the suburbs. For a time they fought for a novel, progressive version of the American dream, only to favor the comfort and security of the dominant model of that same dream. In the meantime, Arthur Garrity controlled Boston schools for eleven years, from 1974 to 1985, before abandoning busing. By 2005, 86 percent of the Boston schools' student population was black and Latino.[45]

For a long time now, it's been said that the antibusing campaigns that occurred all over the country—from Boston, Charlotte, and Detroit to Baltimore, Milwaukee, and Los Angeles and beyond—exhibit Americans rejecting "big government" and starting down the path to embracing conservatism. But that is an oversimplification. In fact, the anger expressed in these campaigns grew out of an exhaustion with government in general: big or small, federal or local, executive, legislative, or judicial, it did not matter. Government at all levels failed to offer adequate solutions, leaving Americans to devise their own. The common denominator was emotion—anger and despair, a sense that they had to fight to hold on to whatever promise they believed came with being American.[46] That spark of emotion drove the front porch political organizing ethos in the 1970s and 1980s.

When American politics moved from schools and neighborhoods into homes—into kitchens and bedrooms—a variety of activists further affirmed the logic of front porch politics as they searched for effective ways to confront and solve what were, to them, life-and-death questions.

3

Sexual Politics, Family Politics

●

It seems hard to believe now, but in the middle and late 1970s, readers could find serious political questions discussed in the pages of *Playboy*, America's best-known "men's" magazine. Feminists criticized *Playboy* for objectifying women and evangelicals denounced it as pornography, but thanks to the temper of the times, it succeeded in providing a forum for debate on a broadening set of political issues.[1] Consider the May 1978 *Playboy*. In this one issue, readers could find a story on New York's "public sex palaces," a column of brief interviews with male celebrities about how "women's lib" had affected their lives, and an interview with the entertainer and leading pro-family activist Anita Bryant. On one extreme, the magazine led readers on a tour, in words and images, of Plato's Retreat, a place where, for thirty dollars admission, a couple could go to have sex, alone or in a group. On the other extreme, the Bryant interview opened another world to readers, one in which citizen Christians characterized feminists and "militant homosexuals" as a clear and present danger to God-fearing traditional families. And in the middle, the male celebrity interviews offered a little balance on the question of women's liberation: the stuntman and huckster Evel Knievel sneered at "women's libbers" as "the ones who've had problems with men" and said, "If I catch one, I try and screw her a little harder"; meanwhile, Cincinnati Reds catcher Johnny Bench acknowledged that he had grown to appreciate feminism for liberating both women and men—"I think the changes are for the best: All people are freer."[2]

By the 1970s, new battles over sex and sex roles pulled a new kind of politics out of bedrooms, out of kitchens, and out of closets into the open.

Struggles over women's rights—particularly the right to physical security—and over gay rights—especially surrounding gays and lesbians in the classroom—revealed how the most intimate experiences and ideals could influence national political contests over recognition and meaning, and national electoral fights for policy and elected office. When, in the 1970s, politics slid under America's sheets, the debate turned on perceptions of choice: women choosing not to submit to husbands, to take jobs outside the home, to terminate pregnancies; gays "choosing" a same-sex lifestyle, "coming out" of the closet to others, demanding equal protection under the law. Unlike so many front porch activists, feminists and gay activists understood the home as a site of abuse and inequity rather than as a site to defend. And yet their politics was equally personal. They saw the very essence of who they were as human beings threatened as they mobilized to secure treatment equal to that of their male and straight counterparts.

This new chapter in American discord included the arrival of an army of self-consciously Christian activists. Although scholars and pundits tend to frame their appearance in ideological terms—describing the new Christian *right*—the fact is that for all but some of their leaders, ideology and political labeling signified little. What mattered was that they saw their families, and by extension the institution of the nuclear family, in danger. At a time when a Gallup poll reported that one-third of all Americans claimed to have had a religious conversion experience, and when evangelists on more than a thousand radio and television stations preached to audiences numbering in the hundreds of thousands, Christians stepped forward as a willing army of grassroots political activists.[3] For the average pro-family activist-in-waiting, the phenomenon worked something like this: first, through observation in his community, he sensed a threat or threats to his family; then the perception of threat was reinforced by an evangelical authority, echoing and giving voice to the front porch concern that his family (and the American family writ large) faced imminent danger; finally, thanks to a growing religious political infrastructure, he organized with other like-minded souls and voted for like-minded candidates.[4] Indeed, Paul Weyrich, one of the nation's leading Christian political strategists, believed that in order to win public support, every political question could be "reduced to right and wrong."[5] This proved to be an enormously important insight that helped shift electoral patterns in the United States; at a time when Americans were being challenged on multiple fronts, one historian notes that many of them "found great solace in moral certainty, unambiguous sexual and familial relationships, and divine forgiveness."[6] Reassurance, at a time when the nation needed reassurance, turned out to be a powerful political salve.

By the late 1970s, a front porch political pattern had emerged. A movement's success would prompt its antagonists to mobilize, rekindling the very conflicts it sought to resolve. As a result, front porch political campaigns—particularly over social and cultural issues—often reinforced one another. Just as title bouts in heavyweight boxing are so often followed by rematches, American political culture was increasingly defined by cycles of protest and counterprotest.

Today it is hard for most Americans to imagine a time when the nature of their personal lives was not, in some way, open for political discussion. Yet until the 1960s, only a small fraction of the nation's political activists dared to suggest as much. On questions of civil rights for African Americans, the goal had always been equal treatment in public accommodations, housing, and employment; and when women demanded "equal rights" earlier in the century, the majority of activists meant only that they wanted the vote. Personal lives became political in the 1960s when second-wave feminists demanded changes not only in public treatment of women—equal pay, equal access to education, bank credit—but in private—an end to domestic violence, control over their own bodies, and a more equitable division of labor at home.

At roughly the same time that citizen groups were modeling community organizing for a nation of would-be activists, the women's liberation movement was similarly pioneering the sensibility of front porch politics. The movement's slogan, "The personal is political," captured a politics based on experience. Women made it plain that the various crises one faces in one's own life, in one's community, or even in one's household can be viewed through a political lens. "The personal is political" established a new way of thinking about politics that soon extended beyond questions of women's rights and gay rights, a way of thinking that a broad swath of Americans (including those who opposed feminism and gay liberation) soon adopted.

Coming out of the civil rights movement, the New Left, and the peace movement, thousands of women devised an organizing strategy called the consciousness-raising group. Every week, in hundreds of gatherings across the country, women got together in small groups to talk about the discrimination they faced in their daily lives—discrimination practiced even by the men they loved. Here, in these groups, women empathized with one another as they described personal experiences—how husbands, fathers, brothers, and boyfriends expected them to play second fiddle, to limit themselves to certain types of work, to take extraordinary measures to make themselves beautiful according to standards set by men. This is how the personal became political.[7] In time, increasing numbers of women began to stand up to men not so much on the front porch, but behind the front door, quietly challenging—and slowly changing—American culture. Later, *Ms.*, the magazine founded by Gloria Steinem, built its long-term success in part by providing a forum for readers to describe their own epiphanies. They sent letters describing moments when they suddenly realized their second-class status not only in society but in their own homes. They often ended their letters with "Click" to signify the "click of recognition" when they realized that something they had long tolerated was in fact evidence of their own oppression as women. *Ms.* went a long way toward mainstreaming feminism in the 1970s and 1980s and was among the first publications to discuss— among many other issues—domestic violence, abortion, and women's health. These were all questions about control of, or security for, women's bodies, and they were essential to establishing a political model based on personal experience.[8]

At times, women put their bodies directly on the line. In 1972, President Nixon signed the Education Amendments Act, which included a vaguely worded provision prohibiting sex discrimination in any educational program at an institution receiving federal funding. In time, the Department of Health, Education and Welfare ruled that under Title IX, federally funded educational institutions had to provide equal access to sports for both men and women.[9] School administrators did not exactly jump to enforce Title IX. Consequently, female athletes found themselves having to educate school officials on their rights under the provision. Yale University, which had only recently admitted women, continued to privilege men's sports over women's. Although one could join the women's crew, for example, tensions with the men's crew made the women's lives miserable, even as the women proved more successful in competition. Rowing in the New England elements can be grueling, particularly during the freezing months of winter and early spring. At the time, Yale did not provide showers or bathrooms for the women's crew at the boathouse (a thirty-minute drive from campus). While the women sat on the bus, their icicle hair dripping, the men took hot showers in the boathouse. Some women rowers fell ill just as they were expecting to be training for the upcoming season and the 1976 Olympics. Led by captain and future two-time Olympian Chris Ernst, and driven by anger at this daily injury, the women's crew essentially dared each other into a dramatic protest. With a *New York Times* reporter in tow, nineteen women's crew members marched unannounced into the office of the Yale women's athletic director and stripped naked. On their chests and backs, they had written TITLE IX in Yale Bulldog blue. "These are the bodies that Yale is exploiting," Ernst read from her prepared statement. "On days like today, the ice freezes on this skin. Then we sit for half an hour as the ice melts and soaks through to meet the sweat that is soaking us from the inside." When a story about the protest appeared on the front page of the *Times*'s second section the next day, startled alumni called to demand action. "Embarrassment is a wonderful thing," Ernst said years later. "The deal was that they were just pretending we weren't there, and our protest was: 'Yoo-hoo, here we are.'" Where government regulations had failed to achieve equality, this front porch tactic made inequality visible; from there, solutions followed.[10]

The Title IX protests were a bridge between the by-now-familiar politics of legal equality and a nascent cultural politics concerned with the control and protection of women's bodies. New political mobilizations revealed the prevalence of domestic violence and rape, and the patriarchal nature of American medicine, and as a result brought private lives to the forefront of the movement's campaign for liberation.

The national success of *Our Bodies, Ourselves*, a book about women's medical and health issues that originated as a Boston Women's Health Collective course readings packet, challenged traditional deference to the male medical profession. By seizing control of expertise about their own bodies, the Boston women tapped into a national hunger for self-determination; indeed, when Simon and Schuster won the chance to publish the book commercially in 1973, *Our Bodies* sold more than a million copies in its first five years.[11] The questioning of the status quo may not have involved marking a ballot or marching in protest, but it contributed to a wider awareness of sexism that further fueled the women's liberation movement. By 1975, when a coalition of women's health organizations formed the National Women's Health Network, it included more than fifty feminist health centers.[12] In challenging the medical establishment's entire structure of care for women, feminists began to show that women did indeed make up their own kind of oppressed class.

On two other issues—rape and domestic violence—they could even better rest their case. Most Americans in 1970 had no idea that, as one scholar has reported, an American woman "stood one chance in three of being sexually abused before the age of eighteen." At college age, "the chances were one in five that she'd be raped on a date." For a variety of reasons, such staggering statistics eluded public attention. Rape victims often experienced shame and did not think others would believe them. Most cases—estimated at 70 to 90 percent—went unreported. Worse, in some states the legal system favored the rapist, as victims were often assumed to be complicit; fifteen states required a witness in order for the case to go to court. In New York, a victim needed *two* witnesses to support her story and evidence that she did not consent. Finally, defense attorneys routinely introduced the victim's sexual history as a way of impeaching her credibility. As a result, in 1971, 2,415 rape complaints in New York City led to a grand total of eighteen convictions.[13]

The women's movement took two courses of action in confronting the rape scourge in America: consciousness raising and rape crisis services. At speak-outs and conferences and in writing, feminists exposed the pervasive presence of rape as a crime against women in America. In the mid-1970s, women's groups successfully lobbied state legislatures to rewrite their rape laws, removing the corroboration requirement and prohibiting defense attorneys from sifting through a victim's past sexual history. Similarly, local groups prodded police departments to establish, for the first time, sex crime units, which were often staffed with women cops.[14]

At the same time, other activists started rape crisis centers as a public service to victims. The first, the D.C. Rape Crisis Center, formed in the nation's capital in 1972, started as a twenty-four-hour hotline in American University student Karen Kollias's apartment. Four years later, more than a hundred rape crisis centers dotted the national map.

Still, the progress made in building this infrastructure of service and protection had to be measured against stubborn ignorance on questions of violence against married women. Until the 1970s, for example, most states defined rape as a crime committed against a woman "not the wife of the perpetrator." Legislators seemed unable to grasp the idea that a husband could rape his wife, and if he did, why a woman would not just leave.[15] But they missed the point. The real question should have been what kept her from staying away. Battered women had few options even in the mid-1970s. Married women, with or without children, often had nowhere to go; before 1972, there were no battered women's shelters in America. In addition, women who left faced the daunting challenge of staying afloat financially. They sometimes could not qualify for welfare because their abusive husband's income made them ineligible, and it was very difficult to get credit without a husband's consent. Women with children sometimes needed both a job and day care services. Beyond economics, some women took seriously their "in sickness and in health" marriage vows, while others exhibited the shattered self-confidence that so often follows from physical and psychological abuse. The batterers often succeeded in isolating their wives from their own families; with little chance for rebuilding self-esteem, many women concluded that the abuse they suffered was somehow their own fault.[16]

The first battered women's shelter in the United States grew out of a St. Paul, Minnesota, VISTA program that offered information on divorce and custody over the phone because women had no other source of such information. In time, Susan Ryan and Sharon Vaughan realized that a lot of the women calling about divorce had been beaten and had nowhere to go. Although Minneapolis–St. Paul had thirty-seven emergency shelters for men, it had nothing for women and children except a one-night-in-a-motel option administered through Emergency Social Services.

Vaughan and Ryan started Women's Advocates in March 1972 and at first took battered women into their own homes. This happened quietly, and consequently largely under the political radar, even though it was a purposefully political act. When the women purchased a large Victorian home on Grand Avenue—the first of four not far from downtown St. Paul—in July 1974, circumstances changed. The men from whom battered women fled often came to the house; some broke into the home, others threw rocks through the windows or phoned in bomb threats. Police did nothing because, as Anne Enke points out, they "assumed that even when women owned a property, men retained a right of access to 'their' women and children on that property." After repeated efforts, including an August 1976 protest march on the Capitol to demand a change in police policies, the police department gave in. Under new policies,

Women's Advocates henceforth led police training sessions, teaching new recruits about domestic violence and the options available and unavailable to women. In 1978, the National Coalition Against Domestic Violence was formed, and by 1982, more than three hundred shelters offered refuge to battered women.[17]

Thus the women's movement succeeded, if in fits and starts, when its central concern was health and physical safety. Some Americans may have been slower than others to support campaigns focused on athletics, medicine, rape, and domestic violence, but few stood up against them. All of that changed, however, when the subject turned to abortion.

Abortion grew into a political issue slowly. Calls for abortion rights intensified following the 1962 case of Sherri Finkbine, a pregnant women who was taking the sleeping pill Thalidomide when research revealed the drug caused serious birth defects. Finkbine's doctor scheduled her for an abortion, but when a newspaper reporter to whom Finkbine had spoken (hoping to spread word of the dangers of Thalidomide) described her case without identifying her, the publicity caused the hospital to cancel the procedure. In desperation, Finkbine went to Sweden for the abortion (and lost her job in the process). In the next two years, a rubella outbreak caused an estimated thirty thousand birth defects, leading some states to liberalize their laws by allowing abortion in cases in which birth defects were likely or the mother's health was endangered. By 1967, *Life* magazine—that most mainstream of American periodicals—stunned its readers by reporting that five thousand American women died every year from self-administered or back-alley abortions. That year, activists formed the National Association for the Repeal of Abortion Laws (NARAL) to begin lobbying not for more reform of abortion laws but for their repeal.[18]

At the same time that groups like NARAL sought solutions through legislation, other activists took the front porch approach of relying on themselves for solutions. Following the *Our Bodies, Ourselves* model of independence, the women of Jane, a Chicago feminist collective started by Heather Booth (who later established the Midwest Academy for community organizers) and others, set up an underground organization that referred women to an abortion "doctor" (who was not, in fact, a licensed physician). Soon women in Jane learned how to do the procedure themselves, and the collective performed as many as thirty abortions a day. Women seeking the service would meet Jane members at a "front" apartment and would later be driven to another apartment for the procedure.

These meeting and procedure locations constantly changed to keep the authorities guessing. In May 1972, police finally busted Jane as it finished a long day in a posh apartment overlooking Lake Michigan, but the group managed to make the service available again within six weeks. Eventually, thanks to the Supreme Court's *Roe V. Wade* decision, the charges against Jane were dropped. The collective estimated that between 1969 and 1973, it performed ten thousand to eleven thousand abortions.[19]

The lawyers who argued *Roe* before the men of the Supreme Court, Sarah Weddington and Margie Hames, began with the principle that every person should be entitled to make decisions about what happens to his or her body without interference from the government. They pursued the case along narrower (and more cautious) constitutional grounds, however, by arguing that the implied right to privacy affirmed by the Court in the past should apply to decisions about one's medical condition.[20]

On January 22, 1973, the United States Supreme Court ruled 7–2 in favor of the *Roe* plaintiffs in one of the most important cases in its history. Justice Harry Blackmun wrote the majority opinion and effectively supported the plaintiff's contention that the right to privacy prohibited the intervention of the state in the absence of a compelling reason. "We recognize the right of the individual, married or single, to be free from unwanted governmental intrusion into matters so fundamentally affecting a person as the right of a woman to decide whether or not to terminate her pregnancy," he wrote. At the same time, the Court rejected abortion on demand. Instead, based on careful study of all the available medical research, Blackmun laid out a complicated standard for assessing all future cases: in the first trimester of pregnancy, the state could not interfere in the decision being made by a woman and her doctor; in the second trimester, the state could intervene only to protect the mother's health; and in the third trimester, when a fetus became viable, the state could even prohibit an abortion (unless the mother's health was at stake).[21]

The *Roe v. Wade* case still stands as one of the women's movement's most important victories, but its singular importance lies just as much in the countermovement it helped mobilize. Although some turned out against abortion in state battles leading up to *Roe*, it took the Supreme Court's decision to fully galvanize a nationally organized opposition. Throughout the 1970s, as public opinion polls generally showed overwhelming support for the right to an abortion, the antiabortion movement gradually built its strength. As the historian Robert Self has recently described it, making abortion legal put women ahead of the family, and that, for many Americans, was a clear example of moral decay. "Because abortion undermined their understanding of motherhood and family and constituted the taking of a 'life,'" Self writes, "for them, it could never be the basis for women's equality."[22] It could only bring down the American family and thus the nation itself.[23] In short order, then, abortion opponents fought back. In 1976, they succeeded in getting Congress to pass the Hyde Amendment, which prohibited the use of Medicaid funds to pay for an abortion except when the mother's life was in jeopardy. In 1978, Congress extended the Hyde Amendment to deny health coverage for abortions to government employees, members of the armed services, and Peace Corps personnel. By the time voters elected Ronald Reagan president in 1980, as we will see in this book's final chapter, antiabortion activists had become one of the most important wings of a larger pro-family movement, with sophisticated telephone and direct mail campaigns financed by the National Right to Life Committee's eleven million members and countless others. The lines were being drawn in an increasingly intense culture war.[24]

Indeed, by the mid-1970s, time and circumstance conspired to push the women's movement back on its heels and open the door to a powerful opposition. In part, feminists' success at confronting American society with a wide range of issues and offering a variety of services had spread the movement too thin. But more than that, to their surprise, they met an opposition that understood equal rights in a very personal way, too, but as a threat to the very women they were meant to protect.[25]

Although the struggle for the Equal Rights Amendment, as a contest over a proposed constitutional change, took place on a national scale, the state-by-state campaign revealed how opponents, in particular, perceived the amendment as an intimate and a personal issue. The idea for the ERA originated with Alice Paul and the National Women's Party in 1923. Both major parties had endorsed it in their party platforms as early as the 1940s, and in the wake of the civil rights movement's various 1960s successes, the wording of the ERA hardly seemed controversial: "Equality of rights under the law shall not be denied or abridged by the United States or by any State on account of sex." And yet the ERA became the focus of the highest-profile battles over women's equality in the 1970s. In the abstract, to supporters, the ERA campaign seemed to be just one more effort to confront ignorance: Who would not agree that women should be treated equally with men? In practice, the amendment would not even apply to private companies or private educational institutions— both places where women lagged far behind men; instead, its importance lay in the principle of asserting, as a nation, that the psychological and cultural structures that propped up inequality would not be tolerated.[26] It turned out that those American psychological and cultural structures were not so easily overcome, however. The ERA battle was ultimately fought not over political equality but over the perceived cultural implications of gender equality.

Although ordinary Americans campaigning in key ratification states would later determine the outcome of the ERA struggle, the first articulation of opposition in front porch terms came from Senator Sam Ervin. Three years before he presided over the Senate Watergate hearings, the grandfatherly North Carolinian waged a sustained effort to amend the proposed language of the ERA in order to "protect" the traditional rights of women. If the law treated women like men, his argument went, motherhood would no longer be protected. The ERA would, in his view, discriminate against women who wanted to remain homemakers. And if their marriages dissolved, they would no longer be entitled to alimony and child support. Even more shocking, he claimed, the ERA would mandate unisex bathrooms in public places, unisex prison cells for male and female inmates, and, at a time when the Vietnam War raged on, conscription for women as well as men. In short, Ervin cast the ERA as a constitutional amendment that would destroy the family. Although Ervin failed to win changes in the ERA's language, he framed many of the terms of the debate for the coming national struggle. In March 1972, the Senate passed the ERA, 84 to 8; the House of Representatives soon after voted 354 to 23 in favor. Within a year, thirty state legislatures had voted for the ERA, and ratification seemed inevitable.

And yet, in 1973, the seemingly unsinkable ERA ran headlong into a political iceberg. Over the next nine years, the pro-family movement, a massive, previously unseen political force, capsized the ERA. Just as women's liberationists tried to frame their arguments in front porch political terms—showing how unequal treatment shaped their day-to-day lives at home, at work, and at school—the pro-family movement likewise placed their arguments against the ERA in front porch terms, arguing that the amendment amounted to an attack on families. Later, pundits saw this debate as representative of the "culture wars" and a deepening split between liberals and conservatives in the United States, but for activists on both sides, labels were irrelevant. What mattered was how both sides saw their lives and dreams under attack.[27]

To the chagrin of feminists, the anti-ERA movement was led not by cartoonish Archie Bunker–type men clinging to notions of male superiority but by women advocating on behalf of women. Such activists made formidable opponents. Ignorance was not the problem. The women who opposed the ERA believed in standing up for women, too, but they thought the ERA would hurt, not help, women. Pro-family activists would transform American politics in the 1970s by using issues such as the ERA, gay rights, and abortion to awaken a wider public to an organizing framework long advanced by feminists: that the personal is political.[28]

The woman most associated with leading the charge against the ERA, Phyllis Schlafly, began her career as a laissez-faire conservative but was arguably most responsible for taking Sam Ervin's critique to the streets. Schlafly came from a bootstrapping background. Growing up in the 1930s, she watched her mother work to support the family when her father lost his job. Schlafly paid her way through Washington University by working night shifts testing ammunition at the St. Louis Ordnance Plant.[29] She later earned a master's degree in political science from Radcliffe and twice ran losing campaigns for Congress. She first came to national attention in 1964 when she wrote *A Choice, Not an Echo*, a critique of the Republican Party's recent history of nominating moderate presidential candidates; the book sold more than three million copies and boosted the far-right candidacy of Barry Goldwater that year.

Perhaps because Schlafly came late to the ERA battle—she was focused on the Cold War as the ERA moved through Congress—the amendment's supporters did not take her seriously at first. But the feminists who dismissed Schlafly as blindly defending tradition misjudged her. As one writer observed, "seldom has one person played such a large role in changing the direction of a policy that seemed to be foreordained."[30] More important, feminists failed to recognize that Schlafly represented a large grassroots movement then mobilizing in defense of the family.

Using *The Phyllis Schlafly Report*, a monthly newsletter typically focused on national security issues, Schlafly singlehandedly led her own kind of consciousness-raising campaign in which she outlined a politics of hypothetical experience. Schlafly and her allies pointed to statistics on divorce and unwed mothers and fueled their campaign with predictions of family and national decline. The "Christian tradition of chivalry," she claimed, "obligated men to support and protect their wives and children." Passing the ERA, putting men and women on the same footing, would, in Schlafly's view, absolve men of that obligation and leave women and their children without protection. The ERA would "abolish a woman's right to child support and alimony" in the event of divorce. At the same time, Schlafly and other anti-ERA women made it clear that they supported equal opportunity and equal pay for women, but they believed that existing legislation already provided for both. In reasoned tones, Schlafly and her supporters stood up for women who chose to remain at home as guardians of family and hearth.[31]

Schlafly and her supporters repeatedly proved themselves to be master organizers. Unlike their feminist counterparts who expended a tremendous amount of energy trying to reach consensus on most every decision, the anti-ERA forces embraced a hierarchical organizing structure. As the states took up ratification, Schlafly organized a national network of women in opposition to the amendment. The *Phyllis Schlafly Report* mailing list grew from three thousand to thirty-five thousand, and according to Schlafly's recent biographer, the recipients "brought an evangelical enthusiasm that energized the entire anti-ERA movement and impressed state legislators with their commitment to stop ERA from being ratified." The evangelical quality is worth noting because evangelical Christian women had hitherto entered the political arena mainly to speak out against Communism; Schlafly brought them to the ERA. In fact, except for the high level of church membership, the STOP ERA rank and file mirrored the National Organization for Women (NOW) membership: overwhelmingly white and middle class, 50 percent over thirty years old, and 66 percent holding college degrees. But where only 31 to 48 percent (depending on the data) of pro-ERA women belonged to churches, 98 percent of the anti-ERA women did.[32]

In a matter of months, Schlafly outorganized the pro-ERA forces for the coming ratification battles in the remaining states. She coordinated the first national conference of STOP ERA (for Stop Taking Our Privileges) in St. Louis in September 1972, and by early 1973 had established chapters in twenty-six states.[33] Schlafly ran news and organizing suggestions every month in *The Phyllis Schlafly Report*, and updated voting estimates for each state legislature in each issue. Most important, she ran workshops for women in each battleground state, and STOP ERA took a page from the early civil rights movement in which well-dressed, well-mannered, articulate activists argued points calmly and in reasoned tones. The critical tactic was to act like a lady, which played well with the white male legislators, most of whom were middle-aged or older and leaned, temperamentally, toward the traditional. In Ohio, pro-family women wrote letters to legislators (often accompanied by homemade bread, pies, or cookies): "We are a group of wives, mothers and working women vitally concerned with how the Equal Rights Amendment will affect the status of women and the fundamental respect for the family as a basic unit of our society . . . Those women lawyers, women legislators, and women executives promoting ERA have plenty of education and talent to get whatever they want in the business, political, and academic world. We, the wives and working women, need you, dear Senators and Representatives, to protect us. We think this is the man's responsibility, and we are dearly hoping you will vote NO on ERA." It was a winning recipe.[34]

In fact, as a number of scholars have noted, behind the disdain for feminists and their alleged assault on the family there stood both "an underlying distrust of men" and a concern about the effect on children of "blurring" gender roles. Phyllis Schlafly frequently asserted that if the nation ratified the ERA, married men would abandon their wives and run off with younger women; with no child support or alimony laws on the books, the "cast-off" wife would then struggle to fend for herself and her children.[35] In addition, if the ERA passed, pro-family activists predicted that the resulting "gender-role blurring"—boys and girls playing Little League baseball together, men and women using the same bathrooms or imprisoned in the same cells—would make children unable to "see the difference between the sexes." And that could only lead to more homosexuality.[36]

Apocalyptic visions of unisex restrooms should have seemed silly—all of the legislators who supported the ERA had made clear that the ERA would not undermine the Constitution's implicit right to privacy—but they were useful in producing outrage among the amendment's opponents. And the idea of women in combat dogged the ratification process at every step. Although the ERA's legislative record on women's military service was somewhat ambiguous—women would certainly be drafted, but would probably not serve in combat roles—the ERA's opponents painted vivid pictures of women drafted out of the safety of their own homes, getting bayoneted on the front lines, and returning home maimed or in body bags (feminists, for their part, essentially said that, yes, they expected women to be drafted and serve equally—because equality is equality).[37]

These front porch concerns over women's and children's safety and security were supplemented by an analysis that saw in the decline of the family the decline of the nation. Many of the women in STOP ERA took inspiration from a number of high-profile evangelical women—Anita Bryant, Marabel Morgan, Beverly LaHaye, Phyllis Schlafly, Tammy Faye Bakker—some of whom (Bryant, Morgan, Bakker) could point to their own front porch experience of coming from broken homes; each defined the family as the foundation of society, a microcosm of the wider civilization that, when healthy, guaranteed the health of the republic. Within the family, husbands, in their positions of authority, were not expected to change or conform for the health of the family. Rather, women derived their power in society from their responsibility and unique qualities to adapt, nurture, and care for their husbands and children.

After winning ratification in thirty states in one year, only three more states voted for ERA the next year, and Tennessee's legislature voted to rescind its earlier ratification vote. Building on the success of the first two years of STOP ERA organizing, Schlafly founded the Eagle Forum as an "alternative to women's lib" and began putting out the *Eagle Forum Newsletter*, a more colloquial version of *The Phyllis Schlafly Report*.

By comparison, the pro-ERA forces were not nearly as well organized. It took until 1976, when it seemed suddenly that the ERA might fall several states short, before a national organization, ERAmerica, was formed to counter Schlafly and her army. And even though ERAmerica counted more than 120 other organizations within its coalition, NOW stayed away and instead mounted its own pro-ERA campaign. Neither national organization came close to mobilizing the number of activists at the grass roots that STOP ERA did.[38]

By 1977, the International Women's Year, the ERA was in trouble. Elizabeth Holtzman, congresswoman from New York, introduced legislation to extend the ERA ratification deadline, and after more than a year and a half of lobbying and a march of a hundred thousand people on Washington, Congress granted an extension to June 1982.

In the end, it did not matter. STOP ERA's kitchen sink strategy of raising every possible negative outcome that could come from passing the ERA, realistic or not, had taken hold in the public mind. In May and June 1982, ERA supporters resorted to desperate measures in Illinois, the last battleground. Eight women fasted at the statehouse for thirty-seven days—confronted at one point by antifeminists who dismissed the fasters as "dieters" and ate pizza and hot dogs in front of them—to no avail. Another seventeen women chained themselves to railings in the Illinois Senate chamber for four days. STOP ERA won as the vote fell four short of the three-fifths majority required in Illinois for ratification. The Equal Rights Amendment was dead.[39]

The battles over Title IX, women's health, domestic violence, and the ERA showed that front porch politics worked. Women took the lead in demanding—and winning—recognition of a wide array of physical dangers and inequities, and, largely by relying on themselves (instead of those in power), they made significant changes that ultimately gave women more security and autonomy. In the more high-profile ERA wars, the pro-family movement proved that adopting a front porch political sensibility of its own could be a valuable national strategy. The key was to counter the politics of experience with a more ominous politics of moral decay. At any time in the nation's history, Americans could point to evidence of moral decline, but the pro-family movement saw moral decline in front porch terms, particularly in terms of protecting children's welfare. These activists pinned the blame for family (and national) decline on feminists—and, as we will see, on homosexuals—by "front-porching" the threat: by giving countless hypothetical examples of how the abstract weakening of the family would look and feel to American women and children.

Beyond the campaign against the ERA, few issues spurred the growth of the pro-family movement as much as gay rights. And, in an archetypal case of the protest-counterprotest cycle that governed American cultural politics in the 1970s, nothing spurred the renewed growth of the gay rights movement as much as pro-family activism. The two movements were effectively mutually reinforcing, seeing in each other mortal threats that had to be met with fierce organizing. For the mostly religious activists in the pro-family ranks, gay rights represented not only an abstract threat to the traditional family—and therefore an assault on American life—but also, if the nation was going to tolerate gay men and women living their "chosen" lifestyle out in the open, a more acute and direct danger to their children. For gays and lesbians, the dream of equal treatment under the law that seemed within grasp by the mid-1970s suddenly came under withering attack from pro-family forces who seemed intent on not only forcing homosexuals back into the closet but on destroying their livelihoods. By decade's end, both sides had chalked up victories and in the process established themselves as dominant forces in American politics.

The gay and lesbian civil rights movement of the 1970s emerged from a convergence of the old homophile movement of the 1940s and 1950s with the New Left and other movements of the 1960s. To those standing outside the movement, it seemed to come out of nowhere and grow quickly. In part, this was because gays had so successfully been kept invisible through the 1960s, but it was also because the new tactic of "coming out," leaving behind the secret life to claim equality in both public and private, mobilized the more committed activists.[40]

The sudden appearance of gay liberation on the national political scene contributed in certain ways to the movement being somewhat more controversial than its sister movements. Segregated behind blacked-out windows in gay bars located in marginal neighborhoods, gays had posed little threat to the American way. Out of the closet, they suddenly became a guerrilla army, a sexually deviant Viet Cong. No matter how strenuously activists presented themselves as combating ignorance, as women's liberationists did, some significant segment of the public would never buy it. And since the question of the origins of gayness continued to be subject to debate, many Americans—particularly those who sought counsel from the Bible—would forever see homosexuality as a choice. And God did not approve of such choices.

As in the women's movement, in the gay liberation movement, divisions between young and old, militant and moderate, appeared at the outset. Older members of the homophile organizations such as the Mattachine Society pleaded for peace and quiet. For them, the fight had always been "about being left alone to live a discreet life as a homosexual man or woman." But they were answered by younger activists calling for "gay power"; these men and women were not interested in living discreet lives, but rather saw liberation in "defining themselves to society as gay men and lesbians." They wanted the same civil rights as everyone else.[41]

Among the younger activists, a range of organizations formed at both the local and national levels, representing varying degrees of militancy. Following the rhetoric of the Black Panthers and third-world rebels, the new activists spoke of liberation and revolution and mostly protested the closet as a culturally enforced quarantine that kept them from being gay in public, from forming their own families, from getting work, and from having access to the full measure of American life. Stepping out into a society that recognized them as full and equal members became the essential goal of their social and cultural revolution. But in arguing for their cause mostly through revolutionary rhetoric—the most prominent new organization, the Gay Liberation Front (GLF), borrowed its name from America's Vietnamese enemy—the most militant groups offered a perspective that was not well received by the wider public. "We are a revolutionary group of men and women formed with the realization that complete sexual liberation for all people cannot come about unless existing social institutions are abolished," the GLF manifesto read.

> We reject society's attempt to impose sexual roles and definitions on our nature. We are stepping outside these roles and simplistic myths. We are going to be who we are. At the same time, we are creating new social forms and relations, that is, relations based upon brotherhood, cooperation, human love, and uninhibited sexuality. Babylon has forced us to commit ourselves to one thing—revolution!

Although the GLF won some victories by following the models of the civil rights movement and women's movement—in Los Angeles, for example, the GLF's nightly sit-ins and demonstrations outside Barney's Beanery led owners to take down the sign in the restaurant's window reading FAGOTS [sic] STAY OUT—it came to be regarded as too radical to represent the whole gay community.[42]

A more moderate group of activists broke away to form the Gay Activists Alliance (GAA). In its constitution, GAA members demanded the right "to feel attracted to the beauty of members of our own sex and to embrace those feelings as truly our own, free from any question or challenge whatsoever by any other person, institution or moral authority." But their most effective tactic, the "zap"—public confrontation by activists—succeeded best in confronting their oppressors over concrete issues such as employment. When New York GAA activists zapped Mayor John Lindsay on the steps of the Metropolitan Museum of Art and during the taping of his own television show to get him to commit to supporting a gay rights ordinance in the city, Lindsay, rather than continue to be embarrassed, quietly began discussions with the GAA and a year later came out in support of legislation banning employment discrimination against gays.[43]

In spite of such successes, and in spite of the gay rights movement growing from fifty advocacy groups in 1969 to thousands by 1979, momentum proved difficult to sustain.[44] In October 1973, the GAA morphed into the National Gay Task Force (NGTF), in part to professionalize the movement and take attention away from movement radicals. Modeled after the integrationist approaches of the NAACP and NOW, the NGTF focused on lobbying by middle-class professionals, and they chose the physician Howard Brown to bring "gay liberation into the mainstream of the American civil rights movement." Even so, raising money remained a constant struggle and successes were episodic. The movement needed an organized opposition, something to fight against.[45]

Inevitably, the persistent calls for gays to come out of the closet raised the consciousness of straight Americans about the pervasive presence of gays in American life. By relinquishing their invisibility, the historian John D'Emilio has written, gays and lesbians "made themselves vulnerable to attack, and acquired an investment in the success of the movement in a way that mere adherence to a political line could never accomplish."[46]

In the early seventies, the gay liberation movement singled out for confrontation the American Psychiatric Association (APA). The association's *Diagnostic and Statistical Manual* (*DSM*) had long listed homosexuality as a mental illness. But a close reading of the *DSM* showed that the diagnosis was based not on science but on social stigma; gays, it said, were "ill primarily in terms of society and of conformity within the prevailing social milieu." Throughout the postwar years, the conservative APA, made up of "businessmen psychiatrists," had ignored the few critics who claimed the *DSM* was wrong on homosexuality. Therefore, from 1970 to 1973, panels at various psychiatric conferences became sites of struggle, with activists from both outside and within the APA pressing psychiatrists to question their own assumptions.[47]

Much of the psychiatrists' confidence in their diagnosis came from the work of New York Medical College's Dr. Irving Bieber. In his 1962 study, based on a survey of seventy-seven doctors who provided information on one hundred homosexual patients, Bieber concluded that homosexuality resulted from a combination of "closebinding mothers" and "detached, rejecting fathers." Bieber thought he was helping homosexuals by identifying the source of their illness and suggesting that they could get treatment for it. But the treatment included electric shock and an aversion therapy in which doctors injected gay men with apomorphine to make them nauseous—à la *A Clockwork Orange*—when they looked at images of nude men.[48]

At the APA's 1972 meeting in Dallas, following two years of sustained pressure from outside the association (mostly from the GAA and GLF), a new challenge came from within the APA itself. A panel on psychiatry and homosexuals included not only two gay activists but Dr. H. Anonymous, a gay psychiatrist dressed in baggy clothing and a distorted Nixon mask and equipped with a voice-altering microphone. To the surprise of most in the crowd, Dr. Anonymous announced that more than two hundred gay psychiatrists were attending the meeting and that they even had their own group, the Gay PA. Given the *DSM*'s designation of homosexuality as a mental illness, these gay psychiatrists had to remain closeted: "We must make sure we behave ourselves, and that no one in a position of power is aware of our sexual preference," he said (in fact, Dr. Anonymous was John Fryer, a psychiatrist who had recently been dismissed from a hospital under suspicion that he was gay; concern for his career prompted the costume, and he did not reveal his identity as Dr. Anonymous until 1994). When he finished, the room rose in a standing ovation.[49]

In short order, the APA's Nomenclature Committee, the one that oversees *DSM* designations, heard evidence that homosexuality was not a sickness. Dr. Charles Silverstein first noted that Alfred Kinsey's 1948 sex surveys showed that 37 percent of all men had had physical contact to the point of orgasm with other men. Silverstein then presented more recent research conducted by the UCLA psychologist Evelyn Hooker, who had been the first to observe that every study of homosexuals to date—including Irving Bieber's—relied on data from homosexuals already in treatment (in therapy, prison, or otherwise hospitalized). No one had studied well-adjusted homosexuals until she, through one of her gay students, conducted research on thirty gay men who had never been in therapy and thirty straight men, all of comparable education, IQ, and age. She administered the same personality tests, including the Rorschach, to each and gave the results to three other psychoanalysts for their assessment. It was impossible to tell from the tests who was gay and who was not. Silverstein concluded his presentation by saying, "It is no sin to say you have made an error in the past, but surely you will mock the principles of scientific research upon which the diagnostic system is based if you turn your back on the only objective evidence we have."[50]

When APA president Albert Freedman announced at a press conference that the association had dropped homosexuality from its list of mental disorders, he also reported that the APA board of trustees had passed a resolution condemning "all public and private discrimination against homosexuals in such areas as employment, housing, public accommodation and licensing." Now, the APA ruled, no scientific basis existed for treating homosexuals differently than heterosexuals. In the National Gay Task Force newspaper, the headline ran, THE EARTH IS ROUND.[51]

The combined effect of the APA's dramatic announcement and more and more gays coming out of the closet created a sense of tangible success. The right to privacy first upheld by the Supreme Court in *Griswold v. Connecticut* (and later extended beyond marital relationships in *Eisenstadt v. Baird*) prompted some states to repeal sodomy laws because legislators believed they would no longer hold up under constitutional scrutiny. New York, Washington, Minneapolis, Detroit, Boulder, Seattle, Ann Arbor, and East Lansing passed gay rights ordinances prohibiting discrimination in jobs and housing. San Francisco, in turn, extended its antidiscrimination authority to businesses with city contracts.[52]

Without realizing it at the time, the gay liberation movement had reached a peak by the end of 1973. In part, a pervasive complacency brought on by the initial successes had set in; fewer people turned out now for demonstrations or even gay rights Freedom Day parades. In the midseventies the movement fizzled. Few activists realized that their successes would soon mobilize Americans—against them.[53]

If Phyllis Schlafly painted feminism as threatening the American family, Anita Bryant cast out-of-the-closet gays as a danger to American children. A former Miss Oklahoma (and second runner-up in the Miss America

Pageant), Bryant was a well-known singer and popular entertainer in the mid-1970s. She performed at both Democratic and Republican conventions, had traveled with the USO to entertain troops in Vietnam year after year, and joined the broadcast team every year at the Orange Bowl football game. Indeed, most Americans knew Bryant primarily through her role as spokesperson for the Florida Citrus Commission (for which she was paid $100,000 a year). "A day without orange juice," she would sing in ubiquitous television ads, "is like a day without sunshine!" In 1977, at age thirty-seven, however, Bryant became identified more for her anti-gay-rights activism than for flogging breakfast juice.[54]

In January 1977, the contest in South Florida began when the Dade County Metro Commission introduced an amendment to a civil rights ordinance that would protect gays from discrimination in employment, housing, and public accommodations. Such provisions were becoming, as we have seen, commonplace, but Anita Bryant's minister, Bill Chapman, convinced her that the amended ordinance might compel private schools—such as Northwest Christian Academy, where her children went—to hire openly gay teachers. From her front porch perspective, Bryant was shocked that her motherly rights and her ability to protect her children had been targeted for attack by the commission. "If this ordinance amendment is allowed to become law," she wrote to the commissioners, "you will in fact be infringing upon my rights or rather discriminating against me as a citizen and a mother to teach my children and set examples and to point to others as examples of God's moral codes as stated in the Holy Scriptures." Hence, just as some opponents of busing resisted the state's interference in parents' decisions on where to live and send children to school, Bryant saw the state as depriving her of her rights as a parent. When the commission, despite Bryant's plea in writing and in person, voted to pass the amended ordinance, Bryant and others felt steamrolled. What kind of democratic institution, they wondered, denies the will of the people? A group of parents left the commission meeting after the vote and regrouped at Reverend Chapman's to plot strategy over banana sandwiches.[55]

With evangelical zeal, these mostly first-time activists decided to form an organization called Save Our Children (SOC) and collect petition signatures to force the commission to either repeal the ordinance or hold a binding referendum on the issue of gay rights. Immediately, Bryant took center stage in a grassroots effort not unlike that seen in local organizing against the ERA. SOC won the support of the Dade County Federation of Women's Clubs, which included fifty clubs and more than ten thousand members. When Bryant hit the Christian tele-airwaves, appearing on the Reverend Jim Bakker's *The PTL Club* (PTL stood for "Praise the Lord") and the Reverend Pat Robertson's *700 Club*, an "avalanche of [supportive] mail" poured in, carrying hundreds of small donations from all over the country. Meanwhile, in Miami, SOC set up offices all over the city, and a small staff supervised an army of volunteers from nearly every religious denomination. "Someone had to answer the phones, commiserate with worried parents, lick envelopes, and get the word out," Bryant later reported. "Someone had to canvass the supermarkets, shopping centers, businesses, and the streets of Miami to gather signatures. Day in and day out, the petitions flooded Dade County." To Bryant, the overwhelming grassroots support proved that in a nation afflicted by "pornography, abortion, TV violence, ERA," and militant homosexuals, there were millions "who had been praying for a long time for revival in this country and survival of the nation." In no time—less than a month—Save Our Children collected more than sixty thousand signatures in support of repeal, even though it needed only ten thousand to force the issue.[56]

In collecting those signatures, Bryant and SOC employed two arguments. First, they dismissed the notion that homosexuals were in fact subjected to prejudice. "Homosexuals do not suffer discrimination when they keep their perversions in the privacy of their homes," Bryant stated in a full-page newspaper ad. "They can hold any job, transact any business, join any organization—so long as they do not flaunt their homosexuality and try to establish role models for the impressionable young people—our children." Second, Bryant and her followers saw homosexuals as fundamentally predatory, implying that they might prey on children not so much as pedophiles but rather as recruiters. "Homosexuals cannot reproduce," she repeatedly said. "So they must recruit. And to freshen their ranks, they must recruit the youth of America." If openly gay men and women could teach in their children's classrooms, the argument went, then they could, like B-movie vampires and zombies, lure kids into their depraved lifestyle.[57]

The sixty thousand signatures gathered by Save Our Children turned Miami, in the spring of 1977, into ground zero in a war over gay rights versus parents' rights. Although Miami was home to a large gay and lesbian population, activists were not well organized in the run-up to a

June 7 referendum on whether to repeal the Dade County Metro Commission's vote. They could not match the telegenic Bryant or the outside support SOC received from national figures such as Phyllis Schlafly, Ronald Reagan, Senator Jesse Helms, and the Reverend Jerry Falwell.[58] More than ten thousand people packed the Miami Beach Convention Center in a show of solidarity with Bryant and Save Our Children. Meanwhile, Bryant suddenly found herself presiding over a bonding experience for rank-and-file women volunteers in the Miami area (she named scores of ordinary Miamians who had joined the Save Our Children campaign in the acknowledgments of her book about the experience)—all learning, mostly organically, that this is how front porch politics works.[59]

On election night, Anita Bryant and Save Our Children won in a landslide; 69.3 percent voted for repeal of the gay rights ordinance, and 30.6 percent voted to retain it. "The people of Dade County—the normal majority—have said 'Enough! Enough! Enough!'" Bryant proclaimed at a victory party full of cheering supporters. "We will now carry our fight against similar laws throughout the nation that attempt to legitimize a lifestyle that is both perverse and dangerous to the sanctity of the family, dangerous to our children, dangerous to our freedom of religion and freedom of choice, dangerous to our survival as a nation."[60]

For gay men and women, the Miami vote could be viewed only as a devastating setback. Bryant and Save Our Children became models for local organizations in other cities such as Minneapolis–St. Paul, Wichita, and Eugene, where, in a series of stunning reversals in the spring of 1978, voters repealed each city's gay rights ordinance. Meanwhile, the Oklahoma legislature passed a bill making it illegal for gays to teach in public schools. In Arkansas, officials proposed legislation to keep gays out of teaching, pediatrics, psychiatry, child psychology, and youth counseling. When a Tacoma, Washington, school fired a teacher for being gay, the Supreme Court refused to take the case.[61]

And then, in a return to the cycle of protest followed by counterprotest, gay and lesbian activists began to fight back. Across the country in San Francisco, Harvey Milk, the city's leading gay public figure, looked out over a crowd of more than three thousand protesters gathered on Castro Street the night of the Dade vote and declared, "Anita's going to create a national gay force!"[62]

In 1977 and 1978, the highest-profile contests over gay rights shifted to California, and at the center of them all stood Harvey Milk. Born in

1930, Milk grew up in Woodmere, Long Island, and by age fifteen knew that he was gay. After a stint in the navy, Milk worked in insurance and then made it big as a Wall Street stock analyst for Bache and Company. According to his biographer, Milk was, at the time, a "hard-boiled conservative in the laissez-faire capitalist mode" who, like Phyllis Schlafly, campaigned for Barry Goldwater in 1964.[63] But Milk was restless, too. In time, he got involved with avant-garde theater in New York, and he eventually moved to San Francisco with the road production of the counterculture musical *Hair*. In the early 1970s, Milk opened a camera shop on Castro Street and soon became a fixture in the neighborhood. He ran for office three times between 1973 and 1976, losing every time. But he got more and more attention with each successive campaign. Along the way, he won the support of the city's unions because he led a boycott that got Coors beer ousted from nearly every bar in San Francisco (in protest of the brewer's antilabor tactics). Meanwhile, although Milk lost a race for city supervisor in 1975, George Moscone narrowly won the mayoral election thanks to the gay vote. Moscone, Milk, and others soon joined forces to do away with citywide elections—dominated by business elites—in favor of district elections in which, as in Charlotte, neighborhoods could elect one of their own to represent their interests. In November 1977, after running under the new district election scheme, Milk won a seat on the city's board of supervisors. He was the first openly gay official of any major city in America.

Meanwhile, in Southern California, John Briggs, a state senator from Fullerton and a prospective Republican candidate for governor against the liberal incumbent, Jerry Brown, had returned to California from Anita Bryant's Holiday Inn victory party hoping to capitalize on the antihomosexual sentiment that he believed existed everywhere. Since the legislature had not passed a statewide gay rights law, Briggs proposed a bill that, if it became law, would explicitly prevent school districts from hiring gay teachers. For a little-known state senator, it was a smart way to get attention for a possible statewide campaign. When the bill met with a distinct lack of legislative enthusiasm, Briggs moved to get a referendum—Proposition 6—on the November 1978 ballot. The referendum text said that school boards "shall refuse to hire as an employee any person who has engaged in public homosexual activity or public homosexual conduct, should the board determine that said activity or conduct renders the person unfit for service." Briggs, like Anita Bryant, presented homosexuality as a simple moral question, a personal choice with potentially far-reaching consequences for the community. In fact, the referendum was far more sweeping in its aims than Briggs acknowledged. It defined "public homosexuality," for example, as "advocating, soliciting, imposing, encouraging or promoting private or public homosexual activity directed at, or likely to come to the attention of school children and/or other employees." It targeted not only out-of-the-closet gays but anyone, gay or straight, who went to a gay pride parade, assigned a book by a gay author, or went to a meeting at which gay rights were discussed—all of which qualified as "encouraging" gay activity and could get you fired.[64]

In both strategy and tactics, Briggs followed Anita Bryant's successful example. He established the California Defend Our Children Committee and trafficked in the same parental front porch rhetoric. "Children in this country spend more than 1,200 hours a year in classrooms," he wrote in a *Los Angeles Times* editorial. "A teacher who is a known homosexual will automatically represent that way of life to young, impressionable students at a time when they are struggling with their own critical choice of sexual orientation." As in Dade County, such arguments found a receptive audience in churches throughout the state. Early in the campaign, polls showed that 75 percent of Californians supported the initiative.[65]

Harvey Milk, for his part, became the public face of the "No on 6" campaign. Milk believed at first that, as in Miami, the gay community would lose, but he hoped to have a good showing in San Francisco. He received piles of hate mail and no small number of death threats.[66] In public speaking engagements, Milk sometimes read lofty passages about freedom and equality from the Declaration of Independence, and the Emma Lazarus inscription on the Statue of Liberty, but his primary concern was with the immediacy of financial danger—in lost jobs—and physical danger, too. Milk believed that persistent discrimination against gays could, if unchecked, lead beyond marginalization to persecution and possibly extermination. At times, he alluded to concentration camps. Seeing ignorance as the root of prejudice, Milk became the nation's highest-profile figure calling on American gays to come out of the closet. He had seen the polls that showed Americans who knew a gay person were twice as likely to support gay rights as someone who claimed not to know anyone gay. For Milk, coming out not only served to alert straight Americans of gays' presence all around them; it also served as a kind of preemptive moral witness. "At what point do we say 'Enough!'?" Milk asked in a gay newspaper column. "At what point do we stand up—as a total group—and say we will not allow it to happen any more? . . . Should we wait until the Bryant camps are built?"[67]

John Briggs and the Reverend Ray Batema countered Milk by founding Citizens for Decency and Morality. Like Milk, Briggs invoked the loftiest of American ideals and based his campaign on a larger analysis that ongoing "moral decay" would soon bring about the end of American civilization.[68] But to reach Californians where they lived, Briggs and Batema, as in the Dade campaign, conjured images of homosexual teachers as vampirelike recruiters who would invade their homes. Briggs asserted that, like pornographers and "dope addicts," "homosexuals want your children" because "they don't have any children of their own . . . [they] have no means of replenishing." By this reasoning, gays wanted to be teachers to "serve as role models and encourage people to join them."[69]

Beyond Harvey Milk's high-profile scrapes with John Briggs, California gay and lesbian activists managed to mobilize behind a unified message that they believed all Californians would find appealing. Rather than lobbying under the banner of human rights (though Milk still invoked it), grassroots activists emphasized the right to privacy in a campaign led by the New Alliance for Gay Equality (New AGE). David Mixner, a longtime liberal activist, electoral campaign strategist, and professional organizer who was himself gay, joined with others in Southern California to set up New AGE; and, in time, the organization folded itself into the statewide "No on 6" campaign. Mixner and his colleagues, based in Los Angeles, excelled at fundraising, particularly among the Hollywood / Beverly Hills glitterati.[70]

But the real breakthrough came when Mixner managed to get an audience with former governor Ronald Reagan. A closeted aide to Reagan had reached out to Mixner, thinking that the privacy issue might make sense to the man who had, for eight years in the governor's mansion, vowed to veto any bill that decriminalized gay sex. In a meeting that lasted more than an hour, Mixner and another colleague told Reagan that the Briggs initiative would "create anarchy in the classroom." As Mixner described it in his memoir, he suggested to Reagan that "any child who received a failing grade or was disciplined by a teacher could accuse that teacher of being a homosexual." In that climate, Mixner said, "teachers will become afraid of giving a low grade or maintaining order in their classrooms." Reagan seemed surprised: "I never thought about that," he said. "It really could happen, couldn't it?"[71] At the end of August, the future president released a statement condemning Proposition 6 for both its "real potential for mischief" and "the potential of infringing on basic rights of privacy." Later, when Reagan commented that "whatever else it is, homosexuality is not a contagious disease like measles," Briggs dismissed the former governor as part of "the whole Hollywood crowd." Yet, to Briggs's dismay, the polls began to shift against the initiative.[72]

In the end, it turned out that the No on 6 strategists were right to gamble on the privacy issue trumping family values. On November 7, 1978, California voters went to the polls and, by a margin of 59 to 41, defeated Proposition 6. It marked an impressive turnaround. Even in Orange County, Briggs's conservative base, the referendum garnered only 46 percent of the vote. In Seattle, on the same day, a similar measure went down to even greater defeat, 63 to 37. George Moscone, San Francisco's straight mayor who supported gay rights, joined Harvey Milk in the Castro to celebrate. That night, in the glow of victory, Milk issued a call that "every person must come out" to show straight America "that we are indeed their children, we are indeed everywhere." Only then, he said, will "every myth, every lie, every innuendo . . . be destroyed once and for all."[73]

Three weeks later, Milk was dead, assassinated, along with Mayor Moscone, by former city supervisor Dan White. In their short time together on the board of supervisors, White and Milk frequently disagreed—White was, for example, the only supervisor to vote against a Milk-penned gay rights bill aimed at ending discrimination in employment, housing, and public accommodations—and when White resigned abruptly from the board but then changed his mind, Milk saw a political opportunity and pressed Moscone not to reinstate him. Upon learning that he would not be reinstated, White went to City Hall and shot the mayor and Milk methodically, execution-style. Forty thousand San Franciscans joined a silent candlelight march through the city. Five months later, the mood turned. When a jury deliberated for only thirty-six hours before convicting White of voluntary manslaughter—and not first-degree murder—spontaneous protests erupted outside San Francisco's City Hall. Harvey Milk's friend Cleve Jones told a reporter that the verdict meant that "in America, it's all right to kill faggots." Angry citizens went on a vandalism spree, smashing the building's windows and burning all the police cars lining a block outside. In a scene that looked more like Paris in 1968, police arrived in riot gear to confront protesters hurling missiles and building barricades. A rioter told a reporter, "Dan White's straight justice is just the last straw. We're not a bunch of fairies. We can be as tough as they were in Watts." For a moment, the struggle over gay rights and the family looked like an urban street riot.[74]

If one bothered to keep a scorecard of such things, at the end of the 1970s, the decadelong fight over gay rights essentially resulted in a draw. Certainly, no one could deny the gay rights movement's successes: the change in the *DSM*, the dozens of local gay rights ordinances passed, repeal of sodomy laws in more than half of the states, and the high-profile thumping of John Briggs's initiative. At the same time, however, the pro-family movement could claim victory for the repeal of a number of those gay rights ordinances, including the devastating knockdown in Dade County; moreover, the movement could thank its very existence and growing strength in large part to the campaigns to defend the traditional family from militant homosexuality. And in spite of the Briggs initiative defeat, the pro-family army marched on as it began to understand its growing power in American politics. As Phyllis Schlafly later noted, the pro-family movement brought together not only STOP ERA, but also other Christian activists who were "motivated by a cluster of moral issues," including abortion, pornography, prayer in school, and homosexuality. In short order, that movement—founded on its own version of "the personal is political"—became an important base for national candidates like Ronald Reagan.[75]

Going into the 1980s, it would not have been an overstatement to use the word "epic" in describing the political contests over women's health, security, gay rights, and the family. The fight over the ERA, after all, lasted more than a decade; the contests over gay rights ordinances played out like a seesaw tennis match as each side won one game only to lose the next. The cycle of protest and counterprotest, driven by the perceived dangers posed by each side's respective opponents, prompted only greater commitment and organizing. But it also guaranteed a kind of war-weariness among many Americans. As early as 1977, the *Washington*

Post columnist William Raspberry wrote that most Americans found activists on both sides of these social divides to be extreme and wished they both would just "shut up about it."[76] After all, for many Americans, feminism and gay liberation seemed like distractions from the tightening circle of hazards—the energy crisis, unemployment, rising prices, and pollution (to name a handful)—threatening *their* families.

PART 2

The Environment

● ●

In popular memory, the national environmental movement in the 1970s appeared suddenly, as though it jumped out from behind a tree and gave the professional activists of the Sixties something to do once the civil rights and antiwar movements tailed off. That is a myth, of course, though like many myths it includes a few kernels of truth—many opponents of nuclear energy, for example, did come out of those earlier movements, and a small proportion of them did live on communes. And it is true that the nation's environmental consciousness rose rapidly. Indeed, public opinion polls showed that in 1969 only 1 percent of Americans regarded "pollution/ecology as an important national problem"; a year later, that number jumped to 25 percent. Similarly, whereas reducing air and water pollution ranked ninth in national priorities in 1965, those concerns ranked second in 1970.[1] Most pundits attributed this apparent turn in public opinion to several high-profile environmental disasters, including the heavily polluted Cuyahoga River spontaneously bursting into flames in Cleveland in 1969; the Santa Barbara oil well blowout, also in 1969, that brought images of seabirds dripping with oil—then still a shocking sight—to American television; and several serious air pollution alerts in New York City.

The problem with this theory of Americans stunned into recognizing the environmental crisis confronting them is that it does not take into consideration all of the ways that Americans were more directly exposed to environmental damage by the late 1960s. Although dirty air and water faced a lot of competition for the American attention span— what with the escalating Vietnam War, cities burning, and the economy faltering—it was hardly the case that Americans were oblivious to their dying environment. Most could see evidence of ecological breakdown all around them: businessmen in steel cities like Pittsburgh brought an extra shirt to work each day because the soot in the air could turn their white shirts gray by noon; Lake Erie was declared a "dying sinkhole"; pollution in lakes and rivers killed off fish and other life; trash was casually tossed along the country's highways. Thus, the public's increased attention to environmental concerns came not so much from headline-grabbing disasters as from the routine pollution of the air, water, and soil in their own communities.

How had the government failed to protect the very air we breathe, the water we drink? Big business may have complained that it was overregulated, but any American could see that industry had been allowed to spew waste into the nation's formerly blue sky and poison its waterways for longer than anyone could remember. With government an unreliable sentinel, Americans launched a dizzying constellation of campaigns to pressure industry as well as local and federal government not only to stop the devastation and clean it up, but to prevent it from happening again. Industry later criticized some of these campaigns—particularly those against nuclear power or the building of toxic waste facilities—as selfish and parochial, turning the term NIMBY (for Not in My Back Yard) into an insult. But the activists did not back down. Indeed, although they suffered their share of defeats, the front porch environmentalists of the 1970s and 1980s put together a string of victories over corporate polluters.

4

Energy, Health, and Safety

●

In the 1970s, few Americans knew the unsung history of the environmental movement. In the first decade of the twentieth century, as Teddy Roosevelt established the national parks system and took measures to preserve huge tracts of land, a classic disagreement between John Muir and Gifford Pinchot effectively defined the terms of the ecological debate in America. Muir, the founder of the Sierra Club, argued that the greatest gift the government could give to posterity would be the preservation of pristine wilderness so that Americans hundreds of years from now could still experience, say, the Grand Canyon the way Muir did in 1900. Pinchot, Roosevelt's forestry chief, thought Muir naïve and argued instead for the "wise use" of the environment, in which resources could be extracted from the land, but not recklessly.[1] From Muir's time through the Second World War, this division between preservationists and conservationists dominated environmental discourse. Although there were local exceptions—New Yorkers who formed antismoke leagues (not cigarettes, but smog and soot) managed to get air pollution ordinances passed—the most effective lobbyists for the environment were sportsmen; the Sierra Club itself became primarily a hiking club.

After the war, the seeming invincibility of the U.S. manufacturing economy, driven by mass consumer society, also produced in parts of the country a filthy Dickensian landscape. All of the technological advances and material abundance brought "urban crowding, suburban sprawl, pollution and smog, clear cuts and dammed rivers, cancer and nuclear fallout"—a sudden case of what the cultural critic Kirkpatrick Sale calls "future shock."[2] The postwar suburbanization of the United States, especially, required the construction of large-scale energy facilities—oil refineries, electrical transfer stations, coal mines—in the countryside to feed the suburbs and cities.³ It also led to massive logging in the nation's forests in order to mill the lumber used to build all of those houses.

But the whole point of Americans moving to the suburbs had been to escape the crowding, filth, and dissonance of the city for a tranquil, purer natural world. Outdoor recreation and quality of life became more palpable concerns for Americans after the war, the kinds of interests that only prosperity on a large scale could bring. When confronted with evidence of ecological spoiling, the new suburbanites grew testy. As a result, the nation saw a shift in cultural attitudes regarding the environment—from Muir's concern for wilderness to protecting humans in their own habitat. As the dean of environmental historians, Samuel Hays, has noted, "public interest in environmental affairs" is simple to understand: "It stems from a desire to improve personal, family, and community life."⁴

At the same time, in the Cold War years of the liberal consensus, most Americans believed the government could solve serious societal problems by funding armies of experts who would analyze the problem, come up with a plan, and hand it off to managers to implement. On environmental crises, however, the government did not have a good track record of deploying experts. The dying lakes and rivers, the smog-blanketed cities, the sprawling suburbs—all could be traced to government agencies catering to the interests of the businesses that were largely responsible for those conditions. The Agriculture and Interior Departments of the federal government, the Army Corps of Engineers, and the Atomic Energy Commission—to name just a few—were criticized as industry shills. Consequently, the power of business vis-à-vis environment went largely unchallenged until the 1960s. As one official remarked in the 1970s, the poisoned landscape's "stench was overpowered by the stronger perfume of money."⁵ Distrusting the axis of business-government cooperation, the American people in the 1960s proved a receptive audience for independent experts; by the 1970s, many had become front porch environmentalists-in-waiting.

One of the first independent experts to sound the alarm of approaching environmental doom was the biologist Barry Commoner. Later dubbed the "Paul Revere of Ecology" by *Time* magazine, Commoner was on the faculty at Washington University in St. Louis in 1958 when he joined the Nobel Prize–winning chemist Linus Pauling and others in founding the Committee for Nuclear Information. Commoner's studies of baby teeth showed that radioactive strontium 90, found in the atmosphere from nuclear weapons testing, was being absorbed into human bones and teeth via the food chain. This was the start of Commoner's environmental activism as he increasingly focused on the ecological and human health costs of America's technological advances. His maxim became "Everything is connected to everything else," and with his 1971 book, *The Closing Circle*, a bestseller that argued against all the technologies that damaged the environment (including cars and plastics), he did more than anyone but Rachel Carson to bring people to environmentalism.[6]

Carson remains the most frequently cited catalyst of modern environmentalism thanks to her 1962 book *Silent Spring*. A marine biologist working on a federally funded Fish and Wildlife Service research team in Patuxent, Maryland, Carson found that pesticides such as the popular DDT got into water and were absorbed by fish, which were then consumed by birds; as a result, the birds laid eggs with shells too thin to hold a hatchling to term. Bird species living in the beautiful Chesapeake Bay area were, as a result, dying off. By extension, she wrote, "we spray our elms and the following springs are silent of robin song, not because we sprayed the robins directly but because the poison traveled, step by step, through the now familiar elm leaf–earthworm–robin cycle." Scientists had a name for this "web of life—or death," she wrote: ecology. Like Commoner, Carson understood the interconnectedness of all life on the planet. She called for alternatives to pesticides—for instance, the use of biological controls (using one species to control the population of another) instead of chemicals—and for government to intervene via regulation of the pesticides industry. At least one historian has called *Silent Spring* "the *Uncle Tom's Cabin* of modern environmentalism." Industry called it rubbish and smeared Carson as a Communist.[7]

The stakes were high. Pesticides had, by the late 1950s, become firmly established in the public mind as a "miracle product." Industry ad campaigns boasted of "Better Things for Better Living Through Chemistry." By the time Carson published *Silent Spring*, pesticides had, according to one scholar, "fully supplanted all other pest control methods and insect eradication campaigns." Manufacturers, as a result, were very keen to see their products' continued use and brought their considerable political influence to bear on state legislatures and the regulating agencies. Farmers liked DDT and other pesticides, too, because they saved them money on labor. Desperate, industry not only branded Carson a Communist but campaigned against her, suggesting she was a lousy scientist, a lesbian, a fearmonger, and a hysteric. The pesticide manufacturer Velsicol Corporation threatened to sue Carson and her publisher even before the book came out.

But Carson's work informed and outraged Americans who were increasingly looking at the environment from a front porch perspective— not merely for its beauty, but for the way that the environment's health bore a direct relation to their own and their families' health. As a result, Carson's work informed a developing front porch political sensibility in the 1960s and 1970s. She likened pesticides to radioactive fallout, and most important, she argued that science and expertise had to be accountable to the public. "It is the public that is being asked to assume the risks that the insect controllers calculate," Carson said in a 1963 interview. "The public must decide whether it wishes to continue on the present road, and it can do so only when in full possession of the facts." As the environmental historian Robert Gottlieb notes, Carson recognized (in a way the general public did not yet) that "the rise of pesticides was indicative of 'an era dominated by industry, in which the right to make money, at whatever cost to others, is seldom challenged.'" Although Carson died from breast cancer the following year, the public heard her and spoke, initially via representatives, when Congress outlawed DDT in 1972.[8]

A few years later, Ralph Nader, calling pollution "different from street crime only in that the cause and effect is not immediate," used the money he won from his settlement with General Motors to establish the Center for Responsive Law, which promptly challenged corporate polluters.[9]

Nader's name and reputation for integrity inspired those living in polluted, toxic environments. In Pittsburgh, for example, a group of forty-three residents founded the Group Against Smog and Pollution (GASP) to fight the Pennsylvania Air Pollution Commission's acquiescence to the steel industry in setting air quality standards. Although studies showed that death rates for people over age fifty increased dramatically "when particulate levels in the air exceeded 80 micrograms [per cubic meter of air]," the commission decided to allow the average to be 100 micrograms. Using a letter-writing campaign to every public official who could weigh in on the issue, GASP succeeded in pressuring the commission to drop its standard to 65 micrograms. The group then recruited scientists— experts who could counter industry claims—to get stronger regulations passed. And when companies stalled in complying, GASP handed out

"Dirty Gertie" awards to the city's worst corporate polluters. By 1976, GASP had grown to more than five thousand members, with a mailing list of more than a hundred thousand. This kind of grassroots activism, coupled with Nader's more nationally prominent efforts, prompted expansion of the Clean Air Act in 1970. GASP and other groups like it ended up inspiring Nader—who had first inspired them—to start up Public Interest Research Groups across the country. Suddenly, the environmental movement gained an important new model for organizing.[10]

By the late 1960s, a rising concern for the environment could be heard above the din of the war, poverty, and segregation. The cumulative effect of a few maverick experts such as Commoner, Carson, and Nader speaking out on environmental issues resonated with a public that could at least see pollution all around and was already distrustful of government and industry. Even Richard Nixon, the evangelist who tried to sell faith in American industrial and technological might to Nikita Khrushchev, acknowledged in his 1970 State of the Union address that the 1970s "absolutely must be the years when America pays its debt to the past by reclaiming the purity of its air, its waters and our living environment. It is literally now or never."[11] For many Americans, the famous photograph of Earth as seen by Apollo astronauts, which was first released in 1969, seemed to confirm Commoner's and Carson's claims of one whole interconnected environment, too.

Two events in 1970 marked the environmental movement's national coming out party: Earth Day and the establishment of the EPA. The idea to borrow the antiwar movement's tactic of a teach-in for a day, creating a twenty-four-hour nationwide discussion on environmentalism, started, not coincidentally, with Senator Gaylord Nelson of Wisconsin. Nelson had been an early Senate opponent of the Vietnam War and had also been behind some of the first significant pieces of postwar environmental legislation, including the 1964 Wilderness Act. Earth Day also mirrored the antiwar movement's Moratorium events of the previous fall in that it was a national event that was defined locally, at the grass roots. Nelson and others started Environmental Teach-In, Inc., and chose April 22, 1970, because he thought most college students would be past their midsemester exams. Very quickly, though, Earth Day took on a force and direction all its own. Years later, Nelson reflected that in the six months prior to Earth Day, the event grew of its own accord, "carried by its own momentum."[12]

Earth Day organizers deliberately sought the attention and participation not only of America's organized activists but also of the country's front porchers. When April 22 finally came, an estimated 20 million people participated in demonstrations and events across the country. The biggest rallies were held in New York, San Francisco, and Washington, D.C., while more than fifteen hundred college campuses and countless communities large and small took part. In New York, residents pulled abandoned appliances out of the Bronx River and Mayor John Lindsay closed Fifth Avenue to vehicular traffic. In Tacoma, Washington, more than a hundred high school students rode horses on the highway as a way of drawing attention to automobile exhaust. A group in San Francisco poured oil into the reflecting pool outside the Standard Oil Building. And University of Illinois students interrupted a Commonwealth Edison speaker—many utilities used the day to claim their "greenness"—by "throwing soot on each other and coughing vigorously." For the most part, however, organizers aimed to minimize confrontation. "We didn't want to alienate the middle class," Denis Hayes, the twenty-five-year-old Harvard law student recruited by Nelson to serve as the main organizer of the event, later said.[13] In time, as the sociologist Denton Morrison argued, the environmental movement "came as something of a relief to a movement-pummeled white, middle-class America." Compared to the Black Panthers, the Weathermen, and other militants in the capital-*M* Movement, environmentalism emerged in the public perception as "clearly the safest movement in town."[14]

This acceptance came more easily to environmentalism in part because the goals of protecting the ecological balance had been codified, at least in the abstract, by Congress and sanctioned by the president. The National Environmental Policy Act (NEPA) of 1969, signed into law by Nixon on January 1, 1970, became the foundation for almost all other environmental legislation in the 1970s and 1980s. Six months later, Nixon corrected a significant flaw in the legislation—the absence of a dedicated regulatory agency to enforce the act—by establishing the Environmental Protection Agency. Starting with a staff of six thousand and a $455 million budget, the EPA opened for business in 1971; ten years later, the staff had more than doubled, to thirteen thousand, and the budget swelled to $5.6 billion. And yet the agency was quickly overwhelmed. Congress pumped out eighteen major pieces of environmental legislation in that first decade, all of which were assigned to the EPA for enforcement.

Environmental law firms in turn began filing lawsuits against polluters for alleged violations of the NEPA; industry responded by filing more than ten thousand environmental impact statements (as required by the new law) between 1970 and 1979. Through it all, the agency found itself under siege from both industry—which lobbied hard to have its authority reined in—and environmentalists—who found it too soft on corporate polluters.[15]

Taken together, Earth Day and the passage of the NEPA helped establish a national infrastructure for lobbying, litigating, and legislating on environmental issues. In addition to older organizations like the Sierra Club, the Audubon Society, and the Wilderness Society, the mainstream environmental movement saw permanent national organizations such as the Environmental Defense Fund, the Natural Resources Defense Council, and the Environmental Policy Center established. They received foundation monies from the Rockefeller, Ford, and Mott Family Foundations (among others), which they often used to focus on the enforcement of legislation.

Though occasionally a thorn in the side of industry, these national organizations were for the most part more acceptable to corporate interests than were the grassroots groups. The latter were unpredictable. The lobbyists and lawyers, on the other hand, were more moderate, willing to work with industry on market incentives, for example, instead of pushing for more regulatory legislation.[16]

In the 1970s, then, a clear divide grew between mainstream environmentalism and grassroots organizations. At times, the two were mutually reinforcing, but just as often they were at odds. As the national environmentalist lobby grew, that growth came at a cost that most activists at the grass roots were unwilling to pay: playing within the rules of "the system." At the national level, the Sierra Club, the EDF, and the NRDC were visibly influencing policy, and that brought them additional members and further influence in the corridors of power. The five biggest organizations grew from a total membership of 841,000 in 1970 to 1,485,000 in 1980. And as John Adams of the NRDC noted in 1989, that level of growth brought results. "In 1970 there were no environmental laws," he said. "There were zoning laws, public health laws, but no real environmental laws. Now we have forty or fifty statutes. Today we have laws across the United States—every county, every town, every city."[17]

At the local level, however, the impact from such legislation was uneven. To an anxious mother frightened by the immediate conditions in her neighborhood, a new federal law often offered little solace. And that is what made that mother, and other spontaneous activists like her, so potent a political force. The corporations or government bodies responsible for the presence of health hazards in a community soon came to understand that residents suffering or threatened by adverse health effects possessed a moral legitimacy that was difficult to overcome politically. Grassroots movements arising in such communities were therefore just as formidable in the political arena as national organizations.[18]

What made environmentalism a pressing personal issue for a majority of Americans was a combination of the energy crisis—and all the complicated politics behind pursuing more oil, coal, and nuclear-generated electricity—and epidemic-like revelations about pollution and toxic waste *nearby*. Before the mid-1970s, learning about the various ecological crises from maverick intellectuals and Earth Day events was like trying to understand the horrors of the Vietnam War just by watching the nightly news. One only began to understand environmental dangers when they hit home, the way one's understanding of Vietnam truly snapped into focus when a neighbor's kid—or your kid—came home from the war in pieces. In the case of environmental dangers, by the end of the decade thousands of local groups had formed in response to the various immediate threats—strip mines, nuclear reactors, toxic waste dumps— placed in their midst. This was archetypal front porch politics. The danger to one's family could be sensed from the top step, with no public official acting to provide protection or redress. These Americans were on their own to raise hell to protect their families, homes, and communities.

In the days before cable and satellite television, long before one could scroll through a thousand programs on a plasma screen bolted to the wall, American children awoke on Saturday mornings to manually click their television dials through a handful of local channels in search of cartoons. Beginning in the middle 1970s, those kids were rewarded with a bonus—*Schoolhouse Rock!*—three-minute musical cartoons, a little education complete with catchy songs. These cartoons slipped lessons on grammar, math, science, and civics in between the regular animated series that ran all morning. In the most popular of these, children learned about conjunctions, nouns, adverbs, the planets, the Preamble to the

Constitution, and how a bill becomes a law. In a post-Vietnam, post-Watergate America, in the midst of stagflation and other national challenges, the songs projected sunny, upbeat messages, presented over simple but clever animation. And an entire generation was hooked: when a *Schoolhouse Rock!* producer played "Conjunction Junction" to an audience of nine hundred Dartmouth College seniors in 1990, almost the entire class drowned out the video as they sang along about the virtues of "And, But, and Or."

But not all of the songs encouraged optimism. At least one, "The Energy Blues," which first aired in 1978, captured the gathering energy crisis in a downbeat tune sung by a cartoon Earth who mourned Americans' wasteful ways. "Energy . . . you'd think we'd be saving it up," he lamented the way an old bluesman might from his front porch rocking chair. Following a succinct history of energy use, from wood to coal—"It looked like it just might last forever"—to oil—"No one knew . . . so many cars and trucks would come to cause a crisis"—the Earth says it's time to find new sources of energy. If "nuclear, thermal, and solar" do not solve the problem, the Earth warns, "we'll get colder and colder." In the meantime, "till we find a fuel that never runs out," the moral of the story for kids is conservation: "Don't be cross when Momma says turn that extra light out." Over images of house lights flicking off and cars slowing to 55 miles per hour, Earth declares, as though it's got no choice: "Energy—we're gonna be stretchin' you out."[19]

By the time American kids heard the sobering "Energy Blues," Americans had been at war over energy for over a decade. All across the country, people watched the quest for cheaper, abundant energy encroach on their own front porches. Few Americans would have contested the need for more and cheaper energy in the 1970s—only 6 percent of the world's population lived in the United States, yet it consumed one-third of the world's energy output—but fierce disagreement arose over the environmental cost. Strip mines, pipelines, high-voltage electrical lines, and nuclear power plants prompted full-scale resistance and rebellion in some quarters—and in each case it came from concern for a very specific environment: the "backyard," writ large, of a particular community.

The energy shortages that began in earnest in the winter of Richard Nixon's second inauguration and were exacerbated by the 1973–74 OPEC oil embargo had such a profound effect on the economy that they seemed to last the rest of the decade. When gas lines reappeared late in 1978, they conjured a familiar anxiety. The resignation, anger, and fear that Americans felt over the energy crisis and the inflationary economy it spawned dragged across four presidential administrations. The situation started to feel permanent. By one measure, the price of gasoline increased eightfold over seven years. By another, the images of families shivering in their living rooms in the first oil crisis were replaced by images of families feeding woodstoves to heat their New England homes in the second.

No one doubted that the country needed greater supply, but from where? Getting more fuel from abroad would only increase dependence on capricious foreign interests. The United States already got one-third of its fuel from other nations. The consensus, then, was to focus on conservation and developing other energy sources at home. But that's where it got tricky. By creating incentives for oil, coal, and utility companies to find more domestic fuel, essentially putting the nation's energy future in the hands of industry, President Nixon seemed to be going back on the environmental reforms he had supported. In the contest between environment and industry, it seemed clear that the government would throw in with the industries. Meanwhile, the American public showed that its commitment to protecting the environment had limits in an age when its wallets had limits, too.

Take, for example, the Trans-Alaska Pipeline. New oil discoveries made in 1968 near Prudhoe Bay on Alaska's North Slope prompted a consortium of oil companies led by Atlantic Richfield Corporation (ARCO) to propose a 764-mile pipeline that would carry 2 million barrels of oil a day from the source to Valdez in the south. Even before the OPEC oil embargo, ARCO pitched the project as a way to decrease American dependence on foreign oil; it would also, ARCO promised, boost the Alaskan economy. But the pipeline would have to cross 641 miles of federal land—roughly the distance between Minneapolis and Oklahoma City— and environmentalists objected that the oil, which comes out of the ground hot, would heat the permafrost and destroy plant life as it traveled through pipes four feet in diameter. In addition, they raised concerns about caribou migration patterns and asked how the consortium would prevent oil from spilling all over the tundra in the event of an earthquake.

This political battle, pre-OPEC embargo, was a test for the new National Environmental Policy Act, which required environmental impact studies of any project that affected public lands. Environmental groups took advantage of the act, using it to force studies on all facets of the proposed pipeline; they succeeded in delaying the project for three years. Industry responded by calling the environmentalists "extremists." Lobbyists pointed out that the people of Alaska wanted the pipeline for the influx of cash and jobs it would bring, and unions flogged the project as a job creator, too. Still, the project was caught in a legal and legislative limbo until the OPEC embargo. When the embargo hit, in November 1973, Congress cast all environmental concerns away and passed the Trans-Alaska Pipeline Authorization Act, which effectively ended all lawsuits and delays. And that was that. No more worrying about caribou.

By 1975, twenty-seven thousand workers flooded into Alaska like it was the next Gold Rush. First they built a 360-mile-long road through the ice and wilderness to Prudhoe Bay. As in the Old West, work camps—twenty-nine of them—popped up along the way, complete with saloons, gambling, and prostitution. Unions agreed not to strike in exchange for higher wages and for the companies and authorities tolerating the frontier mayhem. The final cost of the pipeline came to $8 billion, but it started pumping oil in 1977 and had, by 2005, moved more than 15 billion barrels of oil across Alaska. The environmentalists' years of resistance did not go completely for naught: designers did build long stretches of the pipeline off the ground to prevent thawing and insulated the pipe and its supports. In the end, the most significant environmental consequence of the pipeline came not over land but on the sea, when the *Exxon Valdez* tanker ran aground in 1989 and spilled 11 million gallons of oil into Prince William Sound (it remains the largest oil tanker spill in North American history).

Most important, though, the green-lighting of the pipeline showed how front porch concerns drove Americans' perceptions of the oil crisis. Alaskans chose jobs over protecting flora and fauna. And for most of the rest of the nation's citizens, gas in the tank was more important to the family than possible environmental damage in a distant Alaskan wilderness. No mass movement against the pipeline materialized as Americans fretted over the cost of heating their homes and fueling their cars.[20]

Sensing an opening, the business community began to beat the drum for rollbacks in environmental and other regulations, too. "At first glance, the time seems ripe for major concessions to business," *Business Week* asserted in 1975. "The costs of compliance—at least $130 billion by 1982 . . . —are biting just when the nation is reeling from the worst economic crunch since the Depression."[21] By the time Jimmy Carter entered the White House, most Americans felt that the oil and utility companies were the only ones doing well in Recession America.

The rest of America felt defeated, sitting in smog-choked traffic on a hot summer day. As John Updike wrote in the opening line of his 1979 Pulitzer Prize–winning novel, *Rabbit Is Rich*: "Running out of gas, Rabbit Angstrom thinks . . . The people out there are getting frantic, they know the great American ride is ending." A Gulf Oil executive likewise remarked, "I could feel it everywhere. It was the ebbing of American power—the Romans retreating from Hadrian's Wall."[22] More gas lines, rising heat and electric bills, and a White House that seemed unable to solve the riddle—all combined to shake the American self-image.

Jimmy Carter campaigned for president promising always to be honest with the American people—unlike Nixon and Ford, went the logic—and promising solutions to the energy and economic crises, all while protecting the environment. Given his predecessors' dismal records on energy, Carter didn't have to do much to make a showing. Congress similarly had done little other than pass the Energy Policy and Conservation Act—which set mileage standards for cars and efficiency standards for appliances and established the Strategic Petroleum Reserve.[23] Carter, by contrast, made a good first impression. He not only made energy a focus of his campaign, daring even to say that solar power could account for 20 percent of the nation's energy production by the year 2000, but when he got into office, he named bona fide environmentalists to key posts in the administration—including the new Energy Department—and framed energy policy as the "moral equivalent of war." In Carter's first televised address, he appeared seated in an armchair in the library, wearing a cardigan instead of a suit, and promised a "comprehensive long-range energy policy" to the American people.[24]

But this bold vision was never fulfilled.[25] Instead, the national debate turned primarily on the virtues of either relaxing regulations as a way to spur domestic fuel production or pushing for a new culture of conservation that would both protect the environment from more extracting damage and draw down demand (which would also bring down prices).

Although some of Carter's energy plans succeeded—manufacturers made more efficient cars and appliances, and the nation's per capita energy consumption dropped 10 percent from 1979 to 1983—his larger plans were no match for the simple pro-growth, pro-development message coming from the energy corporations. And his own Council on Wage and Price Stability effectively shot down most new Carter regulation as too costly. The modest plans of the president, along with his national standing, began to unravel.[26]

Indeed, the decade's second oil crisis brought both the public's priorities and Carter's failings into sharp relief. Sparked by unrest in Iran (which shortly led to the Iranian revolution), no oil flowed from Iran to the West from December 1978 to the autumn of 1979; even though Iranian oil accounted for only 5 percent of the oil consumed in the United States, other oil-producing countries took advantage of the shortages and raised their prices.[27] While the White House and Congress fought each other over proposed solutions, oil prices doubled within six months. There were again massive shortages. On Sunday, June 23, 1979, some 70 percent of the nation's gas stations closed for lack of fuel. Americans once more stopped taking weekend trips for fear of not being able to find enough gas to get home. In California, as many as five hundred cars lined up at a station to pay the then-outrageous price of over $1 a gallon for gas. A riot broke out in Levittown, Pennsylvania, and 60 percent of all long-haul trucking just stopped. Carter's approval ratings plunged to 25 percent. Following a week of meetings with dozens of people from all walks of life, the president went on television on July 15, 1979, and diagnosed the American people as suffering from "a crisis of confidence . . . that strikes at the very heart and soul and spirit of our nation . . . threatening to destroy the social and political fabric of America." Crucially, Carter concluded, as Americans looked for solutions to the crisis, they had "turned to the federal government and found it isolated from the mainstream of our nation's life." Americans, it seemed, had given up on (or were at least fed up with) government's inability to solve their problems.[28]

Indeed, most Americans heard Carter's crisis of confidence speech as too little, too late, too complicated, too gloomy, and perhaps irrelevant to the difficulties they were facing. Worse, by the end of 1979, the oil crisis and the economic fallout blurred together with the Iranian hostage crisis, in which student revolutionaries in Tehran took more than fifty staff members of the American embassy hostage, holding them, ultimately, for 444 days. A failed rescue attempt only added to the image of Carter as weak. Americans felt only more acutely the impotence of government, the drought of solutions coming from Washington. Carter's bid for a second term was doomed.[29]

Ronald Reagan, the actor turned politician, understood the value both of projecting a strong image and of making an audience feel good about itself. "Those who preside over the worst energy shortage in our history tell us to use less," Reagan mocked. "American's aren't losing their confidence. They are losing their shirts." Even those who did not like Reagan had to admit the guy could deliver a line. For Americans looking for a leader who, instead of analyzing the nation's confidence, projected confidence himself, Reagan seemed suddenly to have all the answers. That quality would carry him into the White House.[30]

Reagan's attack on big government also resonated. By 1980, Americans were already convinced that government did not have the answers. What Americans wanted was relief, and they did not care if it came from Democrats or Republicans; and despite having largely given up on government solutions, they continued to appeal for them. When no such solutions were forthcoming, a great many citizens were prepared to work outside "the system" to find solutions on their own.

Given the failures of government to fight for the people, the energy wars extended down to the community level, where citizens felt they had no choice but to mobilize to protect their own interests. Of course, activists differed as much in their interests as in their approaches and results. Starting in the mid-1960s, citizens in Kentucky, West Virginia, Ohio, and Pennsylvania rose up against the big coal companies that were then strip-mining all around their homes. As the historian Chad Montrie has shown, "the campaign to abolish stripping was primarily a movement of farmers and working people of various sorts, originating at the local level."[31] These people believed in the hallowed ideal of private property; they were not radicals. In Knott and Perry Counties in eastern Kentucky, however, mining companies had often acquired mineral rights fraudulently, for no more than $1 an acre, and when residents saw the land being destroyed, it sickened them. "Strip miners were boring, ripping, and tearing away at the topsoil to get at the coal underneath, and in the process rolling stones, boulders, trees, and dirt down onto private property, homes, and land," Montrie writes. Worse, the "inevitable acid water which follows the auger and strip mining" killed fish, trees, and grass and bled its way into drinking water.[32]

As one would expect from most any homeowner, residents did not take such threats to their health and safety lightly. Clarence Williams, a farmer from Hazard, Kentucky, explained in a letter to the editor of a local newspaper that his land and everything on it had been destroyed by strip-mining machinery and debris. "On tops of the mountains all you can see are acid wastes and stagnant pools," he wrote. "With the heavy rains beating down these bare hillsides what will hold the soil? . . . The poor people in the valleys will be covered with the filth leaving no farm land to grow crops." Williams, like most of his neighbors, was angry and not prepared to let the mining continue uncontested. "I don't intend to sit idly by and see the resting place of my ancestors covered by spoils from the strip mine destruction. This is my home . . . They yell out to save jobs and industry. They don't realize their jobs mean destroying what the other people own." At first, being law-abiding citizens, local residents tried to work through legal channels. They petitioned and protested politely to the companies and their elected representatives, calling for an eventual abolition of strip-mining. When that got them nowhere, and as they watched the soil continue to slide, they turned to direct action: blocking trucks or occupying a mining site the way Sixties radicals had occupied campus buildings. In other cases, direct action morphed into sabotage and armed standoffs as bulldozers and other mining equipment exploded into twisted wreckage. The locals had grown up with labor disputes, picketing, and threats from company gun thugs when workers went out on strike; they felt perfectly comfortable squaring off against mining company personnel as they sought to preserve the land and their property.[33]

In time, such protests attracted sufficient attention in the halls of Congress that legislators passed new regulations to limit strip mining (a bill aimed at abolishing strip mining failed), only for President Ford to veto the law, claiming it would cost jobs and raise utility bills for consumers. When Jimmy Carter entered the White House, he signed the compromise Surface Mining Control and Reclamation Act. But activists felt defeated: although companies could no longer dump debris down the slopes of the mountains they stripped, the practice of taking off an entire mountaintop was explicitly recognized as a legal mining method. Even so, the example of the Appalachian working class in challenging the mining companies on environmental and human health and safety grounds predicted a decade of similar activism across the nation.[34]

In contrast, activists who organized primarily as energy consumers met with mixed success. The Citizen Labor Energy Coalition formed in 1978 to take on the big oil companies and their supporters in Congress. CLEC pointed out that the oil companies had donated a total of $547,000 to the campaign committees of nine members of the Senate Finance Committee; no wonder, then, that Congress approved tax breaks for the industry in 1977. At first, CLEC's organizing focused on natural gas, the price of which had been set by the federal government since the Great Depression. That had worked just fine until the early 1970s, when the industry, claiming shortages, succeeded in getting the Federal Power Commission to raise the price of gas by more than 300 percent. As Americans suddenly received much higher heating bills, senior citizens and the poor turned their heat off. "My feet froze up in January," one elderly Philadelphia woman told CLEC, "but I didn't have enough money to put the heat back on." With President Carter caving to pressure from industry to decontrol gas pricing—and considering doing the same for oil—CLEC attempted to organize by bringing consumers and the labor movement together to protest rates they found obscene. They demanded the return of price controls on gas and oil, the breaking up of oil conglomerates, and energy subsidies for poor and low-income Americans. "This is more than a matter of dollars and cents," argued William Winpisinger, a labor movement veteran and CLEC's first president. "This is a question of who owns America. What our country stands for. Where we are going."[35] A statement like that smacked of an ideological stand, but for those living in freezing homes, it was a practical statement of survival.

Protests aimed directly at utility companies—specifically at preventing utilities from shutting off heat and electricity in cold-weather months— proved more successful. In Baltimore, when residents could not pay their bills, Baltimore Gas and Electric just shut off their gas and electricity. At the time, the city's unemployment rate stood at close to 20 percent, so the company's policy affected not only the poor but others who had historically been able to earn a paycheck and pay their bills. Ed Montague, a community organizer from northeast Baltimore, explained, "We went to the utility and said, 'These are people who would normally pay their bills. They've successfully participated. You've got to give people credit.'" In a scene that could have been conceived for a film, Montague led a delegation of fifteen from CLEC to meet with the chairman of the BG&E board, Bernard Treushler. When Montague started the discussion, Treushler interrupted him: "Who gave you permission to chair this meeting?" Montague bristled. "It was a question of someone looking at me as a black man and figuring I had to have permission," he later explained. "It made me angry." Montague told Treushler that he could leave his own office if he didn't like it. "Who the hell are you," Montague shouted, "to give me permission to do anything?" Montague prevailed that day, and the automatic shutoffs for nonpayment stopped. CLEC won similar bans or limitations on winter utility shutoffs in at least twenty-three states; direct rate relief for residential customers in several states; and more equitable rate structures in twenty states. Taken together, it amounted to a pretty convincing victory for front porch politics.[36]

By comparison, a though mobilizing at the national level made for great theater, it did not get the same results. On October 17, 1979, CLEC launched "Big Oil Day" with upwards of a hundred thousand people protesting in 120 cities across the country. One thousand senior citizens rallied outside the offices of the American Petroleum Institute (API) in Washington, while seven thousand turned out in the Federal Plaza in Chicago. Despite this showing, Big Oil Day failed to stop Congress from accepting Carter's decontrol order on oil prices and passing a compromise—that is, smaller—windfall profits tax. The protests did not stop. CLECers famously crashed a swank party being hosted by the American Petroleum Institute in the restaurant at the top of the John Hancock Tower in Chicago. Bedlam followed. Executives hid as the protesters fanned out, looking for Exxon chairman Clifton Garvin. The next day, on November 9, 1981, more than five thousand protesters from all over the country descended on the API convention site to protest the oil industry's efforts to further decontrol prices.

The demonstration brought together a diverse array of Americans. "Young and old, black and white, unionists and farmers and housewives came together to tell the oil companies our lives and futures are at stake," reported one senior citizen organizer. "We're ready to fight." Indeed, by 1981, CLEC had affiliates in forty-three states, and in the battle over gas price decontrols, they mobilized a door-to-door canvassing campaign that reached nearly 2 million homes and targeted the oil companies' allies in Congress in midterm elections. CLEC organized "accountability sessions" with elected representatives in two hundred districts to put them on notice that their constituents expected them to vote against decontrol. For a consumer activist initiative, it was a staggering organizational achievement. But it wasn't enough. The opposition mobilized, too. Mobil Oil paid for full-page ads in *The Washington Post* and *The New York Times* that specifically rebutted CLEC's claims about corporate profits. The Natural Gas Supply Association spent $1 million to start a faux citizen group, "Alliance for Energy Security," that also went door-to-door and did phone canvassing. Moreover, the battle over legislation dragged on for years, and despite CLEC's efforts to keep the focus on fair energy pricing—an issue every consumer could understand—the policy complications became such that the public's attention waned. By the end of the 1980s, gas prices were fully decontrolled. CLEC's victories and defeats exposed the promise and limits of a front porch political approach. Its hallmarks of simplicity and immediacy were strengths in some contexts—in struggles over local utility rates, for example—but were weaknesses on the bigger national stage, where the opposition's resources and tactics were overwhelming.[37]

This is why the Minnesota power line wars are so revealing. Fought out between mighty utility companies and not-so-mighty farm country citizens, and fed by the locals' sense of being abandoned by their elected officials, the sustained clashes turned not so much on consumer concerns as on matters of health and safety.

The conflict began in 1973 when two cooperative utilities announced that they planned to build an electricity-generating plant at a lignite mine near Bismarck, North Dakota, and construct high-voltage power lines that would bring the plant's electricity 430 miles east to the Twin Cities. The project was financed by the Rural Electrification Administration, one of the brighter stars in the New Deal galaxy, and according to the utilities, it promised to bring more energy to urban areas. But the farmers who first encountered surveyors siting the path of the power line through their land and their neighbors' land objected vigorously. Even though the utilities would pay them to put up the towers and run the line through their land, the farmers worried about the effect of the line on the farm environment—what it would it do to crops and livestock—and the prospect of high-voltage electric shocks. There had been no long-term studies on the impact of such high voltage of direct current, and farmers trusted only other farmers to tell them what they experienced. "Those damn lines, on a wet day, can throw shocks all over the place,"

Kenny Thurk, a thirty-eight-year-old farmer from Villard, told a journalist. "We've had reports from farmers in Ohio that they can't even drive near the thing without worrying about their hair standing on end." At the same time, the people in these communities were also furious at being left out of making decisions that could have a profound effect on their families' day-to-day lives. Finally, as Paul Wellstone noted, "somehow health and safety always becomes *the issue* in the public debates," and that proved true in Minnesota. There was limited but frightening evidence of an increased likelihood of cancer and other ailments among people who lived near high-voltage power lines in Colorado and upstate New York. The Minnesotans feared being cast—unwillingly—as guinea pigs in some mad scientist's laboratory study of low-level power line radiation.[38]

Given the ongoing energy crisis—with foreign oil that could be capriciously withheld at any time and nuclear power facing its own challenges—Minnesota utility and government officials got firmly behind coal-powered electricity. The decision had been made and there seemed no room to discuss it. A power line would be built across a great many Minnesota farms, it was true, but the farmers would be compensated. No alternative was offered. But the fear of unknown, unpredictable health hazards and the seemingly willful attempts to exclude the farmers from the approval process drove them to act.

The first arrest came in June 1976, just after the state Environmental Quality Council ruled in favor of the power line. Until that point, the farmers felt they had done everything the correct way, registering their opposition through the appropriate legal channels. But on June 8, when surveyors showed up on Virgil Fuchs's land, he hopped in his tractor and ran them off, smashing their tripod for good measure. The next morning, the prosecutor charged him with two felony counts and the judge set bail. Fuchs refused to pay, daring them to leave him in jail overnight with an angry mob outside. They let him go.

The arrest and arraignment galvanized the farmers from Grant, Pope, Meeker, Traverse, and Stearns Counties. There is a long agrarian protest tradition in Minnesota and other parts of the Midwest, and it surfaced with force that June. Unrepentant, farmers next coordinated their intimidation of surveyors; one farmer would see a surveyor and put out a call on his CB radio, and suddenly fifty or sixty people would appear to see the surveyor take off running. In Stearns County, the players in this game of cat and mouse soon learned they would have to play without a referee. The sheriff said he would not, in effect, enforce the law. "I will not point a gun at either the farmer or the surveyor," he said. Bad news for the mice, who next moved to Meeker County, only to be surrounded again by farmers and ignored by the sheriff. In the meantime, Counties United for a Rural Environment (CURE), an umbrella group for power line opponents, filed an appeal of the companies' construction permits, and a Stearns County judge stayed construction.[39]

With no one to enforce the law, the companies sent out surveyors the size of professional football linemen. When one farmer stood in front of a surveyor's optical level with a sign that read KEEP HEALTH HAZARDS OUT, a fight broke out, forcing the sheriff to arrest two surveyors and a farmer. "I can assure you that the board of directors of UPA has said the surveying will be done," a United Power Association spokesman said flatly. "If it requires violence to get that done, that's what it's going to take." One could almost hear the gauntlet hit the floor.

Shortly thereafter, a Meeker County judge sided with the utilities and issued an order prohibiting interference with the surveyors. But in Pope County, November brought more confrontations. When Sheriff Ira Emmons accompanied the surveyors and started to read a warning, the farmers responded by singing "America the Beautiful," "The Star-Spangled Banner," and "We Shall Overcome." Emmons had to arrest five of them that day, but he seemed to understand them. "I think that the feeling of most of the people out here that were doing the protesting was that was the only thing they had left that they could do. Not that they wanted to. I'm sure a lot of them didn't want to, but they felt that was the only way they could protect their property."[40] Indeed, the farmers backed off when the new Democratic Farm Labor governor, Rudy Perpich, took office in December 1976 and personally intervened to try to mediate. After a while, though, with the process dragging on, the farmers got discouraged as they watched the political power of the companies at work. Jim Nelson, one of the first farmers to learn of the plans to put the power line right through his property, summed up the skepticism. "Although we might be down in St. Paul as often as once a week, the power company lobbyists had the other four days to work on the legislators," he observed. "They made good use of the other four days." In September 1977, the state supreme court ruled against them in a case that had consolidated all of the suits against the utilities. The farmers seemed then to have run out of options.[41]

Except that they could follow the example of civil rights activists and commit civil disobedience. On January 11, 1978, Dennis and Nina Rutledge decided to be civilly disobedient. "We didn't want to have any incidents with the surveyors," Dennis Rutledge, a thirty-five-year-old former navy officer, recalled. "We wanted to have a symbolic arrest . . . We felt it was extremely important that my wife and I get arrested on our land confronting the surveyors. We felt that was important personally." Joined by six others who "stood together in the middle of the snow-covered field," the Rutledges were arrested and charged with "obstructing legal process." By all accounts, this refusal to submit to the will of the state was dignified and moving. "I started to cry," Nina Rutledge remembered. "I was scared and I was happy. It was all kinds of feelings mixed up—I was really confused. I felt strong about what I did, but I still had confusing emotions—even feeling guilt, that I had done something wrong, because of the way I had been raised." Going to jail and getting fingerprinted, she later said, "was very trying." But in a dramatic turn of events, the Pope County prosecutor, C. David Nelson, announced his decision to resign rather than prosecute the Rutledges and the other six. "They're not criminals, and that's the point," he told the press. "The law is clear and they are breaking the law as far as I can see, but I don't agree with the law." None of the other six county attorneys was willing to prosecute them, either, and so another legal vacuum opened up. Faced with more and more civil disobedience, the police started arresting more and more farm folk, but hundreds more kept turning up in the fields. The governor had already sent 215 of the state's 504 troopers to Pope County, and it wasn't enough.[42]

In the "battle of Stearns County," the scene looked like the rural Minnesota version of Chicago during the 1968 Democratic National Convention. On Math and Gloria Woida's farm, from February 13 to 15, 1978, the confrontation between tractor and trooper escalated each day. On the thirteenth, Math Woida and others chased the surveyors off his land with a huge manure spreader. The next day, when the surveyors returned with state troopers, Math, from the seat of his tractor, pushed snow up onto the troopers' patrol cars, all but burying them. When Woida's friends tried to use the manure spreader again, the police maced them. That set up events for the fifteenth, when two hundred people gathered at the Woida farm; they had brought in a huge tank of anhydrous ammonia—their own mace, industrial strength—which is dangerous to touch or breathe, and they gave the police a taste of their own medicine. Farmers and state troopers confronted one another in the snow, wearing gas masks, and the police again ran off. Public opinion of the farmers dipped briefly after that episode, but those who maced the cops made no apologies. "I hate to tell you my position during the Vietnam War," Gloria Woida said. "I was totally against all that protesting, but now I see that war as the same as what . . . the Government is doing to us with that power line. I realize we're all at the mercy of the government."[43]

Tactics that used physical force could be justified, therefore, because the power line threatened the farmers' very existence and because the government both failed to protect the farmers and in fact seemed actively to be working against them. When John Tripp was convicted for an action in which he blocked police, he spoke to the simple front porch issues he hoped the judge could understand—that the farmers wanted only to do their jobs. "This line jeopardizes our jobs by ruining our farm fields and makes our place of work unsafe," Tripp said. "Our jobs, our homes, our health . . ." His voice drifted off. "Is the law right when it stands beside corporate giants and pushes our vital concerns aside?" Later that winter, on a cold Sunday, eight thousand people took part in a March for Justice, a modern update of the Farmers Alliance caravans of the 1890s. A tractor waving an American flag led the way, followed by a casket labeled with the word JUSTICE and a towering papier-mâché "Corporate Giant." They marched from Lowry to Glenwood and in the process demonstrated their numbers and commitment.[44]

Sensing their strength, the farmers encouraged Pope County's own Alice Tripp, John's wife, to run against Rudy Perpich for governor in the DLF primary. A fifty-nine-year-old former English teacher, Tripp had been arrested at her farm in January and became a favorite with the press for her "blunt, incisive comments." She might have been good for a sound bite, but during her low-budget candidacy, she articulated clearly how she and so many others became reluctant activists.

What happened to the farmers of western Minnesota is happening to all of us . . . In energy, in agriculture, in health care, in almost everything that matters to people, the same pattern of power is evident. Partnerships of large corporations and entrenched bureaucracies dominate the vital decisions that affect our lives and shape our future. Corporations call the tune; the government—our government—helps them carry out their plans. This is not democratic. The corporate planners and government bureaucrats who decide policies are not accountable to the American people.

She described not only how a lot of Minnesotans felt but how a lot of Americans felt. "Who sacrifices, who benefits, and who decides?" she asked. After spending only $5,000 on her campaign, Tripp managed to win 20 percent of the vote.[45]

By late summer 1978, the farmers could see that the construction of the power line could not be stopped. Tower after tower stood like sentinels over their farms. With no legal remedies available and feeling exhausted from the direct action campaigns, the farmers knew at last that they had lost. Even so, they did not go down without a fight. Recalling the Boston Tea Party, power line opponents moved stealthily at night to remove the bolts from the towers (which ranged in height from 150 to 180 feet tall). In time, at least 685 towers in Minnesota alone—most falling or listing on farmers' land—felt the effects of the so-called "bolt weevils." The company had no choice but to send out repair crews night after night, and they offered a $100,000 reward for information on the perpetrators. As the company and police paid more attention to the towers' security, someone figured out that the power could be interrupted by vandalizing the glass insulators on the lines. As one might imagine, farm people are good with a slingshot, and they shot out more than 5,500 insulators in less than a year. Police learned that picnics and barbecues often preceded a night of bolt weevils and wrist rockets, and in at least one case they tried to break up a big picnic before the sabotage began. Eighteen squad cars descended on the picnic and the state troopers ordered everyone to disperse. Predictably, the farmers refused. Then, as one journalist reported, "they blinded the police with high-powered lights [and] opened fire with makeshift slingshots known as 'wrist-rockets.'" According to one chuckling resident, when it ended, "I'd say there wasn't a single window left on those cop cars . . . those cops never knew what hit 'em." Even after the line went live for commercial operation in August 1979, towers occasionally fell and insulators shattered mysteriously.[46]

In the end, Minnesota farmers lost the power line war. Front porch politics ran up against the massive, glacial shifts in the nation's political economy: in the name of growth and development, government sided with business. The Falkirk Mine in North Dakota still produces coal that is burned at the nearby Coal Creek Station, yielding electricity that is still transmitted by that same power line across the northern prairie to Delano, on the edge of Minneapolis–St. Paul. The utility companies' political clout—lobbying five days a week—could not be overcome. Moreover, most public officials, as well as many Minnesotans outside the affected counties, truly believed that given the dire circumstances facing the state and the nation—energy shortages, the potential dangers of nuclear power—the power line was the least of all energy evils. Without the power line, some feared that the Twin Cities would, like New York City, soon experience blackouts. Clear evidence of the power line's dangers to human health could not be marshaled during the controversy, though studies conducted in the 1980s established a correlation between the electromagnetic fields associated with high-voltage power lines and childhood leukemia.[47]

In spite of the political defeat, the campaign against the power line established a potent precedent. It showed that just as the body's immune system will marshal every available defense against a virus, it is in the natural order of things for ordinary citizens to rally against health hazards in their immediate environment. It also demonstrated that even in a losing campaign, those in power—at the utilities and at all levels of government—could be called to account. Maybe most important, as a defeat for front porch politics, the power line campaign showed that in late-twentieth-century America, life during political wartime sometimes meant losing battles, and maybe even losing the war. But the fight, like countless others over questions of energy and the environment, was evidence of the state of American political culture. In the 1970s, 1980s, and beyond, the public expected to have a role in the decisions that affected their daily lives.

5

No Nukes!

●

As the power line battle raged in Minnesota, a much bigger front in the energy wars opened up. As in similar conflicts over power lines and toxic waste, the struggle over nuclear power plants was fought by a range of citizens, moderate to militant, without much concern for partisan politics or ideology, but in defense of themselves and their families. These were Americans who felt that they had no choice but to organize, fighting to reclaim the right to participate in the decisions that affected their families' day-to-day lives. In a time of economic despair, however, the No Nukes movement sometimes struggled to overcome the competing desire, felt by many Americans, for cheap energy.

In 1970, the United States derived only 1.4 percent of its energy from nuclear power, but thanks to the first oil crisis, nuclear energy's future looked promising. President Nixon, in his major energy speech of April 1973, called on Congress to accelerate nuclear development and licensing. Utility companies purchased 140 new reactors between 1970 and 1974, leading analysts to predict that nukes would provide 25 percent of the nation's energy by 1980 and 50 percent by the end of the century. The "postpetroleum era" seemed to be dawning.[1]

Except that all had not gone smoothly in the short career of nuclear power. Troubling connections to nuclear weapons echoed loudly in the public's ears when the University of Pittsburgh scientist Ernest Sternglass published findings claiming that infant mortality rates in the United States, long in decline, had started to rise again during the era of nuclear testing and that four hundred thousand infant deaths across the country could be attributed to the Nevada atomic weapons testing in the 1950s. A defensive atomic energy commissioner, Glenn Seaborg, asked John

Gofman, then head of the Biomedical Research Division of Lawrence Livermore National Laboratory, to conduct his own research and write a rebuttal. Gofman and his colleague Arthur Tamplin concluded that Stern-glass's numbers were inflated, but that the Nevada tests still had caused four thousand babies to die. For most Americans, that was four thousand too many. The Atomic Energy Commission, which had promised Tamplin and Gofman complete autonomy, pressured the scientists to publish their research without the four thousand figure, but they refused. A few months later, Gofman and Tamplin published the even more controversial finding that if nuclear power plants continued to operate at AEC standards, thirty-two thousand Americans would die each year of cancer. By 1979, when the Three Mile Island accident occurred, George Wald, the Nobel laureate biologist, put it bluntly: "Any dose of radiation is an overdose."[2]

In addition to pointing to potentially lethal radiation exposure, critics also decried nuclear power plants for producing thermal pollution. At the time, nuclear plants wasted 70 percent of the energy they produced in the form of heat. Since nuclear plants must always be located near bodies of water from which they draw to cool the reactor, environmentalists—including no small number of fishermen—complained that waste heat killed or harmed marine life where they fished. Proponents dismissed such claims as unscientific.[3]

In addition to their difficulties with radiation emissions and thermal pollution, nuclear power plant manufacturers and operators have never solved the problem of what to do with the radioactive waste that is a by-product of every plant's operation. Once every year, operators have to remove and replace the spent uranium fuel rods used in nuclear fission. These rods are incredibly radioactive. They have to be removed mechanically by remote control and are cooled in water for a year before being sent off to a plant where they are partially recycled. After uranium and plutonium are extracted for reuse, the remaining radioactive material has to get stored somewhere. But where? As John Gofman noted at the time, this is not a project that anyone really wants because "you must contain and isolate [the radioactive waste] better than 99.99 percent perfectly in peace and war, with human error and human malice, guerrilla activity, psychotics, malfunction of equipment . . ." It is a tall order. The half-life of radioactive waste can be from ten thousand to a hundred thousand years. "Do you believe that there's anything that you'd like to guarantee will be done 99.99 percent perfectly for 100,000 years?" Gofman asked.[4]

Americans expecting the federal government to oversee and minimize such hazards did not take much comfort from the Atomic Energy Commission's record. As early as 1959, residents on Cape Cod discovered that the AEC had long allowed the illegal dumping of radioactive waste in the Atlantic. And in the 1960s, news broke that the AEC had authorized the Climax Uranium Company to sell two hundred thousand tons of radioactive uranium tailings to construction companies that turned around and used them as fill "on which to pour a concrete floor." The concrete, alas, did not stop the deadly radon gas emitted by the tailings from seeping up through the floor. "Babies and toddlers who remained home all day and played on the floor received the heaviest doses," one energy expert later noted. "They, along with the unborn, were the most vulnerable to genetic damage from the gamma rays." The AEC's dismal safety record arose because it served the dual function of regulating an industry that the federal government also charged it with promoting. All of this went a long way toward seeing that a new agency, the Nuclear Regulatory Commission (NRC), replaced the AEC in 1974.[5]

Even with a new regulatory agency, however, the possibility that a nuclear reactor core might melt down remained, through the 1970s and 1980s, not only the main concern of environmentalists but certainly of anyone living in the vicinity of a nuclear plant. Given the growing deluge of applications for NRC operating licenses—there were 42 operating nuclear power plants in 1973, 71 in 1980, and 112 by 1990, and all of the new ones had to go through the NRC's licensing evaluation process—residents living near proposed nuke sites naturally sought information on past accidents. They found a surprisingly long list, dating back to the 1957 Windscale Pile Number One accident in England. There, a routine shutdown somehow led to a fire, which destroyed some of the containment safety equipment, causing radioactive emissions to escape into the atmosphere, poisoning the milk from cows in a two-hundred-square-mile area downwind. The British government had to buy up all the milk and destroy it. A similar fire occurred at the Fermi I reactor near Detroit in October 1966, resulting in a partial meltdown at the 300-megawatt plant. No radiation escaped, but government officials seriously considered evacuating Detroit, forty miles south of the plant. The operators and AEC succeeded in keeping the public largely in the dark about this accident until John Grant Fuller's book, *We Almost Lost Detroit*, was published in 1975. The year that book came out, a worker at the Browns Ferry, Alabama, nuclear power plant accidentally started a major fire when he held up a candle to test airflow and set the insulation alight. The fire raged for seven hours and ultimately caused $100 million in damage. The plant's emergency system worked, but as one General Electric official said, "We really weren't very close [to a meltdown], but I'd just as soon not be that close again."[6]

In the United States, prior to the 1970s, the building of nuclear power plants met citizen resistance at every turn. In 1963, after five years of citizen organizing, the U.S. Geological Survey showed that earthquake faults ran perilously close to Bodega Head, forty miles up the coast from San Francisco, where Pacific Gas & Electric had begun to build what would have been the world's largest nuclear reactor. PG&E backed out of the project the next year.[7] In Eugene, Oregon, after voters approved the funding of a new nuclear power plant in 1968, a group of citizens formed an opposition group, the Eugene Future Power Committee, which, after educating the community on the region's actual energy needs (not sufficient to justify the plant, they argued), succeeded in getting voters to reject it. In Ohio, by contrast, the Coalition for Safe Nuclear Power and a Bowling Green State University student group registered to protest the proposed Davis-Besse reactor at a public inquiry, but the AEC limited what could be discussed at the hearing. In spite of Ernest Sternglass's appearance at a later hearing to discuss his findings on radiation levels near nuclear power plants, the AEC, in March 1971, approved construction.

The Ohio defeat offered citizen activists some key lessons. First, they would need more money and more resources to fight future local battles against nuclear power; second, working within the bureaucratic system was rigged in favor of the utilities because they always positioned themselves as the true experts. Experts presented by activist groups got the brush-off while the AEC greeted the utility's experts like geniuses.[8]

By the mid-1970s, a loose coalition of No Nukes groups began to form. In November 1974, no less a prominent public figure than Ralph Nader convened the first Critical Mass conference, bringing together many of these local organizations. Nader had been increasingly critical of the AEC since the late 1960s; the agency's dual role of regulating the industry while simultaneously promoting it smacked of the kind of rigged corporate arrangement that he relished exposing. Then, in 1972, Henry Kendall and Dan Ford of the Union of Concerned Scientists approached Nader; they knew that they had at their disposal tremendous technical and scientific expertise, but they did not have the media relations skills to carry their findings about nuclear power's danger beyond their small community of scholars. Nader, then at the peak of his influence, agreed to serve as a spokesman, identifying nuclear power as the "number one" threat to public safety in the United States.[9] Just as consumer groups and local corporate and government watchdog organizations were happy to claim Nader as an inspiration and ally, No Nukes activists saw him as a useful weapon on the national stage, complementing their work at the local level.

Nader and the other high-profile experts on the side of the No Nukes movement gave the campaign, nationally and locally, an important boost, and drove the industry to respond. In August 1975, for instance, the UCS presented to President Ford a petition signed by twenty-three hundred scientists describing nuclear power risks as "altogether too great." The industry answered by forming the Atomic Industrial Forum and budgeting $1.4 million for public relations. The AIF ran a ghostwriting campaign to place pro-nuclear "articles" directly in the press and kept dossiers on prominent nuclear critics. Meanwhile, some utility companies spied on antinuclear activists as well (the Georgia Power Company, for example, hired nine private investigators).[10] Last, the industry did well to educate kids in school. A 1978 survey of business-funded educational materials showed that

> more than any industry group, the electric utilities provide extensive multi-media materials on energy issues . . . These energy education efforts notably target the elementary grade levels through the use of films, comic books, cartoon graphics or simple phrasing. This emphasis on the lower grades seems aimed at cultivating a future constituency in support of the electric power industry in general and nuclear power in particular.[11]

In addition, the nuclear power industry responded to criticisms by marshaling experts of all sorts to beat back the opposition. Industry experts portrayed opponents as Chicken Littles predicting an imminent collapse of the sky, while economic experts largely succeeded in convincing the general public that stopping atomic power would lead to lost jobs and higher energy bills. "With a combination of facts, half-truths, and outright lies," John Gofman later said, "industry effectively hammered out a case aimed at the average voter's economic self-interest." Even in the face of growing opposition, such tactics proved extraordinarily effective at the front porch level, where issues central to the household economy—jobs and bills—occupied most people's attention.[12]

More difficult for the industry to combat were the whistleblowers who, especially when they got national press attention, effectively undercut the industry's credibility. Since the control of expertise strongly influenced the nuclear power debate, it made a powerful impression when three nuclear engineers resigned from General Electric in 1976, saying in a statement that "nuclear power is a technological monster that threatens all future generations." A few days later, the NRC engineer Robert D. Pollard also resigned over his frustrations that the NRC was not doing more to ensure the safety of the Indian Point nuclear power plant twenty-five miles north of New York City. *The New York Times* reacted by calling for operations at Indian Point to be suspended and criticized the NRC for being just as much a rubber stamp for the industry as the AEC had been.[13] The American people hardly needed any more reasons to not trust the government or other "experts."

Although anti-nuclear-power measures failed in seven states in 1976, the fact that such ballot initiatives gained any traction at all shocked the industry. Even *Forbes* had to admit that "the antinuclear coalition has been remarkably successful" and that it had "certainly slowed the expansion of nuclear power."[14] If that's what the industry thought, No Nukes activists felt they had accomplished little, that they were losing on nearly every front, while the nuclear industry, if not popular, had claimed a certain inevitability for itself. As a result, by the mid-1970s, the groundwork had been laid for an opposition movement to mobilize at the grass roots, but on a national scale.

Direct action against nuclear power started in 1974 in New England, where, as in New York, residents had the highest average electric rates in the nation. As oil prices went through the roof, more and more New

Englanders turned to heating their homes the old-fashioned way, with woodstoves, and in turn they seemed more susceptible to the promises of cheap and clean nuclear energy. As the industry expanded, however, it ran into serious resistance. In December 1973, Northeast Utilities announced a plan to build a $1.5 billion two-reactor plant in Montague, Massachusetts. It would be the biggest nuclear power plant in the country. The utility put up a weather monitoring tower at the site where the plant would be built, but on February 22, 1974, a local farmer named Sam Lovejoy used a crowbar to take it down. As one observer reported, Lovejoy walked away from "349 feet of twisted wreckage" and hailed a police patrol car to turn himself in. At his trial, to his frustration, the judge ordered the jury to find Lovejoy not guilty on a technicality: the charge of "destruction of personal property" did not actually fit the crime because the tower was not personal property. Still, Lovejoy's actions and trial soon inspired thousands of others.[15]

The mass movement that came to be associated with names like Seabrook, Diablo Canyon, and Barnwell formed on behalf of individual communities, but also formed more as experiments in community. This is why so many see environmentalism as carrying on the work of the 1960s: the No Nukes movement, especially, counted many alumni from the peace movement, marked by the trademarks of the counterculture (e.g., the long hair) and armed with the rhetoric of the civil rights movement's "beloved community" ideal. As Barbara Epstein noted about the movement, "A community that is formed in the process of struggle is a very precious thing, and fulfills a lot of needs that are not met in daily life . . . When people made the decision to step over the line and get arrested, they found that they also made the decision to step into a community that felt fulfilling and liberating." Like the New Left, the No Nukes movement practiced a "prefigurative, utopian approach to politics," living by the standards it expected the ideal society would have. Decisions were always made by consensus, and the movement emphasized civil disobedience and mass arrests as tactics that would win public support.[16]

Beyond these utopian ideals, though, the movement also spoke a language of practical resistance to illegitimate authority. As one participant noted, No Nukes activists "found the same kinds of cover-ups, lies, vested corporate interests and inhumanity involved in nuclear power as in the war issue." In fact, she said, some spoke of nuclear power as "the Vietnam War brought home," and that was an issue that any American living near a proposed plant site could relate to. Sam Lovejoy—who may have been the No Nukes answer to Rosa Parks—lived on a commune in Montague, one that had grown out of the 1960s, and he spoke at length at his trial about communities rallying to defend themselves. Such arguments resonated strongly with locals not because of utopian visions—you cannot see utopia from your front porch—but from a sense that the cooling tower that residents *could* see from their front porches represented a direct threat to their communities and families.[17] Consequently, the No Nukes movement attracted both moderates and militants, the practical and the idealistic, united, if not in a utopian vision, in commitment to human and environmental health.

In the small coastal town of Seabrook, New Hampshire, population 5,700, one of the nation's fiercest fights over nuclear power began with a utility company steamrolling the community. A 1972 poll commissioned by the Public Service Company of New Hampshire (PSNH) showed that the state's residents approved of nuclear power, but when offered a choice between economic growth and environmental protection, 70 percent chose the latter. The poll results seemed not to matter to PSNH, which went ahead with plans to build two 1,150-megawatt reactors in Seabrook. As Henry Bedford later noted, the utility executives somehow missed the "eroding confidence" in the authority of industry experts. They still believed that the people of New Hampshire would trust them and see the appeal of cheap nuclear energy. But by 1976, one could find evidence that even people in conservative New Hampshire questioned received wisdom. Moreover, the state has long been known for its fierce independent streak. With no broad-based statewide tax system, towns levy their own taxes to pay for their own schools, police, fire, sanitation, and snow removal. And although most towns liked the idea of attracting industry to the state (to help pay those local taxes), the lure of supposedly cheap electric rates provided by a nuclear-fed grid did not stop Seabrook voters from voting against the plant in 1976 by a margin of 55 percent to 45 percent.[18]

From the start, the Seabrook Station faced opposition from locals. The Seacoast Anti-Pollution League (SAPL) led the way for several years, arguing three key points: (1) the cooling tunnels that would draw over one billion gallons of ocean water into the cooling towers each day and then recycle it back into the sea 30 to 40 degrees warmer would surely affect the marine life on which local fishermen depended for their livelihood; (2) evacuation in case of emergency seemed impossible in an area where a hundred thousand people hit the beaches in Hampton and Salisbury every weekend during the summer, and where motorists could drive up the coast or due west only on two-lane roads; (3) Seabrook is located near the Boston-Ottawa earthquake fault lines, and the plant's initial designs did not take into consideration a serious earthquake. For the most part, PSNH either downplayed or ignored such concerns.

In June 1976, after the town voted against the plant, PSNH nevertheless received permission from the NRC to begin construction. The opposition quickly crystallized. Within weeks, a coalition of fifteen groups committed to stopping the plant from being built—even if it meant breaking the law—formed the Clamshell Alliance, named for the clams that are a staple of the seacoast diet and that would be threatened by thermal pollution. About fifty people came together at the first meeting, representing a range of constituencies: Guy Chichester, a builder and SAPL activist who grew tired of the League's timidity; Sam Lovejoy from Montague; Elizabeth Boardman of the American Friends Service Committee in Boston; and a mix of local people who had been involved in trying to stop the plant with the referendum in conjunction with no small number of antiwar and "radical ecological counterculture" activists who had moved to northern New England.[19]

With their well-defined worldviews and out-of-town residences, the mass of people who would, over the next two years, occupy the Seabrook construction site in several major No Nukes actions did not really represent the front porch political ethos. Consequently, they drew suspicion from locals and even a mocking critique of their sincerity from otherwise liberal journalists. "We appreciate you kids coming up here," one longtime resident of Seabrook said to a younger activist at one protest, "but some folks wonder just what kind of people have the time and money to come up here for four days." Tracy Kidder, writing in *The Atlantic Monthly*, emphasized the countercultural types and the divide between them and the seacoast locals. Kidder attended one of the Clamshell Alliance's nonviolence training sessions and mocked the role-playing exercise in which one activist played a demonstrator and another played a police German shepherd. These were easy targets. So was the woman at one demonstration who belonged to the Movement for a New Society, a utopian group, Kidder wrote, that practiced the "politics of nice." On the other hand, he wrote, a small business owner who acknowledged "there are a lot of crazies here" had to admit that "probably if it wasn't for them this [rally] would not be happening."[20]

The series of occupations that the Clams (as members of the Clamshell Alliance were known) held starting in August 1976 took as their inspiration the 1975 protests in Wyhl, West Germany, on the Rhine, where twenty-eight thousand people occupied a proposed nuclear reactor site. The plant was never built. In New Hampshire, on August 1, eighteen activists went to the Seabrook site to plant pine and maple saplings where the reactors were to be built. When police arrived to arrest them, the protesters sat down. The police dragged them two hundred yards through mud and bushes to the police vans and charged them with criminal trespass, disturbing the peace, and resisting arrest. Four days later, a group of a dozen elderly Seabrook residents held up groundbreaking ceremonies by sitting in chairs spread across the road to the site. On the same day, in Manchester, the state's biggest city, presidential candidate Jimmy Carter responded to the protests by saying that he believed "there's a place for nuclear power in the future" but that "it ought to be a last resort." Carter, who as a naval officer had participated in a frightening reactor cleanup at Chalk River in Canada (and received a year's worth of radiation exposure in a minute and a half), called for "tough safety precautions," for standardized designs for nuclear plants, and for plants to be "located where people don't live, where the environment will not be destroyed."[21]

A second Seabrook occupation occurred on August 22, when a group marched from a rally of fifteen hundred people on the Hampton Falls town common to the Seabrook construction site. Police again swept in, but this time arrested 180—ten times as many as they had arrested at the first occupation. This incredible growth in the number of people prepared to risk arrest galvanized nuclear opponents across the country. It seemed a model that others could follow.

Within the Granite State, however, public officials like Governor Meldrim Thomson and ordinary citizens dismissed the protesters as a bunch of clueless antiprogress nuts. "Just because there are a few 'kooks' around here," Mrs. Benjamin Brideau of Rochester wrote to the NRC, "who want to stop progress so they can have the woods to themselves does not mean we in New Hampshire are all stupid." Following the lead of William Loeb, editor of the conservative Manchester *Union Leader*, some started to label the Clams Communists. Others simply saw them as elitists, out of touch with most ordinary Americans then struggling to pay their electric bills. Meanwhile, PSNH was equally dismissive of the Clamshell Alliance's environmental concerns, saying that Seabrook would bring jobs and cheap electricity (which would attract more industry for the tax base) to the state. Besides, a PSNH lawyer argued, the marsh already had a railroad and U.S. Route 1 running through it, all within sight of the ramshackle carnival and amusements lining the seashore. "We bring this out not to denigrate the area," the PSNH lawyer said, "but to point out that Seabrook is not sited in an unspoiled glade previously populated only by nymphs and leprechauns."[22]

The pressure over thermal pollution produced its desired effect, however, when the EPA's regional office revoked temporary approval of the Seabrook cooling system. An environmental impact statement would be needed to move forward, it said. Investors began to pull out of the project, and with estimates that the plant would now cost nearly $3 billion (the original budget totaled $900 million), it looked as though PSNH could go bankrupt.[23] In addition, by March 1977, all of the surrounding towns had voted against building the nuclear power plant at Seabrook.[24]

As the utility company stumbled from this unexpected bureaucratic setback at the hands of the EPA, the Clamshell Alliance continued with plans for a massive occupation of the Seabrook site. Led by Quakers with experience in direct action, the Clams held a series of intensive nonviolence training sessions employing the tactic of affinity groups.[25] In practice, affinity groups are made up of eight to fifteen people who are already acquainted and can rely on one another during an action and afterward, perhaps in jail. The Clamshell Alliance made it clear that only people who belonged to affinity groups and had gone through the Clams' training would be allowed to participate in the occupation planned for April 30.[26] Alliance organizers were smart enough to know they did not want to give the authorities any extra reasons to attack them, and therefore they did not allow marijuana or alcohol on the site.[27]

This did not stop the governor and the editor of the only statewide newspaper from smearing the Clams as Communists and the demonstration as a "cover for terrorism." Governor Thomson liked to say that "New Hampshire is what America was," and he played up that nostalgia in appealing to the commonsense folk of his state to oppose these Seabrook rabble-rousers. Thomson was also the one who changed the slogan on the state's license plates from the gentle "Scenic New

Hampshire" to the overtly political "Live Free or Die." These commie Clams were, by this equation, limiting New Hampshire citizens' freedom to live with cheap nuclear energy and needed to be squashed. Fortunately for the Clams, one voice of reason emerged to represent the state on the scene: Col. Paul Doyon, head of the state police, had been present for the August arrests and effectively worked out with the Clams how the arrests in April would go down.

On Saturday, April 30, 1977, affinity groups approached the Seabrook construction site from six different directions. The sight of twenty-four hundred activists meeting and setting up "village" camping areas led to massive press coverage, with journalists drawing explicit parallels with the movements of the 1960s. Harvey Wasserman, both participant and freelance rapporteur, later called it a "watershed event in the direct-action politics of the 1970s." Indeed, except for the Minnesota farmers, no other group mobilized so many people for a mass arrest in the 1970s.[28]

The next morning, the National Guard and police arrived. They lined up just a short distance away from the occupiers, on the other side of the fence surrounding the site. Across the marshes, more than four thousand people attended a No Nukes rally at Hampton Beach State Park. The seacoast crackled with tension. Governor Thomson made a dramatic entrance, arriving by helicopter dressed in army fatigues, resembling a New England Yankee version of Fidel Castro; with Colonel Doyon, the governor met with six representatives from "Occupation City" and ordered everyone to disperse within twenty minutes or face arrest. As planned, about a thousand demonstrators complied. The rest, 1,414 occupiers, stayed. The police did not expect so many to accept arrest and, lacking the resources to move more swiftly, took twelve hours to get everyone into custody. The police also did not quite know what to do with so many people in handcuffs. Some spent the night in army trucks, while others were farmed out to various armories around the state. When a Portsmouth judge processed and released the first small group of protesters, the governor again appeared by helicopter and pressured prosecutors to call for $1,500 bail from each. Now the Clams, who had expected to spend maybe one night in jail, realized that since most were unable or unwilling to pay such high bail, their time in custody could be much longer.[29]

The demand for bail turned out to be a political blunder, as it guaranteed national press attention for the Clamshell Alliance's cause. For the next two weeks, the state held protesters in five National Guard armories.

The extended detentions worked almost entirely in favor of the Clams. "It was like the state had given us five free conference centers," said one detainee, and they made the most of it. The arrests thus became an occasion for community-building among No Nukes protesters—hardly the outcome the governor or PSNH sought. In the meantime, the cost of detaining all of these people—estimated at $50,000 a day—became itself a political issue in a state with hardly any tax base and a tiny budget. Prosecutors attempted to start trying the Clams, if only to get them out of the armories and off the front pages, but that backfired, too. When a judge in Hampton found a handful of Clams guilty but gave them suspended jail sentences and a $200 fine, Attorney General David Souter—later a United States Supreme Court justice—intervened and pressed the judge to stop suspending the jail time. "Giving the defendants a suspended sentence is tantamount to no punishment at all," Souter said. The attorney general expected all of these cases to be appealed, but he also expected them to be dropped on appeal because of the case backlog at the state superior court. Therefore, he said, "justice can only be done by imposing sentence right now." This scared enough Clams that some began paying the bail to get out of the armories before trial; the number of detainees dropped below six hundred by May 12. In the meantime, with pressure mounting over the cost of detaining so many people for so long and anticipating further extraordinary expenses in trying fourteen hundred people, the Rockingham County prosecutor, Carleton Eldridge, negotiated the release of all remaining detainees on personal recognizance if the Clamshell would accept mass trials. As one scholar later wrote, "the state emerged from the contretemps poorer and without much dignity." In the end, the April 30–May 1 occupation came to be regarded by many opponents of nuclear energy as a turning point for the movement. It garnered more media attention than the movement had ever before received, and given the apparent success of nonviolent direct action at Seabrook, the direct action approach quickly proliferated all over the country. As soon as August 6, more than 120 demonstrations and occupations took place all around the country, including occupations at Diablo Canyon in California and the Trojan plant in Oregon.[30]

In spite of the impact of the Clamshell Alliance occupation, a month later, the EPA approved the Seabrook cooling system. Construction could move forward. In celebration of the EPA decision, and as a counterdemonstration to the Clamshell occupation, three thousand people gathered for a march and rally at the JFK Arena in Manchester. They wore T-shirts that said NUCLEAR POWER: THE POLLUTION SOLUTION and NUCLEAR ENERGY: SAFER THAN SEX and marched through the city, some carrying union banners and others shouting "Nukes! Nukes! Nukes!" "It's good to see the silent majority being heard," a PSNH spokesman crowed to the rally, though it later emerged that the utility had paid for the buses and food to get most participants—ordinary ratepayers and labor union members—to go to Manchester.[31] Unions, typically reliable critics of un-restricted capitalism, emphasized jobs and took the side of industry, not the environment. The Clamshell Alliance moved into the fall of 1977 buoyed by the national perception that it was the vanguard of the No Nukes movement but also facing new challenges. In November, in the first trial stemming from the May 1 arrests, Judge Wayne Mullavey re-jected defendant Carter Wentworth's "competing harms" defense. Al-though such a defense—in which one argues that it is acceptable to break a law if, in doing so, one is preventing an even greater harm from occurring—is allowed under New Hampshire law, Mullavey found Went-worth guilty and made an example of him by sentencing him to four months in jail when the prosecution had recommended only sixteen days.[32] Elsewhere, nuclear energy opponents fared better in court. In Or-egon, where 81 members of the Trojan Decommissioning Alliance were arrested for conducting a thirty-eight-hour sit-in at the gates of the Trojan nuclear power plant on August 6, 1977 (and another 124 were arrested in November), the judge allowed a competing harms defense. Norman Sol-omon later recalled that he and his fellow defendants essentially argued that the "threat of nuclear power outweighed the wrong of trespassing." In exchange for trying all of the defendants at once, the judge allowed expert witnesses, including Ernest Sternglass, who testified on the effects of radiation. With the media spotlight on the courtroom, the jury found the defendants not guilty, a finding that led the industry to fear more oc-cupations.[33]

Following the New Hampshire trials, as the Clams moved toward the next planned occupation, scheduled for June 1978, fractures in the Alli-ance made consensus impossible. Disagreeing over whether to accept the state's offer to hold a legal rally, the Clams divided into several factions.[34] But even though the decision to go forward with the legal rally ultimately crippled the Clamshell Alliance, few could argue that it was not a huge public relations victory. On June 25, 1978, more than six thousand Clams, including many who had come from all over the country, arrived at Seabrook and built a small city on eighteen acres. As in the occupation the year before, the Clams set up tent villages and roadways, but they also put up a wide variety of exhibits on alternative energy sources. In what looked like a cross between a medieval carnival and a junior high science fair, windmills, solar panels, and a geodesic dome shared space with displays on recycling and conservation and stalls selling food and T-shirts. The next day, an estimated twelve to fourteen thousand people visited this new energy fair and got to hear music from the likes of Pete Seeger, Arlo Guthrie, and Jackson Browne to boot. Across the state in Manchester, another pro-nukes rally attracted a crowd of five hundred— much smaller than the last one—to its "Clambake." "Come up here, son. How old are you?" an MC said to a kid in the crowd. "Nine? What do you think of nuclear power? Did you hear that, folks? That was from a nine-year-old: 'Nuclear power means jobs.' Did you hear that down in Washington, Jimmy?"

Both sides claimed victory the next day. Governor Thomson said the Clamshell rally did not stop construction for even a second, and the Clams said that they had just hosted the largest No Nukes demonstration in American history. As one journalist wrote at the time, the Clams felt "vindicated by the high turnout, largely sympathetic media coverage, and renewed local support." Several days later, on a Friday, the day after fifty-six Clams were arrested in Washington on the steps of the NRC, the agency ordered construction at Seabrook halted pending EPA approval of the plant's cooling tunnels. It seemed like an astonishing victory for grassroots participatory democracy.[35]

And yet construction began again in August. The dramatic grassroots victory did not stop the wheels of bureaucracy or Wall Street investment, which just ground on and on. The Clams, still split from the disagreement over the June rally, seemed suddenly unable to respond effectively. Instead of another mass occupation, a number of smaller local Clam-affiliated groups carried out a series of small civil disobedience actions. Police arrested maybe sixty participants over several weeks. Clams for Direct Action at Seabrook called for more occupations, including one in October, when two thousand people showed up and cut through the fence at the site but balked at crossing the line. Over the next couple of years, there were more actions, but they carried less weight. Supporters of the No Nukes cause may have taken comfort each time a new protest took place at Seabrook, but to outside observers, it started to look like the tired act of a mimic.[36]

To the everlasting frustration of the Clamshell Alliance—whether moderates or militants—the model established by German activists at Wyhl turned out to be far too ambitious for them. The occupations at Seabrook never came close to attracting twenty-eight thousand people prepared to break the law by taking over the site. In later years, scholars credited the Clamshell Alliance with establishing an American model that many groups followed around the country, carrying on the tradition of trying to build a "beloved community" within and beyond the movement. "The greatest contribution of Clamshell," Barbara Epstein has written, "lay not in containing the growth of the nuclear power industry, but in the creation of a mass movement based on nonviolent direct action and infused with a vision of a better world, which it attempted to prefigure in its own practice." The Clamshell activist and writer Anna Gyorgy agreed, but blamed that emphasis on community for overshadowing the primary goal of "stopping the nukes." For a lot of people in the movement, she said, "the process became more important than the product, the means became an end." In the 1970s, with the economy in the gutter—high prices, high unemployment, high fuel costs—working toward utopia did not win political battles. From the front porch, the distant view was usually clouded by any number of immediate economic hazards. And while the Clamshell Alliance basked in the glow of the beloved community it was building, PSNH and the investors that backed it settled into a strategy that tolerated losing battles in the court of public opinion and taking occasional bureaucratic hits. Through steady commitment and seemingly endless resources, they simply outlasted the opposition. Going into the 1980s, Seabrook Station's containment domes slowly surfaced like a dual moonrise over the marshes.[37]

At the same time, the Clamshell Alliance did spawn a national movement of Alliances all over the country. In Indiana, the Paddlewheel Alliance formed in 1977 in opposition to the Marble Hill nuclear power plant, twenty-eight miles upriver from Louisville, Kentucky. The Great Plains Alliance, meanwhile, succeeded in leading a lobbying campaign against "construction work in progress"—where ratepayers help pay for a nuclear power plant's construction long before it starts producing energy—in Missouri. In Texas, activists formed the Lone Star Alliance, and in Kansas, the Sunflower Alliance. New Mexico and Colorado were home to actions mounted by the Cactus Alliance, and Washington and Montana saw the formation of the Crabshell Alliance and the Headwater Alliance, respectively. In Barnwell, South Carolina, the Palmetto Alliance launched the biggest No Nukes protests in the South. More than 1,500 people turned out on April 30, 1978 (the first anniversary of the big Seabrook occupation), 285 of whom were arrested at the gates of the spent nuclear fuel reprocessing plant at Barnwell (adjacent to the huge Savannah River nuclear weapons site). Over the course of a three-year campaign, using direct action and a variety of legal interventions, the Palmetto Alliance succeeded in preventing the fuel reprocessing plant from ever operating (though it later became one of the few low-level radioactive waste dumps in the country, processing more than 27 million cubic feet of radioactive waste by 2007).[38]

In California, the No Nukes campaign lasted longest, thanks to Diablo Canyon and the Abalone Alliance. In the state where resistance to nuclear energy got its start at Bodega Head and where no less a personage than the governor, Jerry Brown, labeled nuclear power "the next Vietnam," the battles over Diablo Canyon became the movement's longest war.

In the 1960s, the coast that lay west of San Luis Obispo, almost exactly midway between San Francisco and Los Angeles, remained basically untouched. Any campaign to stop the construction of a nuclear power plant had to start with educating the public, and at Diablo Canyon, as in the Boston busing crisis and Miami's Save Our Children campaign (and, as we will see, at Love Canal), it began with the voices of mothers. As late as August 1975, 75 percent of San Luis Obispo residents favored building the 2,212-megawatt twin reactor plant. Starting in 1973, however, Mothers for Peace, previously preoccupied with ending the Vietnam War, came up with a strategy that began to undercut the utility's promises.[39] Led by Liz Apfelberg and Sandy Silver, the Mothers shifted the terms of the debate over Diablo from environmental preservation to a focus on human health and safety. In 1975, the U.S. Geological Survey helped their cause by announcing that an earthquake of as high as 7.5 on the Richter scale could occur only 2.5 miles from Diablo Canyon at the Hosgri Fault. The plant's designers had planned for it to be able to withstand only a 6.75 quake. When the NRC still permitted construction to go forward, resentment in the area began to simmer.[40]

More important, Mothers for Peace introduced a maternal rhetoric that carried over from previous campaigns against nuclear weapons, the draft, and napalm. As the historian John Wills points out, the Diablo plant "seemed part of a broader atomic patriarchy" that the Mothers were ideally suited to fight. "The Mothers focused not upon the promises of new schools or cheaper electricity, but instead on their own role as protectors of children," Wills writes. Indeed, they "interpreted the nuclear-powered invasion of their homes as a radioactive threat" and nothing else. PG&E mocked them, of course. At one NRC hearing, an engineer from the utility dismissed Mothers for Peace as "a bunch of frustrated housewives." But as Sandy Silver later recalled, "Our tag was there's radiation, radiation hurts children, in particular the fetus and young children, and that was our concern." Seeing political work as an extension of their parental responsibilities was an archetypal front porch approach, even if it did not persuade everyone.[41] In June 1977, inspired by the Clams, a coalition led by the Mothers and other opponents of the Diablo plant (which first called itself People Generating Energy) took the name the Abalone Alliance in honor of the thousands of abalone that had been killed in the summer of 1974 when the Diablo plant's cooling system had first been tested (the company later replaced the copper pipes in the cooling system—which made the water return toxic to the abalone—with titanium).

The Abalone, like the Clamshell, also took the Wyhl occupation as its model and planned to increase the size of its nonviolent direct action protests in stages: the first two would be small and largely symbolic; the third, organizers hoped, would be more like Wyhl and succeed in shutting Diablo down. On August 7, 1977, as scores of other nuclear energy protests unfolded around the country, fifteen hundred people turned out at Avila Beach, south of the plant site, to hear activists including Barry Commoner and Daniel Ellsberg speak. Afterward, a relatively small group of protesters got onto the plant site. Police arrested forty-six of them, including two undercover cops. One year later, on August 6 and 7, 1978— just weeks after the huge energy fair at Seabrook brought out 20,000 people—more than 3,000 attended another rally before 487 were arrested at the gates. Despite Governor Brown's sympathy for the cause, prosecutors cracked down: all 487 received sentences of fifteen days in jail and $300 fines. Meanwhile, the Alliance started to make plans for a third action and planned to put it in motion if, as expected, the NRC granted the operating license for Diablo Canyon.[42]

Before Diablo got its license, though, American attitudes about nuclear energy quite suddenly changed. First, *The China Syndrome* opened in movie theaters on March 16, 1979, and focused much of the nation's attention on the possible perils of nuclear power. The film's title derived from the premise that if an accident at a nuclear power plant led to a reactor core meltdown, the core would become so hot that it would melt all the way through the foundation of the plant, into the earth, and not stop melting until it bored its way to China. Early in the film, a California television film crew witnesses a near-meltdown at the Diablo-looking "Ventana" nuclear power plant; the cause at first appears to have been human error. Later, however, we learn of fundamental flaws in the plant's construction that the utility now covers up at great risk to public health. Regulators seem easily fooled. The nuclear power industry's "defense-in-depth" philosophy of having backup systems for backup systems is shown to be no match for industry deceit. And then, two weeks after the film opened, many Americans began to think of *The China Syndrome* as weirdly prophetic when the most serious nuclear accident in American history occurred at a plant in the middle of Pennsylvania's Susquehanna River.

Around 4:00 a.m. on March 28, for reasons still unknown, pumps stopped at Metropolitan Edison's nuclear power plant on Three Mile Island. As designed, an automatic shutdown began when the reactor "scrammed" and the control rods entered the reactor core to stop the nuclear fission process. Somewhere, though, a valve that was supposed to close remained open. Water that should have been cooling the reactor now fled via the open valve. Fortunately, the Emergency Core Cooling System then kicked in (an element of the nuclear industry's vaunted "defense-in-depth" approach to designing redundant safety systems), and the system sent in coolant to keep the reactor from getting too hot. Plant designers had not taken into account, however, the possibility that even a very experienced operator, a veteran of the navy's nuclear programs, would make a mistake. When the shift foreman, not realizing the nature of the plant's problems, shut down the ECCS pump and another pump, the core started to heat and then melt. By 7:00 a.m., radiation alarms were ringing and operators declared an emergency with a possible "uncontrolled release of radioactivity." If, as Jerry Brown had said, nuclear energy was America's new Vietnam War, Three Mile Island may have been its Tet Offensive.[43]

It would be an understatement to say that all hell broke loose in Pennsylvania that day. Plant operators, Metropolitan Edison and NRC officials, and local and state government scrambled to figure out what, exactly, was going on and whether it posed a threat to the health of residents in surrounding communities. The Met Ed spokesman, an engineer named Jack Herbein, immediately downplayed any threat to public health. But Lt. Gov. William Scranton III and other state officials who were gathered in the state capitol at Harrisburg (just miles upriver from the plant) did not feel confident in Met Ed's assurances. The NRC, for its part, could not get information because it had never set up a plan for emergencies. With no command and communication structure in place, the NRC could not even talk to a plant operator because the regular phone lines were all tied up. It kept getting busy signals. In the meantime, plant operators tried one solution after another—mostly by pressurizing and depressurizing the reactor; at times they seemed to slow the meltdown, but at others seemed to restart it. By 8:00 p.m., they had managed to settle the plant down.[44]

For the most part, local residents had favored the arrival of the Three Mile Island plant. Located in Dauphin County, near Bethlehem Steel and Hershey's chocolate factories, and in the middle of a mostly rural county, TMI had benefited from the locals' mind-your-own-business conservatism. Most welcomed the plant as a source of jobs and local tax revenue. A year before the accident, in February 1978, the NRC had approved the license for the second reactor at Three Mile Island (TMI-2) and the reactor started generating power on December 30, 1978. Despite the ongoing No Nukes campaigns at Seabrook, Diablo, and elsewhere, the $700 million TMI-2 went online uneventfully. On the day the meltdown began, the reactor contained about 100 tons of uranium in 37,000 twelve-foot-long fuel rods. As rumors circulated that even the 36-foot-high containment domes—with walls nine inches thick—might not actually be containing the radiation, the thousands of residents who had supported the plant began to wonder what to do.[45]

Within twenty-four hours, any observer could tell that the industry and government agencies responsible for regulating had poorly thought through emergency planning. In the second day of the crisis, on the twenty-ninth of March, the NRC advised Governor Richard Thornburgh to order an evacuation. Thornburgh, fearing a public panic, hesitated as he tried to get a straight answer out of the supposed experts on the severity of the situation. "If my wife were pregnant and I had small children in the area," NRC chairman Joseph Hendrie told Thornburgh, "I would get them out because we don't know what is going to happen." At 12:30 p.m., the governor advised all pregnant women and pre-school-age children living within five miles of the plant to evacuate. He also closed all twenty-three schools in the area. Chaos ensued as television screens broadcast images suited to one of those other 1970s disaster movies like *Earthquake* or *The Towering Inferno*, complete with long lines of ordinary-looking American refugees who, through no fault of their own, happened to be living through this disaster-prone decade. An exodus of packed cars crawled or otherwise stood still; people with strained expressions clung to their children, many of whom had scarves wrapped across their faces, presumably to stop them from breathing radiation. Later estimates put the total number of people evacuating within a fifteen-mile radius at somewhere in the vicinity of 144,000.[46]

In Washington, President Carter, the former nuclear engineer who had attended to a nuclear accident while in the navy, grew weary of Met Ed's and the NRC's failure to seize control of the situation.[47] Following a day of concern about a possible leak or explosion, President and Mrs. Carter visited the site to see the plant for themselves. The president and First Lady toured the control room and other parts of the plant. The public hysteria almost immediately calmed down, and the crisis gradually subsided. A few years later, when cleanup crews finally went into TMI-2 again, they found that 70 percent of the core had been damaged and that half of it had melted. It took four years to clean it up, ten years to defuel the reactor—all at a cost of $1 billion.[48]

Unlike previous nuclear accidents in England and Detroit and at Browns Ferry, Three Mile Island changed the debate over energy "too cheap to meter." The much higher degree of public awareness about the events at TMI made the difference. Polls showed that 98 percent of Americans had heard about the accident, and the percentage of Americans favoring "further development of nuclear power" fell from 69 percent to 46 percent. Most important, it taught the public that the utilities and the government could not be trusted to regulate nuclear power. "What shook the public the most was seeing the men in white coats standing around and scratching their heads because they didn't know what to do," NRC commissioner Victor Gilinsky later said. "The result was that accidents were taken seriously in a way they never had been before."[49]

In the prevailing narrative of the period, Three Mile Island killed the nuclear energy industry, but that is just not so. In the immediate aftermath, the NRC stopped granting licenses and shut down similar plants around the country. It could do no less. President Carter appointed the obligatory blue-ribbon committee to investigate the accident, which issued a 2,200-page report that blasted Babcock and Wilcox (the reactor's manufacturers), Met Ed, and the NRC, all of which it said shared the blame for the plant operators' failure to avert human error.[50] Even so, President Carter, in accepting the report, went out of his way to reassure the industry: "We do not have the luxury of abandoning nuclear power or imposing a lengthy moratorium on its further use," he said.[51] Carter's stance left the door open for the industry to launch a massive public relations campaign proclaiming the relative safety (compared to smoking, driving, and flying) of nuclear power. Utility executives fanned out to hit the television talk shows, hold press conferences, and make themselves available to the public.[52]

The No Nukes crowd did not take this lying down, of course. After Three Mile Island, the movement against nuclear power became *the* political issue of the moment. Just days after the crisis subsided in Pennsylvania, over the weekend of April 7–8, 1979, at least ten major demonstrations took place around the nation. On May 6, an estimated seventy thousand to one hundred thousand people gathered in Washington, D.C., to demand an end to nuclear power. "The history of the nuclear power industry is replete with coverups, deceptions, outright lies, error, negligence, arrogance, greed, innumerable unresolved safety questions, and a cost-plus accounting system that taxes our citizens as consumers and taxpayers," Ralph Nader told the throng. "There has to be a better, safer way to heat water."[53]

Jackson Browne, Bonnie Raitt, Graham Nash, and John Hall formed Musicians United for Safe Energy (MUSE). Building on sporadic benefit concerts held in California since 1976, MUSE held a series of shows—the No Nukes Concerts—with a star-studded lineup at Madison Square Garden in September 1979. Over the course of a week, close to a hundred thousand people attended the five straight nights of shows, and then another two hundred thousand turned out for a final free show at the Battery Park landfill. As one reporter noted at the time, "Nearly everyone connected with the event knew that the 300,000 people who attended the concerts and rally came to hear the music, to enjoy but not necessarily to enlist." Still, the concerts raised an estimated $750,000 for the cause.[54]

Whether or not the awareness of some had been raised, the political struggle between those favoring and opposing nuclear power continued through the 1980s, with neither side able to claim a clear victory. Both sides in this "modern-day holy war"—as Samuel Hays called it—thought that they were right and "that theirs [was] the moral and just cause, and that therefore they [were] destined to triumph while their opponents [were] destined to fail."[55] The public stood somewhere in the middle, worried about both the energy shortages and the threat to their health and safety posed by radiation. At Diablo Canyon and at Seabrook, the reckoning came.

The reality that nuclear power plants already under construction would be hard to halt became obvious first at Diablo. Immediately after TMI, Governor Jerry Brown wrote to the NRC and asked the agency to keep Diablo Canyon shut down until (a) a comprehensive review of its ability to withstand an earthquake could be done and (b) the state could come up with improved emergency plans for nuclear plants. Shortly thereafter, on June 30, 1979, more than forty thousand people turned out for a No Nukes rally in San Luis Obispo at which the governor described the Abalone Alliance as "a growing force to protect the earth." It seemed, as one scholar has recently written, that "momentum appeared firmly on the side of nuclear protest." Not to be outdone, Pacific Gas & Electric organized Citizens for Adequate Energy, a faux grassroots organization to counter the Abalone's efforts. "We're working very hard to establish local chapters," PG&E spokesman Thomas Saunders said. "Because, believe me, they have about eight thousand times more credibility with their peers than some voice out of San Francisco or Washington." It organized Nuclear Energy Education Day (NEED) on October 18, 1979, just a couple of weeks after the MUSE concerts in New York, and claimed that a hundred thousand people had participated in more than fourteen hundred events on that day, including a thirty-five-mile "energy jog" that featured runners wearing NUKES KEEP AMERICA RUNNING T-shirts.[56]

But after a while, the conflict subsided as both PG&E and the Abalone waited for a licensing decision on Diablo. For the company, the delays cost millions of dollars. For the Alliance, it cost momentum. Not until 1981 did licensing seem imminent, and across that summer, more than five thousand activists took part in nonviolent direct action training. The whole state began to brace for the coming showdown. On September 10, 1981, the NRC granted an operating license for the Diablo Canyon plant. Governor Jerry Brown, a nuclear opponent and Abalone fan, called in 500 National Guard troops and 270 California Highway Patrol cops to the site. Within five days, more than two thousand protesters had arrived. Many camped on land offered by a local rancher in what one newspaper said looked like "a sort of eco-activist Hooverville." The campers set up their own village to prefigure the kind of society they wanted to build: solar generators powered the lighting, sound, and hot water. "By saying 'No' to Diablo," one Quaker activist observed, "everyone was in effect saying 'yes' to building a beloved community, to caring for one another, to caring for the earth and future generations." Over the course of the next two weeks, more than nineteen hundred people were arrested at Diablo, some for blocking the main gates or the main road from Avila Beach, others for hiking overland to the plant or for rafting ashore from boats that had dropped anchor. On Sunday, September 21, more than five thousand local residents marched on the plant's gates. The protests began to peter out after two weeks, however, and the Abalone announced a face-saving "stage two"—a plan to go home and regroup. Quite by chance, as the demonstrations wound down, PG&E announced that inspectors had found an error in the plant's blueprints that had led the contractors to install "certain pipes in Unit One" as "duplicates of corresponding pipes in Unit Two, rather than mirror images of those pipes as they should have been." The NRC suspended the plant's operating license indefinitely, and the Abalone Alliance, rather unpersuasively, claimed credit. In fact, the suspension of the license effectively undermined the Abalone as activists went off to work on other campaigns. Over four months in 1983, in reaction to the NRC's authorization of fuel loading at Diablo, 537 people were arrested, but this paled in comparison to the 1981 encampment. The Abalone Alliance, spread too thin, lost the initiative. In April 1985, Diablo's Unit 1 went online; Unit 2 went online in August. Three Mile Island's Unit 1 went back online that year, too.[57]

To the extent that scholars have written about Diablo Canyon, they have tended to evaluate the Abalone Alliance in one of two ways: either they have tied its failure to stop the plant from operating to the general failure of the entire No Nukes movement to achieve the mass appeal of the civil rights and antiwar movements of the 1960s, or they have given it credit for victories that from local residents' front porches seemed somewhat hollow. Barbara Epstein, for example, tried to put the best spin on it by arguing that "the credibility of the nuclear industry had been seriously damaged, a powerful movement had been built, and participants had moved on to other things with a sense of accomplishment." But it is hard not to read that as rationalizing defeat. What the end of the Abalone Alliance campaign really showed was that nuclear power plants already under construction and on their way to operation could not be stopped. Three Mile Island did not matter. The governor's opinion did not matter. And the Abalone Alliance did not matter, at least not when it came to stopping a mostly built nuclear reactor from running.[58]

But the story doesn't end there. Following the disaster at Three Mile Island, the utilities quietly lost a string of contests through the 1980s that essentially wiped out the industry. This time, the industry's antagonists were not direct action activists but well-informed officials in municipal and state governments. The expertise of this new class of opponents, combined with the industry's own errors and wider economic and performance issues, held back the advance of nuclear energy in the United States for the next twenty years.

At Seabrook, where construction had largely stalled before work could begin on the second reactor, PSNH, like other utilities nationwide, had real reason for dread. Instead of facing down hippies and grandmothers, industry lawyers now squared off against public servants who, after Three Mile Island, were much more alarmed about the proximity of their towns and neighborhoods to proposed nuclear power plants. As the transpartisan Not in My Back Yard (NIMBY) phenomenon swept through communities outraged over various toxic waste disposal plans, it made a late appearance in debates over nuclear power, too. Although industry and the media later came to use NIMBY as a pejorative term, it was at first used in approving tones to describe citizen efforts to stop the construction of physical plants that they saw as vessels bringing harmful contaminants to their communities. By that definition, officials in several southeastern New Hampshire towns and several northeastern

Massachusetts towns waged, ultimately, an eight-year NIMBY campaign to get safe, secure emergency plans for Seabrook. Public officials would never have done such a thing before Three Mile Island, when most felt sympathetic to the industry for investing so much money in the plant. But with images of refugees fleeing Middletown, Pennsylvania, fresh in their minds, the public servants seemed suddenly more interested in serving their public.[59]

This made PSNH and New Hampshire governor John Sununu nuts. Both argued that opponents were now, in their NIMBY strategy, trying to refight the siting battle—the battle to prevent a plant from being built on the New Hampshire seacoast at all—that they had already lost in the 1970s. How could the utility be expected to go back on siting when so much money had already been spent to build the station? When Massachusetts governor Michael Dukakis announced that since, in his state's view, there would be no way to come up with a sufficient evacuation plan for Seabrook, he would not prepare one, PSNH responded by dropping its emergency radius from ten miles to one mile. Local activists pointed out that a one-mile radius would not even protect the security guard at the plant's main gate.[60]

It turned out that PSNH and the utilities still had allies in the NRC and in the Reagan administration, however. In February 1987, the NRC declared that it would not be fair to a utility company if, after all its investment, the "utility has substantially completed construction" only to be stymied by the "non-cooperation" of local public officials. Given the "serious financial consequences" for the "utility, ratepayers, and taxpayers," they could not allow the "forced abandonment of a completed nuclear plant." Thus, the NRC essentially put licensing approval ahead of emergency planning, ruling that it would approve a utility's emergency plan with the expectation that states and towns would then have to come up with even better plans once the plant got its license. Governors Dukakis and Mario Cuomo of New York protested vigorously, with Cuomo citing President Reagan's pledge not to have the federal government override local government on such issues. The administration proved slippery, though. The industry had been hopeful about Reagan's replacing Carter in the White House because he had been an outspoken advocate for nuclear power, even after Three Mile Island; in campaigns, he often pointed out that "since the first nuclear power plant went online twenty years ago, there has not been a single nuclear injury" and blamed the "placard-carrying demonstrators" ("unwitting victims of Soviet designs," as he smeared them) for undercutting the industry. Once in office, he decried the federal government for creating "a regulatory environment that is forcing many utilities to rule out nuclear power as a source of new generating capacity" and called for a streamlining of the licensing process. This was in 1981, two years after Three Mile Island.[61]

In late 1987, Reagan ordered the Federal Emergency Management Administration to prepare emergency plans if towns and states would not, overriding his alleged commitment to states' rights. Too little too late for PSNH, though. The utility went bankrupt in 1988, leaving one containment dome (for Unit 2) to rust on the Seabrook site. Later, Northeast Utilities bought the single-reactor plant (Florida Power and Light now owns it), and Unit 1 received its license in 1990 and went online. The total cost came to $6.4 billion for one reactor, and is still being paid for by New Hampshire ratepayers in their higher-than-national-average electric rates. Not too cheap to meter after all.[62]

By the time Seabrook reached its inglorious end, the nuclear industry in the United States had become the corporate equivalent of a patient on life support. Wall Street had, by the mid-1980s, largely stopped blaming the No Nukes movement for the industry's decline and instead took a dim view of the manufacturers and utilities themselves. Seabrook had been typical in that a significant movement to stop the plant from operating failed; its demands for safer operation only delayed operation. Instead, experts concluded that "nuclear power was killed, not by its enemies, but by its friends." No one among the manufacturers, utilities, or the NRC paid enough attention to the spiraling costs of building these plants. As James Cook wrote in *Forbes*, "A company that ties up 'close to 80% of its capital in a construction project,' especially one that cannot produce income until complete, ought not to blame others for wounds that were self-inflicted."[63]

The No Nukes movement legitimately took some credit for adding to those costs through the interventions that dragged out the NRC licensing process for many years, but other structural forces hurt the industry, too. Amid the energy crisis, utilities rushed to place orders for new plants. Instead of standardizing capacity and design, though, manufacturers tried to outmuscle each other by building bigger, more powerful plants, each one more expensive than the last. Custom-built plants—as almost all were—made the licensing reviews take longer, and that added to the expense, too. Finally, the energy crisis, which many thought would be a boon to the nuclear industry, also contributed to its decline, and early: it drove up the price of uranium; inflation soared, leading the Federal Reserve to raise interest rates and make borrowing more expensive. In 1975, even before the first protests at Seabrook, 122 of the 191 nuclear plants in the works saw construction deferred; nine others were canceled altogether.[64]

In the end, the battles over nuclear power ended in a draw. As one scholar noted, "for the uninvolved public, it was a tale of unrelieved incompetence" on the part of industry, government, and opponents.[65] Meanwhile, seven years after the accident at Three Mile Island, an explosion blew the containment dome off the nuclear power plant at Chernoybl in the Ukraine. An enormous radioactive debris cloud drifted around the entire planet, dozens died, and hundreds fell ill of acute radiation poisoning. The full health effects of the explosion may not be known for another generation, but the potential dangers posed by the technology seemed to confirm the No Nukes movement's critique that nuclear power simply carried with it too many risks.

Accidents such as those at Three Mile Island, Chernobyl, and, more recently, Fukushima, made nuclear power into a front porch issue, if fleetingly. Indeed, for No Nukes activists, the difficult lesson learned was that if a campaign could not make the invisible dangers of nuclear power less abstract, it would be almost impossible to stop the building of a nuclear power plant (particularly if construction had already begun). Here we see one example of the limits of front porch politics. When one front porch issue—the health of one's family potentially under threat—went up against another front porch issue—the economic health of one's family in difficult times—persuasion turned on just how acutely a family felt each. In an age of stagflation and soaring home heating oil costs, more Americans worried about their ability to pay the rent or their mortgages than about a possible nuclear accident. If No Nukes activists could have shown that nuclear power had *already* poisoned the air and soil in a community, the way toxic waste had, the energy wars might have ended differently. Instead, the industry and its allies in the two major parties saw opportunities in Americans' dread of higher bills and continued to promote nuclear power as cheaper than oil and gas over the long haul.[66] In this way, it turned out that these contests over nuclear power had much in common with other front porch struggles that had little to do with energy and the environment but a lot to do with the economies of home and community. In the meantime, battles over the worst kind of pollution—toxic waste dumping—dominated environmental struggles.

6

Toxic Waste in the Basement

•

As the energy wars unfolded in the 1970s, millions of Americans could see from their front porches evidence of pollution in the air, on the ground, and in the water. And they did not have to go far in many places to see the worst kind of pollution: chemical and toxic waste.

In the decade after *Silent Spring*, Americans sensed that pollution of all sorts was creeping closer to their own homes. When the soapsuds from chemical detergents formed mountains of foam three hundred feet high in some places on Lake Erie, one scientist spoke for most when he said, "In this day and age, in a society which is so affluent—to have to paddle in its own sewage is just disgusting." It took a little longer for most to realize that if these substances could cause such damage in other parts of town, they could reach one's home, too.[1]

But some Americans were starting to put two and two together, particularly in poorer and working-class neighborhoods. The 1960s saw, for example, widespread scares over the presence of lead in all kinds of household products, prompting local activism that in turn contributed to the antitoxics campaigns of the 1970s and 1980s. Use of lead had increased dramatically between the 1930s and the 1970s: it was present not only in household paint, but in batteries, pipes, television glass, dishes, utensils, and cookware. The result, according to one scholar, was an "epidemic of low-level lead exposure" by the 1960s. In the mostly black community of East Garfield Park in Chicago, residents formed the Citizens Committee to End Lead Poisoning (CCELP) in 1965, and started going door-to-door to educate neighbors about the threat in their midst. CCELP won immediate media attention, and played it as a winning issue for local politicians, too. Other groups sprang up in dozens of other cities, and when screenings began to show conclusively that the lead poisoning rate was much higher in children than expected, the U.S. Congress began holding hearings to investigate. Similarly, facing pressure from local and national environmental groups, the EPA had to reckon with how leaded gasoline bore most of the responsibility for airborne lead—which was especially dangerous in cities and near expressways. The oil companies fought it, but the EPA established regulations to phase out the lead content in gasoline; by the mid-1980s, the levels of lead in Americans' bloodstreams had dropped by 50 percent. Mitigating the lead paint threat proved more difficult, as it retained the stigma of a problem centered in the inner city—one of the first hints of the widespread environmental racism that became a focus of activism by the 1980s.[2]

Like the farmers in Minnesota who took their protest through every stage of the county commission process before turning to civil disobedience, the communities that found poison in their air, water, and soil evolved over the course of their struggles. Furthermore, they did not have the scruples about participation in the political process that more utopian groups such as the Clamshell and Abalone Alliances did. Working-class communities afflicted with toxic waste, like Love Canal, New York, and Warren County, North Carolina, wanted results: cleanup, evacuation, compensation, or any combination of the three.

Also like the Minnesota farmers, they began with a New Deal–style expectation of relief. They presented evidence of the threat in their midst and expected the government—local or federal—to do something. The seeming promise of government aid did not lie in the distant 1930s, either. Congress, in fact, passed two key pieces of legislation in 1976 that seemed to extend that promise. The Resource Conservation and Recovery Act spelled out requirements for recycling waste; the Toxic Substances Control Act authorized the EPA to do premarket testing and screening of any compound that might prove toxic before it wound up in products sitting under someone's kitchen sink. But the chemical industry fought the provision, claiming that it would lose billions of dollars in profits (Dow Chemical alone expected to lose $2 billion). And so Congress passed a compromise act that allowed prescreening but kept the products and the companies under review secret. Moreover, the EPA pledged that it would make enforcement of the law "as palatable as possible" by testing no more than two hundred of the more than one thousand chemicals marketed each year.[3]

In short order, citizens in communities with toxic waste problems learned that they could not trust Congress, or the mainstream environmental groups either. National environmental organizations, with interests in a range of ecological concerns all over the country, had a habit of negotiating settlements through compromise that local groups found objectionable because, for them, the personal stakes—their children's health—were so high. Indeed, while the nuclear energy question featured powerful forces arguing in favor of nuclear power plants because of jobs and clean energy, few tried to articulate an economic upside to dumping. Anyone with common sense could tell that.[4]

In the early 1970s, Love Canal, the upstate New York neighborhood with the Sixties-sounding name, included about two hundred new homes built mostly in the last ten years for working-class families. Most of the new residents felt lucky to be there, what with the economy and cities in decline. Against the odds, they had moved into their own little Levittown and were holding on to their slice of the American dream—living within a small city, Niagara Falls, but in what they thought was a pastoral setting. Just as post–World War II parents rhapsodized about moving out of the big city to the suburbs where kids could grow up with grass stains on their pants, Love Canal resident Luella Kenny recalled being so thrilled to live on one acre of land "with all these oak trees" and a creek running nearby, all within city limits. Her neighbor Marie Pozniak said she saw Love Canal and thought immediately that it "looked like a good place for kids to grow up," for a family to settle down. "There were lots of young people who had young children with buggies and Big Wheels," Lois Gibbs later said. "It was vibrant and it was alive and people had little yards with manicured little flower boxes. And it was exactly what I wanted."[5]

The Love Canal dream began to wither starting in 1977, when, on the heels of drenching rains and the Blizzard of '77 thaw, basements and yards began to swell with toxic groundwater. Plants and trees died. Caustic vapors stung the noses of children and pets. It seemed unsafe to walk on the grass. Slowly, residents began to realize they were living in a lethal chemical cocktail not of their own making. And many of them, up one block after another, were falling sick. None of the Love Canal residents knew the history of the area, but as it turned out, others did: representa-

tives of Hooker Chemical, a major employer in Niagara Falls, as well as
city officials.

As concerned residents soon learned, Love Canal got its name from
a nineteenth-century capitalist dreamer named William Love, who had
hoped to build a canal that would carry a steady torrent of water, de-
scending three hundred feet over several miles, to power factories along
its banks—the result would be not unlike the older mill towns of New
England. When the depression of the 1890s dried up Love's investments,
he abandoned the partly dug canal. In 1920, the city began to use the
would-be canal as a municipal dump site, and in 1942, Hooker Chemical
company began dumping its waste there. Hooker bought the site five
years later and over the course of ten years disposed of twenty-five thousand tons of chemical waste in a hundred thousand drums at the site.[6]

Hooker knew that the canal should not be used as a playground, but
that did not stop it from deeding the property to the city school board for
a dollar in 1953. The board had been looking for a space for a new
school. The Hooker site, in a part of town where future population growth
seemed likely, made sense. Fully aware of what it was doing, the company took quiet measures to cover its liability. "The premises above described have been filled, in whole or in part, to the present grade level
thereof with waste products resulting from the manufacturing of chemicals by the grantor at its plant in the City of Niagara Falls, New York," the
deed to the school read, "and the grantee assumes all risk and liability
incident to the use thereof." Elsewhere, language in the deed mandated
that the soil on top of the dump not be disturbed. If ever it was disturbed,
the deed stated, Hooker would not be responsible.

The board built the 99th Street School at one end of the canal and
opened it in 1955. Soon developers thought it would be a good idea to
build homes near the new school, and over the next ten to fifteen years,
they did. At no time did Hooker or the city government raise the possible dangers of building near the company's old chemical dump. That
question—whether Hooker and the city did more or less than necessary
to protect the public's health—suddenly came up with every popping
drum in 1977.[7]

The reporter Michael Brown had heard about the problems at Love
Canal and wrote a series of investigative reports for the *Niagara Gazette*
that exposed the city government as unresponsive to residents' complaints. Brown also learned, independently, that a 1976 study had found

polychlorinated biphenyls (PCBs)—a chemical compound that, like dioxin, does not break down; instead, it accumulates in the soil, enters the food chain, and winds up in our fatty tissues, as it did at Love Canal. Reluctant to alienate Hooker (which remained employer to more than three thousand), city officials did nothing. But Congressman John LaFalce, alarmed by Brown's reports, brought the EPA to Love Canal to test the neighborhood's air quality. In its report issued in May 1978, the EPA announced that it had found benzene in the air in some Love Canal basements. Since benzene can pass from the soil or water into the air, and is highly carcinogenic, the study confirmed the worst fears. Brown now called Love Canal "a full-fledged environmental crisis." The combination of obviously shocking facts and official indifference brought forth a new group of accidental activists, led by women like Lois Gibbs.[8]

Gibbs had been reading Brown's newspaper reports in 1977 and 1978, and she felt there must be a link between her own children's ailments and the conditions reported in the paper. Gibbs and her husband, Harry, came from hardworking families—Lois's father had been a bricklayer, her mother a homemaker—and owning their own home marked a major achievement in their families. "I had the picket fence," she later recalled. "I had the swing set. I had the mortgage. I had two cars . . . I had a school three blocks away. It was literally the American dream in every aspect of what society perceives the American dream to be." When her son Michael seemed to be developing epilepsy in December 1977, only three months after he started at the 99th Street School, Gibbs began to question the dream. Michael was diagnosed with a low white blood cell count. "I kept on talking to my pediatrician," she remembered. "I mean, I was the Suzy Domestic housewife who did everything. My whites were the whitest whites and the cleanest cleans, the foods were right and the kids got the sunshine and took their naps and I didn't overload them with junk. It just didn't make sense to me." Later, Michael required surgery for urinary problems, and doctors also diagnosed his younger sister, Melissa, with a different blood disorder.[9]

Lois Gibbs's activism began when she got nowhere with the people in charge. In May 1978, right around when the benzene test results came out, the school superintendent told Gibbs that she could not move her son to another school, even though she had brought letters from doctors recommending it. If he allowed one kid to move, he feared there would be a stampede. Gibbs started down her block, door-to-door, with a petition. Although she had been too shy to give a book report in front of her high school English class, she mustered the courage to approach neighbors and strangers. Few gave her the cold shoulder because it turned out that they had their own tales of woe—stories of sick children, miscarriages, birth defects—that formed an immediate bond between neighbors trying to make sense of something terribly wrong. It was a classic case of how front porch activists are made. The people in Love Canal never aspired to participate in grassroots politics, but as they pieced together the evidence that something sinister was poisoning their landscape and that the city would do nothing about it, defending their families meant leaving their homes and engaging. For leaders like Lois Gibbs, it meant learning a whole new set of skills: running meetings, planning rallies, meeting with government officials, attracting media, and raising money by selling T-shirts and holding bake sales. It amounted to a personal working-class revolution, the kind later mythologized by Hollywood in films like *Erin Brockovich* (2000).[10]

Unlike the situations in the Minnesota power line battles or in the No Nukes campaigns, the evidence of danger at Love Canal could at times be seen and touched. When residents met with New York Health Department officials for the first time in June 1978, the state asked for air, water, and soil samples from residents' homes; it also wanted blood samples. In the question-and-answer session that followed, people started to ask about some of the obvious, if inexplicable, dangers they felt around them. When the health officials hedged, urging residents to be cautious and not to eat food from their gardens, one man erupted. "Look, my kid can't play in the yard because her feet get burned," he yelled. "We can't eat out of our garden. What's going on here?"[11]

In August 1978, the Department of Health reported that the samples taken in June showed the presence of ten carcinogenic substances in the air inside Love Canal homes, ranging in levels from "250 to 5,000 times as high as those considered safe." It also reported a high proportion of miscarriages and birth defects. "The people who had lived in the area the longest had the most problems," the department concluded. As a result, the state health commissioner, Robert Whalen, declared that the "Love Canal Chemical Waste Landfill constitutes a public nuisance and an extremely serious threat and danger to the health, safety, and welfare of those using it, living near it, or exposed to the conditions emanating from it." Given the "pervasive, pernicious, and obnoxious chemical vapors and fumes" penetrating residents' homes, he recommended that pregnant women and children under the age of two move away from the canal. Whalen obviously thought he was doing the right thing, acting in the public interest. But to the people of Love Canal, his recommendation was damning. "If the dump will hurt pregnant women and children under two," Gibbs shouted at him, "what, for God's sake, is it going to do to the rest of us?"[12]

Five days later, Governor Hugh Carey finally visited Love Canal—he was running for reelection at the time—and offered another incremental and, to the residents, unsatisfactory resolution. Carey promised to buy the homes of the people living in the "inner ring" (239 families who lived closest to the canal on 97th and 99th Streets) and shut down the 99th Street School. A state task force would knock down the school, tear up the canal, and rebuild it with a tile drainage system that would stop the leaching and thereby make it safe. But this "solution" left out hundreds of "outer ring" families who also had evidence of miscarriages, birth defects, and various ailments. If Carey had thought he would win the hearts and votes of Love Canal that day, he was mistaken.

By that August, the outlines of the coming struggle were in place: Love Canal residents were living in a poisoned landscape not of their own making; the parties responsible seemed long gone; and any expected government assistance seemed feeble or not forthcoming. Over the summer of 1978, residents had been divided over how best to organize. Early on, strategic differences could be seen along largely gendered lines. Many of the men in the community emphasized the economic problems that the toxic waste created, particularly the plummeting value of their homes and the resulting decline in the city's tax base, while many of the women focused on the health of their families. When, after the health department announced its detection of carcinogens, residents formed the Love Canal Homeowners Association, they used the word "homeowner" deliberately. But the LCHA, made up of five hundred families, wound up being led mostly by women. Shortly after the organization formed, a vote removed Tom Heisner, one of the men stressing housing values over health issues, and the LCHA soon followed Lois Gibbs's strategy of emphasizing the health issues. This approach won media and public attention and gave the community an issue around which everyone could unify. It held the group together.[13]

It turned out that the women's leadership in the Love Canal struggle shaped its outcome in many ways, but class and race played critical roles in the saga, too. Working-class and minority residents regarded the big environmental organizations with skepticism, thinking that they were more interested in saving the planet than in cleaning up the toxic waste in an upstate New York neighborhood. Global environmental preservation seemed like a luxury to the people at Love Canal. "Our movement represented the farmers, workers, and mothers," Gibbs said. That movement had its own preservation goals, but those involved preserving its members' health, quality of life, and slice of the American dream.[14]

The most overlooked aspect of the Love Canal story is the role of the mostly African American residents who rented apartments in the public housing project, Griffin Manor, that stood adjacent to the former dump site. When activists like Tom Heisner initially stressed relief for homeowners—and tried limiting membership in the LCHA to homeowners—the Griffin Manor residents took it as a deliberate slight, and a racist one at that. With help from the NAACP, renters formed the Concerned Love Canal Renters Association in September 1978 and demanded the same kinds of health studies already conducted on nearby houses. Gibbs later speculated that state officials actually tried to cultivate this racial divide, but she and others soon realized their mistake in excluding the Griffin Manor residents. They rewrote the LCHA by-laws to include "all residents of the Love Canal area" and called not only for relocation of homeowners but for "relocation for all apartment residents in comparable housing." Public officials continued to prioritize the homeowners' concerns over those of the renters, but by the spring of 1979, both groups, led by women, had found a way to work together.[15]

At Love Canal and in many other communities in what would become a national antitoxics campaign, another kind of women's movement formed. These were not the anarchofeminists of the Abalone Alliance. The Love Canal women not only were not feminists, they explicitly said they did not like feminists. Elizabeth Blum notes that "even as they easily accepted the notions of women's citizenship and public roles, and believed that women had a right to speak publicly and to demand action from the government," they saw 1970s-style feminism as "antifamily" and the women's movement as "exclusive and unrepresentative." Feminists, in their understanding, looked down on women like them for being homemakers. Therefore, instead of framing their participation in this movement and their goals as "feminist," most "consciously chose to use language and actions that reinforced the value of women as mothers and housewives." As such, the Love Canal women co-opted some of the core ideals of feminism while otherwise rejecting these ideals. This helped win over husbands who grew up understanding the gender-coded division of labor typically expected in a working-class home. Debbie Cerrillo's husband, Norman—no feminist—took over much of her work at home because he figured that her efforts with the LCHA were an extension of her responsibilities as a "good wife and a good mother."[16] Furthermore, the Love Canal women's modus operandi of "construct[ing] truth or knowledge out of their experience" is part of a larger pattern central to our understanding of both feminist theory and the front porch political perspective.[17]

For their part, public officials and others who ran up against the LCHA often dismissed the women as clueless, meddling homemakers. When the LCHA brought in the biologist Beverly Paigen to report the results of her study showing that outer-ring families had been poisoned, too, the state department of health rejected the report in ways that echoed PG&E's dismissal of Mothers for Peace, calling it the biased work of a "bunch of housewives with an interest in the outcome of the study."[18]

These kinds of encounters with government officials at first left the LCHA women disappointed—they had expected more from government—and later just made them mad. These women had been confident their government would rescue their families. But disillusioned residents reacted with anger when Governor Carey, who had pledged to relocate all residents suffering from contamination in their homes or illnesses in their families, tried wriggling out of his promise by saying people would have to prove that chemicals in the canal had caused their illnesses. The LCHA built its campaign on that outrage—a sense of frustration that so many Americans who had put their faith in their government, only to be let down, could understand. "There is something about discovering that democracy isn't democracy as we know it," Gibbs remarked years later. "When you lose faith in your government, it's like finding out your mother was fooling around on your father. I was very upset."[19]

Despite being dismissed as unknowledgeable "housewives" peddling "anecdotal" data, the women who led the LCHA in fact countered every announcement or action by the government and Hooker Chemical as though they were grand master chess players. The LCHA set itself up in an office at the now-closed 99th Street School and quickly showed that it had a gift for winning press attention and staying in the headlines. For one thing, Gibbs and others began to rebut the experts employed by Hooker and the state. When Governor Carey demanded that residents prove the connection between the chemicals and their illnesses, Gibbs, with no college credits, stepped forward with a map of the neighborhood and showed that the illnesses clustered along a geographic pattern that followed the swales (the streams that ran through the development). By February 1979, when the state expanded its evacuation order to the outer ring, it quietly acknowledged the validity of the swales theory.[20]

In addition to challenging the "experts," Gibbs and the others waged a sustained campaign in the streets. Critics thought it unseemly to involve children in the protests, to have them hold signs, picket, and take part in marches. But as Gibbs later recalled, the whole campaign focused on "protecting them, and if that's what we needed to do . . . to put a sign in their hand to get them to safety, then that was a small price to pay." Their neighbors followed their lead.[21]

The first pickets began as early as December 1978, when the LCHA tried to block construction workers from entering the work site at the canal—activists worried that digging up the canal could exacerbate the community's health problems, and they also used the protests to bolster their calls for relocation—and they continued through the summer of 1979. During that time, the stakes seemed to be increasing with each passing day. As the state's remediation went on with workers digging up the canal, more and more people in the neighborhood—beyond the evacuated blocks—complained of new symptoms. "It was hot, and the air would just hang there," Gibbs later wrote. "The fumes were thick. They made your eyes water, or you coughed. Someone described it as similar to trying to breathe underwater." When the state announced that it had found dioxin in nearby streams, the LCHA picketed and blocked the entrances again. Police arrested Gibbs for the first time. Even labor union men—from the UAW, the Oil, Chemical and Atomic Workers, and the United Steelworkers—who had long fretted about openly supporting the LCHA for fear of losing jobs (either as reprisal from the company or from industry leaving town), now contributed money and manpower to the cause.[22]

The conflict between Love Canal citizens and the state boiled over in the late summer and into the fall of 1979. A year after state health commissioner Robert Whalen first recommended that pregnant women and young children leave Love Canal, Lois Gibbs put his successor, Dr. David Axelrod, on the spot. Under withering questioning at yet another public hearing, Axelrod acknowledged that the state's data showed that Love Canal women faced a 45 percent chance of miscarrying if they became pregnant. Gibbs's neighbor Marie Pozniak picked up the questioning, asking whether the state, given such data, would relocate all of the families remaining in Love Canal, including hers. Axelrod put his head in his hands during the grilling, but finally said, "No, we're not going to relocate you, Mrs. Pozniak, in light of the dioxin findings." Pozniak, in a fury, stepped forward and told Axelrod he did not deserve the title "Doctor," and then tore his title from his cardboard nameplate and threw it at him.[23]

That same month, the LCHA won a court settlement in which the state agreed to pay for the remaining Love Canal families to stay in motels until crews completed work on the canal's new drainage ditches. But when the state announced in early November that the work was finished and residents could return, it got an unexpected response. Some among those staying at the motels refused to return to Love Canal. They began referring to themselves as "Motel People," a gibe at the United States government that had been so eager to help the Vietnamese boat people, and they pledged to stay where they were until the government came to help them, too. Finally, the New York Assembly approved, nearly unanimously, the purchase of the remaining Love Canal homes and agreed to relocate everyone (except, at first, the Griffin Manor residents, though the state later agreed to move them, too).[24] It took more than a year, but the state seemed to have come at last to the rescue. The LCHA had won.

Except that the saga was not in fact over. On May 19, *The New York Times* reported that Governor Carey and President Carter disagreed over who would foot the bill, and then came reports that the White House might actually block the relocation. All hell broke loose in Love Canal that day. An angry mob gathered outside the LCHA offices. Marie Pozniak, who had torn up David Axelrod's nameplate, used gasoline to spell out the letters EPA on a nearby lawn and set them ablaze. And then it got weirder.

In a case of terribly bad timing, EPA spokesman Frank Napal went to the LCHA offices to discuss a recently released chromosome study (which showed an abnormally high rate of chromosomal abnormalities in Love Canal) on the same day that people in the neighborhood heard the White House might prevent them from moving out of the cesspool. Napal could not answer some of Gibbs's questions about the study and the White House, so he called an EPA doctor to join him. Gibbs then essentially took the two men hostage in the LCHA offices. She said she held them to protect them from the angry mob outside, but then she called the White House and threatened to keep holding the men unless President Carter declared Love Canal a federal disaster area. When FBI agents showed up and spoke of federal kidnapping charges, Gibbs let the men go. Agents then recorded her shouting to the crowd that "the White House better look the hell out" if Carter did not act. "If there isn't a disaster declaration, then today's action will look like a Sesame Street picnic."[25] The next day, Carter widened the area of his emergency declaration and ordered the temporary relocation of seven hundred families from the outer ring. Even still, more delays followed, and the LCHA went to New York for the Democratic National Convention to protest against Carter for "abandoning" them. No fool, Carter, with the election looming, went to Love Canal in September to sign a deal in which the federal government agreed to lend the state of New York $7.5 million and granted another $7.5 million so the state could buy the homes. It was too little, too late for Carter's electoral chances, but it finally got the Love Canal homes bought.

Ultimately, the importance of the citizen movement at Love Canal lies in the example it set for others. It was not the first environmental movement led by working people—Minnesota farmers and Appalachian anti-strip-mine activists came first—but it was the most successful and high-profile to date.[26] And it woke up the rest of the nation to the possibility that if it could happen to those families, it could happen to any ordinary family. After Love Canal, working-class and minority citizens came to make up what one scholar called "America's newest, most radical, and most committed environmentalists." Except that the activists did not think of themselves as radical. They thought of themselves as utterly ordinary Americans who, relying on common sense, saw the danger to their families and acted in a way they expected anyone would in the same circumstances. Similar stories played out all over the country. As Lois Gibbs later wrote, people in communities like Love Canal "know when something is wrong. They observe an increase in disease, dead vegetation, chemical smells, and odd tastes in their drinking water." They did not need experts or extensive studies. When a reporter asked Gibbs why she and the others had to act outside the system, why they had to act like radicals, she replied that "only a person who has never sat with a sick child, tried to work with unresponsive government agencies, and faced huge corporate public relations campaigns could ask such a question." In the end, it came down to a basic calculus, one with which Love Canal residents figured everyone could agree: industry is not entitled to make people sick, and if it does, government is not entitled to ignore it. Finally, the LCHA succeeded in large part because women led the charge. No matter how many times officials tried to characterize them as overreacting housewives, the Love Canal women, acting as protectors of home and hearth, won over the media, the wider public, and ultimately even the skeptical, stingy government officials. If, as one scholar has written, "women are more likely than men to take on such issues precisely because the home has been defined and prescribed as women's domain," they are also more likely to succeed because their stories resonate with a public that easily relates to the maternal instincts at work in the case of Love Canal.[27]

As the Love Canal saga wound down from spring to fall 1980, the likelihood of more Love Canals—more communities sitting on top of toxic waste dumps—combined with additional grassroots pressure drove Congress toward action. It considered legislation that would set up a large fund of money that the EPA could use to clean up the worst toxic waste sites in the nation. "There are ticking time bombs all over," said one EPA official as early as 1978. "We just don't know how many potential Love Canals there are." In fact, before the year was over, another toxic Hooker Chemical site in Montague, Michigan, came to light. Then an explosion at the Chemical Control Corporation plant in Elizabeth, New Jersey, got legislators' attention. Critics claimed that the resulting chemical fire and evacuation of a huge part of the city could have been avoided if only the company had not previously refused to remove the forty thousand drums of industrial waste on the site. Some members of Congress now moved more deliberately to establish a fund to clean up such sites when the responsible parties refused (they could always be sued later). Late in his presidency, President Carter lobbied for the so-called Superfund legislation, telling Congress that the nation could in fact have both jobs and a clean environment. In December 1980, just two months after Carter signed the Love Canal relocation agreement,

Congress passed the Comprehensive Environmental Response, Compensation, and Liability Act, also known as the Superfund law.[28]

In practice, Superfund did not work so well at first. For one thing, the scale of toxic dumping was overwhelming. Like battlefield doctors overrun with wounded, the EPA's Superfund office, facing an estimated four hundred thousand toxic dumps nationwide, went into triage mode from the start. It established a National Priorities List that named the worst sites and those parties responsible (so that they could be sued later to help pay back the cost of cleanup to the fund). But the system quickly bogged down in bureaucratic red tape, not least because the law said that those parties identified as responsible for a toxic site could challenge the designation.[29] As a result, government's approach once again seemed ineffective. Where Americans had seen a federal government in bed with the nuclear power industry, and then absent as communities suffered from toxic pollution, with Superfund, in the early years, it seemed incompetent. This only fueled further the distrust and disenchantment with government that characterized recent years in American life and made possible the election of a new president whose great gift was the ability to echo back such frustrations to the public. "Government is not the solution to our problems," he said. "Government *is* the problem!"

Ronald Reagan saw environmentalism as elitist and antibusiness, and therefore not something most Americans supported. "I do not think they will be happy," Reagan said of environmentalists, "until the White House looks like a bird's nest."[30] For Reagan, the past twenty years of environmental regulations represented government gone big and gone wrong. The message, in short, was that environmentalism had gone too far. The hog-tying of business with too many regulations had to stop.

When Reagan took office, he began dismantling federal environmental protection efforts in two ways. First, through an executive order, he required all federal agencies to provide cost-benefit analyses on all regulations, which were then reviewed by David Stockman, director of the Office of Management and Budget. Stockman wielded his budget-cutting scalpel on all federal agencies, but when it came to the "no-growth, zero-discharge ideology" at the EPA, he used a cleaver.[31] Second, Reagan adopted a fox-guarding-the-henhouse strategy in making appointments to any agencies with responsibility for environmental protection. Most notoriously, Reagan appointed James Watt as his secretary of the interior, the executive department responsible for protection of public lands. Watt had been director of the Mountain States Legal Foundation, a leading organization in the so-called Sagebrush Rebellion that fought federal regulation of public lands in western states.[32] In addition, Reagan put a lawyer from Louisiana-Pacific Corporation—the nation's largest timber buyer—in charge of the U.S. Forest Service, a rancher in charge of the Bureau of Land Management, and a former Colorado state legislator, Anne Gorsuch, known as one of the "House Crazies" for her relentless attacks on federal regulations, in charge of the EPA. By the middle of 1983, the EPA and Superfund were in shambles.[33]

Despite Reagan's claims to the contrary, most Americans disagreed with the new president's approach to the environment, particularly where toxic waste was concerned. Voters may have elected Reagan to two terms, mostly on the promise of returning the country to prosperity (and, by extension, greatness), but pulling a voting lever for a particular candidate did not mean you agreed with all of his policies. A 1982 poll showed that 95 percent of the public regarded "disposal of hazardous wastes" as "a serious problem." Pollsters who conducted an ABC–*Washington Post* survey the next year reported that "even though the large majority of Americans believe compliance with antipollution laws costs business firms at least a fair amount of money, more than three out of four say these laws are worth the cost."[34] Given such statistics, and in light of the unfulfilled promise of Superfund, activists in community after community mobilized to call for a revitalization of Superfund and for the cleanup of the dumped poisons in their soil.

As at Love Canal, women led the way. In fact, in 1981, Lois Gibbs moved from Love Canal to Virginia and established the Citizens Clearinghouse for Hazardous Wastes (CCHW, later the Center for Health, Environment, and Justice); thanks to her national profile, many communities turned to her for advice. "The thing we learned, and we learned it by the seat of our pants, was that these issues are not scientific issues," Gibbs would tell others like her. "They're not legal issues. They're political issues." Early on, the CCHW operated a lot like Phyllis Schlafly's organization, in a pyramid structure in which valuable information on the toxic waste crisis and strategies for combating it got dispersed widely to a receptive and broad base. By the 1990s, Gibbs's organization had worked with more than eight thousand local grassroots groups, or a total of twenty-seven thousand activists. Over the 1980s, the fight against toxic waste became a mass movement. And it *was* a fight—a fight for participatory democracy, in which residents' views would carry as much weight with local government as corporate polluters.[35]

By 1984, Superfund's utter ineffectiveness prompted groups like Citizen Action and the Clean Water Action Project to organize a National Campaign Against Toxic Hazards. Polls showed that 79 percent of Americans thought "not enough" had been done to clean up the toxic waste sites across the country. Groups like CCHW, Mass Fair Share, and the Public Interest Research Groups all over the country made toxic waste a priority issue. More than a hundred grassroots groups in fifty-four cities took part in the National Campaign, pressing to make Superfund more effective by increasing funding to $10.1 billion over the next five years. They also called for a more regular cleanup schedule for the EPA, as well as right-to-know provisions where the disposal of toxic waste was concerned.[36]

On September 26, 1985, the Senate (which could not manage to pass a $6 billion Superfund bill in 1984) passed a bill authorizing funding at $7.5 billion and sent it to the House. The final law—the Superfund Amendment and Reauthorization Act of 1986—not only raised the funding to $8.5 billion but also included a right-to-know provision, mandatory cleanup schedules, and a mechanism through which local citizen groups could get up to $50,000 per Superfund site to hire technical experts. The U.S. Congress, remarkably, seemed to "get it." Given the power and influence of the chemical industry, and the president's ultimately hollow veto threat, the new Superfund law constituted a major victory.[37]

The antitoxics campaign succeeded, ultimately, because no congressman or senator wanted to go back to his district and explain why he had voted against helping families with sick children. It did not matter which party one belonged to, Democratic or Republican, cleaning up toxic waste was party-neutral environmentalism. And unlike the No Nukes or Minnesota power line campaigns, the antitoxics campaign, in confronting a problem that was so widespread, that touched seemingly every part of the country, drove a truly national discussion. As a result, local organizing fed national organizing, and that led to a national solution. It was no mean feat.[38]

The trouble with the various antitoxics campaigns' successes is that they led the industries that produce hazardous waste to seek new ways to dispose of waste, and new places. By the middle of the 1980s, it became pretty clear that most of America's hazardous waste was getting dumped in communities made up of the poor, working-class, and minority populations.[39] Not until the 1980s, however, did the term "environmental racism" arise to indicate deliberate policies taken on the part of industry to dump waste in the backyards of people assumed to have the least political power.[40]

Warren County, North Carolina, for example, should always be mentioned in the same breath with Love Canal. Just seven days after the first network news reports on Love Canal broke, North Carolina farmers complained of a foul, unfamiliar smell on the roadside. It turned out that a waste hauling company, not wanting to comply with new regulations put in place under the Toxic Substances Control Act (TSCA), decided to run its trucks across the state, intentionally spilling waste from the Ward Transformer Company along 240 miles of highway. Waste from the manufacture of transformers is particularly dangerous because it contains PCBs. The problem for North Carolina was what to do with this mess.[41]

The EPA and the state announced a plan to remove the contaminated soil and dump it in a new landfill to be built in Afton, in Warren County, a part of the state that was 60 percent black, 3 percent Native American, and predominantly poor. In doing so, they followed what the historian Robert Gottlieb called the "dominant siting strategy of the period." They chose a "job-starved" site, "away from major urban centers" that would be full of people who could be expected to put up a fight. To policymakers in Raleigh and Washington, Warren County, lacking "any recognized forms of opposition," seemed like an easy solution. But they were in for a surprise. For the next three years, citizens of Warren County and the local county government fought the dumping plan in and out of court. At first, they did not resist this new landfill because they were outraged by the sociopolitical calculation that brought them the PCB dump (charges of racism came later); rather, they resisted in part out of concern for their own health and in part because they expected it would affect the local economy adversely. Besides, they argued, the PCB waste could be sent to an already EPA-approved site in Emelle, Alabama. The EPA and the state found such logic unpersuasive. For one thing, it would cost $12 million to ship the waste to Alabama, versus only $1.7 million to dump it in Warren County. For another, the good people of Emelle, Alabama, did not want the PCBs either.[42]

As at Love Canal, the ensuing battle turned on fear and expertise. The state's experts said that the health risks were negligible, but understanding the residents' anxiety, it pledged to build the "Cadillac of landfills," a state-of-the-art dump that, like the nuclear power industry's vaunted "defense-in-depth" systems, promised "an overabundance of safety features." But the people who made up Warren County Citizens Concerned About PCBs (aka Concerned Citizens) were not buying it. They brought in their own scientists who challenged every component of the landfill's design, from its dual-liner system to its leachate collection system to its monitoring system. Such testimony at public hearings further galvanized the public. Even so, construction on the site finally began in the summer of 1982.[43]

On September 15, 1982, when the first trucks bearing PCB-laden soil began to roll into Afton, residents responded with a change in strategy. Instead of emphasizing the economic and health effects of dumping PCBs in Warren County, Concerned Citizens now charged the EPA and state with environmental racism and decided to protest using nonviolent direct action.[44] Just as in battles over schools and housing in Charlotte, Mount Laurel, and elsewhere, Warren County's toxic waste battle led to the bigger, more uncomfortable question of continuing spatial segregation in post-civil-rights-movement America. Warren County residents responded by resurrecting the civil rights movement for seven weeks that fall, starting on that first morning when the trucks arrived to find two hundred people who had marched from the Coley Springs Baptist Church to the site. The police came and arrested sixty-seven demonstrators for blocking the entrance to the site. Over the next month and a half, hundreds of demonstrators laid down in front of the dump trucks, forcing police to arrest a total of 523, while seven thousand truckloads bearing forty thousand tons of contaminated soil eventually made their way to the dump.

For many in Warren County, the campaign to block the trucks sprang more from a civil rights sensibility than an environmental one. "African Americans are not concerned with endangered species because we are the endangered species," one activist later quipped. And in 1982, anyone could see that the same federal government that had orchestrated a multimillion-dollar relocation package for the majority white neighbor-hood of Love Canal now shoveled toxic waste into the backyard of majority black Warren County.[45]

As a result, the presence and commitment of several key figures from the civil rights movement took on added meaning. On the second day of protests, the North Carolina lawyer Floyd McKissick, the former national director of CORE who had spoken at the 1963 March on Wash-ington, joined the protest and was arrested. The United Church of Christ's Benjamin Chavis, an important figure in the North Carolina civil rights movement, was arrested the day after McKissick. Then Joseph Lowery, of the Southern Christian Leadership Council, got arrested, leading Andrew Young, the mayor of Atlanta and one of Martin Luther King Jr.'s closest contemporaries, to call for the dumping at Afton to stop. Lowery, in particular, kept the group motivated over the coming weeks and succeeded in bringing Walter Fauntroy, the congressional delegate from the District of Columbia, to Afton, where he, too, was arrested. All of these arrests of such high-profile figures guaranteed continued press attention, as did the sixty-mile march from Afton to Raleigh that orga-nizers modeled on the 1965 Selma-to-Montgomery march. By the end of October, however, the trucks had stopped coming, and the landfill was soon capped. Not until 2003 did the state of North Carolina implement a remediation plan to destroy the PCBs under that cap.[46]

In the end, it was Warren County's misfortune to be the site of the first major battle over toxic waste dumping in the era after Love Canal. In addition to the difference in the racial composition of the two com-munities, Warren County differed from Love Canal in another respect: like No Nukes activists, its residents were protesting against the dangers of *future* and *possible* (though *likely*) hazards, not already present and already harmful hazards, the effects of which could be seen, reported, and shown to a sympathetic wider world. Instead of such sympathy, Warren County residents heard charges of being selfish and narrow-minded. Crit-ics accused them of being part of the new, parochial trend nicknamed NIMBY, for Not in My Back Yard.

The NIMBY phenomenon and name did not start out with such negative connotations. At the start of the 1980s, thanks to the shocking news from Love Canal and Three Mile Island, polls showed that more than half of all Americans were unwilling to accept waste disposal plants within fifty miles of their homes, and the percentages were higher when discussing nuclear reactors. No one apologized for putting their communities first. By then, many Americans realized that the early legislation on pollution focused on keeping air, land, and water clean but did not provide disposal rules specific to the type of waste. A frontier system of figuring it out on the fly prevailed into the 1980s, when publicity about high-profile cases unleashed this war in which Warren County turned out to be the first big battle.[47]

In Warren County and elsewhere, industry lobbyists and state officials made a concerted effort to target NIMBYists, sending scientists to reassure communities that "certain risks were acceptable." Usually, they argued that the odds of a dump or incinerator causing health problems were negligible, given the state-of-the-art technology available. But as the environmental policy scholar Eileen McGurty shows, "the risks are real not because of the probability but because of their incalculability." To critics, this is not rational, it is antiprogress, and it holds the United States back in the global marketplace. Business executives also predicted "unprecedented economic paralysis" and wondered if the power of NIMBY would leave "any backyards anywhere for the power plants, pipelines, factories, waste disposal sites, incinerators . . . and scores of other projects that the economy and society as a whole need to keep going."

Others, however, saw NIMBY as the "'white blood cells' of the democratic body politic—small, quickly mobilized, and effective at killing off foreign intrusions." For NIMBY activists, their newfound purpose in opposing something that threatened their families, their children, represented the kind of widespread participatory democracy that student activists in the 1960s had only dreamed of. Even if one was willing to describe NIMBY activism as "parochial" and "self-centered," it was, as McGurty argues, "essential to the subsequent development of the environmental justice frame." Besides, no one among the accidental NIMBY activists suggested that a toxic dump or incinerator should be located in someone else's community. Indeed, Lois Gibbs defended NIMBY as legitimate because it really meant "We don't want this in anybody's backyard." From Love Canal to Warren County to thousands of American communities across the 1980s and beyond, the common perception that government and corporate officials were unworthy of trust when your family's health was at stake fueled environmental justice campaigns everywhere.[48]

This is why a 1992 EPA report described the Warren County demonstrations as "a watershed event in the environmental equality movement." Although the activists failed to block the landfill altogether, their
resistance came to be regarded as a turning point for the environmental
movement. By transforming environmental activism into an extension of
the civil rights movement, Warren County activists raised public awareness of the interconnectedness of race and environment. Almost immediately, the data on environmental racism started to accumulate like heavy
metals in the food chain. In 1984, Congressman John Conyers wrote in the
preface to the 1984 Urban Environment Conference report that "minorities are the targets of a disproportionate threat from toxins, both in the
workplace, where they are assigned the dirtiest and most hazardous jobs,
and in their homes, which tend to be situated in the most polluted communities." Three years later, the United Church of Christ's Commission
for Racial Justice issued a report, *Toxic Wastes and Race in the United
States*. The commission was led by the civil rights leader Benjamin Chavis, who had been born in nearby Granville County. In studying more
than eighteen thousand landfill sites across the nation, the commission
found that three out of every five black and Latino Americans lived in
neighborhoods with uncontrolled toxic wastes. "African Americans were
heavily overrepresented in the population of metropolitan areas with the
largest number of uncontrolled toxic waste sites: These areas include
Memphis, TN (173 sites); Cleveland, OH (106 sites); St. Louis, MO (160
sites); Chicago, IL (103 sites); Houston, TX (152 sites); and Atlanta, GA
(94 sites)." Moreover, the commission concluded, "we have found that
this reality is no accident, no mere random occurrence."[49]

One year later, in 1988, the *Los Angeles Times* reported on one of environmental racism's smoking guns, a four-year-old document written
by a consulting firm for the California Solid Waste Division. The Cerrell
Associates report, entitled *Political Difficulties Facing Waste-to-Energy
Conversion Plant Siting*, offered the ideal profile of neighborhoods least
likely to resist a new incinerator: "All socioeconomic groupings tend to
resent the nearby siting of major facilities, but middle and upper socioeconomic strata possess better resources to effectuate their opposition.
Middle and higher socioeconomic strata neighborhoods should not fall
within the one-mile and five-mile radius of the proposed site." The ideal
site for a plant should be chosen, therefore, not based on environmental
suitability but based on the expected presence and power of a NIMBY

group. Poor people in rural areas—communities with fewer than twenty-five thousand people—with little formal education and lacking "social power" made the best targets. "Communities of color," Robert Bullard later noted, "are far more likely to fit this profile than are their white counterparts."[50]

At the most extreme end of this calculus, one could find American Indians in the Southwest who, for decades, had faced disproportionate risks of radiation poisoning thanks to the uranium mining industry. In 1980, by one estimate, "roughly half the recoverable uranium in the United States [lay] under Navajo land in the Grants uranium belt in northwestern New Mexico." Uranium mining on Navajo and Laguna Pueblo reservations began with the start of the atomic age, and by the 1970s both miners and residents were suffering abnormal rates of cancer and respiratory problems. The more than 90 million tons of tailings that accumulated were particularly lethal as they leached into water supplies. As the mining companies made a killing, they left their Native American miners dying on a dying land. Catastrophe struck on July 16, 1979—just a few months after Three Mile Island—when an earthen dam at the Church Rock mine burst, releasing 94 million gallons of tailings—the waste by-product common to many forms of mining—and radioactive water into the nearby Rio Puerco. One Navajo woman wading in the water at the time developed burns on her legs and later died. The other ten thousand Navajo residents in the area lost all use of the river from which they drew their drinking water. Ten years after the accident, the U.S. Geological Survey found radiation levels a hundred times the maximum allowed; the Church Rock mine remains a Superfund site to this day. In the aftermath, residents formed the Navajo Uranium Radiation Victims Committee and the Navajo Nations Dependents of Uranium Workers Committee to sue United Nuclear Corporation, owner of the mine. In time, they won a $525 million out-of-court settlement. Still, despite the scale of the event and its nature—radioactive poisoning—so soon after Three Mile Island, it got scant attention from Congress or even mainstream environmental organizations.[51]

Most episodes in the growing environmental justice movement featured similar struggles to get more than local attention and were led by Americans who did not fit the usual environmentalist stereotypes. In fact, most of the activists thought of themselves not as environmentalists but as victims (or potential victims) of unscrupulous hazardous waste policies. In Alsen, Louisiana, for example, Mary McCastle, a black woman in her seventies, started the Coalition for Community Action to agitate for cleaner air in the community. Alsen sits north of Baton Rouge, near the northern end of what some environmentalists call "Cancer Alley," an eighty-five-mile stretch of river lined with oil refineries, hazardous waste treatment facilities, and other petrochemical plants. In 1986, the Rollins Environmental Services hazardous waste landfill near Alsen was the nation's fourth largest, holding, according to one expert, "11.3 percent of permitted hazardous waste landfill capacity." For years, residents like Mary McCastle had complained of the fumes emitted by the Rollins site. Locals suffered "skin rashes, eye problems, and breathing problems." As one resident reported, "You couldn't dare get out of your car without covering your face." Workers on the site signed a petition in January 1980 saying that they feared what the fumes might be doing to their health. In time, thanks to such protests, the state investigated and ordered a cleanup at Rollins. The company complied, but it survived and, along the way, tripled the size of its plant.[52]

An hour west of Alsen, in Willow Springs, farmers mobilized when it became apparent that something was horribly wrong with the water. Free-range cattle dropped dead, trees died, dead chickens fell out of trees, and kitchen pots turned green from the obviously poisoned water. It turned out that from 1968 to 1981, Browning Ferris Industries had been disposing of what one observer called a toxic brine from its gas wells (and sometimes other petrochemicals) by dumping it into some man-made pits. By the early 1980s, the resulting lagoons had swelled up, filled with a marmalade of poison. Thanks to the unusual geology of Louisiana, this kind of slop is easily drawn through the soil by the sea level changes in the Gulf of Mexico and what one journalist called the "continuous subsidence of land to the south, part of a natural geologic process." It did not help that the clay in much of Louisiana is not like clay elsewhere; it is porous. As a result, according to one geologist, "there is no acceptable site for a landfill in southern Louisiana." Herbert Rigmaiden, an African American farmer from Willow Springs, testified before Congress, and the residents soon succeeded in getting the poisonous landfills shut down. In 1984, a year after the shutdown, a new health study showed that residents had higher-than-normal rates of boils, rashes, and other skin problems (84.9 percent); blood disorders (25.2 percent); headaches (59.2 percent); and respiratory problems (47 percent).

   As Jim Schwab notes, the Willow Springs activists did not ordinarily sympathize with the environmental movement. They referred to environmentalists as "wildberries" and thought of them generally as untrustworthy radicals. Little did they know (or care), but their own activism helped change the face of environmentalism in the 1980s.[53]

While Louisianans looked to Love Canal as an example of how to deal with an existing public health crisis, two California communities followed the example of Warren County in resisting plans to build toxic waste incinerators within breathing distance. The city of Los Angeles expanded so rapidly through the 1960s that it overtook old landfills formerly located in outlying areas. And as the population grew, the city began to overwhelm its landfill capacity. As a solution, in 1985, the city's Bureau of Sanitation announced an incinerator project—the Orwellian-named Los Angeles City Energy Recovery (LANCER) Project—that would burn 250 trucks' worth of solid waste a day. To no one's surprise, the Bureau of Sanitation did not propose putting the incinerator in Hollywood or Beverly Hills or Westwood. Rather, it proposed building the incinerator in the predominantly black neighborhood of South Central. When the Concerned Citizens of South Central formed, they did their homework. They found that the proposed dioxin emissions for the incinerator were 170 times higher than the allowable limit in Sweden, a country with high health standards. When Mayor Tom Bradley (who ten years earlier had stung the Sierra Club with a jab about neglecting African Americans and other urban dwellers but who supported LANCER) ran for governor in 1986, CCSC members bird-dogged him at every campaign event they could, constantly asking him about the incinerator. When Bradley went to South Central to campaign on what should have been friendly territory, CCSC protesters in gas masks prompted him to flee into a McDonald's men's room. The organization built alliances with people in other parts of the city, too, and in 1987, they targeted the city council elections. Soon after CCSC succeeded in defeating council president Pat Russell, Bradley declared the LANCER plan dead.[54]

   In 1988, residents in the small agricultural town of Kettleman City (population 1,100), about fifty-seven miles northeast of San Luis Obispo, learned that they had been living next to the biggest toxic waste dump in the West. Chemical Waste Management, Inc., set up the dump in the

1970s so that it would be hidden from view behind a set of low hills and not attract community attention. Residents did not know it was there until the EPA began fining Chem Waste millions of dollars for health and safety violations. Once the dump was exposed, Chem Waste proposed building a toxic waste incinerator in Kettleman City; it would burn up to 108,000 tons (or five thousand truckloads) of toxic waste each year. Then, as now, almost all of Kettleman's residents were Latino; 40 percent spoke Spanish only. But they could read the writing on the wall. When they found out that toxic dumps also operated in Buttonwillow and Westmoreland, two other predominantly poor, working-class Latino towns in California, they saw a pattern they had not previously noticed. Kettleman residents formed El Pueblo para el Aire y Agua Limpio (People for Clean Air and Water). In their research, they found that the federal government had not only fined Chem Waste $3.5 million for more than fifteen hundred violations at the Kettleman dump, but that the company had been forced to shut down its incinerator on Chicago's South Side—another poor minority neighborhood—because it routinely overfilled it with waste. Following a series of confrontations at public hearings, El Pueblo won a legal judgment that Kettleman residents had been illegally marginalized. Worn down after five years of fighting, Chem Waste gave up in 1993 and withdrew its application to build the incinerator. "I think they thought we would go away," said resident Mary Lou Mares. "But it was too dangerous to let an incinerator come in here—we had to do something about it."[55]

By the late 1980s, a similar defensive pattern emerged in Native American communities. The Navajos in Dilkon, Arizona, responded in a way that especially helped get the environmental justice movement some national attention. In 1988, Waste-Tech Services came to Dilkon with a proposal to build a $40 million recycling plant. As part of the deal, the plant would not only provide two hundred new jobs, but Waste-Tech would pay Dilkon $200,000 a year, plus $600,000 would go directly to the Navajo Nations for various rents and leases. It seemed too good to be true, and before residents even heard about it, the tribal chair approved the deal. As word got out, however, suspicions bubbled up. Some residents joined together to form Citizens Against Ruining our Environment (CARE) to look into the details. It turned out that "recycling facility" in this case actually meant a toxic waste incinerator designed "to burn chemicals and industrial solvents from oil fields, lumber yards, and hospitals." In addition, the company planned to use the incinerator to burn medical waste, "including human body parts and amputated limbs." Not exactly paper and plastic, bottles and cans. "That's what really turned the stomachs of the Elders," CARE founder Abe Plummer later said. "We have a belief that you respect the dead, and if you cut off a part of the body you put it in the earth with respect—with prayers, not just throw it in the trash." Tribal leaders backed out of the deal. As in Kettleman City, it soon emerged that many Native American communities had been having similar encounters with waste disposal companies that were trying to exploit the confusion over how (or whether) federal and state regulations could be applied on Native lands. In June 1990, Native Americans came to Dilkon from all over the United States to form the Indigenous Environmental Network as a bulwark against these repeated corporate assaults. It remains one of the most important environmental justice organizations in the country.[56]

Whereas many communities facing environmental racism battled in the wilderness, alone and frequently desperate, the sheer number of these contests—in the thousands—inevitably led to the building of national networks. In 1990, as the convergence of environmentalism and civil rights became more obvious, the Reverend Jesse Jackson led a "toxic tour" highlighting environmental racism in minority communities. The next year saw the first National People of Color Environmental Summit held in Washington, D.C. "You can't say it's just a black thing, or a brown thing, or a red thing," Jackson told participants. "For they may dump toxic waste on the poor side of town today, but as surely as the wind blows, as surely as it's one planet Earth, what affects any of us in the morning affects the rest of us by sundown." Finally, in 1994, President Bill Clinton acknowledged the history of environmental racism by signing Executive Order 12898: Federal Actions to Address Environmental Justice in Minority Populations and Low-Income Populations. In doing so, the president ordered all federal agencies to identify and address instances of environmental injustice. From the front porch and the backyard to the White House, arguably the greatest environmental victories were won not by the mainstream environmental movements but by the accidental activists living in poisoned and threatened cities and towns across the country. As Robert Bullard—whose 1993 book, *Confronting Environmental Racism*, helped advance the cause—has written: "People of color have a long track record in challenging government and corporations that discriminate." They do not have to worry about being polite the way the national environmental groups do, and compromise is not on their agenda. Justice is the only item on their agenda.[57]

Thus, by the end of the 1980s, the battles over energy and the environment produced mixed results. From a policy perspective, despite the "morning in America" sloganeering coming from the Reagan White House and all the rhetoric against environmentalism, Americans could still see the smog, still remembered Three Mile Island, Chernobyl, and Love Canal, and were learning of environmental racism and something called global warming. Ultimately, the Reagan administration had to back down from its private market approach, particularly concerning dangerous waste in American backyards. On the other hand, Americans drove into the 1990s riding high in gas-guzzling cars and sport utility vehicles, seemingly without much concern for the environmental impact. When the twentieth annual Earth Day took place in 1990, the most notable difference from the original was the "greenwashing" of all the corporate sponsors seeking to at least appear environmentally conscious.

Ultimately, the various campaigns of those two decades showed a fairly consistent pattern: partisan loyalties and ideology mattered a lot less than finding solutions, and where environmental hazards were real and encroaching on one's family's health, chances were good that a grassroots campaign could persuade the wider public and its representatives that families needed to be protected and the responsible parties held accountable. Where environmental hazards were merely *likely* or *possible*, however, grassroots activists struggled to overcome competing claims from industry or government that jobs were at stake or that they were standing in the way of "progress." Relying on accidental activists who could speak from experience—and were driven by the anger and despair arising from that experience—clearly worked where toxic waste was real and tangible. But accidental activists could accomplish only so much where the danger remained abstract.

Today, we can see the persistence of this trend. The tangible dangers of hydraulic fracturing—or "fracking," as the natural gas drilling method is most commonly known—have mobilized communities in various parts of the country, while the threat of climate change—more abstract or difficult to experience personally—is largely left to be debated by scientists, professional environmentalists, and elite national political figures (such as Al Gore). In fact, opposition to fracking is the rare case in which the pulse of front porch politics can still be felt today. But not unlike the case with nuclear power in the 1970s, fracking retains a front porch appeal for some landowners in West Virginia, Ohio, Pennsylvania, and New York who are looking, in stressful economic times, to balance their household budget; especially in those places where deindustrialization took a heavy toll on the local economy, accepting payment for mining rights on one's land may make more sense than protesting the mining process.[58] One person's front porch danger can be another's front porch opportunity.

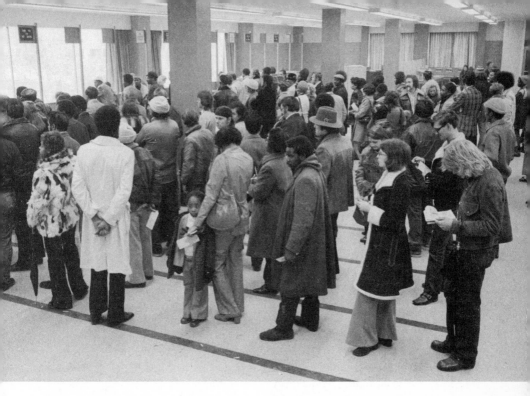

As the economy slumped in the 1970s, images of gas lines and unemployment lines became familiar. Above, the Maryland State Unemployment Office in Baltimore, 1975. Below, a gas station attendant in Maryland directs drivers during the 1979 fuel shortage. (Both images: U.S. News and World Report, Library of Congress)

The citizen movement of the 1970s embodied what the consumer advocate Ralph Nader called an "initiatory democracy." Here, Nader speaks at a No Nukes rally in Boston on June 4, 1979. (Associated Press)

Both opponents and supporters of court-ordered busing engaged in grassroots political campaigns. Here, schoolchildren are bused from the suburbs to schools in Charlotte, North Carolina, on February 21, 1973. (U.S. News and World Report, Library of Congress)

In Boston, anti-busing protesters appropriate the flag. (Boston Herald)

Phyllis Schlafly at a Stop ERA demonstration outside the White House in February 1977. (U.S. News and World Report, Library of Congress)

The entertainer Anita Bryant, leader of Save Our Children, emerges from the voting booth after casting her ballot to repeal Miami–Dade County's gay rights ordinance on June 7, 1977. (Associated Press)

Harvey Milk (at left) on November 7, 1978, awaiting ballot results on a California initiative that would have made it illegal for gays and lesbians to work as teachers in California's public schools. (Associated Press)

A nationwide teach-in, the first Earth Day on April 22, 1970, marked the arrival of the environmental movement. (Associated Press)

On May 1, 1977, New Hampshire State Police arrested 1,414 members of the Clamshell Alliance at the site of the Seabrook nuclear power plant. (Bettmann/CORBIS)

Harold and Hazel Stoner, residents of Harrisburg, Pennsylvania, evacuate with their grandson on March 30, 1979, following news of a radiation leak at the Three Mile Island nuclear power plant. (Associated Press)

Lois Gibbs, the leader of the Love Canal Homeowners Association, standing in front of her home in October 1978. (Washington Post/Getty Images)

In what's widely regarded as the first major action by the environmental justice movement, hundreds of mostly African American residents of Warren County, North Carolina, are arrested in September 1982 for trying to block the dumping of PCB-contaminated soil in a landfill. (Associated Press)

When the steelmaking ceased, citizens of Youngstown, Ohio, asserted a community right to control the shuttered steel mills—including this U.S. Steel plant—that had been the life-blood of the city for decades. (Bettmann/CORBIS)

Cesar Chavez of the United Farm Workers is joined by Baldemar Velasquez (left) of the Farm Labor Organizing Committee during a 560-mile march from the tomato and cucumber fields of Ohio to Camden, New Jersey, on August 8, 1983. (Associated Press)

In December 1977, more than three thousand farmers of the American Agricultural Movement descended on Washington, D.C., in a "tractorcade" to press Congress to pass a farm bill supporting higher prices for agricultural commodities. (U.S. News and World Report, Library of Congress)

Farm families gather at the state capitol in Des Moines in March 1983 for an Iowa Farm Unity Coalition rally. (Bettmann/CORBIS)

Barbara Anderson of Citizens for Limited Taxation used grassroots rhetoric to rally support for Massachusetts's tax-cutting Proposition 2½ in 1980. Like many such ballot initiatives, her effort was bankrolled by a consortium of business interests. (Boston Herald)

In an increasingly tight housing market, tenants in Santa Monica, California, demonstrate in support of Proposition A, a rent control initiative passed in 1979. (Roger N. Thornton, Santa Monicans for Renters' Rights)

In New York City, squatters and urban homesteaders protest the increasing gentrification of the Lower East Side in a May 1989 confrontation with police at Tompkins Square Park. (New York Daily News Archive/Getty Images)

By the mid-1980s, homelessness had become a national crisis. Here, a homeless man lies under a plastic sheet and a blanket in Lafayette Square, across from the White House. (Bettmann/CORBIS)

In Washington, D.C., the homeless and their advocates formed the Community for Creative Non-Violence (CCNV). Here, CCNV serves a Thanksgiving dinner for the homeless on Capitol Hill, November 1988. (Reuters/ CORBIS)

In September 1985, parents of eleven thousand public school students kept their children home on the first day of school to protest New York City's decision to allow a Queens second-grader with AIDS to attend school. (Bettmann/CORBIS)

Outraged by official neglect of the AIDS crisis, activists in the AIDS Coalition to Unleash Power (ACT UP) made a name for themselves with confrontational, nonviolent direct-action demonstrations. (Bettmann/CORBIS)

Anti-abortion activists outside the Atlanta SurgiCenter, where hundreds of Operation Rescue activists were arrested over the course of the summer of 1988. (Bettmann/CORBIS)

In response to abortion clinic blockades, volunteers came from all over the country to stage clinic defenses. Here, activists escort patients into an Atlanta clinic in October 1988. (Bettmann/CORBIS)

PART 3

Resisting the Dismantling of America

● ● ● ● ● ● ● ● ● ● ● ● ● ● ● ● ● ● ● ●

In the middle of the Reagan era, it was hard to find anywhere in America that was a good place to be a blue-collar worker. As Ed Bailey, an employee of a failing cotton gin and farm supply business in Vidette, Georgia, told a reporter, "Seems to me like some folks somewhere are trying to dismantle America—the steel mills, the farms, the textile industry." A farmer friend sitting nearby agreed: "That's become a central theme around here . . . 'the dismantling of America.'" Wynder Smith, a farm supply businessman from nearby Wadley, pointed the finger at Washington and government-set prices: "They are forcing us out of business." The year was 1986.[1]

Two years earlier, Ronald Reagan had won election to a second term in a rout of Jimmy Carter's former vice president, Walter Mondale. These Vidette farmers had helped, voting for the incumbent. But going into the 1986 midterm elections, the Georgia farmers were having a hard time finding a reason to vote Republican.

Presidential politics existed at a far remove from this persistent feeling that "some folks somewhere" were busy dismantling America. For almost the whole of the 1970s and 1980s, most Americans had come to see the dismantling as a steady, merciless process. It did not matter who was president. It mattered only that nearer to home—in fact, *in* one's home, and on one's farm, and down at the factory—the life one dreamed of was being taken away, and not gently. In many ways, the unifying experience of 1970s and 1980s America was this anxiety, the prospect of losing one's job or home—or both. All over the country, factories and mines shut down, banks foreclosed on farms, and high taxes and rents drove residents from houses and apartments.

Like the residents of Love Canal, the factory workers, farmers, farm-workers, homeowners, and tenants featured here felt acutely mistreated because they believed they had followed the unwritten rules for claiming a just portion of the American dream, but as they sat on their front porches and surveyed the changing world around them, they felt duped, swindled, and, as many put it, "screwed." The new poor of the Rust Belt and Farm Belt, the journalist Haynes Johnson later wrote, "had been winners, or so they thought. They had made the 'right' economic moves, had progressed and become confident that tomorrow would always be better than today." But now "their life's hopes were dashed; their once highly paid blue-collar jobs were gone, their farms sold."[2]

Americans did not take this without putting up a fight. They started hundreds of small organizations and launched dozens of campaigns, defending the dream they sensed was being taken from them and fighting powerful forces that included industry and government and often other groups of similarly desperate citizens. They organized to defend and hold on to their jobs and homes in ways that were strikingly similar across the country. It was not a unified social movement per se, but to look back at it now is to see a mass mobilization in defense of jobs, farms, and homes that sprang from the same sense of being denied a piece of the American dream.

7

Fighting for Factory Jobs and Factory Towns

●

For many years now, scholars writing the recent history of American workers have emphasized the declining influence and significance of labor unions in post-1960s America. Most recently, historians have described the 1970s as the time when America "traded factories for finance" and saw "the last days of the working class."[1] There is no question that unions took a beating in these years. Management, aided and encouraged by the federal government under Jimmy Carter and Ronald Reagan, went on the offensive like a resurgent boxer chasing his staggering opponent across the ring, aiming to land the knockout blow (in this case, the one-two punch of hiring replacement workers and closing plants).

Indeed, by the end of the century, the labor movement was all but on life support. Union ranks had dwindled to only 13.5 percent of the national workforce after having once hovered close to 40 percent. Real wages and salaries stagnated for almost all American workers even though most worked two hundred hours per year more than their Canadian counterparts and nearly four hundred more than Germans. The movement's obituary was already written; experts merely waited for it to take its last breath.[2]

It is easy, therefore, to overlook the vigorous campaigns mounted in defense of industrial communities in the 1970s and 1980s. Despite the multivalent assault from business and government, labor activism in fact continued in these decades. As Nelson Lichtenstein reminds us, we do not remember the most significant struggles of the 1970s and 1980s in large part because the more recent struggles "were both physically isolated and ideologically devalued."[3] In most cases, American workers in these years fought not so much for particular concessions as for the survival of their communities, and often as a rearguard struggle, when it seemed to outsiders that the battle had already been lost. Unfortunately, our singular focus on the decline of the labor movement has caused us to lose sight of the way industrial communities mobilized not merely for better wages, hours, and working conditions, but for their towns' very existence.

Once America's mighty midcentury economic engine stalled in the 1970s, and the liberal consensus on which the labor movement had relied came undone, business regrouped and became a formidable force in American politics. The business lobby used its new influence in part to focus attention on the supposed overregulation of industry by the federal government, which it blamed for hurting productivity, creating needless paperwork, stifling innovation and growth, and driving up prices.[4] As a result, President Carter appointed a Regulatory Analysis Review Group to find ways of cutting down on regulatory costs. *The New York Times* noted that "in contrast to 'those heady days of the late 1960s and early '70s [when] anything and everything could be regulated in the public interest,' suddenly, in 1979, 'all the world seems to be against government overregulation.'"[5]

Although deregulation is most often associated with Reaganomics, it started with Carter's deregulation of the trucking, railroad, and airline industries, opening them to more competition (the lower consumer prices promised by deregulation, it is worth remembering, were welcomed by liberals and consumer advocates like Ralph Nader). Reagan, of course, made good on campaign pledges by following up with similar initiatives in the public utility, telecommunications, and banking sectors. The 1980s saw a cycle of reorganization and mergers in the affected industries that led to mass layoffs on a scale not seen since the 1930s. Labor reeled. Matters were made worse by the failure of Carter and the Democrats to get a modest labor law reform bill passed in 1978. The bill would have made it easier for union leaders to organize elections and get them certified by the National Labor Relations Board (NLRB). Nineteen days of filibustering by Senator Orrin Hatch (R-UT) sent the bill back to committee, defeated. "For the first time in twenty years," *The New York Times* commented, "the business community has vanquished organized labor in a fight over a 'gut' issue for labor." As the historian Kim Phillips-Fein notes, the victory marked the arrival of the business lobby.[6]

But maybe more important than the destabilization caused by deregulation and the failure of labor law reform was the growing willingness of government officials—from local to federal—to revert back to a nineteenth-century model of intervening in opposition to the unions. In 1977, Atlanta mayor Maynard Jackson—a civil rights leader close to Jimmy Carter—responded to a sanitation strike by saying, "The employees deserve a pay increase, but we don't have it." When the union—a local chapter of the American Federation of State, County, and Municipal Employees (AFSCME)—went out on strike, Jackson gave workers forty-eight hours to return, and when they did not, to the shock of the union, he fired them. If labor could not hold on in the public sector, dark days lay ahead in the private sector.[7]

Two years later, as Chrysler stumbled toward bankruptcy, the Carter administration decided that the Big Three automaker was too big to fail and put the screws to the United Auto Workers (UAW). In order to save the company and all those union jobs, Carter backed Chrysler CEO Lee Iacocca's efforts to cut wages and cut the labor force. "It's freeze time, boys," Iacocca notoriously threatened. "I've got plenty of jobs at seventeen dollars an hour; I don't have any at twenty." The UAW leadership felt it had no choice but to convince members that it had to share in the sacrifice of saving the company by not only taking the wage cuts but also giving up on its long campaign to get a four-day workweek. Members agreed and gave Chrysler $450 million in concessions. As Nelson Lichtenstein notes, "For the first time in forty years, autoworkers no longer earned the same wages in each of the Big Three auto firms. As the company slashed its payroll and closed many of its older, urban factories, Chrysler employment dropped by 50 percent." Unlike the Atlanta sanitation workers, Chrysler's UAW members could not even contemplate a strike, so weak was their position.[8]

Democrats like Carter and Jackson, therefore, set the labor relations table for Reagan. When the nation's thirteen thousand air traffic controllers went out on strike in August 1981, they had reason to hope. The Professional Air Traffic Controllers Organization (PATCO) had in fact broken ranks with most of the labor movement to back Reagan in the 1980 election, and although the controllers had a no-strike clause in their contract, they believed the president and the public would be more sympathetic to their long-standing complaints of on-the-job stress (arising from staff shortages, long shifts, and outdated technology) than the Federal Aviation Administration had been. And Reagan, after all, was the only U.S. president to have been a union leader. They were mistaken. Reagan cast the controllers' breaking their contract as a "moral issue," and 67 percent of the public agreed. Following Maynard Jackson's example, Reagan gave the controllers forty-eight hours to end the strike, "and if they do not return to work," he said, "they have forfeited their jobs and will be terminated." Reagan spurned offers to mediate the dispute from three former Republican labor secretaries and ignored leaders in Congress and the airline industry who feared a mass firing. Most of the PATCO membership stood firm, too, and after the forty-eight hours were up, Reagan sacked more than eleven thousand of them. He replaced them with retirees and military controllers, and ten days later he assured the public that 80 percent of flights were back to normal; in fact, it took years before the air traffic control system fully recovered.[9]

Most histories of the labor movement in this period point to Reagan's busting of PATCO as a turning point in American labor relations. Employers had long had the right—granted by the U.S. Supreme Court in *NLRB v. Mackay Radio and Telegraph* (1938)—to hire replacement workers, but management worried that such an overt attack on a union would seem too confrontational. After the president of the United States did it, however—and the public seemed to approve—employers brooked no hesitation in moving against unions with replacement workers. Between 1985 and 1989, management brought in replacement workers in one out of every five strikes. Workers could, of course, go out on strike, but if pickets could not keep the replacements out, the strike weapon was practically useless. As a Maine paper factory worker said, "I think it's a shame that this country is allowing the backbone of the country, the working man, the blue-collar man, to be run over, torn down by big business because of a law [the Mackay doctrine] that won't allow them to stand up to big business."[10]

For much of Ronald Reagan's first term, the combination of tax cuts, deregulation, and dramatic cuts in social spending—colloquially called "Reaganomics" by both critics and supporters—did not deliver the promised economic recovery from the recession of 1981–82. The recession often took one industry's productivity levels down so far that it caused a cascade effect ultimately felt by workers in other industries. By 1983, prolonged slumps in housing construction and the automobile industry—the two main users of copper—had caused more than half of Arizona's twenty-six thousand copper miners to be laid off. The miners' unions, led by the United Steelworkers of America (USWA), agreed to unprecedented concessions, including a no-strike pledge for 1983 and a three-year wage freeze; for their part, mining companies promised cost-of-living adjustments (COLAs). But the Phelps Dodge Company, which operated mines in Morenci, Ajo, Clifton, and Douglas, did not sign the agreement. On July 1, 1983, more than twenty-three hundred workers from thirteen unions went out on strike.

To cope with the strike, Phelps Dodge first used supervisors and clerical workers to keep production going, if at a wheezing pace, and within a month declared that it would hire replacement workers. Governor Bruce Babbitt sent four hundred state troopers and three hundred Arizona National Guard troops to escort more than four hundred replacement workers into the Morenci mine (earning the striker nickname "Governor Scabbitt").[11] Eleven months into the strike, the unions were ready to wave the white flag if the company would return them to work and fire the replacement workers. But now Phelps Dodge was committed to breaking the unions and said no. One month later, as strikers rallied peacefully in Clifton to mark the anniversary of the strike's start, Governor Babbitt again sent in the National Guard and state troopers in full riot gear. In a scene from Paris 1968 or Kent State 1970, someone threw a bottle and the armed force lunged forward, firing tear gas and wooden bullets into the crowd. In the end, sixty police were hurt and twenty civilians arrested. Barricades of tires and barrels smoldered into the night.[12] Months later, workers voted to decertify the unions. Phelps Dodge, playing nineteenth-century hardball, had won.

In Austin, Minnesota, the United Food and Commercial Workers (UFCW) Local P-9 took a similar thumping in their battle with processed foods manufacturer George A. Hormel & Company. In the prolonged economic downturn of the 1970s, the meatpacking industry consolidated with plant closings and mergers. UFCW organizers enacted a national policy of "controlled retreat." But when the company tried to negotiate a 23 percent pay cut on the heels of the long wage freeze—while the company seemed to be thriving in spite of the economic climate—fifteen hundred workers, led by Local P-9, went out on strike. Hormel responded first by moving its production to other plants; then, in January 1986, the company announced that it would hire replacement workers. Just as in Arizona, the governor, Rudy Perpich, sent in the National Guard to escort the replacements through the picket lines. Five hundred of the striking workers could see the writing on the wall and returned to those jobs. The remaining thousand workers never worked at Hormel again. Local P-9 was finished.[13]

Finally, in what *The New York Times* called "one of the most bitter strikes of the 1980s," the eighteen-month conflict between the United Paperworkers' International Union and International Paper showed how weak labor had become—leading one historian to call the strike "labor's empty gun."[14] In 1984, IP managers announced that they would put an end to premium pay on Sundays, a staple of the employees' pay package since 1967.[15]

In Mobile, Alabama, when the UPIU would not agree to a new contract that eliminated Sunday premium pay, organizers sensed the IP wanted workers to strike and thus give the company reason to replace them. When the union failed to take the bait, the company responded on March 21, 1987, by locking twelve hundred workers out of the Mobile plant. In a show of solidarity that they hoped would induce management to back down on the Sunday premium pay issue, workers at the Jay, Maine; Lock Haven, Pennsylvania; and DePere, Wisconsin, IP plants went out on strike. When the union twice offered to extend the existing contract, with no changes, IP refused.[16] Instead, IP marshaled its considerable resources to ride out the strike. Given the scale of the company's operations, with forty primary plants around the world and plenty of cash to hire lawyers and public relations experts, IP was well positioned to do so. At Jay, the company moved to replace the workers immediately and claimed to have replaced half of them within a few weeks. In DePere, the whole workforce had been replaced within two months, and by December the company essentially claimed that the strike was over. A spokesman said it was "time for the strikers to get on with their lives and get new jobs."[17]

Using replacement workers to bust unions became a tried-and-true method favored across industry. Just in the early 1990s, Greyhound, Boise Cascade, Eastern Airlines, Continental Airlines, and others used replacement workers to beat down unions in those shops (the latter two had never fully recovered from the early 1980s recession; Eastern finally went under, while Continental reorganized once more under bankruptcy protection). In Decatur, Illinois, aggressive antiunion tactics—including hiring replacements—deployed by Bridgestone/Firestone, Caterpillar, and A.F. Staley broke the back of labor in that community.[18] In the mid-1990s, more than two hundred companies established the Alliance to Keep Americans Working, a lobbying group formed for the sole purpose of defeating legislation that would have banned hiring replacement workers during a strike.

When companies replaced union workers, the whole community—whether Morenci, Ajo, Austin, DePere, Mobile, Jay, or Decatur—died a little. The plants may have continued to operate, but the effort no longer felt like a shared enterprise, with well-paid workers proudly not only making a quality product but building social institutions and relations that announced to the world that they had made it—that they were no longer working-class, but middle-class. In such places, many of the workers who remembered those days were forced out, and for those who remained, it was as if they had returned to an age defined by divided communities, when companies cultivated a worker-against-worker dynamic. In Jay, Maine, Town Manager Charles Noonan remarked some years later that the strike against International Paper had "torn the community apart." Out-of-work strikers either moved away or struggled to survive in a town where most of the people with jobs had been strikebreakers. "Friendships that existed for lifetimes are gone," the town manager reported. "People who went to high school together and grew up together will not speak to each other." As another former paper worker said, "We have no future, really." She was speaking about herself and her husband, but she may as well have been speaking on behalf of the whole community and dozens of others like it.[19]

On the other hand, not all labor disputes in the 1980s ended in defeat for unions. In April 1989, the United Mine Workers of America (UMWA) called a strike against the Pittston Coal Group and its mining operations in Virginia and West Virginia. On April 5, 1,950 miners went out on strike over pension and health issues (as well as Sunday and overtime pay). The union was much better prepared for the strike than the UPIU had been against International Paper. It started with a $100 million strike fund and paid workers $220 a week over the course of the strike. More important, it was prepared to play every card it had, legal and sometimes illegal, to keep the company backpedaling. Workers—almost always dressed in the camouflage fatigues of a hunter or soldier—picketed all Pittston facilities, from mine entrances to processing plants; they marched and held demonstrations; they held sit-ins in Pittston facilities (including thirty-seven women who occupied the company's headquarters in Lebanon, Virginia, for thirty-six hours) and "sit-downs" in the middle of country roads to stop coal trucks from reaching or leaving the plants; they organized their own sluggishly slow convoys to block traffic and further prevent coal trucks from moving; and they built support from more than a thousand unions, churches, and other organizations across the country. Over 270 days, police arrested more than three thousand people—miners and supporters—but the combination of these tactics and the ability of the union to absorb the arrests and fines meant that the company struggled to get enough replacement workers to keep its operations going. In December 1989, the two sides reached an agreement, and in February, UMWA voters ratified the new contract. They went back to work before the end of the month.[20]

The victory at Pittston was echoed in Geismar, Louisiana, and Ravenswood, West Virginia, and seemed to point to new directions for the labor movement. As management went on the offensive and federal and state government aided companies in labor disputes, unions found that they could most successfully push back by expanding their campaigns beyond strikes to appeal to either the local community or the international community, or both. Chemical workers at the BASF plant in Geismar won because they broadened their range of agitation to join with environmental justice activists protesting the company's toxic poisoning of the community. Ravenswood's aluminum workers, meanwhile, took their campaign global, pressuring banks and governments to stop doing business with a company that treated its workers so poorly.[21] Given the multinational structure of so many of these corporations, the global corporate campaign—particularly if organized by a resourceful international union—showed a pragmatic willingness to use any and all tools available. Such campaigns bring a labor struggle far beyond the picket line to hit a corporation in other places in its power structure where it might be vulnerable—with its shareholders, its business partners (such as banks), or its partners in other communities and other countries.

As most of these struggles showed, the central issues of any labor dispute—compensation, benefits, working conditions—are always, either in victory or defeat, front porch issues because they not only affect the worker's life at home but the community's life. Some of the fiercest battles over factory jobs did not, however, involve strikes, but instead saw whole communities—not just the workers—mobilize to stop companies from shutting down their plants and abandoning the cities and towns they had helped to build. Given the long-standing relationship between companies and communities in America's industrial heartland—in places like Youngstown, Ohio; Pittsburgh, Pennsylvania; and Weirton, West Virginia—people living in those cities and towns came to expect that the jobs created by those companies would always be there. For many, this summed up their version of the American dream: steady work, building a product that had no rival, like steel, and building a community where the working class blossomed into a middle class of homeowners who could afford to take vacations and send their kids to college. Lost in all the talk of the basic conservatism of the American working class is the fact that when those firms started to close down their plants and let employees go, these same allegedly conservative workers frequently asserted a community right to private property—a city's right to see factories keep operating. As a defining characteristic of their American dream, such an idea could only be described as radical.

Although some companies had long engaged in moving operations from one city to another—often from the North to the South in search of cheaper labor—it was only in the 1970s that "downsizing" and "reengineering" became standard practice.[22] So common had plant closings and layoffs become by 1984 that the Bureau of Labor Statistics began to use "worker displacement" as a new statistical category. In the twenty years after it started keeping track, the Bureau has counted "at least 30 million full-time workers who had been permanently separated from their jobs and their paychecks against their wishes [and] it did not include the millions more who had been forced into early retirement or had suffered some other form of disguised layoff."[23]

The wave of plant closings and layoffs may have caught workers by surprise, but the fact was that the right to shut down factories was included in almost all collective bargaining agreements. The unions, in their single-minded focus on wages, hours, and working conditions, and for decades working in an environment in which profitability seemed almost always on the rise, did not give enough thought to the shutdown provision in their contracts.[24] Given that concession to management and the isolation of one plant from another, building a mass movement against shutdowns proved very difficult.

Industry succeeded in setting the terms of national discourse by blaming the faltering American economy on unions, the federal government, and foreign competition. In response, a group of more than a hundred labor, civil rights, feminist, and environmental organizations formed the Progressive Alliance in 1978 and funded a systematic study of plant closings carried out by the political economists Barry Bluestone and Bennett Harrison. Following regional conferences on shutdowns in Columbus, Ohio; Boston, Massachusetts; and Portland, Oregon, Bluestone and Harrison gave plenty of ammunition to those who would organize to stop factories from closing.[25] American workers worked harder than ever, they found, and the American government did not collect anywhere near the proportion of GNP in taxes or spend more on social welfare than its peer nations in Western Europe. Moreover, Japanese companies no longer sold their products for less, as they once had, but instead were grabbing more market share because they made "more attractive and better quality products." Those looking to assign blame, Bluestone and Harrison argued, should look no further than the companies themselves. Corporate managers, in the face of greater international competition and shrinking profits, deliberately scrambled to "restore, or preserve, the rates of profit to which they had become accustomed in the halcyon days of the 1950s and 1960s." And that meant shifting capital "as readily as possible, from one activity, one region and one nation to another." As a result, "the industrial base of the American economy began to come apart at the seams." The dismantling of industrial America—and of hundreds of thousands of American lives—grew out of this quest for old profit margins.[26] "In a nutshell," they concluded, "capital has unilaterally ended even lip service to the great postwar social contract."[27]

By 1982, commentators were calling that swath of industrial America that extended from the East Coast through the Ohio River Valley up into Michigan and the Great Lakes the Rust Belt—shorthand for a whole region in which factories had fallen quiet and where, one got the impression, human beings had seized up like latter-day Tin Men. Unemployment in the steel industry alone hit the Great Depression level of 30 percent that year. These were dark days in the formerly heaving, gleaming cities of Youngstown, Pittsburgh, and Weirton. How those communities responded is one of the great lost stories of recent American history.

Over three successive autumns in 1977, 1978, and 1979, Youngstown, Ohio, suffered wave after wave of plant closing announcements. In September 1977, the Lykes Corporation announced the closing of Youngstown Sheet and Tube's Campbell Works, and two months later, Lykes merged with LTV, the owner of Jones & Laughlin Steel. A year later, Lykes/LTV/J&L announced that the Brier Hill Works would be closing, and eleven months later, U.S. Steel announced the closure of its Youngstown Works. As one commentator wrote, "in less than three years, all steelmaking in what had once been the second steelmaking city of the nation, next to Pittsburgh, came to an end." The three waves of closures cost about ten thousand people their jobs, and over the ten years between 1977 and 1987, a domino effect caused the number of manufacturing jobs in the Youngstown-Warren metropolitan area to fall from 63,000 to 38,200. By January 1987, 51,000 persons in Mahoning County (one out of six) earned below the poverty wages of $5,360 a year for a single person or $11,000 for a family of four.[28]

Almost immediately after the first plant closings were announced, members of the community began to speak of community property rights extending to privately owned factories. An Ecumenical Coalition formed in October 1977 with the goal of keeping the Campbell Works open through an employee-community ownership scheme. "As religious leaders we are committed to studying the moral dimensions of this problem," the Coalition declared in its first statement on the shutdowns. "What is the responsibility of an industry to the citizens of the community in which it is located? What is the moral responsibility of management to labor, and labor to management, and of both to the community?" A month later, a Steel Crisis Conference issued a pastoral letter: "Some maintain that this decision is a private, purely economic judgment which is the exclusive prerogative of the Lykes Corporation. We disagree. This decision is a matter of public concern since it profoundly affects the lives of so many people as well as the future of Youngstown and the Mahoning Valley."[29]

As the historian and labor lawyer Staughton Lynd, who would come to play an important role in the struggle, later described it, many in the community spoke of a community property right that develops over time—like common law—based on a manufacturing operation's history with a particular community. Under the circumstances, many now agreed "that private decisions with catastrophic social consequences are really public decisions, that some kind of community property right arises from the long-standing relation between a company and a community, and that the power of eminent domain (the power of government to take private property for a public purpose without the owner's consent) should be used to acquire industrial facilities when corporations no longer wish to operate them."[30] Displaced workers could then put themselves back to work running the operation as their own company. Were these the so-called Reagan Democrats who turned on their own party in 1980 to vote Republican? Maybe—because they certainly felt abandoned by Jimmy Carter and the Democrats for doing nothing to save their factories and hence their communities. But it is hard to imagine Reagan agreeing with their definition of property rights (and although Ohio voted for Reagan in 1980 and 1984, the Mahoning Valley voted Democratic).

The confrontations with U.S. Steel started almost immediately after the company announced the shutdown of the Youngstown Works. On November 30, 1979, workers from the Youngstown plant held an informational picket outside the company's Pittsburgh headquarters, a building distinguished by its brown, oxidized Cor-Ten steel structure. Picket signs bore dozens of slogans, including U.S. STEEL KILLS COMMUNITIES, THE MAHONING VALLEY NEEDS A MARSHALL PLAN, YOUNGSTOWN GHOST-TOWN USA, and in reference to the ongoing hostage crisis in Iran, U.S. STEEL ADDS 13,000 HOSTAGES. At some point, the pickets spontaneously burst through the doors and flowed up the escalators to the second floor; guards cut the power to the elevators to the executive floors, trapping the executives in the building. When organizers first tried to persuade everyone to go back to the street, the crowd burst into the Vietnam War–era chant, "Hell no, we won't go! Hell no, we won't go!" In time, the event ended peacefully. A few weeks later, the union met with management and offered to give up $6 million in incentive pay if it would keep the plant open, but the executives said no. When workers offered to buy the mill, they got no reply. Led by Staughton Lynd, seventy-five workers and a coalition of supporters filed suit against the company, seeking to restrain it from closing the mill and to "make it available for acquisition by its workers."[31] U.S. Steel responded by moving up the closure date to March 11, six days before the trial was to begin.

A combination of emotion—equal parts anger, sadness, and despair—and research on other experiments in employee ownership drove the campaign to buy up the closed plants. At community meetings, laid-off workers passionately described what it had meant to them and their families to make steel and to live in a steel town. Steelworker Len Balluck told members of the Ecumenical Coalition how the same men who had so recently set new production records at the Campbell Works open hearth broke down in tears as they left the mill on its last day of operation, how they wept as they threw their work clothes into the Mahoning River on their way home to face their families. "The only thing I can compare it with is Pearl Harbor," one worker of forty years said. "Most people couldn't believe it," another said of the Youngstown Works closing. "It was so huge and had operated so long and so many people depended on it for their livelihood." There had already been community meetings at which a local attorney and grocery store owner suggested the community buy the steel mill. "Why don't we all put up five thousand bucks and buy the damn place [the Campbell Works]?" the lawyer asked. As steelworker John Barbero wrote soon after in the *Brier Hill Unionist*, "not only should the steel industry be saved but the steel towns must be saved too."[32]

The idea that the workers and other residents could combine forces and buy a shuttered plant began to catch fire throughout the Mahoning Valley. As they learned, employee ownership of reopened companies had become increasingly common in late 1970s America. Lynd listed mines in Vermont and Pennsylvania, plywood mills in the Pacific Northwest, a rubber plant in Indiana, and factories in Maine and upstate New York as precedents known to the people of Youngstown as they made their bid for steel mill ownership. And the South Bend Lathe Company, which four hundred workers had recently reopened under an employee stock ownership plan, in particular, inspired hope in Youngstown. Still, not one of these companies was anywhere near as large as any of the Youngstown steel operations. There simply was no precedent for reopening industrial operations on this scale, or at the cost of buying even one of the plants in the Mahoning Valley. But the biggest obstacle remained U.S. Steel and the other companies, none of which seemed inclined to sell to their out-of-work employees.[33]

Other protests followed. On January 28, 1980, a thousand steelworkers and supporters met at the Steelworkers' Local 1330 union hall, up the hill from U.S. Steel's Youngstown headquarters. "We've been trying to talk to U.S. Steel," shouted Bob Vasquez, the union local president. "They won't listen to us. We've been trying to talk to Jimmy Carter. He won't talk to us. We have to make these people listen! If U.S. Steel doesn't want to make steel in Youngstown, the people of Youngstown will make steel in Youngstown! We're going down that hill!" The crowd stormed down the hill, broke down the front door to the headquarters, and fanned out through and around the building. Some got on the roof with a massive sign reading WORK NOT WELFARE. The workers left once management promised another meeting, but the result remained the same. The U.S. Steel board would not sell the plant to the workers, who could only buy it with government aid, because board members thought it a bad idea to sell to a "government subsidized competitor."[34]

When U.S. Steel would not budge, Lynd and other lawyers filed for an injunction to stop the company from closing the mill on March 11 and consequently brought the city's claim of community property rights to court. "We've done a lot for them [U.S. Steel]," Youngstown mayor Patrick Ungaro said. "A lot of people worked for them and now they're gone. Morally and philosophically I believe they should do something for the community." To the astonishment of U.S. Steel, the judge granted the injunction, seeming to accept the idea of community property rights as at least a valid argument. "Everything that has happened in the Mahoning Valley has been happening for many years because of steel," federal judge Thomas D. Lambros declared. "Schools have been built, roads have been built. Expansion that has taken place is because of steel. And to accommodate that industry, lives and destinies of the inhabitants of that community were based and planned on the basis of that institution: Steel." Did this history not mean anything? the judge asked rhetorically.

> It seems to me that a property right has arisen from this lengthy, long-established relationship between United States Steel, the steel industry as an institution, the community in Youngstown, the people in Mahoning County and the Mahoning Valley in having given and devoted their lives to this industry. Perhaps not a property right to the extent that can be remedied by compelling U.S. Steel to remain in Youngstown . . . But I think the law can recognize the property right to the extent that U.S. Steel cannot leave the Mahoning Valley and the Youngstown area in a state of waste, that it cannot completely abandon its obligation to that

community, because certain vested rights have arisen out of this long relationship and institution."[35]

Even the activists trying to hold Youngstown together could not believe the judge's words. For a moment, it seemed the steelworkers and their families might yet break the cycle of dismantling.

They were wrong. At the conclusion of the March trial, Judge Lambros conceded that the legal "mechanism" to recognize a community property right "is not now in existence in the code of laws of our nation."[36] Youngstown was beaten. Eventually, a group of workers and community organizers managed to support a group of local businessmen who leased the McDonald Works (one portion of the Youngstown Works). That saved fewer than a thousand jobs, though the McDonald Works remains operating today. In the meantime, in early 1982, U.S. Steel blew up its Youngstown blast furnaces, guaranteeing "that local people would never be able to work in a large full-scale steel operation again."[37]

Steelworkers and residents watched this literal dismantling of their livelihood the way one might experience a spouse walking out of a marriage. "Betrayal" was the word most often used. "For a town our size, look what we put out," said Joe Marshall, a former steelworker. "No one could match Youngstown. We helped build America. What they did was rape Youngstown."[38] Unemployment hovered for years near 30 percent; county records showed that child abuse rose by 21 percent and suicides increased 70 percent over just two years. During the worst of it, the city saw two thousand personal bankruptcies in one year and as many as fifteen hundred people a week lining up at one Salvation Army soup kitchen.[39] In the late 1980s, the journalist Dale Maharidge traced the origins of the new hoboes—homeless men and women riding the rails illegally, crisscrossing the country to find work—from Youngstown and other industrial cities.[40] Maharidge's work influenced Bruce Springsteen when he later wrote the bitter Rust Belt lament "Youngstown," which tells the story of highly productive workers making "seven hundred tons of metal a day," only to be cast off by the company because the "world's changed." "Once I made you rich enough," Springsteen sings, "rich enough to forget my name."

As Springsteen suggests, corporate leaders blamed a changed world for the industry's decline. The unions, in turn, saw devastation coming and made every effort to save jobs. But even though the USWA gave up $1 billion in concessions from 1983 to 1985, there was no stopping the slide. By

1985, the number of United Steelworkers of America still employed in the Monongahela Valley, including Pittsburgh, had dropped from 22,500 in 1980 to fewer than 5,200. Industry officials and politicians effectively told the steelworkers that it was time to move on, to get trained in some other skill and find new jobs. In response, the Tri-State Conference on Steel—made up mostly of union members and local Catholics—organized a "résumés for Reagan" campaign. Unemployed workers who had done as they had been told and taken retraining courses, only to find no better work prospects, sent in their résumés to the president of the United States.[41]

The most vital campaign in Pittsburgh mobilized to save U.S. Steel's Dusquesne Works, closed by the company in 1984, and its blast furnace, Dorothy Six. Built in 1966 and named for a U.S. Steel executive's wife, Dorothy was the biggest and most productive and efficient blast furnace in the Monongahela Valley. It stood more than a hundred feet tall and could purify five thousand tons of iron into steel every day; it broke all production records. Even so, the company shut it down, claiming it was unprofitable and had been made obsolete by newer technology. But this did not stop Tri-State workers from making a bid either to find investors to buy it or to find a way for workers to buy it. They waged an eminent domain campaign, making the case that the communities had the power to seize land and property in the public interest. "We like to refer to this as reindustrialization from below," Mike Stout of Homestead Local 1397 of the USWA told a reporter. "We don't just see it as saving jobs; we see it as our patriotic duty. We see the backbone of this country being crushed, and we're saying we're out to save it." It did not seem like such an outrageous suggestion to buy Dorothy Six and get her up and running again. Pittsburgh's mayor and city council endorsed the creation of a Steel Valley Authority that could use eminent domain power to acquire Dorothy and even pledged $50,000 toward SVA's budget. Nine city councils in the area, according to Lynd, "took all the legal steps necessary for final incorporation of the authority in January 1986," and the New York financial consulting firm Lazard Frères & Company conducted a feasibility study that concluded that a domestic market existed for U.S.-made steel, particularly if some of the technology could be improved. But U.S. Steel disputed such claims and refused to sell despite the massive public uprising.[42]

Part of the reason workers in Pittsburgh and Youngstown clung to the hope of communities keeping plants going, against all odds, was because of Weirton, West Virginia. Thirty-five miles west of Pittsburgh,

Weirton, like Youngstown and Pittsburgh, owed its existence to the steel industry. In the 1970s, National Steel, which had owned Weirton Steel since the 1920s, was the second-largest steel company in the United States; it employed twelve thousand workers making beverage cans, garbage bins, and sheet steel for cars, farm equipment, and large appliances. In the early 1970s, Weirton had been highly profitable, shipping more than 3.5 million tons of steel and earning more than $50 million. By the late 1970s, however, Weirton was suffering the same slackening of demand that affected other steel companies: the oil crisis led to manufacturers making smaller cars that required less steel; aluminum overtook steel and tin in making cans; and as farming went into decline, fewer farmers continued to buy heavy equipment. Moreover, in 1973 the International Steelworkers Union had negotiated annual 3 percent raises as well as cost-of-living adjustments in exchange for giving up the right to strike; as inflation spiked in the late 1970s, it drove wages up even further. As a result, like U.S. Steel, National hedged its bets by diversifying its operations into other industries. Thus, when in 1981 it suffered a year of insufficient profits, it laid off 3,000 Weirton workers (leaving only 8,500) and announced that it would begin scaling back the Weirton operation to just a finishing plant that would require a fraction of the existing workforce.[43]

Unlike U.S. Steel and the other steel companies in Youngstown and Pittsburgh, however, National offered to sell Weirton Steel to its employees if they could raise the money. This, according to one reporter, unleashed an *It's a Wonderful Life* scenario.[44] The workers put together an employee stock ownership plan (ESOP) in which, *The New York Times* explained, "a trust is created, and banks make loans to the trust, which buys the company's stock. The company makes payments to the trust to retire debt, and, as lenders are repaid, the trust allocates stock to employees."[45] Such arrangements were rare, and few dared to suggest that they were foolproof; for example, the Rath Packing Company in Iowa had taken the ESOP route in 1980 and was struggling to survive as the Weirton talks took place (and in fact Rath went bankrupt in 1985).[46] Many obstacles needed to be overcome. Weirton had always paid its workers more than the industry average as a way of dissuading union organizing, but the ESOP required a massive pay cut of up to 32 percent.[47]

Moreover, achieving consensus among employees proved difficult. It took more than two years of organizing, but in September 1984,

84 percent of Weirton workers approved the deal. Following a 20 percent reduction in wages, workers agreed to a six-year wage freeze, and in exchange for $194 million paid to National Steel by the new Weirton Corporation, 6.65 million shares of common stock were placed in a company trust; after five years, as the debt was repaid, the trust began distributing shares to employees based on their wage levels. The employees promised no strikes and no lockouts. And National agreed that if the new company failed within its first five years, National would still pay pensions and shutdown costs. The vote "not only will save jobs and the community," ISU president Walter Bish gushed, "but [it] gives us an opportunity to be owners of a Fortune 300 Company, share in profits and be stockholders. That's quite an accomplishment." Not everyone was impressed. Lynd called the wage cut "unexplained and unjustifiable" and the whole deal "just terrible. Worker ownership Wall Street Style." And even though two Wall Street investment firms did feasibility studies that endorsed the sale, *The New York Times* predicted the deal would never work. "The lesson of the last decade is as simple as it is depressing: To be able to produce steel more competitively, the American steel industry must shrink and thousands of steelworkers must lose their jobs . . . [The country needs] a leaner, more specialized steel industry."[48]

But Weirton thrived under new management by cultivating a culture of employee participation in all levels of decision making. In a key innovation, the new company introduced employee participation groups (EPGs), of which there were dozens and which cultivated employee pride in their work and product. The EPGs usually functioned as teams of workers from the same areas of the company, often focused, as employee owners, on examining their own processes and looking for ways to work more efficiently and cost-effectively. To take just one example, the Steel Works Crane Repair EPG built a sixty-ton hot mill crane from recycled parts, thus saving the company half a million dollars. "The starting point," new president Robert Loughead told a Harvard Business School audience, "must be that of first creating a participative environment, where people want mutual involvement, where ideas can flourish rather than get smothered . . . In short, the employee can develop a strong sense of attachment to the job place and the enterprise furnishing it. Who really knows more about the products made or the services provided than frontline employees?" In the end, as predicted by financial analysts, Weirton posted profits for sixteen consecutive quarters. It even thrived, despite ups and downs, into the late 1990s, when another wave of foreign competition finally put it on the ropes. The company went bankrupt in 2003 and was bought by a venture capitalist who then sold it to a foreign competitor. With fewer than a thousand workers still employed making tin products, one could make the case that the ESOP deal only postponed the workers' inevitable doom—and plenty in the community were bitter about being betrayed by a board on which employees held too few seats— but Weirton employees managed to buy themselves twenty more years of employment that steelworkers in Youngstown and Pittsburgh would have been happy to get.[49]

In contrast to the scramble to save factories and jobs in Youngstown, Pittsburgh, and Weirton, the federal government's response to the rash of plant closings was notable for its almost total ineffectiveness. Rescuing Chrysler had been an important exception, but neither the Carter nor Reagan administration showed any interest in bailing out workers in other industries, even in steel. In May 1988, Congress passed the Worker Adjustment and Retraining Notification (WARN) Act, which included a sixty-day notification provision for mass layoffs and plant closings for companies with more than a hundred employees, but President Reagan vetoed it. "I object to the idea that the Federal Government would arbitrarily mandate, for all conditions and under all circumstances, exactly when and in what form that notification should take place," Reagan said. The House and Senate could not override the veto, so legislators removed the notification requirement and passed the bill by more than a two-thirds majority. Reagan still refused to sign, but it became law anyway.[50] Rust Belt workers looked on in disgust. Ten years after Youngstown's Ecumenical Coalition was founded—and four years after the Weirton sale to employees—the best the federal government could do was to pass a weakened retraining law.

It would have been better for steelworkers if there could have been more Weirtons, but the Weirton story ended up an anomaly. Most communities that fought to hold on to their industrial bases lost and went into sharp decline. Yet it is significant that these communities mobilized the way they did—not along party or ideological lines, but simply in defense of their jobs and communities, asserting a collective understanding of what their American dream looked like. Workers in America's industrial heartlands saw the attack on labor coming—the efforts to break their unions, the plant closings—and rallied to defend themselves. And they rallied because they had to, and because they believed they could, in fact, save their communities. No one else, least of all the government, had lifted a finger to help, so they did it themselves.

8

The Heartland Uprising

●

Ever since the nineteenth century, farmers understood their struggles against banks and government within a Jeffersonian vision of citizenship. That is, farmers, in their minds if not in others', occupied a hallowed place in the revolutionary tradition of the founders. "Cultivators of the earth are the most valuable citizens," Jefferson once wrote. "They are the most vigorous, the most independent, the most virtuous, and they are tied to their country and wedded to its liberty and interests by the most lasting bonds." This vision remained relevant even in the second half of the twentieth century. As *Fast Food Nation* author Eric Schlosser has noted, farmers also knew that they had helped win the world wars and outshone the Soviet Union's collective farming model. "You could hardly find a better symbol of freedom," Schlosser says, "than the American farmer."[1] And yet, by the 1980s, farmers could be forgiven for feeling that they had been transported back to a more capricious age as they once again, like their forebears, found themselves fighting to survive.

Since agricultural work is not covered by the National Labor Relations Act, both farmers and farmworkers are usually treated as independent contractors or agents with a measure of control over their circumstances that industrial workers lack. Of course, this notion of independence is fanciful. Farmers have always been beholden to external factors, including volatile prices, government policy, lending rates, shipping costs, and the power of various middlemen. Though farmers made record profits in the early and mid-1970s, they also saw a sudden downturn in their fortunes as fiscal policymakers in Washington tried to get inflation under control. The wave of farm foreclosures that swept the Midwest and elsewhere in the 1980s was not unlike the wave of industrial plant closings; both left behind shattered communities and shattered lives. In both cases, families believed that they had done everything right, played by the rules, and worked hard, only to see the rules rewritten to someone else's advantage. The sense of injustice that sprang from that realization sparked an angry and desperate rural uprising too often over-looked by historians focused on cities, suburbs, and the rise of the right in this period. In fact, the organizing of migrant farmworkers is one of labor's great success stories in this period, and the battles waged by farm-ers in decline stand as some of the era's strongest examples of front porch politics in action.

In the lives of migrant farmworkers and family farmers, both of whom live where they work and work where they live, the politics of their labor is not only about their labor but about how they live from day to day in communities of people just like them. A farm was to a family what a blast furnace was to a steel community; if it ceased to function, so did the family. And when families were forced off farms, formerly vibrant communities in the nation's heartland turned to ghost towns. Of course, even as farmers and farmworkers struggled to endure the same shifting economic conditions—which were often dictated by policymakers, banks, and food processors—they also regarded each other warily and some-times found their interests in direct conflict.

Thanks to Cesar Chavez and the United Farm Workers (UFW), Ameri-cans knew a lot more in the 1970s about the lives of farmworkers than they do now. In the late 1960s, Chavez's name could often be heard ut-tered in the same breath as Martin Luther King Jr.'s, such was his cha-risma, dedication to nonviolence, and status as a leader not only of farmworkers but of Mexican Americans. Migrant farmworkers—the ones who move seasonally with the harvest, picking fruits and vegetables row by row—have historically been subjected to the kinds of employer actions (e.g., summary firings, spying, blacklisting) that are illegal in other industries. And since farmworker unions had always found it dif-ficult to organize a mostly transient workforce, they simply did not have the resources to ride out long strikes. The United Farm Workers, there-fore, did not try to emulate the industrial unions, and instead modeled its approach on the civil rights movement by making boycotts the center of its campaigns for economic justice.

The UFW's overarching goal may have been union recognition and the right to collectively bargain, but that quest was driven by a combination of grievances over workplace and living standards. Migrant workers in California lived in a particular kind of squalor, not unlike the plantation arrangements of old when the only housing was made available by the plantation owner: if migrants were lucky, growers provided housing in rickety Depression-era shacks—tiny tin-roofed structures with no windows—that were never intended to be permanent; more often, they lived in makeshift tents constructed out of gunnysacks or lean-tos made of scrap materials like cardboard and linoleum. The only running water was often one faucet, shared by dozens of people, who also had to share outhouses that were, as Chavez later described them, "always horrible, so miserable you couldn't go there." Even if they could have afforded more than beans and potatoes for their own consumption, few had any way to refrigerate their food and no way to cook it but over an open fire. Medical care was so uneven that many farmworker children went without essential vaccinations. "We are engaged," Chavez said on the eve of the 1965 Delano grape strike, "in [a] struggle for the freedom and dignity which poverty denies us." By 1970, the UFW's successful national boycott of table grapes led to formal contracts with 150 California growers producing 85 percent of the state's grapes. Twenty thousand farmworkers not only got a pay raise but could now claim the same protections as most unionized industrial workers: cleaner and safer working conditions, including a ban on pesticides like DDT; the provision of field toilets and clean water; mandated rest breaks; benefits that included a health plan, the establishment of a fund to assist disabled and elderly farmworkers, and a burial fund; and the institution of a union hall where a worker seniority system would be implemented as well as formal grievance procedures.[2] For Mexican American migrants who didn't have a fixed address or, therefore, an actual front porch, these were nonetheless front porch issues: conditions that affected their daily lives as they moved from place to place following the harvest.

In spite of the union's historic victory, the growers never gave up trying to crush the UFW, and the union, for its part, hamstrung itself as it struggled to make the transition from a social movement to a collective bargaining institution. Later, many who left the UFW blamed the union's reliance on Chavez as both visionary and micromanager; they also pointed to the failure to provide paid jobs to the staff, which hurt as the union now had to run hiring halls and negotiate contracts. As a result, the Grower-Shipper Vegetable Association saw vulnerability, and by the summer of 1973, as UFW contracts expired, the growers took on the union. When two thousand UFW workers went out on strike in the Coachella Valley, strikebreakers—hired thugs and Teamsters, signed by some growers to "sweetheart contracts" to punish the UFW and protect replacement workers—pummeled UFW workers, and police arrested three hundred for violating court injunctions intended to limit picketing. During a long and bloody summer, two UFW members were killed (one was beaten by a police officer following a UFW strike meeting, another was shot on the picket line in a drive-by shooting) and countless injured. Only the commitment of $1.6 million in AFL-CIO money to the UFW strike fund kept the union afloat as nearly thirty-six hundred workers went to jail over the summer. Ultimately, as contracts expired, the growers made no effort to re-sign with the UFW (they were getting by with Mexican immigrant replacement workers organized and protected by the Teamsters). The union which had begun the year with 180 contracts covering 67,000 workers ended the year with only 14 contracts covering 6,500.[3]

The UFW fought back with another boycott of table grapes, lettuce, and Gallo wine while simultaneously waging a legislative battle for more farmworker protections. By October 1975, polls showed that 12 percent of all Americans were boycotting table grapes, 11 percent were boycotting head lettuce, and 8 percent were boycotting Gallo products. The union also succeeded in getting the Agricultural Labor Relations Act passed in California, which guaranteed the right of farmworkers both to vote to unionize and to choose their unions in elections. By the end of 1975, the UFW had rebounded, winning 76 percent of almost 200 elections. In the next two years it went on to win 250 elections, the end of a long crawl back to equal standing of eight years earlier.[4]

Even in the wake of such triumphs, the UFW remained on the defensive in the late 1970s and into the 1980s as the growers settled in for a prolonged war, chipping away, with the help of the state, at the UFW's base. Just keeping the union alive became the central front porch issue for migrant farmworkers; without it, they knew, all other core issues would not be addressed. When Republican governor George Deukmejian took office in January 1983, he was criticized for following the Reagan model of hiring antiunion foxes to guard the state's Agricultural

Labor Relations Board henhouse, declaring that "the board is no longer responsive to the needs of farm workers." With no ALRB protection for the union, growers began to run up a string of victories, particularly with legal challenges, which were very expensive and sapped the UFW's treasury. In other cases, following the Chrysler model, a grower would declare bankruptcy in order to compel union concessions as the business "reorganized." Still others found that if they just did not negotiate new contracts with the farmworkers, the ALRB would do nothing. By 1987, the union held only thirty-one contracts, representing fewer than fifteen thousand workers. Worse, living conditions were deteriorating; cancer clusters in farmworker communities were linked to pesticides, and media reports revealed that countless undocumented farmworkers were living underground, in caves they had dug for themselves, for lack of decent housing. Although Chavez told a graduating class in 1989 that there was nothing that mattered more to the UFW than "the lives and safety of our families," and the union attempted new boycotts and waged massive campaigns to educate the public, it made little headway against a Deukmejian administration so devoted to helping the growers keep the union at bay.[5]

In retrospect, many see this result as a failure on Chavez's part: he was unwilling to make the transition from a social movement representing the interests of Chicanos, Mexicans, and Filipinos to a trade union model, and even worse, he adopted a controversial leadership approach that seemed cultlike and resulted in purges of longtime organizers. By the time Chavez died in 1993, the UFW had contracts covering only five thousand workers. Today, the UFW still exists, but it is a faint shadow of what it was in its heyday. In the end, for California's migrant workers, a front porch political strategy worked only up to a point. To have succeeded over the long term, the UFW needed to win the allegiance of consumers not merely in times of boycott but all the time; it needed consumers to regard working and living conditions for farmworkers as points of principle. But that was a tall order when so many Americans worried about their own troubles.

In the Midwest, migrant workers followed the UFW's model under even more complicated circumstances, but still won landmark victories. Every summer in the 1970s and 1980s, more than sixty-five thousand migrant workers—most Mexican American or legal Mexican immigrants—moved up from Florida or the lower Rio Grande Valley in Texas to the upper Midwest to harvest a range of crops: vegetables, including toma-toes, cucumbers, asparagus, and sugar beets, and fruit, including apples, peaches, cherries, and strawberries. The average family income for these migrants—$6,450 a year—was so low that they had no choice but to move throughout the season, looking for more work and more pay.[6]

Their experience was defined not only by strenuous work for pauper pay but also by the experience of living in camps, in appalling condi-tions, with families crammed into a single room with no running water. Although many farm owners made good faith efforts to provide decent housing, in sanitary conditions, many others did not. Often, a migrant family could expect to share a small house with two other families or, worse, live on their own in converted chicken coops with only three walls and an open front. If they were lucky, they would find toilet and shower facilities in a separate building, shared by many families, but just as often, they were expected to use outhouses and get by without showers, bathing in streams (and all of these facilities could be taken away from a farmworker and his family if he gave the farmer any grief at all). Studies showed that with limited access to proper medical care, and with their nutritional intake limited by their low income, migrant farmworkers could expect to live, on average, only to the age of forty-nine. They experienced higher-than-average rates of infant and maternal mortality, malnutrition, and infectious diseases—to say nothing of the hazards of backbreaking work in an environment soaked with pesticides. Although an important bond of community and solidarity connected migrant farmworkers, they yearned to be a more stable, thriving community—something akin to Youngstown in its prime. "We call on the agricultural industry to recog-nize that farmworkers have legitimate concerns for their families," Baldemar Velasquez, founder of the Farm Labor Organizing Committee, said. His hope, he said repeatedly, was for "a healthy industry in which all workers . . . can earn a living that is conducive to a healthy family." Here, then, was the basis of their unique front porch claim: they wanted to have healthy families, in which their children would grow up healthy, with a good education and a chance to make better lives for themselves than their parents had managed in a life in the fields.[7]

On many farms, however, employers considered the migrants inde-pendent contractors and therefore did not have to pay minimum wage; in many cases, migrants worked practically as sharecroppers, getting 50 percent of the value of whatever they harvested. Worse, for the migrant, the income tax rate for self-employed independent contractors was higher than for wage earners, so their take-home pay—if they knew enough to pay their taxes (and many did not, only to wind up owing large sums to the government)—was squeezed that much more. For many migrants, it seemed that the only way they could assert any control over their own household economy was to take their children into the fields to bring in extra income. This was hardly a recipe for a healthy family or a healthy future.[8]

If the conditions for farmworkers in Ohio and Michigan were as bad as in California, the difficulties in organizing were in some ways greater. The farmers who employed migrants were usually running much smaller operations than the powerful California growers, and as a result, they were themselves under the thumb of corporate food giants such as the Campbell Soup Company, Libby's, and Heinz. Any farmer who negotiated a contract with the migrants risked being judged as unreliable by the corporate food processors to whom he sold his crops. The companies aimed to control as much of the crop production process as possible, from selling seedling plants to the farmers to dictating the use of pesticides and ultimately setting the price for which the crops would sell—all from the top down. As a result, migrant workers needed to negotiate with the farmers who employed them and who themselves had to negotiate with the food processing giants who were little interested in hearing farmworker complaints.[9]

Baldemar Velasquez began organizing migrant workers in the upper Midwest in the late 1960s, when he founded the Farm Labor Organizing Committee (FLOC) in the image of the UFW. Velasquez was born in Texas and began working in the fields among migrant workers at the age of four. When he was six years old, his family settled in Gilboa, Ohio, so that he and his siblings could go to school. In later years, his own experience of childhood poverty—of sleeping with his brothers in a bed in a migrant shack as the snow whipped through gaps in the walls—led him to organize migrant workers who, twenty years on, faced similar living conditions. In the mid-1960s, Velasquez went to college, first at Pan American University in Texas and later at Bluffton College, a Mennonite institution in Ohio. He volunteered with the Congress of Racial Equality in Cleveland, and he learned about Gandhi from his father-in-law, a Bluffton professor who had known the Indian leader. Soon he saw his own calling as organizing the migrant farmworking community of which his

family had been a part since before he was born. In 1967, Velasquez
formed FLOC with his father and a small group of farmworkers. At first,
FLOC won union recognition and better wages from tomato growers, but
they soon found that going after individual growers was pointless when
the tomato and pickle processors controlled the farm economy. The companies acted as though the way they set prices and production terms
with growers had nothing to do with how the growers decided to harvest
their crops. But by the late 1970s, FLOC prepared to take the fight to
some of the biggest food companies in America.[10]

In 1978, FLOC called for something unprecedented in American labor relations: three-way contracts among farmworkers, growers, and the
processing companies. When most of the farmers and all of the companies ignored the union, twenty-three hundred Ohio farmworkers went
out on strike against Campbell Soup and Libby's. They picketed the tomato fields in northwestern Ohio, and the canneries, too. Following
Cesar Chavez's example, Velasquez went on a hunger strike. But the
farmers and the companies fought back. Thanks to a variety of factors,
farmers all over the country were, beginning in the late 1970s, facing
down their own front porch worries, struggling to pay their debts; the
last thing they needed was to be unable to meet their harvest targets. As
they became more desperate to maximize their crop yield, farmers' anger toward the migrants sometimes turned ugly. Some of the farmers
displayed shotguns to intimidate pickets; one sprayed a picket line with
pesticides, and another drove his pickup truck into a line of strikers.
Across a field from FLOC's tent city strike headquarters, someone lit a
cross on fire, Ku Klux Klan–style. In a season of uncertainty, tension blan-
keted the region. When the harvest concluded with 20 to 30 percent of
the tomato crop unpicked, the companies struck back, too: Libby's filed
suit against FLOC for financial losses incurred by the strike, and most
important, Campbell mandated that its ninety tomato suppliers mecha-
nize their harvesting process for 1979. Although harvesting tomatoes
with machines is a bit like conducting surgery with a machete—it takes
up everything, ripe and unripe—and the mechanical harvesters often
got bogged down in the mud, farmers had no choice but to follow Campbell's and other companies' directives. By 1982, only 15 percent of the
tomato harvest was picked by hand. But the move toward mechanization
amounted to a tacit acknowledgment that the processors did, in fact, have

a relationship with the migrant workers and gave FLOC an additional issue around which to organize.[11]

When Velasquez, following Martin Luther King Jr.'s 1963 strategy in Birmingham, Alabama, led a group of children in a nonviolent civil disobedience action by sitting in front of a mechanical tomato harvester, the campaign experienced its worst spasm of violence. Law enforcement arrived at the field and went wild, charging toward the group, swinging clubs and beating parents who had rushed into the field to protect their children. Police arrested sixty people, and when the FLOC lawyer, Jack Kilroy, arrived to arrange bail, a deputy sheriff told him he was under arrest; Kilroy asked why and in reply got jumped by a group of deputies who pounded his head so relentlessly into the pavement that they fractured his skull. Photos of him lying in a pool of blood look like a mob hit.[12]

FLOC reacted to these attacks by continuing the strike indefinitely and, in the summer of 1979, calling for a boycott of all Campbell products and those of its subsidiaries, including Vlasic pickles, Swanson frozen dinners, and Pepperidge Farm products—and later, when Campbell introduced new products such as Prego spaghetti sauce and Le Menu frozen dinners, they were boycotted, too.[13] Organizers also succeeded in getting considerable press attention from sympathetic journalists who broadcast or published reports of inhumane working conditions, child labor, and pervasive discrimination against Chicanos. FLOC operatives went to Florida and Texas, where many migrants lived during the winter, to recruit members and spread word of the strike and boycott. Similarly, in a variation of the corporate campaign that the Ravenswood workers employed, FLOC helped establish support committees in major cities such as Chicago, Detroit, Indianapolis, and Philadelphia; these committees provided the boycott's shock troops, tapping consumer conscience in their areas. In one of the local groups' most effective tactics, boycott supporters attacked Campbell's Labels for Education program, an ingenious marketing operation in place since 1970 in which schools could collect Campbell's Soup can labels from students and exchange them for school (and especially athletic) equipment. Over the 1970s, many kids earned bats and balls, uniforms and cleats, by bringing their chicken noodle soup can labels to school. But thanks to FLOC's work with the local committees and church groups, some twelve hundred parochial and public schools dropped out of the labels program by 1982.[14]

In addition to the boycott, a number of FLOC tactics created enough negative publicity that Campbell changed course. First, in 1983, about a hundred migrant workers marched 560 miles from Toledo to Campbell's corporate headquarters in Camden, New Jersey, garnering considerable press coverage. The publicity led to an Ohio state senate investigation of farm labor and living conditions that found that processors and growers held farmworkers in a kind of "shadow slavery"; the investigation concluded that Campbell and other food processing companies effectively dictated living and working conditions for migrants. The intervention of the National Council of Churches, which could mobilize all of its parishes across the country against Campbell if it wanted to, finally forced Campbell to fold after seven years of struggle. In February 1986, FLOC signed two three-year contracts—one with Campbell and the Ohio Tomato Growers Association, and the other with Campbell and the Michigan Vlasic Pickles growers. The next year, Heinz capitulated and signed a similar contract with its pickle growers and FLOC. The contracts addressed most of FLOC's major workplace issues: better and uniform wages; full transparency in the reporting of pay, expenses, and other withholding and adjustments; $2,000 for each family that had gone out on strike in 1978; establishment of formal grievance procedures; and payment of union dues for workers by the processors. In addition, the parties agreed to more obvious front porch resolutions, including initiating an experimental health program and investigating and resolving problems regarding housing and exposure to pesticides. By 1991, when more than five thousand migrants worked under FLOC contracts and new contracts had put an end to sharecropping and child labor in Midwestern fields, migrant housing had been upgraded, too—from, as Velasquez described the change, "one-room shanties for entire families" to "multi-bedroom units with their own self-contained showers and cooking facilities as opposed to the common-use facilities they had before." Most important, FLOC's success brought stability to pickle and tomato growing, enough so that farmers increasingly worked with FLOC to improve housing and sanitary conditions in and around the fields. Today, FLOC, building on the success of its Midwestern campaigns, continues to work on behalf of farmworkers, with much of its energy now devoted to tobacco workers in North Carolina.[15]

• • •

By comparison, the protracted struggle of family farmers—iconic symbols of freedom, sitting astride their John Deere tractors like frontier cowboys—boasted few successes. Perhaps that is why farm politics has largely been left out of the histories of the 1970s and 1980s. In part, historians' focus on urban and suburban America in the postwar years has left the rural experience in the shadows. In addition, there is a sense that the 1980s marked an end point, the last gasps of desperate independent farmers. But that is far too simplistic. For the family farm movement sprang from the same kind of front porch ethos that drove movements against plant closings, the poisoning of communities by toxic waste, and so on: in each case, Americans became activists because they felt that they had been treated unfairly and abandoned by government, and that that unfair treatment would lead to the end not only of their lives as they knew them but of their hopes and dreams. Far from wanting the government to leave them alone, they wanted it to intervene and ensure that they would be treated fairly. Farmers do not fit the mold of conservative or progressive politics. They were both conservative in their entrepreneurial spirit and eager for a government presence that would ensure a fair shake. And dating at least from the 1930s, they had been able to count on Washington to work with them, with subsidies and crop management programs, to maintain a decent standard of living. In the 1970s and 1980s, however, policymakers were presiding over tectonic shifts in the structure of the nation's political economy that made the family farm expendable.

Maybe the most important thing to remember about the farm crisis of the late 1970s and 1980s is that no one saw it coming. After all, farmers thrived compared to most Americans in the 1970s. Global grain shortages drove the price of American wheat to historic highs, and with the dollar weak, unmoored from the gold standard, foreign governments could afford to buy as much American produce as they wanted. The Nixon administration told farmers to plant "fencepost to fencepost" and fashioned policies to spur further investment in agriculture. American farmers prepared to "feed the world" by expanding their operations—mostly with money borrowed from banks happy to lend it amid such rosy price forecasts.[16]

At the same time, in an inflationary climate, the "value" of farmland soared. Some farmers began to see themselves as investors as much as producers. One told a *New York Times* reporter that he had borrowed so much money to buy so much land that was going up in value so fast that every morning he "woke up $8,000 richer." Many commentators later noted that a new brand of farmer—younger, college-educated, heir to the family farm—saw a bright future in all of this expansion. And in this they were encouraged by so-called experts. "The farm crisis caught most university researchers—along with nearly everyone else—by surprise," the *Chronicle of Higher Education* later reported. "Few agricultural economists foresaw just how quickly or how drastically the agricultural bull market of the 1970s would change in the 1980s." "Everybody was extremely optimistic," a Western Minnesota lawyer and son of farmers remembered. "Everybody borrowed a huge amount of money. We didn't have any sense at the time that this was anything but good. We believed that farmers were going to become people of status in this world . . . It felt good. It never occurred to me or anyone else to say, 'Well, gee, something could go wrong here.'"[17]

By the late 1970s, the fencepost-to-fencepost growing was increasing American farm production even as the success of foreign competition in the face of a stronger U.S. dollar reduced demand. Prices fell slowly at first, then more quickly. From the first half of the decade to the second, the average farm income declined by about 25 percent, and by the mid-1980s, family farm income had dropped by an amazing 83 percent, from $35,174 to $6,000. Inflation caused the wealth, on paper, of many farmers to grow substantially as their land values continued to climb, but the price crisis dried up their cash flow. As a result, many farmers borrowed more from their banks and lending agencies; those institutions figured that making operating loans posed little risk when the farmers' land served as collateral.[18] Then, in 1979, the Federal Reserve Bank moved to stop runaway inflation by restricting the monetary supply and allowing interest rates to go up; for farmers, this meant paying back loans at a higher rate and, when the Fed's initiative succeeded, watching the value of their land spiral downward. As lenders became much less inclined to provide the extra operating money farmers so badly needed, Jimmy Carter made matters worse by imposing a grain embargo on the Soviet Union following its invasion of Afghanistan. Many, perhaps even a majority, of farmers were suddenly carrying more debt than they were worth and had no way to make it up. Massive waves of foreclosures followed, and rural communities across the Midwest began to experience something like another Great Depression.[19] Farmers went from confused to angry. One succinctly summarized the feelings of thousands: "There's a lot of people feeling abused by the system."[20]

The crisis only got worse under the Reagan administration. The huge increase in defense spending during the "second Cold War" of the 1980s required more government borrowing, which drove interest rates even higher and inflation down even further: the national inflation rate in 1979 was 11.3 percent; in 1983, it had dropped to 3.2 percent, and by 1986 it was down to 1.9 percent.[21] Once high interest rates made it impossible for farmers to make payments or seemingly ever to pay down their debt, they turned to the "lender of last resort," the Farmers Home Administration (FmHA)—the New Deal agency set up to help farmers keep their farms—to refinance their mortgages. Moreover, the Reagan team was so confident that their economic package of deregulation, lower taxes, and reduced social spending would put money in American pockets and boost consumer spending that they pressed the FmHA to keep lending to farmers. "I remember our state director when he was still newly appointed coming around to gather a bunch of us supervisors together and saying, 'You *make* these plans work. Use whatever prices you have to, because by fall, the economic program will be working so good that all these will be good loans, you just wait and see.' So we did," recalled one FmHA county supervisor. "Well, it probably took me a year or two before I could see that, hey, year after year, these farmers don't pay their debts—and they borrow more money to cover their last year's bills, and it can't go on." Moreover, borrowing from the federal lender became a humiliating experience; borrowers could do little—even buying seed— without first getting approval from the FmHA.[22]

Farmers who found themselves in trouble felt blindsided. That sense of having been unable to see it coming only added to a general sense of personal failure. Lester and Laura Joens of Manning, Iowa, were typical. They went from being model farmers to going bankrupt practically overnight. Married in 1960, parents of four children, active in their church and community, the Joenses worked Lester's father's farm. When Lester's father died in 1980, they bought his land from other heirs so that they could keep on farming. And then came the collapse in land values and prices. In November 1982, the Joenses' bank demanded repayment of all their notes within ten days. They were stunned. They had no idea that they could be required to pay off all notes—including some that were not due to be paid off for years—on such short notice, but their banker pointed out the fine print: the bank had the right to call in any loan it deemed unsound. Two years later, by the time their story (the Joenses were uncommon in their willingness to speak candidly to the press about their plight) had made them symbols for farmers across the country, the Joenses had declared bankruptcy and quit farming to sell insurance. As Laura described it to a reporter, everyone in her family suffered from the farm's failure, but her husband took it the worst. "It was hard on me, but," she added, "it's doubly hard on a man. They feel so responsible." Lester said that his spirit died on that day that the bank called in those notes.[23]

With bankruptcy came auctioneers and the pain of seeing all of one's possessions—symbols of a family's life on the farm—sold off, one piece at a time. "It was a very hard day," Minnesota farmers Steve and Kathy Schroeder later recalled. By the time a bank decided to auction a farmer's land and machinery, equipment and livestock, everyone in the community—the would-be bidders—knew that with no market to sell to, there were bargains to be had. Thus, the humiliation of a very public bankruptcy was compounded by seeing one's neighbors as vultures. "Everything was going, too," said Kathy. Locals, Steve lamented, scooped up "every damn thing we got." It felt like "everyone was pounding on us," Kathy said, and wept.[24]

The pervasive sense of failure galvanized farmers to organize. They consistently made the point that American farmers had not measurably failed. They had produced as much as or more than prior generations; they had wrung more than anyone else had from their land. (Indeed, critics charged that farmers had obediently done everything expected of them by the government and agribusiness, including poisoning the soil and groundwater with pesticides, using crop management techniques that stripped the produce of its natural nutrients, and slaughtering animals in ways some thought inhumane.) Therefore, it was not the farmers who had failed; rather, the system had failed them. They could not get a reasonable price for their produce—which was not their fault.[25] "A lot of people try to say this is no different from any other business failure," said Mike Hrabe, a Kansas wheat farmer. "I tell you there is a great difference." Hrabe farmed land that had been in his family for more than a century, and he was a proud follower in their footsteps. "Dad and Granddad had both been successful," he told a reporter. "And I was a member of the school board, a member of the church board, a member of the board at the Farm Bureau, and I was a 4-H Club leader. I was pretty well thought of in the community." Pushed to the brink of bankruptcy, feeling humiliated and emasculated in the midst of the farm crisis, Hrabe prepared to take his own life, stopping only when he saw his son's Little League uniform. "There is a certain pride in farming, and the shame of failure is just overwhelming," Hrabe said. "Death seemed better than facing it."[26]

Indeed, the nation's attention turned to the farm crisis in the mid-1980s in part because of the macabre press coverage of the rash of farmer and lender suicides. In Oklahoma, 160 farmers took their own lives from 1983 to 1988, making suicide (rather than accidents) the leading cause of farm deaths. Thumbnail sketches that made it into *The New York Times* included the story of Eugene Copeland finding his fifty-four-year-old wife, Katherine, a kindergarten teacher, lying across a burning trash pile. In the midst of an FmHA foreclosure, Eugene concluded that Katherine "just couldn't see any way to escape. She got desperate." A few weeks later, in Gracemont, Oklahoma, forty-year-old Bill Stalder killed his wife, his ten-year-old son, and his sixteen-year-old daughter, then burned down his farmhouse and shot himself. On the final page of a diary he left in the barn, police found the word "responsible" written over and over. Some bankers, like Bruce Litchfield of South Dakota, feeling the pain of foreclosing on their clients, killed themselves, too. In Iowa, somewhere between forty-five and fifty farmers committed suicide each year from 1980 to 1986. A number of farmers decided to shoot others, gunning down bankers and law enforcement officials in their final desperate acts.[27] Finally, clinicians noted many more examples of domestic violence, alcohol abuse, and injuries to pets. "Veterinarians are treating farm dogs that have had their ribs kicked in," reported a Missouri sociologist. Failure and solitude made a volatile combination. With so many farmers prepared to choose suicide over seeking help, a hundred townspeople in Deuel County, South Dakota, submitted applications for food stamps and heating aid they did not need in order to insulate the few who truly needed help from any sense of public embarrassment or feeling outcast. "A change of culture this revolutionary usually comes from wars," Father Leonard Kayser told *Newsweek*. "But these farmers don't even want their own families to know they're in trouble. They just fail, one by one."[28]

Across the rural Midwest, as farmers failed, so, too, did whole communities. In 1984—a year in which the Agriculture Department found that 214,000 farms could not pay their bills—the number of Americans living on farms dropped by 399,000. Places like Odebolt, Iowa, and the surrounding county "had endured three bank failures, forty farm bankruptcies, declines in school and church enrollments and the loss of two major farm equipment dealerships . . . this was not atypical of conditions throughout much of the Midwest and great plains." As farm values fell as much as 50 percent from 1982 to 1986, on average, 2,109 farms failed each week; nearly 87,000 farms went bankrupt in 1985 alone.[29]

The farmers who mobilized in protest saw the failure of a larger system at work, but not all farmers felt that way. In the insular and competitive culture that defines most farm communities, the long-standing commitment to personal and moral responsibility for one's successes and failures reigned. The anthropologist Kathryn Dudley later called this the ideal of an "entrepeneurial self": farmers, she wrote, are "deeply committed to the cultural logic of capitalism, even as they remain alert to the danger that they may themselves become a casualty of that system."[30] The view that farmers believed they were making and lying in their own beds of financial ruin has dominated scholarly analysis of the farm crisis, but that research presents a skewed version of reality. By focusing almost exclusively on the survivors of the farm crisis, scholars like Dudley have neglected the experience of those who failed. In such an analysis, the farmers who protested are marginal figures, shunned by all those who kept quiet, put their heads down, and worked their way out of the crisis.[31]

Of course, it is much more difficult to find and study a population of farmers who were forced off their farms without much of a fight and to learn about their political experience, but we know that many thousands of farmers did not suffer in silence. They joined in a wide variety of political actions throughout the 1970s and 1980s. In doing so, they joined a tradition that dated back to the nineteenth century and had garnered headlines as recently as the 1960s. The National Farmers' Organization (NFO), founded in 1955, aimed to win contracts with processors that would provide a "reasonable profit," and the group took to a series of "holding actions"—withholding milk, livestock, or produce from market—as a way to pressure the processors and also raise prices. By the time the American Agricultural Movement (AAM), a national organization calling on the federal government to help save the family farm, was formed in 1977, only ten years had passed since the NFO staged milk dumpings. In addition, the counterculture encouraged young people to move to the country, and some of them brought a New Left ethos that called for farmers to have a say in the issues that most affected them. In 1975, some of these farmers founded an organization called Rural America. They launched research projects investigating rural poverty, housing, education, energy, and the environment, and they called for a democratization of the U.S. Department of Agriculture (USDA) and other federal policy reforms that would discourage speculative farm buying and the growth of agribusiness at the expense of family farmers.[32]

The American Agricultural Movement emerged out of this context. The organization was formed in September 1977 by forty farmers who had been meeting at the Branding Iron Café, a diner in Campo, Colorado (often, in farm communities, diners and coffee shops offered a collective front porch politics experience where threats were identified and solutions shared). "This is just a nice little farm community," Don Walker, the mayor of Campo (population 250), told a reporter. "People who live in town know that if the farmers aren't doing well, they won't do too well either." Although livestock yields were up in 1977 and American crops abundant, farmers could see the financial walls closing in on them. The prices they received in 1977 were, on average, down 20 percent from the prices they got at the high-water mark of August 1973; meanwhile, in an inflationary climate, their costs continued to soar. Only more borrowing could keep many of them afloat, and they knew that that was no way to sustain their families. The Campo diner thus became a "forum for cussing and discussing" government farm policy and plotting ways to fight back. "It used to be that we'd all laugh in here about how farmers should go on strike," said Melody Espey, owner of the Branding Iron Café. "No one's laughing now."[33]

Indeed, going into the winter of 1977–78, the AAM called for a farm strike—not so much a strike as a withholding of produce—to press a number of demands. They wanted to create a coalition of agricultural producers to help Congress write the farm bill, and most important, they wanted prices to rise to something approaching parity. Although most Americans might not have understood the meaning of "parity," for farmers it had been a long-standing goal. Parity, as defined by economists dating back to the Depression, essentially measures the prices of farm products against other commodities and in relation to the prices of items farmers have to buy; in 1977, farm prices stood at 67 percent of parity, their lowest level since 1933. Farmers argued that 100 percent parity—when the market value of farm commodities essentially matched that of manufactured goods—had been the norm in the years before World War I (indeed, the parity index was based on 1914 levels) and had later been institutionalized, after 1933, by New Deal acreage limitation programs. In the postwar years, parity translated into stable middle-class status for farmers.[34] It was, in short, the kind of policy precedent that farmers believed in (and that government had been happy to follow in part because it undercut the impetus for rural radicalism).

By the end of the 1970s, with farm commodity prices failing to keep up with prices in other sectors, the AAM blamed the government for designing policies that kept food cheap so that Americans could afford to buy other goods and keep the rest of the economy afloat. "The products and goods and services that we have to buy, they've increased [in price] from 500 to 1500 percent and we're still selling our product at the same old price we had in 1948," said Alan Gains, president of the Oklahoma branch of the AAM. Government policy, he said, could be summed up as "cheap food policy."[35] To reorient the priorities of government policy, the AAM demanded that the federal government make it illegal for farm commodities to be sold at subparity prices and that it establish a National Board of Agricultural Producers made up of family farmers; the board would then help the USDA balance supply and demand in such a way as to guarantee 100 percent parity. Easy enough to demand, but not so easy to get.[36]

The AAM grew from that group of forty Colorado farmers in September 1977 to a national organization with eleven hundred local offices in forty states in January 1978; by then, sociologists estimated that more than 3 million people had attended an AAM rally. More visibly, as the AAM called for a national farm strike—asking farmers to withhold their produce or livestock from market—farmers drove their tractors off their fields and into the streets. The defining image of the movement was the long convoy of tractors known as a tractorcade. Georgia farmers converged in their tractors on President Carter's hometown of Plains when he visited for Christmas. More than eleven hundred tractors formed a twenty-seven-mile parade encircling Lubbock, Texas, as farmers sent a message to their "city cousins" calling for an endorsement of higher prices for farm goods. Another massive tractorcade greeted Agriculture Secretary Bob Bergland when he went to Omaha to meet with AAM strike leaders. And most dramatically, more than three thousand farmers from all over the country descended on Washington, D.C.—some, traveling at only 15 miles per hour, needed nearly twenty days to get there—to demand a farm bill from Congress that would guarantee 100 percent parity.[37] Throughout the winter and into the spring, farmers roamed the halls of the House and Senate office buildings, stalking representatives, lobbying for the bill. For amateur lobbyists, the farmers had a knack for getting good media coverage; they staged rallies, drove their tractors, and positioned "broad-shouldered and heavy-set farmers" at visible locations to distribute literature and catch the television cameras' eye. In one widely covered move, a group of farmers herded goats on the steps of the Capitol Building to attract media and public attention.[38]

Thanks in part to the midterm election cycle, the farmers found many receptive listeners in Congress, and going into March it looked as though they would win a surprising legislative victory. But then the Council on Wage and Price Stability—the Executive Branch office introduced in the Carter years and charged with restraining inflation—declared that provisions designed to improve the prices farmers would get for their goods would lead to a 2 to 5 percent increase in retail food prices, thus sparking cost-of-living wage increases and higher prices for nonfood products—in short, a spike in inflation across the board. Farmers now came under attack for being, as a *New York Times* editorial put it, a "narrow-interest" constituency. They were blamed for living too high on the hog in good times and expecting consumers to bail them out. President Carter responded by threatening to veto the bill, and the House rejected it. The farm strike may not have helped; although there are no firm statistics on levels of participation, experts at the time claimed that most grain farmers had withheld at least part of their crops, which had helped to bring prices up just as Congress was considering various versions of a farm bill. In the end, they got an emergency assistance act that increased price supports by only 11 percent and extended credit to farmers in jeopardy of losing their farms. It amounted to applying a Band-Aid when a tourniquet was needed.[39]

The AAM retreated from Washington disillusioned. Some went home angry, feeling as though the federal government had ignored them. Others charged that the farmers had not done enough to convince the public and Congress of the seriousness of the financial crisis facing them.

Many just wanted to get back to their farms and get back to work. The farm strike fizzled. AAM organizers, meanwhile, set about planning for the following January.

In 1979, farmers once again began the new year with a massive presence in Washington, as some thirty-five hundred farmers came from all over the country, again driving tractors, pickup trucks, and motor homes—but this time they were not so polite. They deliberately blocked traffic, drove onto the National Mall—causing millions of dollars in damage—and into the Reflecting Pool, and tossed a goat over the fence at the White House. Later, after getting bad press in *The Washington Post*, a hundred farmers drove their tractors to the *Post*'s offices and burned stacks of the paper on the sidewalk while a delegation met with the editors. It did little to improve the movement's now-soured image. Almost all mainstream press reports now cast the farmers as being overly aggressive and destructive; reporters routinely claimed that farm income was up in 1978 (true enough, given the rise in prices) and that protests were driven by a minority of "unwise farmers" who had taken on too much debt and "militants" driven by greed. Likewise, they now mocked the notion of parity as "antiquated" and sure to drive retail food prices up.

Combined with images of unruly farmers trashing the Mall, such critiques devastated any public support the farmers may have had. With the farmers' second retreat from D.C., some experts not only declared the farm movement dead but argued that mass protest in general had "simply gone out of style." The national environment had changed. The era of idealism that made so many believe in mass mobilizations for civil rights and peace had given way to an era of confusion. "The country is in kind of a testy mood right now," Congressman John Brademas told a reporter. "I don't think people like to be threatened, and protest tactics can backfire." As Michael Cole of the lobbying group Common Cause said, "The only way to win is to develop the capacity to do things on the inside. Things don't happen solely because outraged people show up in Washington. That doesn't mean the end of demonstrations, but you have to do both."[40]

Such observations reflected competing tendencies in the AAM, and the movement soon split. One faction, keeping the AAM name, became in effect a political action committee (PAC) and, disgusted with the Carter administration's handling of farm issues, threw its support behind Ronald Reagan in the 1980 election. The other faction, known as

Grassroots AAM, made up mostly of the so-called "militants," continued to plan demonstrations, mostly at the local level. In the estimation of some scholars, the AAM failed, ultimately, to translate its policy ideas into "a coherent proposal"; the notion of parity never got traction with the public. Soon it did not matter. The Fed's 1979 restriction of the monetary supply caused farmland values to fall, and President Carter's grain embargo on the Soviet Union following the invasion of Afghanistan cut into farm income. By the early 1980s, with a new administration proving equally, if not more, hostile to farmers and with waves of foreclosures spreading like dust clouds across the prairie, the family farm movement turned from abstract pricing theory to a plea to call off the banks.[41]

Once it became clear that Reaganomics could not stop farm values and farm commodity prices from nose-diving, the Reagan administration blamed the farmers for their own problems. "For the life of me," an exasperated David Stockman, the budget director, complained, "I can't figure out why taxpayers have the responsibility to go in and refinance bad debt willingly incurred by consenting adults who went out and bought farmland when prices were going up and thought they could get rich." President Reagan himself pledged to eliminate farm subsidies altogether, blaming them for creating a culture of "dependency on the Federal Government" and thus "weakening incentives for self-reliance." He also suggested that only a small minority of farmers were facing severe financial distress and implied that that was their own doing. Reagan's agriculture secretary, John Block, declared that the administration would "allow supply and demand to determine price," bringing about "market clearing." Farm advocates called it "farmer clearing," given the acceleration of foreclosures it would unleash.[42]

Most American farmers responded to the president's implicit likening of farm subsidies to welfare checks as an Iowa farmer, Myrna Harms, did: "We don't want a handout," she said. "We want to be producers." Indeed, as one scholar has more recently noted, "AAM members did not want subsidies. In fact, they felt that, given the low prices that they have historically received, it was the farmer that was subsidizing the American public's access to cheap food." For farmers, there was no difference between their seeking a fair price and industrial workers' seeking a living wage. Most of all, they wanted to keep their farms and their way of life, and by the early 1980s, even that was moving out of reach for tens of thousands of families.[43] Indeed, as early as 1981, the U.S. Department of Agriculture predicted the end of the family farm. In less than twenty years, the USDA accurately anticipated, more than a million farmers (about half the total at the time) "will be driven from the land"; predicting the triumph of industrial farming, it added that "only 1 percent of the remaining operators will possess half the nation's arable land and food supply." The implications for both rural communities and food quality have been profound.[44]

Since farmers typically used their land as collateral for their loans, the declining value of their land turned once-sound loans into bad loans. The FmHA and other lenders brought the farm crisis home in the form of countless foreclosures. A class action lawsuit earned farmers an early reprieve, at least from the FmHA. A judge ruled in November 1983 that the FmHA must suspend all foreclosures "until it developed regulations allowing borrowers to defer loan payments in the event of uncontrollable circumstances and for a neutral mediator to hear their case before liquidation procedures could begin." That moratorium lasted until 1988, but it did not help farmers facing foreclosure from lenders other than the FmHA.[45]

On another front, by 1985, farm advocates succeeded in pressuring farm country representatives in Congress to put forward a Farm Policy Reform Bill that would introduce a system for controlling surplus production: farmers would accept the elimination of federal farm subsidies in return for a new system that kept prices stable. The specifics of the bill emerged from a series of hearings organized by Jim Hightower and Jim Nichols—the Texas and Minnesota agricultural commissioners, respectively—and held around the country in 1983 and 1984. The testimony heard at those hearings formed the basis for legislation that effectively "called for a more planned agricultural economy, a more environmentally sound agriculture, and an end to trade wars." In support of the bill, activists organized massive rallies in farm country. In St. Paul, Minnesota, seventeen thousand people converged on the state capitol (thirty-four school districts canceled classes for the day so students could join their families at the rally). Another fifteen thousand turned out in Ames, Iowa, for a rally at Iowa State University's basketball arena. In St. Paul, the farmers demanded state legislation, too, including a moratorium on foreclosures and extension of emergency credit; in Ames, at the

National Crisis Action Rally, one speaker lamented that the rally could turn out to be a "funeral ceremony for our American dream" if Congress and the president did not push through the farm policy bill. Signs in the crowd read SAVE THE HEART OF AMERICA and DOESN'T ANYBODY HEAR US? and a group of farmers hanged Budget Director David Stockman in effigy.[46] After both the House and the Senate passed a separate bill to provide emergency funding for the planting season, however, the national press again turned on the farmers—"No one ordered them to double their debts in a decade," a *New York Times* editorial chided—and President Reagan vetoed it with flair, lumping it into a category with all other "needless" spending. "I will veto again and again until spending is brought under control," Reagan blustered, making no mention of the ballooning defense budget. Soon after, at a public appearance, the president joked that America "should keep the grain and export the farmers," and the sky seemed to darken over farm families everywhere. Senator Tom Harkin responded by planting 250 crosses, each one representing a failed farm, in Lafayette Park, across the street from the White House.[47]

In this climate, although some farmers still campaigned for parity, the politics of the family farm became something more primal. What mattered now was simply holding on to the farms—clinging to the land and a way of life. In reality, farm organizers possessed few tools to fend off the banks, but the few they used made for high drama. In Minnesota, organizers brought back the Depression-era tactics of the "penny auction" and the sit-in with some success and set an example for the rest of the country. Even though Gerald and Alicia Kohnen had never missed a payment on their award-winning dairy farm, in 1982 they received a foreclosure notice from the First State Bank of Paynesville. The bank claimed that "declines in local farmland values had devalued the collateral and jeopardized the security of the loans," and since there was a "payable on demand" clause in most farm loan contracts, the bank demanded repayment of the whole loan. Knowing that no farmer could pay it, the bank prepared to auction off the farm and all of the equipment on it. In response, on the morning of the proposed auction, August 26, 1982, dozens of farm folk mobilized by Citizens Organized Acting Together (formed in 1979 and known locally as COACT) turned up at the Kohnens' farm. They were "determined to convince potential buyers not to bid anything higher than a nickel or a dollar" for anything. The auctioneer, rattled, called off the auction. Two years later, as the lender pressed on with its liquidation plans, COACT filled the bank with protesters. This action produced massive media coverage, particularly when the police finally came and arrested thirty-seven people. The bank's determination was shaken. Ultimately, it agreed to renegotiate the loan, "settling for a $50,000 buyout on a $137,000 obligation." The Kohnens managed then to find another lender to keep them and their farm afloat. In the aftermath, the sympathetic sheriff asked the county to buy a bus because he figured there would be many more such protests and he would need it for mass arrests.[48]

The Kohnens' battle to save their farm served as a model for other farmers who found themselves in similar circumstances, and although there was no hiding the fact that these were acts of desperation, they offered a morsel of hope where there had been none. By 1985, "farm gate defenses" and No Sale auctions garnered headlines from a more sympathetic national press. In Toledo, Iowa, two hundred protesters showed up at the county courthouse, and although they could not stop the Federal Land Bank from proceeding with the sale of a farm, activists drove fifty crosses into the ground: twenty-five were painted white to represent farmers driven out of business by the current crisis, and twenty-five red crosses represented those believed to be "slowly bleeding to death." This symbolism of the death of the family farm rivaled photos of tractorcades as the enduring image of the farm crisis.[49]

That imagery was accompanied by a narrative that held Washington responsible for the plight of family farms. In one widely covered story, nearly a thousand protesters gathered outside the Clinton County Courthouse in Plattsburgh, Missouri, to try to stop the sale of Perry Wilson's farm, foreclosed upon by the St. Louis Federal Land Bank. Wilson, who started farming in 1933, had 820 acres, 700 of which were up for sale in March 1985. Eighteen months earlier, he had missed a payment—the first time in fifty-one years—and now he faced losing his farm. His son, Perry Wilson Jr., pointed to President Reagan (who had just vetoed the Farm Policy Reform Act) as the main culprit. "Nobody, none of these farmers are asking for a forgiveness of this debt," he said. If the president and Congress would give the farmers a decent price—if they doubled the price of wheat, it would raise the cost of a loaf of bread by only three cents—all of the farmers would "pay these debts off." Instead, Reagan administration policy "hasn't been [designed] to help the farmer, it's been to screw him right into the ground off his land." When "people are losing their homes and farms" and "rural towns are disposed of one by one,"

Wilson said, and Reagan does nothing to get farmers a decent price, "there's something wrong with that man. He's got a heart of stone." More ominously, Perry Jr. described "them"—government officials—in ways that echoed the worldview of the emerging militia movement. Congress and the president are "controlling things," he said, but "they want to do away with private ownership in this country. That's all there is to it. They're taking away what our forefathers fought for and our freedom in this country. It's no accident. And the people are getting tired of it. They're getting tired of it."

Outside the courthouse, the sheriff said that he had "worked all week to get this sale called off" but the bank had "stood firm." When the trustee charged with conducting the sale stepped outside to begin, protesters shouted "No sale! No sale!" for twenty minutes, and a scuffle broke out. Police arrested some of them, but shortly, the trustee and the sheriff's men retreated into the building as the crowd cheered. Ultimately, however, the Wilson family lost its entire farm; Perry Sr. moved into a nursing home and Perry Jr. went to work for another farmer.[50]

In another Depression-era tactic, farmers sat in at the USDA office in Chillicothe, Missouri, for months in the spring of 1986. In their view, farmers and industrial workers belonged to a single class of discarded American producers. Some two hundred farmers, many of them on tractors, rolled into the USDA parking lot in frustration that no FmHA official would field their complaints about a hostile FmHA county supervisor. Their immediate concerns were local, but they saw their plight as part of a national pattern of the powerful neglecting and taking advantage of the less powerful. All they wanted, they said, was a fair price, the way industrial workers deserved fair pay. One organizer, Charlie Peniston, had visited Austin, Minnesota, during the Hormel strike and saw an affinity with the striking P-9 workers: "Hormel had the nerve to ask them for a 23 percent pay cut," he explained. "You got to realize Hormel made profits of $84.6 million in the last quarter of 1985. And they did that by stealing hogs from the farmers and labor from the laborers." And yet, in Washington, he said, the president seemed interested only in helping companies, the banks, and defense manufacturers. The epic sit-in brought the Reverend Jesse Jackson, the civil rights leader and presidential candidate, to Chillicothe for a rally that attracted more than four thousand people; weeks later, John Cougar Mellencamp gave a concert to ten thousand there.[51]

In spite of Hollywood filmmakers' efforts to publicize the farm crisis through films like *Country*, a general sense that most Americans knew more about the famine in Ethiopia than the dislocation and deprivation in American farm country led Willie Nelson and Illinois governor Jim Thompson to organize the first Farm Aid concert. Nelson, who grew up on a Texas cotton farm, first got the idea for Farm Aid when he heard Bob Dylan make an offhand remark about not forgetting the American farmer during the July 13, 1985, Live Aid concerts for Ethiopian famine relief. With Governor Thompson's help, Nelson lined up a venue in the nation's heartland, the 78,000-seat Memorial Stadium at the University of Illinois in Champaign, for a show Nelson organized in roughly six weeks. Subtitled "A Concert for America"—perhaps to distinguish it from Live Aid's concert for Africa—the show featured an improbable collection of fifty-four country and rock acts, playing to a capacity crowd (tickets were $17.50) in a fourteen-hour show, broadcast live on the Nashville Network (TNN), then a fledgling cable station reaching 24 million households. Country music stars such as Loretta Lynn, Merle Haggard, Waylon Jennings, Johnny Cash and June Carter Cash, George Jones, Charlie Daniels, Glen Campbell, and Nelson himself appeared on a rotating stage—for quick transitions between artists—with rock and pop royalty such as Bob Dylan, Neil Young, the Beach Boys, and Joni Mitchell; blues giants B.B. King and Bonnie Raitt; underground and punk rockers Lou Reed, X, and the Blasters; and mainstream stars like John Cougar Mellencamp, Billy Joel, Carole King, John Denver, Eddie Van Halen, Rickie Lee Jones, the Beach Boys, Foreigner, Randy Newman, and John Fogerty, among others. Volunteers in Nebraska answered phone calls to take pledges during the concert and ultimately collected $10 million.[52]

The Farm Aid concert stoked the continuing debates about who was responsible for the farm crisis and what should be done about it. Some mocked the $10 million raised as barely a drop in the bucket of the $215 billion national farm debt and dismissed the concert's consciousness-raising efforts as rationalizing a dismal haul of money. A *New York Times* editorial again dismissed American farmers as a special interest and reduced Farm Aid to "one of the biggest and best-covered lobbying efforts in history." Calls to save the family farm were wrongheaded, the paper suggested, when "the American farm sector must shrink" if the structural problems of farm "overcapacity and overproduction" were to be overcome in the interest of the rest of the economy. And as the anthropolo-

gist Kathryn Dudley found, some farmers in her Minnesota cohort—the
ones who were critical of farm activists generally—regarded the "public
cup-rattling" of Farm Aid as an insult to farmers. Organizers in the family farm movement, however, reached a decidedly different verdict. As
one Iowa activist put it, "The reality is that when Willie Nelson and the
other performers at Farm Aid got up and talked about the crisis in American agriculture and the countryside, people listened." Over the next
twenty years, Farm Aid raised $27 million for family farms.[53]

By looking at the farm crisis at a macro level, *The New York Times* and
the president—who essentially shared the view that farm supports should
be eliminated altogether—missed the fiercely local, micro-level perspective of farm politics. The two camps just talked past each other. In the
communities devastated by farm foreclosures and the attendant business
failure, only the view from the farm porches and coffee shops truly mattered. As a result, the most vital political organizing in the heartland involved helping farmers cope with the financial and emotional stress that
the crisis inevitably caused.[54]

By the mid-1980s, as local organizing turned from lobbying for higher
commodity prices to No Sale auctions and sit-ins, many involved found
themselves providing a variety of services to farmers in trouble. Increasingly, the national press picked up on groups like the Iowa Farm Unity
Coalition, Minnesota Farm Advocates, the Kansas Rural Center, the Wisconsin Farm Unity Alliance, and the Missouri Rural Crisis Center (and
countless others), approvingly noting the practical work these groups
did. Formed out of necessity, organizations in each place became aware
of their counterparts in other states and began helping one another out.

The Iowa Farm Unity Coalition (IFUC) "assembled one of the most
comprehensive sets of services," but in some ways it was the least typical.
For one thing, IFUC grew directly out of the New Left–influenced Rural
America, and it operated alongside Prairiefire Rural Action, a church-
based advocacy group. The Reverend David Ostendorf, the director of
Prairiefire and former director of the Midwest office of Rural America,
played a vital role in IFUC from the start. IFUC went out of its way to
"restrain tempers and violence" and any hints of the kind of radical
rhetoric or action that had backfired on the AAM. As a result, it built
a "loosely knit, locally controlled network of farm activists" and, as one
political scientist noted, did not "impose rigid discipline on the rank and
file." In turn, it won the support of Iowa churches that had a tradition of

political engagement as well as the state's union members, particularly
the United Auto Workers, most of whom worked for "agricultural implement manufacturers." In addition to organizing farm gate defenses,
sit-ins, and other protests, IFUC distinguished itself through its social
services: working through local ministers and churches, it helped to form
support groups for emotionally distressed farm folk, got food stamps for
those struggling to put food on the table, and established a Farm Survival Hotline. The hotline effectively built a network of farmers, as callers
were put in touch with other farmers who had faced similar financial or
legal challenges; in time, those farmers often became the next cohort to
man the telephones. In the meantime, accountants and lawyers made
themselves available to farmers referred via the hotline. Although some
hardliners criticized IFUC for focusing its efforts on services rather than
more overtly political protest, IFUC's approach gave it a measure of legitimacy among farm families, the media, and policymakers that the
AAM, for example, had found impossible to secure.[55]

The Minnesota Farm Advocates began with Lou-Anne Kling, who,
with her husband, Wayne, farmed soybeans, corn, and wheat and ran
a "farrow-to-finish" hog operation on their 160-acre farm near Granite
Falls (Wayne also farmed another three hundred acres with his father).
She first tried her hand at political organizing when prices dropped so
low that they feared losing their farm. Lou-Anne and her husband signed
up another twenty farmers for a July 4 Farmers' Independence Day protest, during which they planned to plow under one acre of small grain
and then do the same thing each day for a week, "to show that it was
cheaper for us to plow it under as green manure than it was to harvest it."
But when July 4 came, only a few others plowed under their crops. The
protest was a bust. Since "organizing farmers is like trying to haul frogs
in a wheelbarrow," she later said, she turned to electoral politics and ran
for the state legislature in 1982. She lost the election, but along the way
she found that farmers gravitated to her, and some sought her help on
their individual cases. In response, she and another farmer undertook an
informational tour to tell farmers about their rights with the FmHA and
other lenders. Soon the demand for her advice grew to the point that the
Wheat Growers Association gave her an office in St. Paul. "People were
lined up in the hallway," she later recalled. "It was just such a desperation
for knowledge! . . . I could only spend half an hour or forty-five minutes
with them. They'd lay their paperwork out, and we'd go through it quick.

I'd say, 'Try this and this and this,' and they'd be off." In time, she went to the state legislature and showed them a map indicating all the places in Minnesota where she had advised farmers, urging them to set up a program to help the thousands of other farmers she had not yet met. The legislature allocated $102,000 for her to start up Minnesota Farm Advocates with a staff of thirty-five, many of whom were women farmers from the northwest who farmed all day and then worked the phones all night. Advocacy programs in other parts of the country tried to emulate Kling's Minnesota example; by 1988, Kling had trained advocates in similar programs in sixteen states.[56]

Minnesota farmers could also turn to Groundswell, a nonpartisan grassroots jack-of-all-protests organization that grew out of the 1985 St. Paul farm bill rally. Funded by contributions and grants, Groundswell organized No Sale rallies and sit-ins but also engaged in lobbying the Minnesota legislature on farm policy; additionally, it raised money to provide direct relief to farmers faced with medical costs or household bills and published a newsletter that it distributed to fifteen hundred people. Some of the membership in Groundswell overlapped with the Farm Advocates, and each organization served to support the other.[57]

In the next state over, the Wisconsin Farm Unity Alliance, which functioned much like Groundswell, organizing direct action as well as lobbying, did not have to actively recruit advocates because, as in Iowa and Minnesota, farmers aided by the Alliance just stepped forward to help others. Kitty and Reg Pityer lost their farm in Elroy and eventually moved to Viroqua, where they became full-time advocates. The Pityers reported being so overwhelmed with the number of calls that they could not keep up with the demand. In time, farmers who were turned away on the phone asked if they could help by taking calls.[58] In western Kansas, the Kansas Rural Center began a training program for advocates. After identifying farmers who would like to do more, the KRC would recruit groups of twenty-five or so and bring them to a meeting and, with the help of the Pioneer Seed Company, pay for their meals and lodging. In a series of presentations, the advocates-in-training heard from bankruptcy lawyers, experienced advocates such as Lou-Anne Kling, and other experts on the various problems facing Kansas farmers.

In all of these states, organizations that responded to the needs of the local farm community also thrived thanks to the cross-pollination of ideas from activists and advocates in other states. Social movement scholars label this phenomenon "diffusion," but what it meant was that the front porch perspective not only let farmers see encroaching threats, it also helped them to see solutions that others (though typically not the government) had come up with.[59]

To some, this advocacy work may not have seemed like political work, but to the farmers themselves, any such distinction would have seemed laughable. The various crisis centers and hotlines may have directed all of their energy toward social services, but in practice they represented a community under siege—not unlike antibusing advocates, Love Canal residents, or Rust Belt steelworkers. Working to save a community using any and all tools available was a fundamentally political act, even if most policymakers, Reagan administration officials, and big-city newspaper editors didn't grasp the political case that was being made.

In Missouri, where Roger Allison became something of a local legend for standing up to the FmHA and beating the agency in court, the Missouri Rural Crisis Center represented a microcosm of such political action. A decorated Vietnam veteran, Allison rose to prominence in October 1980 when he physically stood in the way of FmHA officials foreclosing on his father's neighboring farm; he was arrested for his pains, and two weeks later the FmHA county supervisor notified him that he wanted to review Allison's files. "We're gonna sell you out," he said to Allison, and in April 1981, the foreclosure notice arrived. But Allison sued in federal court and won. *Allison v. Block*, a landmark court ruling, compelled the FmHA to give borrowers the opportunity to seek deferrals of their loan principals and interest. "I just want to go back to my farm and farm. I want my dad to be able to farm," Allison told an interviewer. "And I want anybody else that wants to farm to have that opportunity to do it." Allison therefore started the Missouri Rural Crisis Center in October 1985 and, funded by various social justice foundations and Farm Aid, organized job training for nonfarm work; mental health outreach programs; information services for legal and financial advice; and youth services. "We organize farmers, and we coordinate," Allison affirmed. "And we encourage—we don't discourage—farmers to stand together to take control of their lives because there isn't a lot of time left."[60]

Four months after President Reagan's veto of the 1985 farm reform bill, representatives of many of these service organizations, as well as others, met in Des Moines, where they formed the National Save the Family Farm Coalition (NSFFC). Bolstered by the credibility and legitimacy that social service missions brought to so many farm organizations, the NSFFC championed the 1986 effort to pass the Save the Family Farm Act as well as farm credit reform in 1987. By 1988, when the coalition included thirty-seven organizations in twenty-two states, the FmHA changed course and wrote off $7 billion in farm debt, thus allowing a hundred thousand farmers the chance to keep farming. On the other hand, the Reagan administration waited until the November election had passed and then served foreclosure notices on eighty thousand farmers with delinquent FmHA loans. No amount of organizing, local or national, could stop those notices—though, thanks to the Allison suit, the farmers held the right to seek loan deferrals or restructuring.[61]

Although some scholars have credited the family farm movement with isolating the supporters of free markets and holding off a more calamitous collapse of family farms, that is setting a pretty low standard for success. In fact, the legislative victories of the time—such as the Food Security Act of 1985, which resulted in substantial increases in federal aid—mostly helped agribusiness and served to postpone the collapse that finally came in the 1990s. Indeed, despite the NSFFC's best efforts, grassroots organizing could not beat back the influence of agribusiness when it tried to pass the Save the Family Farm Act. Had it been enacted, that law would have stabilized prices, set up a structure allowing producers to control supply, and helped to restructure the debts of many financially distressed farmers. But agribusiness likes oversupply and low prices because it fosters cutthroat competition among small producers that makes those operations vulnerable to takeover. Archer Daniels Midland, ConAgra, and Cargill triumphed in the 1980s and ultimately in the 1990s thanks to "vertical integration"—buying up and merging with small farms and other companies in the food delivery chain. They also engaged in intense lobbying and made large donations to legislators. By 1996, as Thomas Frank noted in *What's the Matter with Kansas?*, the so-called Freedom to Farm Act basically put an end to certain price supports, ended subsidies for taking acreage out of production, and rolled back federal regulations. The multinational agribusiness industry could not have done a better job of writing the law themselves. The family farm was all but finished.[62]

The 1970s and 1980s may have marked the last great grassroots mobilization of American farmers. While the twentieth century began with 39 percent of Americans living on farms, it ended with only 1.5 percent living on farms; and with most Americans giving little thought to where their food comes from before it arrives at the supermarket, any future mass mobilization around farm politics seems a distant dream.[63]

Yet the family farm movement represents a rich and varied local political experience that is at odds with the widespread view that the heartland has always been almost uniformly conservative. Examining colors on a map misses not only the substantial support that the Reverend Jesse Jackson had in farm country but also the fringe elements that gravitated to supporting the extremist presidential candidacies of Lyndon La-Rouche and wound up in militias in the 1990s. Both camps were motivated by seeing a federal government that had once worked with farmers now setting them adrift. Both took this abandonment personally, because the threats from the banks and Washington were not abstract; they met them at their farm gate as they stood on soil that some of their families had tilled for more than a century. The appeal of Jesse Jackson and Lyndon LaRouche to farmers did not, therefore, lie in the soundness of their political proposals so much as in the exhaustion of any other perceived viable options. In the end, though, few placed much hope in electoral solutions. The only option that made sense in the day-to-day of the farm crisis was organizing from one's front porch. For more than a decade, tens (if not hundreds) of thousands of farmers sustained a political movement on the national stage and, most important, kept hope alive for countless farm families at the local level.[64]

9

Revolts at Home

●

Away from the rural heartland, in the nation's burgeoning suburbs, the sense of achievement and entitlement that comes with home ownership did much to shape the American political landscape in the 1970s and 1980s. Homeowners felt under siege, sometimes from bureaucrats and judges crafting solutions to inequality but also from sources like the oil crisis (which drove up the cost of home heating fuel), inflation, and taxes. What often gets ignored in accounts of the so-called "tax revolt" of the late 1970s, however, is that tenants felt the financial pinch as much as or more than homeowners, and like homeowners, they organized into countless social movements in cities across the country.

In some respects, homeowners who voted for lower property taxes and tenants' rights activists (many of whom aspired to home ownership, after all) sang from the same song sheet. Homeowners and tenants both criticized high housing costs and other threats to their household economies; their causes (like those of farmers and farmworkers), however, were sometimes pitted against each other; for instance, landlords who benefited from tax rollbacks sparked rent strikes when they did not pass savings along to tenants. And then there were the truly poor who, without the means to either buy or rent, took to squatting and homesteading in the thousands of city-owned vacant buildings in urban centers all over the country.

The tax revolt of the late 1970s and early 1980s has long been read as evidence of the death of liberalism and the dawn of the Reagan Revolution and the rise of conservatism. Accepting the views of pundits at the time, and indeed the rhetoric of tax revolt leaders, most Americans have assumed that homeowners voting for lower taxes were in fact rebelling against government. When Proposition 13, a tax limitation referendum, passed by two to one in a California statewide vote, journalists like Tom Wicker of *The New York Times* called it a "new revolution" representing a "massive rejection of liberal government as it had developed in the post–New Deal era." Or, as another commentator put it, "What happened is not so much a tax revolt as an anti-government-big-spending revolt." President Carter himself sighed that he saw Proposition 13 as "an accurate expression of, first of all, the distrust of government." But they—and the scholars and latter-day activists who have followed—misread what was behind the tax revolt.[1]

The tax revolt was neither a grassroots uprising nor actually anti-government. Although statewide ballot initiatives mobilized a great many homeowners to vote against higher property taxes, in state after state the vote tally resulted not from genuine grassroots organizing but from its well-crafted *appearance*. As one political scientist has noted, these were "faux populist moments" that shared certain traits: "A tax crusader, acting as a populist entrepreneur," managed to get a tax limitation initiative on the ballot; aside from signing petitions and then coming out to vote, ordinary citizens did not mobilize as, say, farmers or steelworkers did when they acted directly, and in concert, in political action; and although the leading tax crusaders relied on populist rhetoric, the campaigns themselves were driven, organizationally and financially, by "vested special interests" that relied mostly on expensive television and direct mail appeals to win voters.[2] The recognition by vested interests that it was effective to sell their political cause as if organized by taxpayers from the bottom up reflected the fact that front porch politics had truly arrived. At the same time, this co-optation was an early indicator of front porch politics' decline: savvy political operators saw in the emotional power of front porch claims a ticket to contrived authenticity. The mad-as-hell stance, righteous and indignant, could easily be adapted to make a cause look like a broad-based movement.

Such nongrassroots efforts did, of course, win voters to the cause. But recent scholarship shows that homeowners voted for tax limits not because they wanted smaller government but because they wanted a return to the system of informal government subsidies that had kept their taxes low in the pre-stagflation era. In California, the state most associated with the tax revolt, the homeowner vote to limit property taxes originated in what one historian calls the "breakdown of a decades-old 'compact' between homeowners, industry, and city governments." As the state's population doubled between 1950 and 1970, "growth liberalism"—the use of state power "to create, subsidize, and stabilize private markets"— defined the age. In practice, this meant that middle-class Californians got used to a system in which federal agencies underwrote mortgages and took steps to keep undesirables (i.e., the poor, working class, and minorities) out, and in which new industry provided enough munici-pal revenue via taxes "that the homeowner property tax rate could be kept reasonably low." Residents understood that industry thus paid for schools, fueled job growth, and kept individual taxes down. This infor-mal subsidy for the middle class was made even more uneven by unscru-pulous local assessors who assessed homes at a fraction of their value in an implicit trade for votes or campaign contributions. Others gave low assessments for bribes. When, in the 1960s, courts began to find such practices to be discriminatory, reforms standardized tax rates at a per-centage of a home's assessed value. Fair enough—until inflation in the 1970s drove housing values through the roof, and with them property taxes. Stripped of the informal tax privileges, middle-class voters went to the polls to demand their restoration. Far from revolting against govern-ment, voters were in fact appealing to government to act as usual and protect them from the volatility of the market.[3]

While the tax revolt movement is associated with the rise of the right, the first protests against rising property taxes tended to have New Left origins. In Illinois in the 1950s and 1960s, for example, the Cook County assessor calculated homeowners' assessments in inverse proportion to their contributions to Chicago mayor Richard J. Daley's Democratic Party machine. Citizens Action Program (CAP)—which started as Citizens Against Pollution—found, in the course of campaigning for cleaner air, that U.S. Steel's South Works plant was "scandalously underassessed." Most CAP members were low- and moderate-income homeowners, but its main organizers, Leonard Dubi and Paul Booth, had been student activists (Booth was an original signer of the Port Huron Statement, the founding document of Students for a Democratic Society). Protests led to reforms—a modernized, computerized assessment program that played no favorites—but property taxes still went up, driven by inflation. To keep elderly homeowners from having to sell their homes, CAP successfully lobbied the legislature to pass a tax credit for them. Similarly, in Massachusetts, Mass Fair Share not only worked on insurance and utility issues but campaigned through local chapters set up primarily in working-class neighborhoods to lower property taxes for homeowners and shift the burden to businesses. Here again, key organizers Mark Splain and Michael Ansara came out of the welfare rights and SDS movements, respectively, but, like CAP, they worked with a growing army of first-time activists outraged that their taxes were rising when so many corporations were millions of dollars in arrears on their own state and local taxes. When Fair Share won legislative passage of a bill that would have preserved tax privileges for homeowners, Democratic governor Michael Dukakis vetoed it. In the early 1970s, real grassroots credibility marked the first efforts to confront the property tax problem. California changed all that.[4]

In California, as in most of the country, tax policy rarely showed up as a political issue prior to the late 1960s. With the economy chugging along, most Americans paid their taxes without complaint. It seemed that the American economy provided enough to go around—including to the government, which most people trusted to put the money to good use. But by 1978, anger over taxes had been building for more than a decade. Trouble began with a series of corruption scandals in which either whistleblowers or investigators found that elected tax assessors engaged in a variety of unscrupulous practices, including taking bribes to keep assessments on business properties down. In response, the state assembly passed modernizing legislation to centralize, professionalize, and standardize assessment practices. The implementation of standardized assessment at precisely the moment when inflation, invisible and inscrutable, took home prices into the stratosphere resulted in every property, home or business, being "reassessed every three years at 25 percent of market value"—much higher than usual. Most California homeowners felt as though a phantom pickpocket had relieved them of their wallets altogether. BRING BACK THE CROOKED ASSESSOR! bumper stickers could be seen on cars up and down the state.[5]

Many Californians had been lured to the state by the promise of an affordable American dream, but by the early 1970s, the dream was dying. As the California journalist Peter Schrag notes, only a generation before, in the 1950s, one could buy a three-bedroom, two-bath home built in a former citrus grove for $14,000 (with a mortgage payment of $70 a month). By the early 1970s, the value of those homes had increased substantially, even before inflation sent prices even higher. "For nearly two decades it was lovely to see what had been a $12,000 tract house go up to $30,000," Schrag later wrote. "But when it doubled again to $60,000, or tripled to $90,000, and the taxes went with it, it was fun no longer." Inflation saw the average price of a Los Angeles single-family house jump 120 percent in value, from $37,800 to $83,200. It became common, therefore, to see property taxes on a two-bedroom house spike from $400 a year to $1,200. Suddenly, the prospect of losing one's home, particularly for the elderly and others on fixed incomes, became very real.[6] In states that had enacted property tax classification laws, in which business and residential property tax rates were standardized but at different rates depending on the classification, the consequences were less dire. Minnesota tax laws, for example, included thirty-one separate classifications for property taxes, and consequently, Minnesota saw no tax revolt. By the time California voters passed Proposition 13, seven other states had passed classification laws.

Homeowners in California, as in many other states, just wanted relief—and quickly. Recognizing that the housing market and inflation drove up home prices and thus their taxes, they did not attack government so much as appeal to it to ease their pain. For many ordinary Americans, the expectation that the government was there to help them had not died. In the early 1970s, property tax protesters across America came from both the left and the right and sought either a rollback of taxes to previous rates or an abolition of them altogether. Activists lobbied legislatures most frequently for "circuit breaker" laws that would essentially graduate the property tax according to income level; thus, if assessments took a homeowner's property tax too high relative to her income, a "circuit breaker" would cut the tax off. These laws varied from state to state, and they could be very complicated, but by 1978, thirty-one states had passed them. Most of California's first property tax protesters sought only a rollback of reassessments, but in time the veterans of the civil rights and welfare rights movements who founded the Citizen Action League (CAL) lobbied for a circuit breaker law called the Tax Justice Act. If passed, the law would have extended the circuit breaker to anyone with household income under $30,000 a year. Unions and other progressive groups endorsed it, and some protests—such as the April 20, 1977, demonstration in Redwood City at which fifteen senior citizens burned their assessment notices—got considerable media attention. Critics claimed that the legislation was too complicated. The bill fell six votes short in the assembly in September.[7]

By the time the circuit breaker law failed, other parties were well on their way to circumventing the legislature by getting a tax limitation referendum on the ballot. Although President William Howard Taft had long ago offered a biting critique of ballot initiatives as easily "adapted to the exaltation of cranks and the wearying of the electorate," California required only 8 percent of voters' signatures to get a measure on the ballot.[8] Those who favored initiatives argued that even if they fail, they often prompt productive debate and reform; critics, however, saw them as easily abused by powerful interests.

Howard Jarvis had no difficulty enlisting such interests even as he succeeded in casting himself to the public and media as an everyman. Born in a Utah mining town, Jarvis came from a hardscrabble background and built his fortune from scratch. An accomplished athlete, he played semiprofessional baseball and fought twenty-one professional boxing matches before he bought a small newspaper that he expanded (while he was still in his twenties) into a chain. Following the Second World War, he built his fortune in California after starting an appliance factory; when he sold the factory in 1962, he devoted himself to Republican Party politics full-time, describing himself as a "rugged bastard who's had his head kicked in a thousand times by the government." Richard Reeves called Jarvis "the last angry man."[9]

Jarvis tried for years to get a tax reform initiative on the ballot, but it took until 1977 for him to succeed. He joined forces with Paul Gann, a former car and real estate salesman from Sacramento who had started People's Advocate as a neighborhood crime watch group that in time turned its attention to taxes; Gann, too, had failed to get enough signatures for a ballot initiative. By 1977, the year that CAL's circuit breaker law just missed passage, times had changed. Inflation, a still-troubled economy, and Governor Jerry Brown's failure to deliver on promised tax relief set the stage. Gann and Jarvis split the state—Gann took the north and Jarvis the south—and started gathering signatures one more time. They relied primarily on volunteers to collect signatures, but they also benefited from the help of chambers of commerce, real estate agents, and apartment owners (the latter urged tenants to sign with predictions of higher rents if the initiative did not pass). Jarvis became executive director of the Los Angeles Apartment Owners Association and used the association's mailing list to solicit signatures. By December 2, Jarvis alone had collected more than enough—over a million—signatures just in the south. The vote on Proposition 13 was set for June 6, 1978.[10]

The allure of Proposition 13 lay in its simplicity. As written by Jarvis, Proposition 13 would roll back property assessments and freeze them at 1975 levels; the values could then be raised by only 2 percent a year (to account for inflation), and properties could be reassessed only at the time of sale or transfer. All property would then be taxed at a flat 1 percent of its new value, whether based on the annual 2 percent increase or on its recent sale price. Maybe most important (and perhaps most overlooked), Proposition 13 would prohibit any government body—local or state—from raising any new taxes without a two-thirds vote of the governing body. In effect, this new system would mean that an average Los Angeles homeowner paying $2,200 on a $70,000 home in 1977 would see his taxes rolled back to $700 a year, only to rise thereafter at 2 percent per year. That kind of math appealed to a lot of anxious California homeowners.[11]

By brushing off criticism, Jarvis largely succeeded in obscuring the fundamental unfairness of the initiative. He slapped away charges that Prop 13's biggest beneficiaries would be landlords and business property owners who anticipated a savings windfall of $3.5 billion out of a total loss of local tax revenue of $5.5 billion. That is, homeowners, on whose behalf the initiative had allegedly been written, stood to save only $2 billion of the total $5.5 billion in savings. Moreover, since residential properties change hands more frequently than business properties, reassessments at market value were much more likely to happen on homes than on commercial property. Such revaluations of homes, critics pointed out, would also lead to blatantly inconsistent taxation of homeowners living in the same neighborhood where one house might be taxed on its 1975 value, but the house next door, recently sold to a new neighbor, would be taxed on its new market value. Finally, few Californians seemed to grasp that with less property tax to deduct on their federal income tax returns, a significant chunk of their property tax savings would be flipped to Uncle Sam in the form of higher income taxes. Jarvis dismissed any such critique as a "crock of manure" and called his opponents "liars," "dummies, goons, cannibals or big mouths." Gann, for his part, balanced Jarvis's caustic declarations by casting his statements in front porch terms, calling on Californians to "dream the American dream of being safe and secure in our homes."[12]

Some of those who saw Proposition 13 as irresponsible mobilized to put alternatives before the voters. Since the circuit breaker bill had failed, a bipartisan group of state legislators proposed a constitutional amendment that would allow a Minnesota-like classification system. The legislature passed the amendment in February 1978. In order to ratify it, the amendment went on the ballot as Proposition 8, in direct competition with Proposition 13. Complicating matters further, state senator Peter Behr introduced a bill that would cut property taxes for everyone by 30 percent and expand circuit breaker provisions for senior citizens—but only if Proposition 8 passed.[13]

A knock-down, drag-out campaign ensued. If anything, the "No on 13" coalition of teachers, unions, consumers, and good government groups that promoted Prop 8 had more of a grassroots base than the Prop 13 campaign, but that did not stop the media from suggesting the opposite. The press cast Jarvis as leader of a populist uprising and Prop 8 as a government-driven face-saving but too-late effort. Ultimately, Jarvis prevailed. Operating out of the Los Angeles Apartment Owners Association offices, he raised more than $2 million—most of it from apartment owners—and spent it on expensive television ads and direct mail appeals designed to scare already frightened homeowners. A famous television spot featured a jack-in-the-box playing "Pop Goes the Weasel"; as a hand wound the handle and the music played, a voiceover warned that "the politicians have a surprise for you, but they didn't want you to know about it until after the election." When the box popped open, it delivered the revelation that property taxes were about to go up by 100 percent for some homeowners. In one notorious tactic, Jarvis used public records to target homeowners with a direct mail appeal that came in an official-looking envelope, as if from the assessor himself. Inside, Jarvis wrote that he was "shocked to learn" that the recipient's property taxes would double from (here a computer inserted the recipient's actual tax figure for 1977) in the next three years. Despite such underhanded tactics, by April, public opinion polls showed the two propositions running just about even, with some evidence that support for Proposition 13 was beginning to fade.[14]

The turning point came unexpectedly. A new reform-minded assessor in Los Angeles, Alexander Pope, had just completed his first assessment, covering one-third of L.A. County homes. Rather than let taxpayers wait until they got their tax bills at the usual time in October, he announced on May 16—just weeks before the vote on the ballot initiatives—that property owners could visit his offices to learn their new assessments. Then all hell broke loose. It turned out that Jarvis's predictions were not so outrageous after all: the average increase in L.A. County assessments was in fact over 100 percent. Television news cameras captured images of people weeping, screaming in anger, despairing that they would now have to sell their homes because they would not be able to pay the taxes. It did not help that the state of California was flush, with a nearly $6 billion surplus; in the minds of the majority, it seemed the state could weather Prop 13's steep tax cuts.[15]

On June 6, 1978, Californians voted for Proposition 13 by nearly a 2–1 margin, giving it 65 percent of the vote. "Tonight was a victory against money, the politicians, the government," Howard Jarvis crowed. "Government simply must be limited. Excessive taxation leads to either bankruptcy or dictatorship." But as the journalist Robert Kuttner noted shortly thereafter, public opinion polls "did not confirm widespread erosion of public support for government." Save for welfare, "California voters did not want to see public services reduced." Moreover, polls showed that voters distrusted "all remote institutions—big business, big labor, as well as 'big government,'" and that the overwhelming majority simply thought in terms of preserving and protecting their own economic well-being. They understood that "something in the tax system was giving them a good screwing" and they just wanted it to stop.[16]

To call the tax revolt antigovernment is to miss the point. Voters did not approve Prop 13 because they favored tax limitation over, say, classification; rather, they voted for 13 because it offered the most relief, and fast. If CAL's circuit breaker bill had passed nine months earlier, or if Pope had not opened the new assessment figures for public viewing, or if Governor Brown had simply used some of the state surplus to provide tax relief, Proposition 13 would have died on the vine.[17] Anger at the state came second to immediate relief from personal economic hardship. Perversely, Jarvis's pseudo-front-porch tactics prevailed, and in so doing perhaps signaled the eventual demise of front porch politics.

In Proposition 13's aftermath, local government saw more than $6 billion in funding evaporate. The state moved to use its surplus to offset the losses, but even so, municipalities cut services and laid people off. San

Francisco closed twenty-six schools, laid off a thousand teachers, and doubled the mass transit fare to fifty cents. Officials made wholesale cuts to state mental health and developmentally disabled programs, dumping patients into "rooming houses and inadequate nursing homes." Some cities lost their school bus systems and others saw summer school and arts, music, and sports programming cut. Writing twenty years later, Peter Schrag lamented that whereas the state's schools had been "among the most generously funded in the nation," they were now "in the bottom quarter among the states in virtually every major indicator—in their physical condition, in public funding, in test scores." Universities that had once been tuition free became expensive, and the state's infrastructure— the freeway system that had once been the envy of the nation—was "now rated among the most dilapidated road networks in the country." In the meantime, the big winners were the big corporations and commercial property owners: Pacific Telephone saved $130 million; Pacific Gas & Electric, over $90 million; Standard Oil, $13 million in Contra Costa County alone. As critics predicted, the federal government collected 22 percent more in income taxes than it would have if homeowners had been able to claim higher property tax deductions on their federal tax returns; similarly, the state got 14 percent more than it would have before Prop 13. And renters felt hoodwinked. Forty-seven percent of the state's renters, scared by predictions of higher rents if Prop 13 were to fail, voted for the measure, only to find that with the turnover of rental properties, new owners passed their higher tax on to tenants in higher rents.[18]

After Prop 13, democracy in California got knocked off its axis. In a sustained circumvention of representative government, the referendum came to represent "the people." Since Proposition 13, the California state assembly has been largely circumvented by ballot initiatives on nearly every major issue facing the state. As many commentators have noted, referenda only appear populist. They are in practice driven by interest groups with big money, and as one scholar found in a nationwide study, the side that spent the most prevailed 78 percent of the time (though it is worth noting that the November 2012 election saw Californians overturn the two-thirds requirement for a tax increase). Ballot initiative contests rely on very expensive campaigns that pay pollsters, advertising and publicity experts, signature gatherers, and direct mail specialists. The problem with this kind of fake populism is that, as Schrag notes, it is not aimed at improving civic engagement.[19] In that way, such causes are the very opposite of grassroots causes, all the more damning because they can be easily made to look like one.

And that may be the most valuable lesson. The managers of these campaigns recognized as early as 1978 that a broad-based grassroots image affords a level of authenticity and legitimacy that a "special interest" media campaign does not. The crisis of rising property taxes certainly fits the definition of a front porch political issue, but aside from a mass turnout at the polls, it did not lead to even a small-scale front porch political mobilization. What is important in understanding American politics in that era is that it looked as though it did.

The appearance of the people expressing their will en masse drove the national tax revolt narrative that soon swept the nation. Roughly two-thirds of the states had already passed some kind of tax reform law by 1978. In California, they did it by popular vote. In other states, like-minded tax crusaders, seeing a new and sexy way to achieve political change, quickly moved to mimic Jarvis. In Idaho, for example, the retired insurance salesman Don Chance—"the perfect Idaho counterpart to Howard Jarvis," according to one observer—drafted a nearly exact copy of Prop 13, "complete with misspellings and references to provisions that didn't exist in the Idaho constitution," to qualify it for the ballot. It passed by a 60–40 margin.[20]

In Massachusetts and Ohio, citizen groups mounted a variety of tax reform efforts, sometimes with a much broader base of support than in California, but ultimately they were overtaken by the corporate-backed tax revolt fever. For decades, municipalities in the Commonwealth of Massachusetts had taxed industrial and commercial property owners at higher rates than homeowners. In 1979, however, the State Supreme Judicial Court ruled that the system was unfair and ordered that business properties be taxed at no more than 25 percent of their assessed value (the average for residential property). The sudden reduction in commercial and industrial property tax revenue left cities and towns facing huge budget shortfalls, and the only way to make up for it was to raise property taxes on everyone, including homeowners. By 1980, municipalities in Massachusetts (aka "Taxachusetts") took in 53 percent of total revenue from the property tax, second only to Alaska.[21]

Mass Fair Share had turned to the ballot initiative in 1978 after Governor Michael Dukakis vetoed circuit breaker legislation. Joining with mayors from around the state, Fair Share managed to get a classification initiative on the ballot and get it passed two to one by voters despite a well-organized opposition led by Associated Industries of Massachusetts (AIM), a coalition of two thousand companies. But Fair Share faced competition, too, in campaigning for property tax reform. Citizens for Limited Taxation (CLT), founded in 1973 by a handful of libertarian and conservative businessmen, had also been active throughout the 1970s, trying to get an amendment to the state constitution that would limit taxes and state spending. Ideology—more than the acute pain of rising property taxes—drove their legislative agenda. They believed in small government and very limited public spending (one leader, Don Feder, had to step down in 1980 when he said he wanted to eliminate "most public services, including schools, libraries, and fire departments"). Meanwhile, events in California inspired a change of strategy. Soon CLT introduced its own ballot initiative, Proposition 2½, and made common cause with AIM to get it on the ballot. Proposition 2½ called for a cap on property taxes at 2.5 percent and mandated that any municipality presently taxing at higher levels roll back its rate by 15 percent each year until it got down to 2.5 percent. Only a two-thirds popular vote could lift the 2.5 percent cap. "In a year, the scene had changed radically," Robert Kuttner observed. "Where the Left coalition had seized voter grievances in 1978 and made big business the target of popular anger, now the most right-wing of the tax protest groups had the only tax initiative on the ballot."[22]

CLT did not have a cranky Howard Jarvis to lead its campaign, but it did have a kind of proto–soccer mom in Barbara Anderson. A mother and former YMCA swimming instructor, Anderson joined CLT as a volunteer in 1977. By 1980, she took over as executive director. A younger, more attractive version of Jarvis, Anderson became a "darling of the news media." "Our fight is not mainly about money," she declared. "It's about control. *They* have to learn once and for all that it's *our* government." Still, despite Anderson's populist rhetoric and the romantic image of its leader working in a tiny office above a pizza joint, CLT did not mobilize the grass roots. Instead, Anderson courted the Massachusetts High Tech Council (High Tech), a consortium of eighty-six firms that paid for CLT's political consultants and advertising. High Tech argued that it could not attract highly skilled workers to Massachusetts because of the prohibitive property taxes. As in California, however, CLT and High Tech framed "Yes on 2½" as a populist campaign to voters, emphasizing that "100,000 of your friends and neighbors" had put it on the ballot in the first place. It worked. On November 4, 1980, the day the nation elected Ronald Reagan president, Prop 2½ passed by a 59–41 margin. Unlike California, Massachusetts had no budget surplus to bail out the towns and cities, and waves of layoffs and service cuts took place in schools, libraries, and fire and police departments across the commonwealth.[23]

The national news coverage of Prop 2½, coming in the wake of Proposition 13 in California, did a lot to fuel the national perception of a nationwide tax uprising, but it was a mirage. Leaders like Howard Jarvis and Barbara Anderson succeeded in spinning a narrative that explained the ballot results as evidence of a national movement. Americans certainly experienced the bite of rising taxes as an existential threat, and when given the chance, they voted their anger, but if one wanted evidence of a real national uprising over housing, one needed only look to those faced with soaring rents.

Obscured in all of the ink spilled over the tax revolt was the startling fact that the United States of America, the wealthiest and most powerful nation in human history, was in the midst of a housing crisis. A variety of factors had conspired by the late 1970s to drive vacancy rates to all-time lows: the Nixon administration's moratorium on federal housing programs, coupled with inflation driving up the cost of building materials, land, and financing, caused construction of new rental units to grind to a halt—and the soaring purchase price of homes meant that more and more people were competing for rental units. The demand pushed rents to new heights. Some people could not afford to pay and wound up moving in with family and friends or living in shelters or on the street. At exactly the same time, cash-strapped American cities began boarding up thousands of residential properties abandoned by landlords when deindustrialization, suburbanization, and redlining drained tenants away. Such conditions meant that while homeowners voted to roll back taxes, renters and squatters mobilized not so much to claim a slice of the American dream as to claim a roof—any roof—over their heads.

For millions of Americans, the 1970s marked a passing of the American dream of home ownership. As inflation took home prices out of reach, a whole generation of middle-class suburbanites found themselves in the same position as the urban poor, looking to a future as permanent renters. Whereas two-thirds of Americans could afford to buy a single-family home in 1950, less than 10 percent could do so by the early 1980s. Moreover, the rising rents in urban centers meant that more tenants than ever before were paying 25 percent or more of their income for rent. Tenants who think of their apartments as one stop on a longer journey toward home ownership are difficult to organize. Once they saw themselves as a permanent class—an oppressed class, in fact—they set about organizing in opposition to the landlords, real estate developers, gentrifiers, and pro-growth forces arrayed against them.[24]

In some parts of the country, tenants began organizing in the 1960s, often as extensions of civil rights, welfare, and neighborhood campaigns and often in opposition to federal public housing programs designed by liberals to help the poor.[25] Public housing tenants in St. Louis, for example, launched a citywide rent strike in 1969. Collectively, the strikers withheld more than $300,000 in rent on their way to winning tenant management of public housing in that city. Similar events occurred in Newark and Baltimore.[26]

Although New York City introduced rent control to keep rents reasonable in the 1940s, the city saw tenant organizing throughout the 1960s. Rent strikes in Harlem from 1963 to 1965 grew out of civil rights activism and led to the establishment of the National Tenants Organization. A decade later, as the city staggered through its debt crisis, just barely avoiding bankruptcy, tenants at Co-op City, a subsidized housing development for middle-income tenants in the Bronx, erupted in the largest rent strike in American history. A massive complex of more than fifteen thousand units in thirty-five towers and six town-house clusters, Co-op City was so big that it was home to three shopping centers and six schools. The Riverbay Corporation, which administered it on behalf of the state of New York, had raised rents more than 125 percent from 1965 to 1975. With the city and state flattened by the fiscal crisis, government offered no relief to tenants who, faced with their own rising costs, struggled to pay their rent. In June 1975, they began what turned out to be a thirteen-month rent strike, with nearly 90 percent participation; altogether, they withheld $27 million in rent, all of which they put into an escrow account. The state threatened mass eviction, but given the scale of the strike could not possibly follow through. "We said we'd like to know which politician was prepared to hire the army necessary to evict 60,000 people," strike leader Charlie Rosen said. Eventually, in June 1976, the state capitulated, turning management over to a tenant leadership. It was a mixed victory, however. The new management still needed to collect enough rent to pay the rising mortgage interest, and other costs brought rents nearly to the level that had prompted the strike. But for tenants around the country, such a massive show of resistance became a model for dealing with landlords, public or private.[27]

Tenants living in private housing shared some of the same basic complaints as their public housing counterparts—rent increases, unsafe and unsanitary conditions, unlawful evictions—but these were amplified by market conditions. By the 1970s, the independent "mom and pop" landlord had largely given way to the absentee professional landlord who had bought apartment buildings as tax shelters and paid a management company to run them. Unsurprisingly, tenants often grew frustrated with unresponsive property managers and inaccessible landlords. In addition, as tenants got better organized, landlords started to convert rental units to condominiums, at once eliminating their tenant problem and contributing to the shortage of rental units. As housing experts noted, between 1970 and 1979, 366,000 rental dwellings were converted to condominiums nationwide, 71 percent between 1977 and 1979, when both rents and tenant organizing were rising.[28]

The demographics of tenant organizations varied depending on local political traditions and context. In university towns like Ann Arbor, Madison, Berkeley, and Cambridge, for example, students coming out of various Sixties movements played instrumental roles in winning rent control ordinances that set a cap on rents. In other cities, tenants could not boast of such success. Landlords in Boston, for example, fought back and, with the assistance of Mayor Kevin White, managed to get a "vacancy decontrol" law passed in 1976, which meant that when a tenant moved out of a rent-controlled apartment, the landlord could raise the rent to inflation-market rates. Between 1976 and 1982, 80 percent of Boston apartments that had been under rent control were decontrolled. In gentrifying neighborhoods such as Jamaica Plain, it was not unheard of to see rents jump 300 to 500 percent in just a few years. Well-organized tenants increasingly confronted not only a powerful "pro-growth" lobby made up of real estate investors and developers, but a new class of young urban professionals ("yuppies") who, tiring of the suburbs, returned to the cities in large numbers in the early 1980s. Just as most cities cut services in low-income neighborhoods, "over in Gentryville," one Boston activist cracked, "public funds are poured into plush amenities like gaslights and brick sidewalks" to attract more yuppies. To tenants struggling to find a place for a reasonable rent, it looked like most cities were following the same pattern of building "gleaming skyscrapers, brownstone condos, and food boutiques," but leaving "urban prairies"—block after burned-out block of vacant lots and abandoned housing stock—to crumble just out of view.[29]

In New Jersey, tenant organizing began not with former student radicals but with suburbanites and commuters living in large apartment complexes as well as poor tenants in the inner city in Newark and Passaic. Formed in 1969, the New Jersey Tenants Organization (NJTO) engaged in rent strikes and other various forms of demonstrations and protests, but it found the most success in organizing around electoral politics. Throughout the 1970s, NJTO organized tenants as a voting bloc and helped get rent control laws passed in more than a hundred New Jersey communities. It also won places on local rent control boards for tenants themselves, so that they could better guard against condo conversions, vacancy decontrol, and other landlord efforts to raise rents.[30]

Nowhere did the battle for rent control have a more sudden and profound impact than on the Southern California coast in Santa Monica. Tenant organizers had put Proposition P, a rent control initiative, on the ballot in 1978, but it was voted down on the same day that Proposition 13 was passed (partly because many voters believed rent relief would come with the passage of Prop 13). Soon after Proposition 13 passed, however, tenants in thirty-seven different Santa Monica buildings reported rent increases to the city's Fair Housing Alliance. (Statewide, steadily increasing rents after Proposition 13 led Howard Jarvis to join Governor Jerry Brown at a press conference to implore landlords to pass on some of the Prop 13 windfall or face legislation. Cynics started calling Jarvis the "Father of Rent Control.")[31] The Santa Monica City Council was unmoved; the mayor, Donna Swink, was a banker and landlord, and two other councillors were landlords, too. Renters did not back down. "If you think you've seen a homeowners' revolt," one tenant shouted at a city council meeting, "just wait for the coming tenant revolt!"

Organizing tenants—who made up 80 percent of Santa Monica's population—had proven difficult in the past because, like tenants elsewhere, most hoped to one day own a home there. As the urban planning scholar Allan David Heskin noted, renters "referred to their apartments

as their homes and indicated that they felt those homes were threatened."
It was a classic front porch dynamic, as tenants, under threat of losing
their homes in a tight housing market (and unsure of where they could
go) and winning no sympathy from local government, told the council
that they felt they had to form tenant organizations "to defend themselves." At that same council meeting, one tenant reported that she had
no choice but to move three times in one year because of rent increases.
When she declared that she would not move again, the crowd roared.
At some point during the evening confrontations, one councillor said
out loud that he feared the tenants might burn the council chambers
down. He was not joking. A month later, when four of the seven council
members voted to reject a six-month rent control ordinance, the tenants
took to the streets.[32]

Santa Monicans for Renters' Rights (SMRR) put rent control before
the people once again, this time in a far more sweeping initiative called
Proposition A. It called for the establishment of a rent control board
elected by voters and a ban on the demolition of rental units or conversion of them into condominiums, and it conspicuously had no vacancy
decontrol provision. Thousands of volunteers hit the streets and shopping malls, distributing literature on Proposition A and fending off the
accusations of the landlords and their allies. When one landlord suggested that tenants move to a less expensive suburb, they replied: "Unlike
you, we work for a living; our jobs and family needs dictate where we
should live . . . why is it that landlords are able to uproot families, desta-
bilize neighborhoods, shuffle children around from school to school, and
dispossess senior citizens?" These types of arguments won allies. As one
observer noted, wherever the tenant campaigners walked, they were "received like guerrilla regulars in a friendly countryside." Though the opposition outspent the tenants $217,257 to $38,443 and predicted that a
rent-controlled Santa Monica would become "another New York full of
slums and abandoned buildings . . . where rapists, muggers, robbers and
murderers will increase," voters passed Proposition A, 54 percent to 46
percent, and at the same time elected two SMRR leaders to the city council. By 1981, five tenant representatives served on the city council, including a mayor. Two landlord ballot initiatives in ensuing years went down
to crushing defeats.[33]

Landlords fared better in San Francisco. There, a citywide coalition
of homeowners and renters formed San Franciscans for Affordable

Housing (SFAH), a coalition of thirty-five different groups drawn from tenant, civil rights, gay rights, labor, and senior citizen organizations as well as churches. In response to rent hikes following Proposition 13's passage, SFAH lobbied hard for Proposition R, a ballot initiative that would have imposed controls over rents, evictions, demolitions, and condo conversions as well as assistance to low- and moderate-income homeowners. Polls taken two weeks before the November 1979 vote showed that Proposition R would pass, but landlords poured hundreds of thousands of dollars into the campaign in its final weeks. The No on R forces outspent the affordable housing efforts by approximately $600,000 to $45,000; most of the real estate money paid for a saturation television and radio ad campaign, as well as a bombardment of direct mail, making a variety of claims—from predictions of the coming "Bronxification of San Francisco" to claims that the measure would actually cause rents to rise. "Some households reported receiving as many as eight pieces of mail from the No on R campaign in a single day," the urban planner Chester Hartman later explained. When the city supervisors passed a watered-down version of rent control, giving the landlords an appealing "Let's give the new law a chance" argument, Proposition R went down in defeat, garnering only 41 percent of the vote in a 70 percent renter city.[34]

Even in cities where tenants won rent control, and especially in cities where they were defeated, there were plenty of Americans left behind. Countless people "doubled up," moving in with family and friends when they could not afford to pay high rents in tight markets (such people are notoriously difficult to count; one 1989 estimate put the number of New Yorkers doubling up at somewhere between 69,000 and 103,000). And of course, by the 1980s, tens of thousands of Americans lived on the streets, under bridges, and in parks. Indeed, a more accurate name for the homeless would be "the evicted," according to one urban geographer, "since people don't simply fall out of the housing market—they are usually pushed." And the evicted are rarely passive. Some workers who lost jobs to plant closings in places like Youngstown and soon lost the ability to pay their rent became the new hoboes, riding the rails from city to city looking for work. Others were employed but not at sufficient wages to pay rent and support families; many thousands of these people in cities all over the country demanded that local and federal government officials turn over some of the country's tens of thousands of abandoned buildings to those desperately in need of housing. They pledged their own sweat in exchange and built a movement of squatters and homesteaders to carry it out.[35]

Squatting, homesteading, and "sweat equity" work took place all over the country, but these tactics are perhaps most associated with Philadelphia and New York. As the activist Seth Borgos defines it, "to squat is to occupy property without the permission of the owner," and at its heart it is a political act, criticizing a society's failure to provide housing to all who need it. Homesteading and sweat equity programs, in contrast, usually result from a city government reconciling itself to its inability to manage all of the abandoned properties on its hands and in effect licensing squatters to take over buildings if they rehabilitate them. The U.S. Congress effectively legalized homesteading in the Housing and Community Development Act of 1974 as a feeble attempt to help manage the Federal Housing Administration's growing number of foreclosed-upon homes (the number had risen from 21,000 in 1970 to 78,000 in 1974).[36] But the distinction between squatters and homesteaders was usually irrelevant, as most homesteading began as squatting, and the rehabilitation of property took place whether city officials acceded to it or not.

The nation got its first glimpse of urban homesteading in October 1977 when President Carter visited the Bronx as it burned within sight of Yankee Stadium. The South Bronx was one area the city had chosen to let deteriorate in the wake of its near-bankruptcy, and as the number of abandoned buildings grew, unscrupulous landlords set them on fire to collect the insurance. When the president arrived, he saw "utter devastation" and abandonment on Charlotte Street, but he also saw sweat equity work being carried out in buildings on Washington Avenue. A "rash of favorable publicity" for homesteading followed the president's positive reaction—*The New York Times* reported the next day that A LOAN AND SOME 'SWEAT EQUITY' CREATE AN OASIS AMID DESOLATION—and soon churches, foundations, and government agencies moved to support organizations such as the People's Development Corporation (which saw its budget jump tenfold to $4 million almost overnight).[37]

Squatters and homesteaders framed their cause in moral terms. In 1972, Philadelphia city officials estimated that thirty-five thousand housing units—more than 5 percent of the total stock—had been abandoned. Even though it demolished upwards of ten thousand buildings a year, more were abandoned each year, and by one calculation, the city maintained a "constant 22,000 abandoned structures" throughout the 1970s. Against this bleak landscape—and it was bleak, nearly dystopian, as the abandoned structures provided a haven for a burgeoning drug trade and assorted violent crime—Milton Street, an African American hot dog vendor and neighborhood activist with a flair for the dramatic, started mouthing off about the city's priorities. He called out Mayor Frank Rizzo for favoring housing redevelopment in posh upper-middle-class neighborhoods like Society Hill over the poorer parts of the city. When the fiscal crisis hit Philadelphia, the mayor proposed a campaign against "urban blight," a "slum clearance" program that, rather than rehabilitating the five thousand Department of Housing and Urban Development homes that had been foreclosed upon and stood empty in North Philadelphia, would remove twenty thousand dwellings over five years. Rizzo was not alone. The city's business establishment and liberal politicians and city planners all endorsed the kind of "pro-growth" vision for Philadelphia that Boston and other cities also pursued; they hoped to attract investment and bring professionals back to the city to live and spend money. Activists called this the "whitening" of downtown and, led by Street, prepared to fight.[38]

In June 1977, Street and his North Philadelphia Block Development Corporation announced what he called a "Walk-In Urban Homesteading Program," pledging to move hundreds of squatters into empty HUD-owned single-family houses. In fact, with the help of local residents, Street and others had been breaking into abandoned homes in North Philly and moving families in for more than a year. In short order, they settled two hundred squatters into those homes, claiming that they were there to rehabilitate the buildings and prevent further vandalism and neglect. For the most part, the public and the media reacted positively, with the *Philadelphia Daily News* declaring that the program "is putting people who need homes into houses that have stood vacant for too long." And although HUD secretary Pat Harris said the squatters were "no better than shoplifters," HUD proved flexible; many of Street's squatters received title to their houses at low cost, while others received FHA or other mortgages, and the rest entered into rental agreements with HUD. But city officials were unswayed. The city council president predicted that Street's homesteading program marked "the beginning of anarchy," and the council stuck to its program of developing downtown. Ramping up the confrontation, housing activists began protesting at the site of the new Gallery Mall on Market Street in the heart of Center City, and beginning in February 1979, Street and others disrupted city council meetings for two full months, packing the weekly meetings with up to a thousand supporters. "Street's well-scripted antics had become a centerpiece of Philadelphia life and of the regular business of government," the historian Andrew Feffer writes, "and TV viewers were tuning in nightly to make sure they didn't miss the latest episode."[39]

Inspired by Milton Street's example, Philadelphia ACORN activists Fran Streich and Jon Kest began organizing a complementary squatting campaign. Despite Street's success, HUD still had more homes than it knew what to do with—nationally and in Philadelphia—so it began tearing them down, selling them, or handing them over to city governments. ACORN activists decided to target Philadelphia's utterly ineffective homesteading scheme, the Gift Property program. Run by Harry P. Janotti, a corrupt Democratic city councilman, the Gift Property program was supposed to sell houses for $13 to families who pledged to rehabilitate them, but in the course of four years, Janotti had transferred only a few hundred homes, and many of those went to his speculator cronies. While one speculator managed to secure thirty Gift Property houses, more than five thousand program applicants waited to hear something, anything, in response. Sit-ins at Janotti's office did nothing to move him, so ACORN decided to squat in Gift Property houses. "Need a House? Call ACORN," said leaflets posted all over North Philadelphia. Thousands of residents called, and scores of people decided to take the risk of squatting. Kest and Streich insisted that would-be squatters sign contracts that said they understood that squatting was illegal; they also required that squatters get the signatures of 75 percent of the neighbors saying that they would support the squat. Neighbors almost always signed, eager to have a squatting family next door instead of a "shelter for junkies." In addition, the campaign explicitly appealed to American bootstrapping traditions. Squatters were not asking for handouts; they were plainly prepared to break their backs to turn abandoned buildings into homes, ghettos into neighborhoods.[40]

Each time ACORN moved squatters into a home, it had the potential to be a media event. Usually, a rally would be held to demonstrate neighborhood support for the squat, followed by a march to the house. On one typical occasion, marchers strode past houses with banners hanging out the windows reading WELCOME, ACORN SQUATTERS. As television cameras captured the action, the squatters would speak to the crowd. "I decided to squat because . . . we are in Richard Allen project and you know what that's like—the rats and the crime and the stink and all," one young black woman said from the steps of her squat. "I need a house for my children! This is our moment. We are going to fix up this house and make it a place to live." As the crowd applauded, two young men used crowbars to pry sheet metal off the doorway, and the woman entered the house triumphantly. In time, Janotti was forced out by an unrelated scandal, and the city elected a new mayor, William Green, "with a clear mandate to reform the city's housing programs." The path to that reform was not always smooth—one activist defined ACORN's relationship with City Hall as a pattern of "alternating confrontation and negotiation"—but in time a Philadelphia model emerged. Only low- and moderate-income families would be eligible for homesteading, but they would be given three years (instead of the typical six months) to rehabilitate the homes, and one year to deal with "all major housing code defects posing a substantial danger to life and safety," at which time they would get the deed to the property and two more years to finish all renovations. To pay for all of this rehabilitation within three years, homesteaders received low-interest long-term loans. Finally, the city agreed to transfer two hundred houses a month (though, in practice, it never managed more than fifty a month) and to accelerate foreclosures of abandoned property.[41]

Given the success of the squatting campaign in Philadelphia, ACORN went national with a squatter program. By April 1982, more than two hundred ACORN squatters occupied buildings in thirteen cities, including Detroit, Pittsburgh, St. Louis, Houston, Dallas, Tulsa, and Phoenix. The results were not always as positive as in Philadelphia—in some cities, officials cracked down with mass arrests and refused to negotiate—but in time, ACORN took squatting to the nation's capital, where two hundred activists squatted in a tent city in the Ellipse, near the White House. Although President Reagan ignored the protest, the squatting campaign led to ACORN activists testifying before Congress and, ultimately, to the passage of the 1983 Housing and Urban-Rural Recovery Act, which essentially codified many of the provisions worked out in

Philadelphia. "Congress listened to you folks," a HUD official said to an ACORN activist, "and we're going to have to listen to you, too." Perhaps that official really believed that statement, but the Reagan administration did not in fact move to address the problems of abandoned housing or homelessness. Indeed, although Reagan signed the 1983 act into law, cuts in federal housing programs were among the deepest made by his administration.[42]

The fiercest battles over housing took place on Manhattan's Lower East Side, for many years a kind of squatting ground zero. Lots of artists and hippies famously squatted in illegal "crash pads" there in the 1960s, giving the area a reputation for political and cultural radicalism. By the late 1970s, the combination of high rents and abandoned buildings led the city to institute a provisional homesteading program by which homesteaders earned title to their homes at a nominal financial cost but through substantial sweat equity. "Our building has been abandoned for nine years," one homesteader reported. "It was like the neighborhood garbage dump. We pulled cars out of the basement. The garbage down there was impacted, packed so tightly. We did not have a roof; half the building had been burned away so the water would go right down there. We had to work with pickaxes. The garbage was like that on almost every floor except where there was no floor." Such dedication attracted a variety of community organizations. The Lower East Side Catholic Area Conference (LESAC), Nazareth Home, the Housing Development Institute (HDI), Rehabilitation in Action to Improve Neighborhoods (RAIN), and others facilitated homesteading by providing some financial, technical, or legal advice.[43]

Gentrification of the Lower East Side above Houston Street (in what is now usually referred to as the East Village) prompted resistance and, in response, violence. As the geographer Neil Smith has chronicled it, the real estate industry started to promote the area because of its proximity to Greenwich Village, home to Washington Square Park, jazz clubs, and rising rents. But the "culture industry" promoted gentrification, too. Art dealers, gallery owners, artists, writers, and performers moved into the area and "converted urban destruction into ultra chic." Smith quotes the art critics Walter Robinson and Carlo McCormick salivating at the mix of glamour and danger: "As for ambience, the East Village has it: a unique blend of poverty, punk rock, drugs, and arson, Hell's Angels, winos, prostitutes, and dilapidated housing that adds up to an adventurous avant-garde setting of considerable cachet." No small number of commentators compared the East Village to Paris's Left Bank and London's Soho.[44]

The new chic had a predictable impact on real estate values, and in short order an overwhelmingly poor and working-class population in Alphabet City (the East Village from Avenue A eastward), which had seen its population decline by 67 percent in the 1970s, found itself living in gold rush territory. The sixteen-story Christadora building, built in 1928 on the east side of Tompkins Square Park on Avenue B, was a classic example of the real estate wheeling and dealing that became common practice. Once a settlement house, by the 1960s the building was in terrible disrepair, a hollow shell of its former self. In 1975, the city tried to sell it at auction but got not a single bid. A Brooklyn real estate developer finally bought it for $62,500—a sixteen-story building!—hoping to get federal backing to convert it to low-income housing. In the meantime, he welded the doors shut to keep it safe, and it stayed that way for five years. In the early 1980s, as the area became an "avant-garde setting of considerable cachet," others started making offers, and the Brooklyn developer sold the Christadora to another developer for $1.3 million; a year later, that developer sold it for $3 million. Fully renovated and transformed by the next year into 86 condominiums, the four-floor penthouse on top—with its "private elevator, three terraces, and two fireplaces"—alone sold for $1.2 million. As this kind of gentrification swept through even Alphabet City, by the mid-1980s only city-owned slum properties were left. And thus was laid the groundwork for full-scale housing wars in the East Village.[45]

At the heart of the East Village is Tompkins Square Park, and in the late 1980s, it became the epicenter of New York's housing wars. In 1988's long, hot summer, the park became—as it had for past generations—a kind of "outdoor living room" for local residents, but it also attracted a crowd that came in to the city for the scene. That year, the in-migrant gentrifiers started to demand more police presence and enforcement of both noise ordinances and the park curfew. "It's the yuppies moving in on us," one local punk told a reporter. "It's like we scare the rich people." The police finally showed up in riot gear and on horseback on August 6,

1988, the night of a demonstration aimed at keeping the park open past the curfew. According to a *Village Voice* account, the mounted police "suddenly charged up Avenue A . . . radiating hysteria . . . they were sweeping 9th Street and it didn't matter if you were press or walking home from the movies or sitting on your stoop to catch a breeze . . . The cops seemed bizarrely out of control." The battle raged all night, with 450 police squaring off with a mix of "antigentrification protesters, punks, housing activists, park inhabitants, artists, Saturday-night revelers, and Lower East Side residents." Some in the crowd chanted the Vietnam-era slogan, "Hell no, we won't go!" and others sang "This land is your land, this land is our land." The artist Clayton Patterson captured the carnage on four hours of videotape that was later used as evidence against the officers, seventeen of whom were cited for misconduct and six of whom were indicted (though not convicted). When the police finally withdrew at around 4:00 a.m., the survivors celebrated deliriously. They followed the police, applauding and shouting "Every night!" A small group directed its remaining energies on the symbol of gentrification, the Christadora House, busting into the lobby, tossing its potted plants out onto the sidewalk, and yelling "We know who you are!" and "Die, yuppie scum!"[46]

A number of smaller riots followed the big one in the park, usually arising out of either the eviction of squatters or the demolition of a building. On Eighth Street east of the park, squatters occupied two edifices that the Buildings Department claimed were unsafe. The squatters claimed otherwise and argued that they had renovated the buildings at no small cost. More than that, the homesteaders expected the city to serve them with proper eviction notices, but the Department of Housing Preservation and Development said that since the buildings were legally vacant, they could be taken down. On April 1, police removed the squatters and the city demolished one of the buildings by the afternoon. Protesters again hit the Christadora, smashing the glass lobby doors; the incident resulted in nine arrests. A few weeks later, on April 20, the city declared once again that the second building, standing across the street, was unsafe even though the homesteaders had letters from two architects and a contractor saying that the building could be rehabilitated. When the demolition crews arrived on May 2, protesters dumped urine on them and knocked down scaffolding. A street fight broke out between more than two hundred protesters and some three hundred police, leading to sixteen arrests. Three days later, police blocked off the area and the demolition proceeded. Gentrification was winning thanks to the business end of so many police batons.[47]

Meanwhile, police did not consistently enforce the Tompkins Square Park curfew. As a result, by July 1989, nearly two hundred homeless persons lived in the park full-time in what looked something like a Depression-era Hooverville, with lean-tos and other impermanent structures serving as shelter. Police and the Parks Department would, at random, clear the park of its residents and all of their possessions, but they just kept coming back. From the city's perspective, and especially from the point of view of the new, affluent residents, this eyesore could not stand. Mayor David Dinkins finally sent the police in at 5:00 a.m. on June 3, 1991, and cleared the park for good. Rejecting the moral claims of squatters, homesteaders, and the homeless in favor of gentrifiers' moral claims, he ordered an eight-foot-high fence built and posted police around the park perimeter, 24/7. "The park is a park," Mayor Dinkins said. "It is not a place to live." The city then spent $2.3 million on a reconstruction of Tompkins Square Park. Visitors to the East Village or the Lower East Side today can see for themselves that the coalition of gentrifiers, real estate developers, and pro-growth politicians won this housing war.[48] Yuppies own the East Village and the Lower East Side.

To a surprising degree, the politics of the 1970s and 1980s revolved around the politics of housing, and around front porch efforts to seek housing relief. Squatters and homesteaders, renters and homeowners looked outward at a landscape that suddenly looked alien and threatening. Inflation and taxes were obvious culprits in conspiring to make Americans feel they were losing their grip not only on their homes but on their futures. But so were changes in the political economy, when municipal governments—likewise facing inflation, but also deindustrialization and shrinking tax bases—took the side of "growth" and "development" and therefore of business interests, investors, and gentrifiers. For homeowners, tenants, and squatters, then, the obstacles were becoming immovable; hard work no longer seemed enough to guarantee security, for themselves or their families. Just as industrial workers expected to work in the same well-paying jobs in the same factories for the rest of their lives, providing for their families, homeowners and tenants expected to be rewarded for paying their way forward. And just as farmers expected, as producers, to work the land and provide for themselves and their families, tenants and homesteaders believed that hard work would lead to their security, too. This, they all believed, is how America works—or *should* work. But the 1970s and 1980s crushed those expectations and showed just how tenuous the American dream had become.

PART 4

Resisting Nightfall

● ● ● ● ● ● ● ● ● ● ● ● ● ● ● ● ● ● ● ●

Early in 1982, the novelist and travel writer Paul Theroux took readers of the Sunday *New York Times Magazine* on a tour of the city's subway system, conveying the wonders and terror of riding the rails in an era of tight budgets, vandalized subway cars, and roving packs of muggers and purse snatchers. His essay cast the subway system as an exotic, unknowable place; only transit workers and cops seemed to understand its language and customs. He came across people who were "clearly crazy," the subway homeless whom the police called "skells," most having been released from city hospitals in the early 1970s when "it was decided that long term institutionalization was doing them little good." Theroux's treatment of the homeless as colorful but threatening creatures—"They drink, they scream, they gibber like monkeys"—assumed what was by then a common pose. Most Americans likewise viewed the poor, the damaged, the *lesser* ones, as if at a zoo—they were best seen at a safe remove across a trench and behind a fence.[1]

In the 1970s and 1980s, journalists, pundits, and politicians colored the public dialogue on the nation's problems with tales of the exotic and dangerous. There were stories of the "underclass," the "undeserving poor," and yarns about "welfare queens" living high on the social service hog while the unworthy got jobs because they could fill some quota. When *Time* put the "American Underclass" on its cover in 1977, it foreshadowed Theroux's detachment with its own report from what sounded like an urban animal park: "Behind [the ghetto's] crumbling walls lives a large group of people who are more intractable, more socially alien and more hostile than almost anyone had imagined. They are the unreachables: the American underclass."[2]

The United States was home to a lot of unreachables in the 1970s and 1980s, and because they were unreachable, because they were different from other citizens, they became fair game for arguments as to why they were different, how they got that way, and who was to blame. The majority of Americans observed the exotic from their front porch and saw not a citizen neighbor, but a danger.

Consider the homeless. Some, like Theroux, looked at the homeless and saw crazy people, while others, like President Reagan, saw irresponsible bohemians who lived on the streets "by choice."[3] Arguments raged about how many homeless people there were, why they were homeless, and what to do about homelessness. And these arguments erupted within what commentators were increasingly referring to as America's "culture wars"—battles over fundamental moral issues in which both sides claimed to speak for America's most sacred traditions. Abortion, pornography, and popular culture generated considerable controversy in this period. Battles over homelessness joined similar disagreements on welfare, affirmative action, and people with AIDS. The moral questions these issues raised had to do with personal responsibility and how much generosity of both spirit and treasury Americans should direct toward those who, many argued, either brought their circumstances on themselves through their behavior or were likely to take advantage of that generosity.

By the early 1980s, the problems of both homelessness and AIDS had appeared quite suddenly and seemed to leave a trail of victims in their wake. Each winter, the media soberly reported on shelters filled to overflowing with the homeless trying to escape the cold and included the shocking tally of dozens nationwide who had died of exposure on the streets. Similarly, by the mid-1980s, the AIDS epidemic racked up a death toll into the tens of thousands, mostly claiming the lives of gay men and intravenous drug users. Most Americans looked on these people the way Theroux observed the subway "skells"—thinking that most of the homeless were mentally ill or that AIDS victims had brought this plague on themselves; while the homeless deserved pity and maybe some charity, a majority of Americans thought people with AIDS might need to be quarantined to protect the rest of the population. On the other hand, both the homeless and their allies and people with AIDS and their wider communities came to develop a style of front porch politics. They rejected the characterization of themselves as "victims," and in addition to seeking immediate relief from both public and private sources, they sought fundamental change in the fields of housing and public health. They demanded that they not be shunned and ignored. They demanded to be treated with decency and respect. And as in the battles over women's equality, gay rights, and the family, the struggles over homelessness and AIDS brought private issues again into the public domain. As a result, the two campaigns became central to what the sociologist James Davidson Hunter calls the "battle over the moral character of the nation" that defined the so-called "culture wars." Americans who became homeless activists and AIDS activists stood, as if in a postapocalyptic film, on a neighborhood or community battlefield; we can imagine the camera sweeping around them as they stand in the center, looking outward at the bodies of the suffering, dead, and dying, and we watch them as they realize that they cannot stand there and do nothing. For themselves and their communities, they had no choice but to act.

10

The Politics of Homelessness

●

In retrospect, the rise in homelessness in the 1980s is easy to explain. A combination of deliberate policy choices and economic troubles led to declines in the labor market and in the availability of low-income housing. Deindustrialization, particularly in cities in the Northeast and the Midwest, changed the shape of the American labor market; when factory jobs disappeared, they did not come back. When the economy shifted toward service industries and information processing, it did not easily accommodate those discarded factory workers or, more important, those young Americans who would have entered the manufacturing sector had it still existed. Minority men, in particular, suffered acutely from this disappearance of manufacturing jobs.[1] The result was obvious: an absence of steady work at decent wages makes affording a place to live difficult.

The nationwide rollbacks in welfare benefits also played a role. And as *Newsweek* pointed out at the time, the cuts in specific benefits meant poor people would be less likely to pay their bills and consequently more likely to lose their homes. A family of four got only $100 a month in rent allowance in Indiana, for example. Likewise, in Pennsylvania, Governor Richard Thornburgh and the state legislature "moved to restrict all able-bodied men to 90 days on welfare a year." But as *Newsweek* reported, "instead of lessening dependency, as conservatives hoped, it simply made many of them homeless and thus still dependent." And once homeless, with no fixed address, one could not even register for food stamps or receive welfare benefits in many states.[2]

At the same time, the Reagan administration cut federal funding for subsidized housing by 80 percent from 1981 to 1989, from $32 billion to

$6 billion. And, as one scholar has noted, the administration "all but eliminated Section 8 of the Housing and Community Development Act of 1974 which provided low-income renters with housing certificates that guaranteed landlords the difference between a tenant's rent and 30 percent of his or her income." Meanwhile, federal housing starts fell dramatically, from 183,000 in 1980 to 20,000 in 1989. Consequently, by the end of Reagan's second term in office, public housing in the United States accounted for a mere 1.5 percent of the nation's housing. At the local level, cities trying to recover from the economic crisis of the 1970s began offering tax incentives to bring in mostly white-collar business and young urban professionals. The results were stark. Whereas in 1970 there had been 6.6 million affordable housing units available for 5.9 million "very poor" households, by 1990, 8.5 million households competed for 4.3 million affordable housing units. That meant that 4 million households paid a much higher percentage of their income—upwards of 70 percent— on housing than did most Americans.[3] "Appearances may have suggested otherwise," the sociologist Kim Hopper later wrote, "but what the country glimpsed on the streets and in the shelters in the 1980s was not some new species of disorder, but the usually hidden face of poverty, ripped from its customary habitat." The homeless may have been presented as if they were a "distinct, even foreign species," but, really, the vast majority were just like anyone else in this economy, only more unlucky and more marginalized. And they entertained few illusions about the government's failure to help them stay in their homes.[4]

Prior to the 1970s and 1980s, the homeless were not even called "homeless." Most of them were older white men, frequently alcoholics, living on "Skid Row" in single-room-occupancy accommodations or on the streets, labeled "bums," "hoboes," or "vagrants." By the 1980s, the "new" homeless were visibly different. They were much younger, and not merely lone men, but women with children and whole families. Nearly half were African American and nearly one-third were veterans, 40 to 60 percent of whom were Vietnam veterans. One study estimates that children accounted for 24 percent of the homeless.[5]

Some of the fiercest debates over homelessness were waged over just counting them. Through much of the 1980s, activists claimed that at least 2 million people nationwide were homeless on any given night, while the Department of Housing and Urban Development claimed they numbered only 250,000 to 350,000. Policy experts and social scientists picked apart the HUD estimate, faulting the department's methodology, and later studies seemed to confirm that the numbers were in the millions. In a 1995 telephone survey, for example, 3 percent of Americans with telephones acknowledged that "they had been homeless sometime between 1985 and 1990." As one sociologist interpreted it, "when these findings are corrected to include children, a midpoint estimate of seven million Americans said they were homeless" in the late 1980s.[6]

Neither the federal government's economic policies nor local government's scramble to open shelters seemed capable of solving homelessness. Despite the economic recovery that followed the recession of 1981–82, in the winter of 1985, New York City sheltered 8,300 individuals and 4,000 families *in one night*.[7] By 1988, HUD estimated the number of shelters in the United States at 5,019, approximately 2,000 of which were designated for families. Somewhere between 40,000 and 100,000 American families stayed in homeless shelters for at least part of the year in 1988.[8] This was not morning in America; it was more like a long, moonless night.

It is, of course, difficult to describe the "front porch" perspective of the homeless without straining the metaphor; the homeless do not, obviously, have front porches. But because their private experience occurs in public, their very existence is a public issue. Given their experience of personal crisis, their motives for mobilizing were obvious. They sought the immediate provision of shelter to minimize the most immediate, proximate pain, and they also at times demanded wholesale changes to the public housing system and related safety net structures. Meanwhile, with homeless Americans' private lives so readily on display, residents who lived in the same communities mobilized either in solidarity with the homeless or in opposition. Those who joined in solidarity were often jolted by the realization that the existence of so much dislocation so close to home was a disturbing measure of a community's health; it was not unlike finding out that one's neighbors were growing ill from something toxic in the soil or air, only to find that it was an absence of decent jobs and good housing that was proving toxic. On the other side, those who mobilized in opposition were not so much opposed to homeless people per se as they were opposed to what the homeless seemed to represent: an unpleasant disorder in the community, one that harmed its ability to draw consumers or employers or tourists and reflected a widespread anxiety about rising crime rates. Both sides felt that government had failed them.

The grassroots campaigns over homelessness arose in part to fill a vacuum left by a federal government that seemed either willfully in denial or out of touch with reality. "No one is living in the streets," HUD official Philip Abrams declared to a reporter in June 1982, when it was plainly obvious that plenty of people were. Presidential adviser Edwin Meese claimed on the eve of Christmas 1983 that reports of hunger in America were anecdotal and "purely political"; indeed, he confidently asserted that those who went to soup kitchens went "because the food is free . . . and that's easier than paying for it." A few months later, President Reagan himself dismissed concerns over growing numbers of homeless in America because, he said, people living on America's streets did so "you might say, by their own choice." Thomas Main, writing in *The Wall Street Journal*, bluntly asserted that New Yorkers living in homeless shelters were not "truly homeless" but were "exploiting a good housing deal."[9]

The American public's attitudes toward homelessness were likewise unclear and not entirely sympathetic. The most prominent mythology presented the homeless as "lazy, crazy, drunk, or doped," with many echoing the president in contending that the homeless were more like gypsies, living a modern-day bohemian lifestyle. Tangled up in all of these impressions were assumptions that the homeless had no one to blame but themselves. As one scholar wrote, Americans want to believe that "every American who has the pluck and patience and a capacity for hard work can make it into the economic mainstream, that the American dream is there for those who dare to succeed."[10] In contrast, another sociologist summarized, "the homeless are visible symbols of our decline as a nation, and we resent them for it."[11]

In an era that saw the introduction of the term "compassion fatigue," the public seemed happy to combine structural problems and character factors in explaining homelessness. Most Americans just wanted a solution, but with opinion on the causes of homelessness so mixed, none was in the offing. They wanted to both "help and control," though politicians mostly read such mixed signals as the public wanting only that homeless people be controlled.[12]

The task of the homeless and their allies was not only to relieve the most immediate misery, but also to critique the lack of jobs and adequate housing that laid misery's foundation.[13] "It is not sufficient to ask what it is about the homeless poor that accounts for their dispossession," Kim Hopper argued. "One must also ask what it is about 'the rest of us' that has learned to ignore, then managed to tolerate, and now seeks to banish from sight the evidence of a present gone badly awry."[14]

The scale of homeless activism in the 1980s defied expectations. The fact that being homeless was, for most, an episodic event—with many "cycling on and off the streets" multiple times—should have made organizing difficult. In addition, the basic struggle for survival on the streets—which also caused many to move around a lot, within and between cities—was more important than going to a meeting or a demonstration. Finally, if the widespread reports of mental illness and other disabilities were to be believed, then those conditions should have mitigated against organizing, too. And yet the homeless formally organized in more than fifty American cities during the 1980s, participating in a wide variety of tactics, including demonstrations, street theater, marches, and encampments.[15] The Coalition for the Homeless, formed in New York City in 1980, was followed in quick succession by similar organizations in Boston, Atlanta, San Francisco, Phoenix, Minneapolis–St. Paul, Chicago, Columbus, Denver, Los Angeles, Richmond, Seattle, and Tucson. In 1982, these groups banded together to form the National Coalition for the Homeless, which by 1990 represented homeless groups in nearly every state in the Union. Like the NAACP or NOW, the coalition lobbied Congress and state legislatures, ran a legal division that litigated on behalf of the homeless, and also organized public education campaigns. This work, conducted by advocates and allies of the homeless, sometimes only fueled the public perception of the homeless as passive victims, but the homeless organized themselves in many cities as well, forming homeless unions in San Francisco in 1982 and Philadelphia in 1983 and establishing the national Union of the Homeless in 1985; by 1988, it had chapters in fourteen cities.[16]

Much of the homeless organizing and advocacy took an "if only they knew" approach, reasoning that if public officials and the American public understood better the realities of who homeless citizens were and what their daily life was like, solutions would soon follow. The homeless and their advocates—*especially* their advocates—had a faith in documenting the problem not unlike that of Progressive Era muckrakers. In addition to dozens of government reports on the homeless in cities all over the country, the muckraking went mainstream with books like Jonathan Kozol's bestseller *Rachel and Her Children* (1988) and ABC's *God Bless the Child* (1988), a television drama about the life of homeless children. The "implicit premise" in all of this work, one expert pointed out, was that rendering the scale and nature of homelessness would "suffice to prompt corrective action." Certainly, by the time a quarter of a million Americans, including thousands of homeless, traveled to Washington for the HOUSING NOW! rally at the Capitol, any American still unfamiliar with the homeless crisis must have been in a coma for much of the decade. Still, the wait for corrective action continued.[17]

Part of the difficulty was that people on one side of the issue argued for treating homelessness as a housing problem while others argued for helping the homeless overcome the presumed personal shortcomings that led to their being homeless in the first place. Indeed, despite widespread agreement that some form of "transitional housing" (shelters) was absolutely necessary in the short term, opinions differed on their long-term value. Shelters became, for many, an effectively permanent and relatively easy solution—partly because this kind of charitable structure brings in religious and other nonprofit groups that run the shelters and thereby earn goodwill and government grants. Many homeless advocates therefore criticized shelters as actually perpetuating homelessness, not ending it. In building "enough shelters to house their homeless populations," critics charged, municipalities had "become merely more proficient at concealing [the homeless] from public view," undermining any sense of urgency to deal with the larger social structural problems that gave rise to the homeless crisis in the first place."[18] Two forms of front porch politics collided: the existential need for proper housing versus a community's NIMBY-like desire for a better quality of life, free of "vagrants."

The fiercest battles over homelessness took place within view of the White House and the Capitol dome, as Washington's homeless and their grassroots allies took on President Ronald Reagan in an era of glitz and conspicuous consumption. There, the Community for Creative Non-Violence (CCNV) established itself as one of the leading homeless organizations in the country and through a series of dramatic protests, including hunger strikes, won important symbolic as well as practical concessions from the federal government. CCNV had been around since the Nixon administration, founded by the Paulist priest Ed Guigan, who came out of the Catholic Worker movement, and a couple of dozen "Christian anarchists" who wanted to confront the "violence of wasted lives" in their D.C. neighborhood. Initially dedicated to protesting the

Vietnam War, they opened a soup kitchen in October 1972. CCNV members realized that they needed to open a shelter in wintertime, and they appealed in individual letters to eleven hundred local churches, synagogues, and mosques to help provide shelter; by the winter of 1977, two churches sheltered the homeless. At that time, homelessness had yet to be identified as a public issue. Even so, with church shelters filled to capacity, CCNV persuaded the city to open its first shelter, run by the Department of Human Services, and spent the coldest nights of the winter patrolling for D.C.'s homeless. It was a model that the homeless and their advocates would follow in dozens of other cities in the coming years.[19]

Most of those cities did not, however, have a Mitch Snyder to lead them. Beginning in the late 1970s, Snyder emerged as the primary architect and spokesman for CCNV, for homeless organizing in D.C. and, really, for the nation. A master of political theater and what one scholar has described as "moral brinkmanship," Snyder was the skunk at the Reagan Revolution picnic, raising hell and demanding that the nation pay attention to those whom it would rather sweep under the "morning in America" rug. Led by Snyder, the homeless functioned as "spoilers"; countering claims of returning prosperity, they were "insistent reminders of the unruly night outside."[20]

By the late 1970s, Snyder had begun to articulate a front porch political perspective on homelessness; through his Catholic faith, he heard a call to solidarity with the less fortunate. It was important that the homeless people with whom CCNV worked were in fact their neighbors—people they could see every day sleeping on subway grates, in doorways, and on park benches. As people of faith, Snyder and CCNV saw the problem of homelessness right in front of them, could not make sense of it as Christians, and mobilized to solve it.[21] Allies admired Snyder's ability to draw attention to the cause as well as to get private and public assistance for the homeless; others who were sympathetic to the cause criticized him for focusing too much on the Band-Aid approach of opening shelters to the neglect of policy on jobs and housing.

From challenging the spending priorities of Holy Trinity Church, where the Kennedys and other powerful Catholics like Senators Ernest Hollings and Dennis DeConcini, Congressman David Bonior and newsman Roger Mudd, worshipped, to challenging the city to both increase the number of shelters and govern them more humanely, Snyder led CCNV's struggle to confront a community's willful denial of its residents' suffering.[22] Over eight nights in December 1978, CCNV led a homeless occupation of an unused portion of the National Visitor Center at Union Station. Each night, anywhere from 80 to 140 people slept there, sheltered from the cold. The U.S. Department of the Interior at first supported the occupation, but within days they had second thoughts and padlocked the doors. Two days of civil disobedience led to forcible arrests but also extended the occupation's already significant media coverage. In the aftermath, the D.C. Department of Human Resources gave two shelters—one for men and one for women—to CCNV to run, validating the organization's standing and setting a ground floor for further campaigns.[23]

For the next couple of years, CCNV busied itself running the shelters and working toward getting the homeless residents to run them themselves, but the issue of homelessness only grew in both scale and political potency. In the spring of 1980, *The Washington Post* ran a series of articles by Neil Henry on his experiences going undercover as a homeless man for two months. His message could not have been drearier for 1980s America. Henry reported the shelter experience in the most miserable terms—the powerless, down on their luck, getting kicked out at 6:00 a.m. every morning without so much as a cup of hot water (the noncompliant being beaten by staff)—while also describing many of the homeless as damaged or drunk, preferring life on the street. This was the key tension: where some saw a crime against humanity on the sidewalk every day, others saw a public nuisance. For either humanitarian or quality-of-life reasons, both sides wanted the problem solved, but it was hard to move forward when no one could agree on the main causes of homelessness. In exasperation, the *Washington Post* columnist Colman McCarthy angrily denounced the "myth that the dispossessed and rootless prefer life on the street, that vagrancy has its advantages and that this ragged population of 'bums' and 'shopping bag ladies' is too proud to ask for help." Rather, the evidence of an "uncomfortable truth" was there for everyone to see: "America has a permanent refugee class, people driven into the streets . . . from pressures created only recently."[24] Not everyone agreed. How citizens reacted depended on how they interpreted the nature of the threat from their front porches.

From the front porch of the White House, Ronald Reagan seemed bewildered. When CCNV and others fasted in protest of the government's withholding 200 million pounds of surplus dairy in limestone caves in Missouri, the president moved grudgingly to make some of the surplus available even as he admitted feeling "perplexed" about stories of hunger in America. Months later, Reagan's task force reported that hunger levels in the United States had been "exaggerated" and argued that although anecdotal evidence of child hunger existed, it did not amount to a "national problem." Even after Reagan bowed to pressure to turn over to CCNV the old Federal City College building on Second Street to use as a shelter, he made that ill-informed comment on the *Good Morning America* television program that the homeless were homeless "you might say, by choice."[25]

CCNV's sustained campaigns, vigils, and fasts made for high drama and won for Washington an indelible association with poverty and deprivation at just the same time that Ronald Reagan busied himself hailing America as a "shining city on a hill" and attacked the Soviet Union as an "evil empire." It was a difficult act to follow. In some cities, activists followed a vaguely CCNV model, but in others, different circumstances required different responses, and in most cases, activists made it up front porch–style—as they went along.

Certainly, when most Americans thought of homelessness, their minds turned first to New York City. There, although the homeless had won a 1979 consent decree that both established shelter as a right for New Yorkers and also spelled out minimum standards for quality of shelter, by March 1981, studies estimated that thirty-six thousand people lived on the streets while the city could offer only thirty-two hundred beds. Mayor Ed Koch did not deny the problem the way Reagan did, but he was reluctant to set up a system of shelters for fear of how it would affect neighborhoods and his electoral prospects. He also did not want to be seen, at a time when New York's economy still limped along, to be handing out free housing. As early as 1983, Koch introduced a program requiring some homeless to work in the shelters for twenty hours a week in exchange for their room and board and $12.50. "We want to help these people become rehabilitated where we can," the mayor declared. "We're instilling in them a work ethic"—implying that they had become homeless because they were lazy. The possibility that some homeless persons might have lost their jobs or been evicted when they could not pay rising rents seemed beyond his comprehension. Even so, over the course of the 1980s, lobbying and advocacy by a number of charities such as the Coalition for the Homeless pressed the city to provide more shelter and

services. By the early 1990s, on any given night, the city sheltered a staggering number of homeless: 7,000 men and women and 4,500 families
(about 6,500 adults and 8,000 children). In 1993, it created the Department of Homeless Services, which operated 160 shelters with a staff of
1,700 and a budget of $389 million a year. As a result, the biggest battles
over homelessness centered on those who encountered the public outside
the shelters—the men and women sleeping in Tompkins Square Park,
the subway panhandlers. In the subways and in the East Village, the city
government increasingly sided with "quality-of-life" campaigns that
found the homeless either offensive or threatening.[26]

As the 1980s wound down, it became more common to hear Americans speak of compassion fatigue. At the start of the decade, more Americans seemed willing to treat the homeless as a symptom of wider problems
with employment and housing; by the end of the decade, however, it was
more common to see the homeless as the cause of an acute quality-of-life
problem, and a persistent one at that. "Each spring, the army [of homeless people] migrates to the parks," wrote one critic. "Sandboxes become urinals. Swings are broken. Every park bench seems to be owned
by a permanently curled-up dozing alcoholic or perhaps a street schizo-
phrenic. When the cycle is complete, the community withdraws, serious
drugs and criminals move in, and you have what Los Angeles and Washington DC are now calling 'dead parks.'"[27] In Miami, city attorneys argued for clearing the homeless from parts of the city: "It does not take a
scholar to recognize that tourists do not want to pay money to vacation
in Miami and be forced to walk through homeless encampments to enjoy
a city park."[28] In the second half of the decade, residents in some communities began to treat the homeless the way the Minnesota utilities
treated the farmers standing in their way: they wanted the shortest route
to a solution. Local laws enacted to sweep the homeless out of town
sometimes created the "leafblower effect" of simply pushing the homeless from one community to another. The fiercest battles over homelessness, therefore, occurred when homeless persons came to be seen as toxins
in the middle of the community, as obstacles blocking a community's
path to prosperity.[29]

In Los Angeles, the homeless and their allies battled the city and its
business community in a series of sustained tent city skirmishes arising
out of the city's first sweeps in advance of hosting the 1984 Summer
Olympics. Los Angeles County's main approach to managing the home-

less had been an inadequate voucher system; it allowed qualifying individuals to go to a single-room-occupancy hotel and exchange the voucher for a room for the night. If the SROs were full—there was space for only about twelve hundred a night—the county gave out $8 "emergency housing checks" even though no one could get decent housing for $8 a day. In the first challenges to this system, a group of public interest lawyers formed the Homeless Litigation Team and challenged the requirement that the homeless have some form of identification to qualify for the $8 emergency checks, and they also sued the county to keep taxpayer money from funding SROs with any health, fire, or safety code violations. Finally, lawyers sued the county for penalizing welfare recipients who missed appointments or hadn't completed twenty job searches a month by dropping them from the rolls for sixty days; the policy merely pushed those already living at the margins into homelessness and "did nothing for the individual's work ethic and only moved that person further away from being employed and finding permanent shelter."[30]

In the meantime, the pre-Olympics police sweeps of the homeless from their most visible encampments downtown may have cleared the homeless for a time, but they also galvanized homeless organizing. A kind of urban capture-the-flag game developed as the homeless slept in various public places around the city—near City Hall or at the Los Angeles Music Center—only to be cleared each time by police.[31] By 1987, a narrative had developed justifying the homeless hunt the way some made the case against toxic waste: these "shantytowns" were themselves toxic, "havens for crime and disease and simply an embarrassment for Los Angeles," and therefore had to go. In this narrative, the personal shortcomings of the homeless not only made them unworthy of being helped but made them a cancer on the community.[32]

In Atlanta, business groups were convinced that customers and tourists stayed away from commercial areas because of the homeless presence and therefore lobbied to create "safeguard" zones downtown where the homeless would be kept out. By 1985, in response to high unemployment and insufficient low-income housing, and estimates that the number of homeless Atlantans had hit five thousand, religious groups had established more than thirty shelters. Business leaders took a Not in My Back Yard approach, arguing that they did not object to sheltering the homeless, just that they envisioned "meeting the needs of these people somewhere other than downtown Atlanta." For critics, it seemed that the homeless were being treated like a prison population or like a waste incinerator imposed on a neighborhood. Supported by Mayor Andrew Young, the safeguard zone went ahead, even as the homeless marched behind a black crucifix—the "vagrant Christ"—in protest on Christmas Eve 1986. In the meantime, however, a group of thirty design and construction professionals calling themselves the "Mad Housers" conducted a series of surprise covert operations in which they built six-by-eight-by-six-foot huts for the homeless. Each one took twenty minutes to build and, according to a journalist, had the "air of fraternity pranks," but they went a long way toward embarrassing the government for its failure to do more to house the poor. Eventually, the Mad Housers built two hundred huts around Atlanta and went on to build more in Boston, Dallas, Cincinnati, San Francisco, Grand Rapids, and Chicago.[33]

By the second half of the 1980s, cities all over the country saw battles over what to do with the homeless follow the Atlanta example, demonstrating an important shift in the terms of the debate: whereas CCNV had persistently demanded recognition of an unconditional right to shelter—to survival—in Washington, D.C., homeless organizers across the nation now found themselves fighting for the right just to *be* anywhere. Lined up against them were merchants demanding the right to control the environment in which they conducted business, including the sidewalks and public spaces in their neighborhoods. In many cities, public sympathy for the homeless fell away over the course of the decade, and it became common for city councils to pass a variety of "antivagrancy" laws. Santa Barbara enacted no-sleeping and no-camping ordinances; Cincinnati, like New York, cracked down on panhandling; Chicago, Columbus, and Miami followed Atlanta's example in sweeping the homeless from public view.

The homeless fought back in a variety of ways, sometimes through direct action, other times through negotiation with governments and businesses, and occasionally through legal action. In Boston, the Homeless Civil Rights Project (HCRP) grew out of a campaign to stop harassment of the homeless in Boston Common by a particular police officer nicknamed RoboCop. HCRP organized a petition to get the motorcycle officer removed from the Common beat and in the process managed to negotiate representation on the police department's citizen advisory committee and to assist in training officers on how to interact with the homeless. This nondisruptive approach, focused on civil rights, won HCRP allies in Boston's halls of power. As a result, HCRP successfully opposed merchant discrimination against the homeless in Boston. The group documented numerous cases of homeless people being refused service or pushed out of restaurants and coffee shops while other customers "were allowed to linger over their meals." When it prepared to launch a boycott of the Au Bon Pain coffee-and-sandwich shops—a chain which "had a particularly notorious record of such discrimination"—the company's board of directors agreed to sit down and cowrite, with HCRP, a set of guidelines on how merchants should treat the homeless. Citywide, merchant discrimination against the homeless dropped dramatically.[34]

Meanwhile, on the other side of the country, the city of Santa Ana moved forcefully against "vagrants" living near the city's Civic Center, home to most of the services they needed. Orange County's county seat, Santa Ana carried the second-highest housing costs in the United States. In the summer of 1988, the city council declared that "vagrants are no longer welcome in the City of Santa Ana" and established a Vagrancy Task Force to move all homeless people and their possessions out of Santa Ana. As ever, the rationale was "quality of life" and preserving an inviting environment for shoppers and visitors. On August 15, 1990, the police carried out Operation Civic Center in a manner approximating a SWAT raid. Some police, armed with binoculars, took up positions on rooftops and called in the location of homeless people for cops on the ground to bust. They arrested sixty-three people. Following a lengthy booking process, in which many of the arrested were chained to benches and held for up to six hours without food or water, the police finally carted them off to the edge of town and left them there. A judge later found that police had illegally targeted the homeless and ordered the city to pay $400,000 in damages. Emboldened by the court's ruling, the homeless set up a tent city in the Santa Ana Civic Center area; the city council responded by making it illegal to set up tents or use sleeping bags or otherwise live temporarily outdoors in a public space. A seesaw court battle ensued, with the municipal court first upholding the new law, an appeals court striking it down, and the state supreme court again upholding it.[35]

Increasingly, however, the homeless and their advocates won these kinds of court cases. In 1992, a federal judge in New York ruled the city's antibegging law unconstitutional on First Amendment grounds. One month later, a judge ordered Miami to create "safe zones" where the homeless could "eat, sleep, bathe and cook without fear of arrest." This came after years of sweeping the homeless from Miami's public parks to make these settings more appealing to tourists. Judge C. Clyde Atkins ruled, however, that "arresting the homeless for harmless, involuntary, life-sustaining acts" violated their right to due process.[36] And in a number of cities, lawyers working on behalf of the homeless won recognition of their voting rights even though most homeless had no fixed address, hitherto a prerequisite for registering to vote.[37]

By the early 1990s, homeless activists could point to a mix of victories and defeats. Maybe the most important successes arose from their refusal to buy into the "morning in America" or "shining city on a hill" narratives. In the glamour days of the Reagan administration, with television shows like *Dynasty, Dallas,* and *Lifestyles of the Rich and Famous* promoting a narrative of prosperity reclaimed, homeless activists put the intertwined issues of poverty, housing, and homelessness before the American people and would not allow them to be swept under the rug. Public figures and celebrities jumped on the bandwagon, as when comedians Billy Crystal, Whoopi Goldberg, and Robin Williams launched Comic Relief, an HBO benefit that, year after year, raised money to be distributed to homeless organizations. In October 1989, more than 250,000 homeless and their allies—many of whom had marched hundreds of miles like the 1932 Bonus Army—gathered in Washington for a massive HOUSING NOW! rally. Not only did homeless activists' protests achieve a variety of improvements in municipalities all over the country, but the constant action in Washington led to Congress's passing the first law to address homelessness since the Great Depression. The McKinney Homeless Assistance Act appropriated $1 billion in aid for a variety of homeless programs in 1987 and 1988, including allocations for emergency shelters, job training, and health care. In short, it was an acknowledgment that homelessness had become a national crisis. Of course, the McKinney Act and its subsequent reauthorizations passed as emergency measures and did not attempt to solve the structural issues that led to homelessness. Indeed, the scholars who study homeless organizing in this period note that the most common "solution" to homelessness—the shelter—became institutionalized in this period, effectively taking the place of the old Skid Rows, but on a much larger scale. As Kim Hopper has concluded, "shelter neither solves homelessness nor prevents further displacement. Absent an adequate supply of affordable housing—and the jobs and income supports needed to sustain households once relocated—remedial efforts are doomed to an endless round of musical chairs." Moreover, by the mid-1990s, it was clear that the old prejudices against the homeless were alive and well, as when the new mayor of New York, Rudolph Giuliani, declared, "We must stop considering people as homeless, and recognize that they may be mentally ill, substance abusers, undereducated or untrained." Indeed, as a result of Giuliani's quality-of-life campaign, the homeless were as likely to wind up behind bars on Rikers Island as in a homeless shelter. Despite all the gains made by the homeless movement—all the lives saved—"compassion fatigue" opened the door for some in power to go back to the old practices of discarding and denying the homeless, sweeping them from view.[38]

In retrospect, it is easy to see that the homeless wars were fought from two competing front porch perspectives. Both sides wanted homelessness eradicated and mobilized only when they sensed that government seemed incapable of solving the problem. But as they went to battle, one side focused on helping the homeless survive and argued for more (and more affordable) housing, while the other side focused on the personal shortcomings of homeless people and struggled to remove them as a public nuisance. "So few of the resources America spent on homelessness" in the 1980s "went toward the provision of permanent and accessible housing," the sociologist Cynthia Bogard summed up, "while so many went toward studying homeless people's characteristics, 'rehabilitating' homeless people from their deficits, or warehousing them in shelters that are both costly and temporary." In a lot of ways, homelessness "had become a social problem that was primarily *not* about solving the nation's housing crisis." Rather, for many Americans, the main task involved fixing the homeless themselves, or, failing that, sheltering them from both the elements and their own personal deficiencies. The end of the homelessness wars thus showed the limits of front porch politics: both sides were left unsatisfied, as neither the housing crisis nor the question of what to do with so many homeless was resolved.

11

AIDS Politics

•

Perhaps due to the public's keen desire to buy into the "morning in America" fantasy, to believe that America once again stood tall after taking some body blows in the 1970s, many Americans could countenance crisis only in terms of individual failing. Homelessness, intruding so rudely into the Reagan years, could not be explained in terms of macroeconomics but only in terms of the homeless themselves. At best, sympathetic Americans might want to shelter them, but at worst, others were prepared to discard them, since by this reasoning the homeless had to be held accountable for their own lot.

At almost exactly the same time, many Americans reacted similarly to people stricken with the new AIDS plague. Since at first AIDS spread in the United States mostly among homosexuals and drug addicts, the American public did not demand a comprehensive government response in the way that they surely would have had the disease spread at first among heterosexuals (as it did, for example, in Africa). Rather, the Reagan administration's apparent unwillingness to address AIDS or to even dare speak its name in public fueled denial and an impulse to keep such unpleasantness out of public view. This abdication of leadership guaranteed a slow marshaling of resources to combat AIDS and only deepened the widespread perception that government was, in Reagan's own words, "the problem." But for those for whom AIDS suddenly became a front porch and very personal issue, there could be no waiting. AIDS workers in communities hard hit by the disease stepped into the chasm left by the government; they offered services almost immediately, raised money for research and sex education, and, as frustration grew with the official response to the epidemic, turned to an increasingly confrontational kind

of politics to win meaningful change in policy and public attitudes toward people with AIDS. Although veterans of the gay rights movement
played a central role in the fight against AIDS, many AIDS activists followed the same trajectory as the accidental activists at Love Canal or the
farmers fighting the power line or foreclosure: having given up on any
hope that the government might act, they moved unselfconsciously
into a mode of self-reliance, driven by horror and despair, anger and
compassion.

In addition, AIDS activists followed in the footsteps of feminists and
gay rights activists who had articulated and theorized the politics of
Americans' personal lives. People lived with AIDS mostly in private, in
their home lives, with the people they loved, but their political struggle
brought personal lives again into the public arena.

The first indications of the AIDS epidemic appeared in summer 1981,
just months before Paul Theroux published his article on the perils of
New York's subway system. At first, the news of the epidemic seemed as
removed from most Americans' experience as homelessness. Most of the
public responded the way they would to news of an outbreak of cholera
following a South American earthquake—it was something that happened to other people. And in any case, advances in modern medicine
had been so successful in eradicating infectious diseases, it seemed likely
that the illness—whatever it was—could be brought under control relatively quickly. In the gay community, however, a brief period of denial
soon gave way to terror and confusion. From initial reports in June 1981
of five gay men in Los Angeles each afflicted with three infections at
once, and in July of twenty-six gay men in New York with Kaposi's sarcoma (a cancer that usually hit older men but occurred now in men in
their thirties), to, by the end of August, seventy additional cases of
Kaposi's sarcoma or *Pneumocystis carinii* pneumonia, it was clearly an
epidemic. By early 1982, Lawrence Mass, a gay doctor in New York, had
begun describing it as a "disorder of immunity," and some public officials had labeled it GRID, for Gay-Related Immunodeficiency. It would
be another two years before scientists isolated the HIV virus that inhibits
the immune system, in turn opening the door to any number of oppor-
tunistic infections—hence the name Acquired Immune Deficiency Syndrome. By that time, doctors in the gay community had long before
pieced together the circumstantial evidence that the disease spread
through sexual contact and intravenous drug use. And the number of

gay men dying had shattered any hope that the disease could be out-lasted. "I thought that I would be killed by it, that everybody I knew would be killed by it," Cleve Jones, the San Francisco gay rights activist and friend of Harvey Milk, later said. "It was very frightening." Psychologists came up with a new term, "multiple loss syndrome," to describe "the ways that the grief process shut down when individuals experience too much loss without adequate time to grieve." The historian Allan Berube told *The New York Times* in 1987 that he had already lost thirty friends. "I'm learning how to incorporate grieving into my daily life," he said. "It's now as much a part of my life as eating and sleeping."[1]

Almost immediately, fierce debates over how to contain AIDS—even before it was called AIDS—erupted in the gay community. Doctors and some leading lights in the gay community urged gay men not necessarily to have less sex, but to have it with fewer people. Promiscuity, a product of sexual liberation in the 1960s and 1970s, came to be seen as the main culprit. Even David Goodstein, editor of *The Advocate*, who had at first been dismissive of such conclusions on the spread of the virus, conceded later in 1982 that "whether we like it or not, the fact is that aspects of the urban gay lifestyle we have created . . . are hazardous to our health. The evidence is overwhelming." But others heard this argument and sensed the specter of sanctimonious and possibly coercive moralism. Suddenly the debates over AIDS turned into latter-day debates over gay liberation, with some asking what the point of a sexual revolution was if not to have more sex and others responding that sex was not all that gay liberation represented.[2]

Had the virus spread at first among straight men and women, some of the debate over promiscuity in the wake of the sexual revolution would certainly have sounded the same, but the perception of a "gay plague" not only caused division in the gay community, it contributed to official neglect and a new wave of antigay politics. "The sexual revolution has begun to devour its children," the former Nixon speechwriter and future presidential candidate Pat Buchanan wrote in the *New York Post* in May 1983. "And among the revolutionary vanguard, Gay Rights activists, the mortality rate is highest and climbing . . . The poor homosexuals . . . they have declared war upon nature, and now nature is exacting an awful retribution." The Reverend Jerry Falwell agreed, but more than that, he warned his *Moral Majority Report* readers that HOMOSEXUAL DISEASES THREATEN AMERICAN FAMILIES. The public, largely ignorant about the nature of AIDS, worried less about people with AIDS than about whether they or their families could catch it. Could you get it from casual contact, from a kiss, sweat, a mosquito bite? Could you get it at the dentist's or in a restaurant? As late as September 1985, when it had been clearly established that AIDS spread only through bodily fluids—blood and semen—47 percent of Americans still believed AIDS could be spread by sharing a drinking glass, and 36 percent believed it was "unsafe to associate with someone with AIDS" even if one did not have "intimate physical contact." As a result, while only 15 percent polled by the *Los Angeles Times* agreed with William F. Buckley that people with AIDS should be tattooed as carriers, 51 percent did favor quarantining people with AIDS. In September 1985, the parents of eleven thousand New York public school students acted on their own front porch fears and kept their children home from the first day of school to protest the presence of a second-grader with AIDS at a school in Queens. "They send children home if they have lice or chicken pox, but they want to let them in if they have AIDS," one parent told a reporter. "Now what kind of reasoning is that?" In Kokomo, Indiana, Ryan White, a fourteen-year-old hemophiliac who contracted AIDS through a blood transfusion, fought to attend his public school after it had forced him to spend several months of seventh grade learning from home via a telephone hookup; when a court ruled in his favor, he was harassed by other kids at school, and the windows of his house were smashed and the family car's tires slashed. Cashiers at local grocery stores threw his mother's change onto the counter rather than touch her hands. Although pundits credited White's struggle with helping to pierce many myths about AIDS, there remained through the late 1980s considerable criticism of "the gay lifestyle" for the disease's spread and common casual approval of quarantining people with AIDS.[3]

In the meantime, the gay community, faced with a mounting body count and an absent government, reacted the way citizens do after their community is flattened by a tornado or flood; rather than argue the finer political points, they went out to help those who had been hit hardest. Unlike those militant farmers who first turned to radical actions and then moved to set up service organizations, AIDS activists established scores of AIDS service organizations and turned to more militant politics only later. Such a potent threat as AIDS, striking at the heart of their personal and social lives, warranted a comprehensive response, and at the moment when scientists were still scrambling, this first line of AIDS workers set the standard by helping those who had contracted the disease. It helped that the gay liberation movement had, by the early 1980s, started to devote more attention to lobbying and professionalization; the step toward providing services and lobbying over AIDS issues came naturally and really without question. Not unlike the women's health movement establishing the medicine-in-our-own-hands model, it was something that had to be done.[4]

Since New York and San Francisco experienced the epidemic's shock most severely, it made sense that AIDS service organizations first found their footing in those cities. By one tally, New York claimed half of the nation's AIDS cases by 1983; ten years later, it had more cases than the next forty cities combined. Late in the summer of 1981, before most Americans had even heard about a "gay cancer," eighty men gathered in the novelist and playwright Larry Kramer's apartment on Fifth Avenue overlooking Washington Square Park. Kramer was a polarizing figure in the gay rights movement thanks to his relentless criticism of what he saw as excessive promiscuity in the gay community; his novel *Faggots* (1978) seemed to many to be self-hating. According to some observers, Kramer "seemed to be always angry, and it was difficult to tell how much of his rage reflected his sour judgment of gay male culture and how much resulted from his resentment at the way it had treated him." In any case, on that night in Kramer's apartment, those in attendance decided to form Gay Men's Health Crisis (GMHC). At the outset, opinion divided over how the organization should function. Kramer led a minority who argued that GMHC should be a political organization, demanding government action in both combating the illness and in serving those who had contracted it. The majority, however, won the day with their vision of self-reliance; they set out to build a first-rate service organization dedicated solely to helping those with AIDS and educating the rest of the gay community about AIDS and how to avoid getting it. Through a variety of leaflets, newspapers, and public forums, GMHC took the message to the community and, as the sociologist Susan Chambre notes, the "lessons were not abstract." Two thousand people showed up at (and another five hundred were turned away from) a New York University auditorium for GMHC's second public forum in November 1982. At the event, physicians described to the crowd what they knew so far about AIDS, using a slide show; when one of them projected an image of a Kaposi's sarcoma lesion on the screen, a distressed voice in the balcony exclaimed, "Oh, no!" in recognition.[5]

Maybe most important, GMHC grew in response to an acute need, with activists essentially making up their mission on the fly. "We are Gay Men's Health Crisis," the group's first newsletter began. "We are volunteers concerned about a growing threat of diseases in our community." Like families in Love Canal comparing notes on their families' ailments, the writers promised to pass along information about these diseases once medical investigators started to figure it out. At the same time, from the start, GMHC operated a Patient Services Committee "to help these men through what must be, in the best of circumstances, a terrifying moment in their lives." By 1983, the menu of services GMHC offered had expanded to include "a hotline, crisis intervention counseling, a buddy program, and a financial assistance department to help with welfare, food stamps, and Social Security . . . recreation services, support groups, and patient advocacy." Farmers in Iowa would have recognized the array of service offerings as if they had been organized by the Iowa Farm Unity Coalition. The GMHC's volunteers who designed and delivered its services "viewed AIDS as a personal and as a communal issue." In time, GMHC mobilized thousands of volunteers to tend the sick and raised millions of dollars for research and education; it is safe to say that the vast majority of those volunteers joined the battle because AIDS had touched their lives personally. As one volunteer recalled, he got involved with GMHC because he "wanted to be where there were caring and informed people doing something about what was happening." GMHC volunteers described the situation as an emergency. "The feeling was that everything was on fire and that we had to do something about it," GMHC volunteer Alex Carballo-Dieguez recalled. "We couldn't turn our backs to it and say 'I am going to do something else.'" Not to act was not an option.[6]

GMHC's variety of services met a host of needs that many felt the government should have been meeting. Working at first out of donated space in a welfare hotel on West Twenty-Second Street, the hotline rang off the hook, from over a hundred calls its very first night of operation to twenty thousand calls a year in 1985 to fifty thousand calls in 1987. Much of the work involved advocating for people with AIDS (known as "PWAs") as they struggled to overcome discrimination in health care; in the early years, hospitals and ambulance services tended to treat patients like

lepers, refusing to deliver food or push patients in wheelchairs unless
they were dressed in gowns, mask, and gloves. In 1985–86, the GMHC
ombudsman mediated 485 cases with health-care providers; two years
later, the number had nearly tripled, and often, proper service could not
be won without lawyers getting involved.[7]

As critics continued to blame gay men for bringing AIDS on themselves, GMHC and other service organizations went out of their way to
show that in fact the gay community could act responsibly by providing
reasonable and compassionate care to those who needed it. The sociologist Deborah Gould calls this the "trope of responsibility," playing into
the "shame-imbued idea that gays, somehow undeserving, had to be
'good' in order to get a proper response to the AIDS crisis from state and
society. Respectability, on straight society's terms, was the price of admission." But as we have seen with other political mobilizations in the
1970s and 1980s, many also felt that they had been good citizens, only to
be abandoned. "I love my country. I've worked hard for it. I've paid my
taxes, voted in every [election], and I never threw garbage in the streets,"
GMHC volunteer Robert Cecchi declared in a 1983 candlelight vigil in
New York.[8] Indeed, increasingly, GMHC cast its work as dedicated to helping decent people just *survive*—physically, financially, spiritually, and
emotionally—because no one else was helping. Here, support groups such
as Gay Men with AIDS (GMWA) were especially important. "We talk
about how we're going to buy food and pay rent when our savings run
out . . . how we are going to earn enough money to live when some of us
are too sick to work . . . how it feels to get fired from our jobs . . . the pain
we feel when our lovers leave us out of fear of AIDS . . . the friends who
have stopped calling . . . what it feels like when our families refuse to visit
us in the hospital." Michael Callen, founder of GMWA, told a New York
congressional delegation in the spring of 1983, "Mostly we talk about
what it feels like to be treated like lepers who are treated as if we are morally, if not literally, contagious. We try to share what hope there is and to
help each other live our lives one day at a time. What we talk about is
survival." For the first six years of the epidemic, this existential concern
dominated all others, and the same held true in most other cities.[9]

In San Francisco, Cleve Jones and others founded the Kaposi's
Sarcoma Education and Research Foundation in April 1982 in the Castro and pretty quickly managed to secure funding from the city's Department of Public Health (and, later, state funding). By 1984, ten staff

members ran the operation and had changed its name to San Francisco AIDS Foundation (SFAF). One activist described the importance of "owning" AIDS: "It's our disease (our sickness and dying) and how we deal with it is our business. What's more, it's our business to deal with it." Of course, ownership brought its own perils, potentially letting government off the hook for failing to address the crisis if the gay communities "owned the disease too completely." In San Francisco, however, the city partnered with service organizations from the earliest stages of confronting the disease—in a way that other cities such as New York did not. It helped that gays in San Francisco were already an important part of the political establishment dating back to Harvey Milk days. It also helped that, unlike New York in the early 1980s, San Francisco's budget—despite the damage wrought by the tax revolt—could accommodate spending on AIDS.[10]

SFAF led the nation in devising a remarkably successful sex education campaign that dramatically cut the number of AIDS infections in the city. Since safe-sex practices were widely perceived as making sex less pleasurable, SFAF had to come up with a way to sell using condoms to its audience. Under the direction of Les Pappas—who famously declared, "Until recently gay men had as much interest in condoms as Eskimos do in air conditioning"—SFAF came up with a campaign that effectively eroticized AIDS prevention. The HIV infection rate in the city dropped dramatically from a peak of 21 percent of uninfected gay men becoming infected in 1982 to less than 1 percent of the gay male population infected annually by 1985.[11] And in the meantime, despite objections from some quarters of the gay community, the city shut down fourteen bathhouses—widely regarded as laboratories for the spread of AIDS; another six had already closed following a significant drop in business. As one historian has noted, "their patrons were either dead, dying, or afraid of dying." By 1987, SFAF employed eighty-five people and had extended its services to include a hotline, counseling and advocacy programs, a food bank, and housing assistance.[12]

As SFAF grew dramatically during the epidemic's early years, it overshadowed the self-organizing AIDS service efforts of other demographic groups. The sociologist Nancy Stoller reminds us that AIDS activism extended to many people who, thanks to the attention on gay white men with the disease and their political debates, were left out of public discussion and who have been largely left out of the historical record. But

Stoller's work recovers a variety of AIDS organizations dedicated to serving women, African Americans, Latinos, prostitutes, and prisoners that essentially showed the same self-reliance impulses as SFAF or GMHC, but to an even greater degree, since public and private funding were harder for them to come by. AIDS work happened not only in the Castro but in neighborhoods all over the city.[13]

In the Tenderloin, San Francisco's red-light district, prostitutes organized the California Prostitutes Education Project (Cal-PEP) to promote safe sex practices and keep AIDS in check among sex workers and their customers. The project got its start when the Centers for Disease Control (CDC), interested in mapping prostitutes with HIV, approached COYOTE (Cast Off Your Old Tired Ethics), an organization advocating the decriminalization of prostitution, for help. COYOTE agreed, and soon the prostitutes who participated became AIDS experts, counseling their peers and, from Cal-PEP's maroon van, handing out condoms, spermicides, and bleach kits to decontaminate needles. By 1987, Cal-PEP, with the support of the CDC and the state department of public health, had become a model for public health campaigns as it extended its brief beyond sex workers to other street people. A thirty-two-foot-long RV became a mobile clinic, complete with counseling rooms, an examination room, and a lab; it rolled through parts of the city where SFAF dared not tread. As Gloria Lockett, the former prostitute who became the executive director of Cal-PEP, reported, Cal-PEP was committed to hiring people who were formerly prostitutes, drug addicts, and homeless, because they knew better than anyone else what life at the margins was like. "The work that we want to do, and that we cherish doing, is working with what other people call the losers," Lockett said. "But to us they're our people. So basically we have moved from being this prostitutes-only organization to being an organization that works with people on the street." Cal-PEP's approach in time caught on with public health officials. Later in the AIDS crisis, the San Francisco Department of Public Health, for example, followed Cal-PEP's example by expanding its services from the Castro to the poor and predominantly African American Bayview–Hunter's Point neighborhood, where there had been a sharp rise in HIV/AIDS since 1987.[14]

In other cases, the persistent perception that AIDS service organizations like SFAF failed to meet the needs of certain constituencies led to breakaway groups. Mainstream organizations provided few pamphlets in Asian languages. But Asian activists in San Francisco formed the

Asian AIDS Task Force in 1986 (it later became the Asian/Pacific AIDS Coalition, or A/PAC); other groups included the Chinese AIDS Prevention Project, Japanese Against AIDS Project, West Bay Filipino AIDS Project, Southeast Asian AIDS Prevention Project, Korean Community Service Center, and Gay Asian Pacific Alliance. Likewise, a group of self-described anarchist hippies started a needle exchange program among intravenous drug users in the Tenderloin in 1988, eventually building it into Prevention Point, the largest program of its kind in the nation. At least once a week, they turned up in the Tenderloin with needles and exchanged one clean one for each dirty one brought to them. In the first ten months, Prevention Point exchanged more than a hundred thousand needles, and by 1992, that number had risen to more than a million as the group took the program to five locations in the city. The program generated controversy, of course, because critics saw it as undermining efforts to get drug users off drugs altogether (the complaint was heard from many black leaders, who feared that needle exchange would keep, in Stoller's words, "the black community endlessly chained to drugs"). Still, there was no question that it helped keep the spread of AIDS in check.[15]

AIDS activists in these service organizations worked themselves to the bone, partly out of sympathy and compassion but mostly out of desperation to just put an end to the dying. Overwhelmed as they were, few proposed more militant responses, though there were exceptions. Larry Kramer still stands as the most prescient of all AIDS activists, effectively predicting the government neglect that would follow the outbreak of AIDS and demanding that those affected harness their outrage and direct it toward those with the power and resources to do the research and find a cure. As early as March 1983, Kramer published the landmark article 1,112 AND COUNTING in the *New York Native*, the most widely read gay newspaper in the city. "If this article doesn't scare the shit out of you, we're in real trouble," he wrote in the opening line. "If this article doesn't rouse you to anger, fury, rage and action, gay men have no future on this earth. Our continued existence depends on just how angry you can get." The Boston activist Cindy Patton made a similar appeal to channel anger into action in the June 18, 1983, issue of the *Gay Community News*, urging readers to reject straight society's message that they somehow deserved this "punishment" for leading a "terrible lifestyle." "We have to turn that around now, and say: This society is not going to kill us anymore."[16]

At first, these pleas for action were rarely heeded.[17] Given the scale of the epidemic and the dying, the first priority continued to be caring for others. Over time, though, as months turned into years, and the epidemic grew with no signs of stopping, no signs of a cure, many who had been touched by AIDS saw their anger catch up with Larry Kramer's and moved to more militant political action. The federal government, most egregiously, seemed to be responding to the crisis in slow motion. Whereas the CDC had spent $9 million within months of the 1976 Legionnaires' disease outbreak (which killed thirty-four people), it spent only $1 million in the first year of an AIDS epidemic that had already claimed the lives of more than two hundred. By the middle of 1983, the City of San Francisco had spent $3 million on AIDS, which was more than the National Institutes of Health (NIH) had allocated for "extramural AIDS research" nationwide to that point. By 1985, when the number of AIDS cases had cleared eleven thousand and the number killed had topped six thousand, the president of the United States had not once uttered the term "AIDS" in public. Meanwhile, the CDC was by then estimating that half a million to a million people were already infected with HIV "and that AIDS cases would double over the next year." For anyone concerned about AIDS, it slowly became impossible to tolerate the government's apparent willingness to sit back and watch as the relentless onslaught of the epidemic unfolded.[18]

Most histories of the AIDS crisis rely on Randy Shilts's exposé *And the Band Played On* (1987) to portray the Reagan administration as not only willfully negligent in failing to address the AIDS epidemic but as beholden to certain segments of the New Right. And certainly it is true that the administration did next to nothing about the disease during Reagan's first term. But, as the historian Jennifer Brier reminds us, the "historical record points to a more complicated, and internally contradictory, administrative reaction to AIDS," especially after 1985. Brier emphasizes a split within the administration, with Secretary of Education William Bennett and his undersecretary (and later presidential domestic adviser) Gary Bauer squaring off against Surgeon General C. Everett Koop and a presidential commission on HIV/AIDS.[19]

Not until December 1985 did President Reagan ask Koop to write a special report on AIDS, emphasizing that "AIDS must be dealt with as a major *public* health problem" as opposed to a political problem. That made sense to Koop, an evangelical Christian known for his staunch antiabortion beliefs. But the surgeon general surprised many in the administration when he issued a report in October 1986 aimed as much at prevention as at addressing those who already had the disease. Koop's report laid out an educational program for adults and children that sparked an uproar within the administration, mostly because he called for blunt discussion of AIDS and sex among young Americans.[20]

Koop's views ultimately prevailed when a presidential commission established by Reagan at Bauer's request—in hopes it would approve of Bauer's approach to AIDS—came back with a report that more or less endorsed Koop's educational program as well as a massive increase in funding of AIDS research and services for PWAs. It also praised the "homosexual community" for "the development and growth of community-based organizations" such as GMHC and SFAF that had for so many years been carrying the can for the government and treating people with AIDS.[21]

As the federal government dithered, and as critics like Senator Jesse Helms became more strident in blaming homosexuals for AIDS, the conditions that made more militant activism possible began to come together. For one thing, there were new reasons for the gay community to feel under siege. The June 1986 Supreme Court decision in *Bowers v. Hardwick*, which upheld an 1816 Georgia sodomy law, sparked protests all over the country, including the largest spontaneous gay rights demonstration—three thousand people blocking traffic around New York City's Sheridan Square near the Stonewall Inn—since the original Stonewall riots. Now, it seemed, the government had the right to invade one's bedroom and police one's sex life. Furthermore, by 1987, AIDS had killed at least twenty-eight thousand people in the United States. Hate crimes against gay men and women more than doubled nationwide, and in 28 percent of these cases in New York City, the perpetrators "taunted the victims with comments about AIDS." Taken together, the *Hardwick* decision, the government's failure to do anything about AIDS, and a rise in hateful rhetoric and violence all added up to, as one scholar phrased it, "evidence that state and society viewed gay men as expendable—indeed, as better off dead." This was just what Larry Kramer had warned of. In October 1986, at the national March on Washington for Lesbian and Gay Rights, organizers began calling for civil disobedience. Over the course of the weekend, wave after wave of protesters demonstrated at the steps of the Supreme Court, and police arrested more than eight hundred of them as thousands of supporters applauded and cheered. It was just the beginning.[22]

In February 1987, the Centers for Disease Control hosted a meeting of CDC officials, doctors, and representatives from every major gay and AIDS organization in the country, and they worked out an agreement on promoting HIV education instead of HIV testing. It was an orderly, professional affair, an important and seemingly historic conference. But there was a fly in the ointment. A group calling itself the Lavender Hill Mob (after a 1951 British film starring Alec Guinness) showed up at the end-of-meeting press conference dressed as concentration camp prisoners, in gray prison shirts with the pink triangle the Nazis used to single out homosexuals, and mocked the government officials and AIDS workers alike. A little agreement on promoting education was, in the face of so much death, barely worth a mention as far as the Lavender Hill Mob was concerned. Indeed, such an event was only marginally different from the more general national silence then hiding from view the growing "holocaust" of AIDS deaths.[23]

The Lavender Hill Mob action reflected a growing sense of outrage among many AIDS workers, particularly anger toward AIDS organizations that seemed calmly committed to merely managing the AIDS epidemic rather than stopping it cold. One activist told a reporter that people were "getting tired of candlelight vigils when, in fact, blow torches may be necessary."[24]

From this bubbling cauldron of fury and indignation came the AIDS Coalition to Unleash Power (ACT UP). Just as Larry Kramer was present at the creation of GMHC, he now sparked the founding of this new organization with a speech at the Gay and Lesbian Community Center in Greenwich Village. He who had once been seen as a hysterical, screaming madman now returned as the "redeemed prophet." "I have never been able to understand why for six long years we have sat back and let ourselves literally be knocked off man by man without fighting back," he shouted at his audience. "How many dead brothers have to be piled up in front of your faces in a heap before you learn to fight back and scream and yell and demand and take some responsibilities for your own life?" In a matter of weeks, ACT UP had established itself as a group of mostly young professionals who had been affected in some way by AIDS; they brought experience in government, public relations, journalism, and the arts, as well as ties to veterans of the gay rights movement, to bear on their work. As Deborah Gould has argued, the key to this new mobilization was emotion; in short order, ACT UP saw to it that anger replaced grief, militancy replaced mourning. "ACT UP is a diverse, non-partisan group united in anger and committed to direct action to end the AIDS crisis," read the group's statement of purpose. "We protest and demonstrate; we meet with government and public health officials; we research and distribute the latest medical information; we are not silent." By the early 1990s, more than eighty ACT UP chapters organized in the United States, with more than thirty others working in other countries.[25]

ACT UP made a name for itself by pursuing a steady campaign of aggressive, nonviolent direct action demonstrations—all as vehicles for demanding long-overdue government action (even after years of official neglect, as in so many other movements in this book, activists turned to the nearest tool at hand—some kind of government intervention). At its first action, on March 24, 1987, hundreds of ACT UP demonstrators held a die-in on Wall Street in front of Trinity Church, holding up traffic for hours. Police arrested seventeen people, and the press picked up the story (Larry Kramer acknowledged that they had no specific complaint with Wall Street, but the location was useful in attracting the media). They issued demands that soon became familiar: an immediate release of AIDS drugs by the FDA, and at reasonable prices; a "massive public education" campaign to help prevent AIDS; and the "establishment of a coordinated, comprehensive, and compassionate national policy on AIDS." When Dr. Frank Young, the head of the Food and Drug Administration, who had been hanged in effigy on Wall Street that day, several weeks later approved a speedier drug approval process, the media "credited ACT UP's pressure tactics for this success."[26]

At the same time, ACT UP made it clear that the sudden change in tactics, the move toward militant action, came really as a last resort. "For six years our community has stood virtually alone in waging the war against this epidemic," declared Ralph Payne, a San Francisco AIDS Foundation board member who spoke at the June 1, 1987, ACT UP demonstration at the White House.

> We have developed the services . . . We have lobbied our elected officials demanding action. We have fought back lunatics wanting to put us into concentration camps. We have conducted the funerals. We have conducted the funerals! And we have exhausted all of the avenues available

to us within the system. We must let the system know that it is failing us, and that we can no longer stand by and watch our people die. If we have to, we will break the law—non-violently. Filling up the jails is preferable to filling up the hospitals. We are not going to just die.

As with so many front porch mobilizations in the 1970s and 1980s, an existential threat pushed people who had not previously thought of themselves as activists out of their homes and into the streets.[27]

ACT UP members took part in nonviolent direct action even as an extensive committee structure provided a host of organizing opportunities. The Majority Action Committee and Women's Caucus focused on people of color, who were the majority of people with AIDS, and on women with AIDS. The Majority Action Committee, meanwhile, showed that "only 9 percent of the participants in New York's AIDS Program trials were black even though they accounted for 33 percent of the city's AIDS cases." In January 1988, the Women's Caucus occupied the offices of *Cosmopolitan* magazine and got it to retract an article by the psychiatrist Robert Gould headlined REASSURING NEWS ABOUT AIDS: A DOCTOR TELLS WHY YOU MAY NOT BE AT RISK, which essentially suggested that straight women had little to fear from the disease. The Women's Caucus also succeeded in getting the CDC to change the definition of AIDS to include ailments that were unique to women. "Many women had been dying of bacterial pneumonia, which was ridiculous, like it was an epidemic of bacterial pneumonia," the scholar and activist Maxine Wolfe recalled. "But it wasn't. It was HIV, really." ACT UP also got the CDC to acknowledge that AIDS manifested itself in women in incidents of cervical cancer, tuberculosis, and a low T-cell count that had previously been left out of the agency's definition. The Housing Committee, meanwhile, worked to show the link between AIDS and poverty, and pressed for better housing and health care. Maybe most important, members of the Treatment & Data (T&D) Committee effectively became experts on all of the most recent research and used that expertise to challenge the FDA and the National Institute of Allergy and Infectious Diseases (NIAID) on how they conducted their drug trials. Eventually, T&D published the *FDA Action Handbook*, which laid out the way the FDA worked and how its drug approval process—with testing done not by the FDA but by the NIH or by the pharmaceutical industry under the FDA's supervision—kept lifesaving drugs from the patients who needed them.[28]

As in the women's health movement of the late 1960s and 1970s, T&D put citizens forward as experts who might know the science as well as the scientists.[29] One T&D member, Jim Eigo, came up with the idea of holding "parallel" drug trials that would greatly expand the number of people able to take the drug. Maybe they did not qualify for the official trial because they were too sick or on other medications, but under Eigo's proposal, they would still be able to take the drug while the researchers would benefit from the added data. The point was that the FDA was overly concerned with safety when they could be testing new drugs on people who were already dying with no other options. To press this campaign on the FDA, ACT UP took the fight to the agency's headquarters in Rockville, Maryland, in October 1988. Fifteen hundred protesters laid siege to the building and covered it in signs and banners, including one with a bloody handprint that read THE GOVERNMENT HAS BLOOD ON ITS HANDS and ONE AIDS DEATH EVERY HALF HOUR. Over the course of the day, small groups of activists blocked entrances and others managed to get inside; they held die-ins and hanged President Reagan in effigy. When police arrested 176 people, others blocked the police buses as they tried to depart for the jails. Within two weeks, the FDA issued new regulations for a speeded-up drug evaluation process, and seven months later, Anthony Fauci, the head of the National Institute of Allergy and Infectious Diseases, adopted Jim Eigo's parallel track proposal. AIDS activists had, *The Washington Post* observed, "demanded a revolution," and in dramatic fashion, they got it. The testing time on AIDS drugs was cut in half, and over time, the *Post* said, FDA officials started to sound so much like ACT UP activists, they could have been working for the group.[30]

On the same weekend as the FDA demonstration, the organizers behind the Names Project Memorial Quilt displayed the quilt for the first time in Washington, across from the White House. The Quilt project had begun in 1987, with the idea that sewing together the panels, each of which represents someone who has died from AIDS, would help to dramatize the scale of the epidemic. Cleve Jones and other Names Project founders hoped that by using the "traditional American" craft of quilting, they would be able to touch American heartstrings and their "pocketbooks." Jones claimed publicly that the Names Project was "completely non-political" and that it had "no political message at all," though it might be more accurate to say it was open-endedly political: the historian Christopher Capozzola shows convincingly that the quilt's "framework of memory was consistently democratic in ways that could encompass its multiple constituencies and their varying definitions of politics." Family, friends, and lovers of those lost to AIDS could create quilt panels with any visual or textual content they wanted; there were no restrictions other than the size. At each public viewing, organizers read all of the names aloud, a process that, in 1987, already took more than three hours. On the weekend of the FDA demonstrations, ACT UP tried to turn the quilt into a source of anger and mobilization. Activists handed out leaflets: SHOW YOUR ANGER TO THE PEOPLE WHO HELPED MAKE THE QUILT POSSIBLE: OUR GOVERNMENT. The text on the flip side read: "The Quilt helps us remember our lovers, relatives, and friends who have died during the past eight years. These people have died from a virus. But they have been killed by our government's neglect and inaction . . . More than 40,000 people have died from AIDS . . . Before this Quilt grows any larger, turn your grief into anger. Turn anger into action. TURN THE POWER OF THE QUILT INTO ACTION."

Here was perhaps the clearest indication that the outlook among AIDS workers had changed. Where previously activists had little energy to do more than tend the sick and mourn the dying, now those experiences fueled their anger and mobilization. "We were saying, 'Mourning's fine. No problem. Make your space for mourning,'" recalled Carol Hayse of ACT UP / Chicago. "But then, you know, get out, grab a rock and throw it through the window of the FDA."[31]

Or blacken the eye of a drug company. Since Burroughs Wellcome, the maker of azidothymidine, or AZT, effectively held a monopoly on what was then the only AIDS drug on the market and charged huge sums to use it, ACT UP targeted the company, demanding price cuts. After the company responded to relatively light pressure by cutting AZT's price by 20 percent, ACT UP waged a series of further protests against the company to press for greater price reductions. Most dramatically, in September 1989, ACT UP activists dropped a SELL WELLCOME banner from the balcony above the New York Stock Exchange trading floor at the start of a day's business. Just four days later, the company agreed to cut AZT's price another 20 percent, from about $8,000 a year to $6,400.[32]

Taken together, these concentrated bursts of political theater directed at both the government and the drugmakers seemed to at last affect those with the power to address, if not solve, the AIDS problem. As in so many grassroots battles in the 1970s and 1980s, this change in the political landscape would not have occurred without the efforts of those people most directly affected by the crisis at hand. "If people weren't sitting in at FDA, and chaining themselves to the wall of Burroughs Wellcome," one scientist told *The Wall Street Journal*, "none of this"—none of the fast-tracking of drug trials, none of the reductions in drug prices— "would be happening."[33]

Given ACT UP's success in shaming the government and companies like Burroughs Wellcome into taking steps to improve treatment and make it more accessible, the group soon turned its attention to its political opponents. From the start, ACT UP had made President Reagan the poster boy for silence and indifference in the AIDS crisis, but in the late 1980s, it likewise targeted individuals like John Cardinal O'Connor in New York, and Jesse Helms and his corporate supporters, and soon took the battle to Reagan's successor, President George H. W. Bush. Dozens of ACT UP activists staged a die-in outside New York's St. Patrick's Cathedral in December 1989 while, inside, affinity groups disrupted O'Connor's mass by throwing condoms in the air, parading up the aisles with CARDINAL O'CONDOM placards, and chaining themselves to the pews. The NYPD arrested 111 people that day, and the media became sharply critical of ACT UP and its tactics: disrupting a religious service crossed an invisible line of propriety. "Because we went inside the cathedral, we denied the Catholic parishioners their freedom of religion," one participant remembered. "Their rights became the focus; our life-and-death issues were secondary." Increasingly, ACT UP got more attention for disruption than for its political message, but not always. During Mario Cuomo's State of the State address in January 1990, the governor interrupted his speech to ask the sergeant at arms, who was dragging away an AIDS protester, to let the man speak. Cuomo responded by defending the state's AIDS policies, but to the astonishment of many in attendance, he then commented to the assembly that "you can argue with [the protester's] timing and his taste [but] you cannot argue with his sincerity." Larry Kramer said he burst into tears when he saw the exchange on television. "It's just so moving to be taken seriously, to see Cuomo actually let the guy speak," Kramer told the *Times*. In addition, protests that same year targeted Jesse Helms—including a kiss-in in the senator's

Washington office—and Philip Morris, the tobacco company, for campaign donations to Helms. After a nine-month boycott, Philip Morris announced it would double company contributions to AIDS research and education.[34]

Increasingly, though, those in power found sympathetic hearings in the press when they complained about ACT UP's adversarial tactics. San Francisco ACT UP organizers had been rubbing authorities the wrong way for a couple of years—with a blockade of the Golden Gate Bridge, a disruption of the San Francisco Opera's opening night, and a Castro Street blockade—when, in June 1990, they decided to protest the Sixth International Conference on AIDS. Even before the convention began, they blocked the Marriott Hotel doors, demanding to participate in the conference. When Health and Human Services Secretary Louis Sullivan was to speak to the conference, ACT UP shouted him down, to the point that he could not go on. Later, more than 500 demonstrators blocked Market Street downtown, stopping traffic until police arrested 140 of them. All of this, particularly the harangue directed at Sullivan, drew negative comments from the press. "It's not as if society had turned its back on AIDS and those whom it strikes," a *New York Times* editorial began, implausibly. The paper admonished ACT UP for failing to see that shouting down the HHS secretary was counterproductive. "If ACT UP's members would only keep their faith in education and hard lobbying and put down their bullhorns, they might find their rage surprisingly well understood, and effective when focused in the right way on the right targets." President Bush likewise chastised ACT UP for its "totally counterproductive tactics." To the extent that AIDS "should be treated as a health question," he said, "they work even against that because of their outrageous actions," which had included mass die-ins near the president's vacation home in Kennebunkport, Maine. Some in ACT UP did in fact express reservations about these tactics and the possibility that they would alienate a lot of people, but they were in the minority. As one organizer remarked, "We do a lot of really nasty things, but it gets stuff done. I don't see how you could stop at anything if someone you love is dying and that can be changed and you feel that not enough is being done."[35]

The ongoing confrontation with George Bush led to an escalation in tactics. Bush, long annoyed by ACT UP's tactics, had further provoked the group by being more outwardly antagonistic than President Reagan had been. Where Reagan had stayed mostly silent on AIDS and had quietly promoted a "public health crisis" approach, with little regard for the civil rights of people with AIDS, Bush more overtly put the blame for AIDS on the victims and implied that he had more important things— dealing with an economic recession in an election year, for example—to tend to. "I'm in favor of behavioral change," the president said. "Here's a disease where you can control its spread by your own personal behavior." ACT UP/NY responded by inviting AIDS activists to Washington on October 11, 1992, just a few weeks before the election. "You have lost someone to AIDS. For more than a decade, your government has mocked your loss. You have spoken out in anger, joined political protests, carried fake coffins and mock tombstones, and splattered red paint to represent someone's HIV-positive blood, perhaps your own," the invitation read. "George Bush believes that the White House gates shield him, from you, your loss, and his responsibility for the AIDS crisis. Now it is time to bring AIDS home to George Bush." ACT UP planned to bring AIDS home to the president with a funeral procession that would conclude with "an act of grief and rage, and love" at the White House: the faintly sacramental spreading of ashes on the president's lawn. "Join us to pro- test twelve years of genocidal AIDS policy."[36]

Organizers deliberately juxtaposed this adversarial tactic with the Names Project Memorial Quilt, implying that grieving alone achieved little. "George Bush would be happy if we all made Quilt panels," one ACT UP/NY member said. "We're showing people what the White House has done: they've turned our loved ones into ashes and bones." Indeed, as Avram Finkelstein, the artist who came up with the iconic SILENCE = DEATH poster, later described it, "the procession was the Quilt come to life—walking, shouting and storming the White House." At the end of the march, "the ash bearers charged the gate [and] a fog of ashes blew through the fence and the urns were hurled." The ashes action, as stunning as Vietnam Veterans Against the War throwing their medals over the fence at the U.S. Capitol in 1971, represented everything that ACT UP stood for—following one's anger and indignation from the front porch into the streets, where others who shared that anger awaited. The ashes procession may not have influenced policymakers, but it "defined AIDS memorials for me," Finkelstein concluded. "It connected me for the first time to the anger and grief of thousands of others, and recon- firmed what I have always known . . . action is the real Quilt."[37]

A variety of forces conspired to bring about ACT UP's eventual decline. Inner conflicts led some committees such as Treatment & Data and the Housing Committee to peel off and form their own organizations. Perhaps more important, the organization's success in winning key demands, such as the removal of clinical trial red tape and greater funding for AIDS services, undercut the impetus for militancy. Furthermore, as in any intense political climate, individuals burned out and could not sustain the same level of engagement and militancy over many years. By the early 1990s, as treatment options began to improve, ACT UP could legitimately take some credit for concrete scientific and bureaucratic improvements. No less than the National Institutes of Health's Anthony Fauci credited ACT UP with improving the "way we design our scientific approaches" to testing new drugs. Experts have partly credited AIDS activists, too, for the advances that led to the 1996 discovery of protease inhibitors that are, to date, the most effective treatment of AIDS. The organization did not, on the other hand, succeed in keeping the treatment costs down—try $20,000 a year for protease inhibitors—and that financial reality, in time, led many AIDS organizations to turn their attention to the global south, where AIDS still runs rampant and where too few drugs are available because of the cost.[38]

All told, activists working on AIDS and homelessness brought the intimate, personal approach to politics typical of the front porch perspective into the streets and living rooms of mainstream America. Even more than other aggrieved groups, the homeless and people with AIDS were marginal because so many in mainstream America—and particularly in the halls of power—preferred not to see them. Discarded and disregarded, people with AIDS and the homeless—along with their supporters and allies—first made sure that they got the services necessary for survival and decent, dignified treatment; and then they made sure that they would not, in fact, be ignored. They refused to stay in the shadows, and in so refusing, they executed the most basic political act: they joined the ranks of a nation of activists.

PART 5

Saving America from Itself

● ●

Activists in nearly every political battle chronicled in this book—whether it involved busing, the family, gay rights, women's equality, toxic waste, farmers and tenants, the homeless and people with AIDS—couched their claims in moral terms because each battle tapped into a sense of moral outrage. Outrage about suffering wrongs, about having expectations dashed, and unfairly, is a moral outrage rooted in a sense of injustice. But in the so-called "culture wars" of the 1980s, morality itself came into question. What is and is not moral? The answer depends on one's world-view. Regardless of how one answers, one is almost certainly convinced—just as those who mobilized out of a sense of being wronged were convinced—of the rightness (and righteousness) of one's cause and its consistency with American values.

In the 1970s and 1980s, questions of morality—and related questions of decency and obscenity—permeated public discourse. How could America maintain its constitutionally guaranteed right to freedom of expression without damaging traditional mores that insulated children from the obscene, pornographic, and *immoral*? As we saw in chapter 3, the battles turned primarily on questions of choice, on decisions made by individuals in their private or family lives. In this way, the 1970s battles over women's equality, gay rights, and the family anticipated continuing struggles in other areas of private and family life. Choosing to become pregnant is, of course, a deeply personal decision, and so is choosing to terminate a pregnancy. Teaching children about sex and sexuality is not a matter to be taken lightly, and most parents expect some control over when and how those lessons are taught. And allowing children to experience certain works of art or entertainment—visual, theatrical, or musical—can, depending on the content and context, also be a fraught choice for parents.

As battles over abortion, pornography, and decency in popular culture raged in the 1980s, much of the fight focused on *who* had the control. Who had the right to make these decisions? Who defined what is immoral or legitimate? Who defined what is obscene, indecent, or artistic? Some thought that every decision should be made by individuals, while others felt that a whole community (local, state, or federal) might in some cases make certain decisions in the interest of the whole community or society. Usually, in the end, no middle ground could be found. For both sides, the stakes for the nation seemed too high. In any and every culture war battle, Americans on all sides can be counted upon to be certain that they are aiming to save America from itself.

12

Abortion Wars

●

Few who knew Randall Terry could have predicted that he would, in the 1980s, become one of America's most prominent culture warriors. Terry had grown up in a liberal middle-class family in upstate New York, the caricature of a guy who showed up too late for the Sixties party. A musician who wished he had been born ten years sooner, he hitchhiked through the South, hoped to make it in the music business, dabbled in drugs, and then gave up; he made his way back to central New York and became a born-again Christian. Terry later said that the Lord put the vision in his heart not only to "rescue babies and rescue mothers, but to rescue the country," but actually it was a film that did it. He had wept after seeing *Whatever Happened to the Human Race?*, a film based on the evangelical thinker Francis Schaeffer's book of the same name, described by one scholar as the "*Birth of a Nation* of pro-life politics." Binghamton and nearby Vestal, New York, would be Terry's Lexington and Concord. In the parking lot in front of Southern Tier Women's Services clinic in the spring of 1984, Terry and his wife, Cindy, leafleted against abortion and spoke to women about giving their children up for adoption to couples who, like the Terrys, had been unable to conceive (one woman agreed and let the Terrys adopt her baby daughter). On June 8, 1984, as Southern Tier, faced with the politically motivated loss of their Binghamton lease, planned to move to Vestal, Terry and six others pressed past the Binghamton clinic's staff and entered a procedure room. Police arrived to find that the activists had chained themselves to equipment and furniture in the room. Terry, by then a department store tire salesman, refused to pay bail and, like the civil rights activists he so admired, spent thirty days in jail. There, he considered his position and the movement he wanted to lead. You get nowhere by being nice, he thought. Better to follow the example of Gandhi and King and create "the tension and upheaval necessary to produce political and social change." Like civil rights organizers, Terry's moral compass read silence as complicity. "We have sinned as Christians by letting this holocaust go on," he said. "We need to act like it's murder."[1]

In the sustained grassroots war over abortion, one side saw the right to terminate a pregnancy as an attack on the family, which was the bedrock of American life, while the other side saw the abolition of abortion as an attack on women's autonomy and on the American promise of equality. In both cases, it seemed to activists, the American immune system was failing and the entry point of the fatal illness could be found in the abortion debate. Randall Terry and the antiabortion organization he eventually founded, Operation Rescue, represented a politics of morality that not only emphasized protecting the family, especially children, but equally claimed to be saving America from its own decline, moral and otherwise. Of course, that representation was built on top of a worldview that privileged men's power over women and religious authority over women's autonomy, and that saw in feminism an attack on motherhood, the family, and the nation. Pro-choice activists, in contrast, articulated a defense of liberty that not only emphasized control over one's own body but as fervently claimed to be saving America from a backward slide into nineteenth-century structures of inequality. Many of the earliest advocates for the legalization of abortion mobilized because they lived in a society where, when they became pregnant, they were acutely aware of the limited options available to them—or had experienced an illegal and maybe unsafe abortion; by the 1980s, however, the pro-choice movement included many Americans who had not faced that kind of crisis personally but who saw the cause as part of the larger project of women's equality.

The politics of pregnancy and abortion is perhaps uniquely associated with the 1970s and 1980s, mostly because before the Supreme Court's 1973 *Roe v. Wade* decision, pregnancy was largely a private matter. The Federal Communications Commission and network executives would not allow the word "pregnant" to be uttered on 1950s television—even on *I Love Lucy* when its star, Lucille Ball, was, as one expert has since noted, "visibly *expecting*." But *Roe* changed all that as larger battles over the family and equal rights for women—most notably over the Equal Rights

Amendment—morphed into what the sociologist Kristin Luker has called "a struggle over the concept of motherhood." For pro-life/anti-abortion activists, "motherhood tends to be viewed as the most important and satisfying role open to a woman. Abortion, therefore, represents an attack on the very activity that gives life meaning." Pro-choice activists, in contrast, are more likely to see motherhood as just one role alongside others, such as a career outside the home. Therefore, while pro-lifers cast motherhood as the highest aspirational role for women, pro-choice women see pregnancy as a potential "hardship." According to Luker, "abortion in this context is a means of liberating women from the burden of unplanned and unwanted childbearing and childrearing." Luker points out that as late as 1950, a major textbook on marriage and family noted that "although it was very difficult to predict what a man would be doing at the age of twenty-four, one could predict what a woman would be doing at that age with virtual certainty." This was more prescription than description, Luker concludes. But thanks to the women's movement and postwar shifts in American economic life, women started to expect to be able to work for most of their adult lives in the same way that men do. As a result, an unplanned pregnancy "came to be seen as a tragedy." Women therefore needed to be able to have control over their bodies, not be told by the state that they were legally obligated to give birth.[2]

Within this debate, the view of the embryo was tied to one's worldview. That is, "to attribute personhood to the embryo is to make the social statement that pregnancy is valuable and that women should subordinate other parts of their lives to that central aspect of their social and biological selves." If one sees the embryo as a fetus, on the other hand, "then it becomes socially permissible for women to subordinate their reproductive roles to other roles, particularly in the paid labor force." The conflicting worldviews vis-à-vis abortion were therefore not unlike the much older battles over "separate spheres," which turned on assumptions about gender difference: men are better suited for the public life of work and politics, while women are born to work in the private sphere of home and family. In the post–women's liberation years, pro-choice men and women clearly rejected that model, while traditionalists saw in it something worth preserving.[3] As a result, for both sides in the struggles over abortion, the perception of danger arose as much from visions of women's role in American life as from direct experience; both sides introduced experiential evidence—advocates of abortion rights re-counted tales of the dark days before *Roe*, and their opponents deployed photographs of fetuses—in the service of a more abstract belief.

Across the 1970s and 1980s and beyond, the fight over abortion has been fought on two fronts, one involving legal challenges and the lobby-ing of government officials, the other at the grass roots. Pro-choice orga-nizations, for example, dedicated much of the 1970s to lobbying, working to protect the *Roe v. Wade* decision that legalized abortion from en-croachments at the state and federal levels. One of the first questions to arise after the Court's decision in *Roe* was how it would apply to poor women on Medicaid. Most legal observers did not think that if a state paid for pregnancy-related health care for poor women, it would be con-stitutional to then deny payment for their terminations. Nevertheless, Congress passed the Hyde Amendment (named for Congressman Henry Hyde) to the Social Security Act of 1976 removing federal funding for Medicaid recipients' abortions. When the Supreme Court upheld the amendment in *Harris v. McRae* (1980), it concluded a process by which, in one expert's analysis, the government turned abortion into a market issue. The Court ruled that *Roe v. Wade* had not established a constitu-tional right to abortion. Rather, it had established the right of women to make a decision about abortion without the "unduly burdensome influ-ence" of the state. Therefore, the historian Rickie Solinger notes, while the "government would not criminalize abortion . . . neither would it pay for it." Poor women were expected to save up so they could pay for it themselves. The Democrats, for their part, were of little help to the pro-choice cause; Jimmy Carter, the born-again Christian president, had no stomach for the issue.[4]

Pro-choice organizations left reeling by the Court's ruling on the Hyde Amendment now had reason to regroup and plot a new strategy. By the time voters put Ronald Reagan in the White House, many pro-choice activists felt that they had lost the initiative, that pro-lifers controlled the terms of the debate and now had in the president a powerful ally. The National Abortion Rights Action League (NARAL) turned its attention to fundraising, using some of the direct mail techniques pioneered by Richard Viguerie for conservative causes, dramatically increasing its membership numbers and financial standing. NARAL then started chan-neling some of that money into building local branches, state by state. Going into the 1980 elections, it mounted an electoral campaign based on its I'M PRO-CHOICE AND I VOTE signs and bumper stickers, and put the slogan on postcards for voters to send to their elected representatives. This amounted to local organizing but not a lot of local action. NARAL showed little enthusiasm for demonstrations at clinics, for example, where, increasingly, pro-life protesters were showing up to make their stand. "Politically, things like pickets have zero effectiveness, but volunteers like them," one NARAL organizer said. "So occasionally we'd do them for the volunteers, to rev people up when they need a boost. They really like pickets—I don't know why, I can't stand them myself. Usually, we tried to channel energies into more productive things like campaign work, which volunteers also like." Other pro-choice groups were not so hesitant. In Chicago, when the Cook County Board of Commissioners decided to shut down the abortion clinic in the Cook County Hospital— the only one available to poor women—Women Organized for Reproductive Choice (WORC) turned out more than a hundred protesters demanding hearings. When the commission granted the hearings, some two hundred WORC protesters showed up. Although the commission still shut down the clinic, the protest hinted at more to come. In Cleveland and elsewhere, pro-choice activists would show up at pro-life speaking engagements by the likes of Phyllis Schlafly, "posing as the barefoot, pregnant members of organizations like 'Ladies Against Women' and carrying signs with slogans like 'You're nobody till you're Mrs. Somebody' and 'Sperm are people too.'"[5]

Ultimately, this kind of pro-choice organizing did less to protect *Roe* than did court decisions. The city of Akron, Ohio, had in 1978 passed a series of strict abortion ordinances requiring, for example, "a waiting period, parental consent for minors, and a lecture on the developmental state of the fetus to be given to the woman by her physician." In 1983, the Court reaffirmed *Roe* and struck down most of the Akron ordinances and thus put an end to local governments moving to restrict abortions (at least for the time being). In the meantime, most pro-choice groups continued to work primarily on electoral politics, and after the Akron decision, even that was hard to sustain. Only when the pro-life movement escalated its abortion clinic blockades and "rescues" did pro-choice grassroots organizing stage a comeback.[6]

Although Operation Rescue got the most attention, clinic blockades actually began nearly ten years before Randall Terry's Binghamton action. Most of the early direct action demonstrations were planned by

Sixties veterans, usually Catholic antiwar types following in the tradition of the Berrigans and the draft board raids. The so-called "father of
the rescue movement," John O'Keefe, was a devout Catholic and pacifist
who had been granted Conscientious Objector status during the Vietnam War. Shaped intellectually as much by the Catholic Charismatic
Renewal, a Catholic counterpart to Protestant evangelicalism, as by Gandhi and King, O'Keefe carried out his first abortion clinic sit-in in January 1977 in Norwich, Connecticut, and went on to plan a number of
others, inspiring many followers across the country.[7]

St. Louis, Missouri, fast became the "vortex of sit-in activity," in part
because of a similar cast of Catholic activists but also because the community, including the authorities, did not seem very interested in enforcing the law of the land. As the journalists James Risen and Judy Thomas
reported, "the antiabortion protest movement in the United States has
never enjoyed, either before or since, the kind of broad public and political backing it had during a few brief months in late 1979 and early 1980
in St. Louis." St. Louis University student Samuel Lee, like O'Keefe a devout Catholic, founded People Expressing a Concern for Everyone
(PEACE) to carry out sit-ins at local abortion clinics. PEACE pioneered
the use of a typical Catholic left antiwar legal defense strategy—the
necessity defense—in which they argued that they broke the law in order
to prevent a greater and graver crime. In their first deployment of the
necessity defense, they put physicians on the stand who testified that life
began at conception and put a woman on the stand who testified that she
did not have an abortion after a sit-in. They were acquitted. One juror
said that the jury "accepted the students' argument that they believed
trespassing was necessary to save the lives of unborn human beings."
Having established that the necessity defense could work, thus making
prison sentences less likely, Lee soon drew far more people to his cause.
In Lee's St. Louis, unlike O'Keefe's Northeast, a large number of fundamentalist Protestants joined up with the Catholic protesters. By 1980, the
politics of abortion dominated St. Louis, as evidenced by sixty thousand
people turning out for a pro-life march through the city that summer
and most of the area's major politicians, including Congressman Richard
Gephardt, publicly declaring themselves to be pro-life.[8]

The continued success of the necessity defense led PEACE to initiate
dozens of clinic blockades in conservative St. Louis County. Police arrested Samuel Lee fifty times before a court ever convicted him. The

police, prosecutors, and judges all seemed sympathetic to the cause. On one occasion, the judge who handled most of the cases, Harold Johnson, "bundled fifty arrests against fourteen protesters that had built up over the previous year and dismissed all of the charges." A combination of legal appeals and the arrival of a new Catholic archbishop finally slowed St. Louis's pro-life campaign. The new archbishop, John May, came to St. Louis in March 1980 and took a dim view of Catholics breaking the law so wantonly, particularly on an issue where it appeared the national majority stood against them. Moreover, the clinics had gotten wise and turned to the courts to get injunctions to keep activists away; this did not always work, but it guaranteed stiffer penalties for those who dared violate the court orders. In time, the Missouri Court of Appeals ruled that the necessity defense was invalid in antiabortion cases; abortion, the court matter-of-factly stated, is a "constitutionally protected activity and therefore legal and its occurrence cannot be a public or private injury" that might justify someone's committing a lesser crime. John Ryan, another Catholic and sometime social worker, kept the pro-life flame lit in St. Louis through the mid-1980s, blocking clinic doors at least once a week and racking up more than four hundred arrests. He later formed the Pro-Life Direct Action League, a group willing to resist arrest and to destroy clinic equipment if the opportunity arose.[9]

Far to the north, in Fargo, North Dakota, the announcement that a women's health clinic would soon open sparked controversy. Almost immediately, pro-life and pro-choice citizens formed their own organizations, unaffiliated with any national groups, and settled in for a long standoff. The LIFE Coalition and Partners in Vision did their best to prevent the clinic from opening, while Citizens for Reproductive Choice rallied in opposition, to defend the clinic and the community's right to have it opened. When the clinic opened in spite of protests, the LIFE Coalition launched a prayer vigil (in which activists called themselves "Prayer Vigilantes") and spent at least two hours a week pacing back and forth on the clinic's sidewalk, praying.[10]

Thanks to the anthropologist Faye Ginsburg, who, in the midst of the Fargo abortion battles, did in-depth interviews with dozens of the city's pro-life and pro-choice activists, we know that few were veteran activists; rather, most of the women who joined either side of that campaign did so primarily based on their own personal experience. Kay Bellevue, the woman who started the women's health clinic at the center of the controversy, had herself had an abortion. She and her husband had four small children (the youngest was eighteen months old) when she became pregnant by accident. The pregnancy came at a particularly stressful time in her life (her own parents were going through a divorce and one of her children "was having problems"). With no women's health services available in Fargo at the time, she went to another state to terminate the pregnancy. "In my experience, people who have made the choice to have an abortion made it because they want a strong family," Bellevue told Ginsburg. "How bringing an unwanted child into a family strengthens it is something that I have never been able to understand." Another activist with Citizens for Reproductive Choice, Sherry, came to her views on abortion after her own difficult pregnancy resulted in the birth of a severely handicapped daughter who died in the delivery room. It made her angry to hear pro-life activists talking about other women's pregnancies when "it wasn't their experience." The pro-lifers "weren't there for me when I needed support," Sherry said. "They're out there talking and . . . carrying on about the life of the fetus and not one of them is concerned about me. If I don't say something for myself, it might not get said. I don't want to have to leave the country because my own country has made it illegal for me to do what is best for my life." As Ginsburg summarized, the generational experience was particularly important for these activists, in part because they came of age in the 1950s and 1960s, witness to powerful social movements, but also out of the "experience of life-cycle events related to reproduction."[11]

Similarly, pro-life activists in Fargo articulated their views about abortion through their own pregnancy and motherhood stories, and they did not often come across as caricatures of traditional motherhood. In fact, several of Ginsburg's pro-life activists said they were in favor of birth control and, by extension, of choice. But, as one activist who favored women's rights said, "once that's done"—once one is pregnant—then "you've already made that choice." She said that when feminists "lumped together" abortion with "women's rights, like equal pay, I get really upset." Similarly, Peggy Jones, a Catholic pro-life activist, told Ginsburg that it's "about being responsible for our actions . . . It's like getting in the car," she said. "One of the risks you take is having an accident."[12]

For others, the experience of a near-abortion inspired their opposition to the abortion clinic. A woman named Helen recounted how when she was in the womb, her mother grew ill because she was grieving over the death of Helen's older sister, who had died recently in a car accident. "My mother . . . couldn't eat and they said if you don't eat we're gonna have to take that baby because you're gonna die," she said. "They wanted to abort her, and she said, 'No way.'" Here, Helen's mother's perseverance in bringing her into the world both saves her life and is a model of commitment that she relates to the pro-life movement. A friend of Helen's named Corinne told Ginsburg of how she became pregnant with her second child when her first was only six months old and just as her husband left her. "I didn't want that baby [but] I would never have thought of an abortion although I knew it was available," she said. "I believe in choice, in picking a career, or whether to buy this or that. But I don't believe anyone has the right to kill another human being." For Corinne, a baby is a human being "from conception on."[13]

As Ginsburg concluded, these pro-life women told stories that were "much more complex than the stereotype" of them as "reactionary housewives and mothers passed by in the sweep of social change." Most favored equal rights for women, and most of them worked outside the home, and many of them, in emphasizing the importance of nurturing children, expressed ideas that would have been received coldly by conservative ideologues such as Phyllis Schlafly. One mother of three, for example, argued for "flexible job hours" and "shared jobs," asserting that "companies should hire people in ways that will allow mothers and fathers to take care of their children." Widespread acceptance of abortion was typical of a society that valued consumerism over everything else, thus compelling both parents to work so as to eliminate any obstacle (such as an unwanted pregnancy) to acquiring more stuff. That was the kind of grim view of the clinic as representative of America's decline that led the "Prayer Vigilantes" to the sidewalks outside the clinic.[14]

Pretty soon, though, it became clear that the prayer vigils accomplished little. The LIFE Coalition therefore hired a "problem pregnancy counselor" and began a "sidewalk counseling program," approaching visitors to the clinic, handing out literature, and generally suggesting that women consider other options. In time, this led the LIFE Coalition to lead the movement in a new tactic—establishing a "problem pregnancy center." In the spring of 1984, the LIFE Coalition opened the Abortion Action Affiliate Problem Pregnancy Center to target the "young unwed mother." Nationally, in the mid-1980s, some two thousand of these centers "counseled" pregnant girls and women, urging them to consider giving up their as-yet-unborn child for adoption. The centers served another purpose, too, in that they answered the criticism that the antiabortion movement "had no concern for pregnant women." In their advertising, the clinics presented "problem pregnancy" and "crisis pregnancy" services, without any hint that the menu of services did not include abortion. Thus, unsuspecting women, thinking they were entering a clinic where they could learn more about abortion services, found themselves watching an antiabortion slide show or film "that sometimes includes pictures of bloody aborted fetuses." Pro-choice activists in some cities managed to penetrate these centers cloak-and-dagger-style. They then exposed them to the press and filed lawsuits to prevent misleading advertising.[15]

At roughly the same time, pro-life organizing in Fargo and elsewhere grew increasingly militant and forceful, and against a backdrop of escalating violence directed at clinics nationwide, it became harder and harder to distinguish ordinary pro-life protesters from the violent, apocalyptic ones. Arsonists had first hit abortion clinics in Eugene, Oregon, and Minneapolis in 1976 and 1977, respectively (the latter came as little surprise, since the local Catholic diocese had repeatedly referred to the Minneapolis clinic as "Little Dachau"). A year later, the first clinic bombing took place in Cincinnati. By 1984, however, the number of arson and bomb attacks nationwide had risen to 30, with a total of 319 "acts of violence" (including vandalism) against 238 clinics tallied between January 1983 and March 1985. And in these same years, militant pro-lifers first targeted abortion doctors directly, with Don Benny Anderson and two other members of the Army of God kidnapping the Edwardsville, Illinois, doctor Hector Zevallos and his wife at gunpoint and holding them for more than a week in an old ammunition bunker. Anderson later said that he "agreed with pro-choice groups" that bombers and other more violent pro-lifers were "encouraged by the absence of direct condemnations of their activities" by President Reagan, who remained silent on abortion clinic violence through his first term. The president, Anderson said, had effectively given the "green light" to clinic bombings. On Christmas Day 1984, the twenty-one-year-old evangelicals Matthew Goldsby and James Simmons, calling themselves the Gideon Project, bombed three Pensacola, Florida, abortion clinics, all within minutes of each other, as a birthday "gift to Jesus." The two had in fact bombed another clinic in June and, having eluded capture, then plotted the bolder Christmas attacks.[16]

This level of violence followed a sharp turn in abortion politics rhetoric in which pro-lifers became increasingly apocalyptic as the years since *Roe v. Wade* passed. Prior to the 1980s, more moderate claims about the "human quality of prenatal life" marked pro-life rhetoric. By the mid-1980s, however, more and more pro-lifers saw the struggle over abortion as "America's Armageddon." The historian Carol Mason scoured pro-life writings in this period and found that proponents described abortion not only as "an apocalypse" but "a revelation of just how immoral America [had] become." More than slavery or the Holocaust, abortion to these pro-lifers is "the ultimate of human atrocities and signals the end of humane society." The existence, by 1982, of nearly three thousand abortion-providing facilities, coupled with public opinion polls consistently showing that more than three-quarters of Americans approved of a woman's having the right to choose an abortion, thus signaled societal doom. Consequently, the battle over abortion became not only a war to stop these atrocities but a war to save America from itself. Militant antiabortionists thus combined the typically nonideological front porch approach, rooted in self-reliance and defense of family and home, with a religious worldview as catalyst and sustaining force. At its most extreme, some abortion warriors overlapped with the budding militia and survivalist movement that viewed the American government as conspiring to deny liberty to its citizens—which, in this case, extended to the unborn—from whence it was just a short step to justifying violence in the pursuit of stopping abortions. Whereas moderate pro-lifers had been hesitant to label abortion "murder" before the 1980s, the more apocalyptic types now saw no distinction and extended the reasoning behind the necessity defense to "killing for life." Later, from 1993 to 2002, at least seven abortion doctors and clinic personnel were assassinated.[17]

In a place like Fargo, pro-life activists gradually expressed their opposition to abortion in more intimidating fashion. The more militant activists founded Save-A-Baby (similar to Jerry Falwell's organization of the same name, but allegedly not tied to it) and escalated their tactics to include confronting anyone entering the clinic with biblical quotations and images of bloody fetuses. Later, they took to stalking and harassing both patients and the clinic's doctors and staff, including picketing the doctors' homes. They also engaged in smaller-scale legal harassment, suggesting that the clinic disposed of fetal remains improperly and did not keep its building in code with local fire regulations. This kind of sustained campaign brought out the clinic's defenders, however, in a way not usually seen. Not only did the clinic and its supporters sue to maintain access to the clinic, they hired security guards and organized "a steady round of volunteers to escort patients through the intimidating line of protesters in front of the facility." Even the newly overt and hostile environment on the streets in front of the clinic did not stop the flow of traffic through its doors. It did, on the other hand, garner national news attention, such as when ABC's *20/20* newsmagazine program came to Fargo in the fall of 1984 and all but ignored moderate voices in favor of examining the most extreme spokespersons in Save-A-Baby. The added attention did cause the district court to issue an injunction against Save-A-Baby requiring that it change the name of its "Women's Help Clinic of Fargo"—an obvious attempt to confuse women who really wanted to reach the Fargo Women's Health Organization—and inform callers that it did not offer abortion services.[18]

By the time of the Pensacola bombings on Christmas Day 1984, it seemed that the abortion wars might actually end, as many Americans now viewed the pro-life cause as a vehicle for terrorism. Just weeks before the Pensacola attacks, even the pro-life leader John O'Keefe, a pacifist, found his cause undermined by violence. O'Keefe led a blockade of a clinic in Wheaton, Maryland, on November 17, 1984, with more than a hundred participants, forty-six of whom were arrested—the largest nonviolent blockade to date—but two days later, a rogue terrorist named Thomas Spinks bombed the very same clinic. He might as well have strapped TNT to the movement, so successful was he in making the blockade and the bombing appear related. Nor did it help pro-lifers to have leaders such as Joseph Scheidler, a former Catholic seminarian and founder of the Pro-Life Action Network, speaking to the press in terms that seemed to accept that pro-life terrorism was inevitable and unstoppable. "I don't condone, I don't advocate, but I don't condemn," he told a reporter. Scheidler "appeared to the public to be like the Sinn Fein leaders in Ireland," James Risen and Judy Thomas observed, serving "as a political front" for clinic bombers the way Sinn Fein did for Irish Republican Army terrorists. If that kind of militancy alienated much of the public, it also left open the door for a savvier leader, someone who under-

stood the history of social movements and how to make pro-life direct action echo movements that had won more favor with the public in the past.[19]

It turned out that Randall Terry, the Montgomery Ward tire salesman and former used car salesman, was that man. Terry believed that
the pro-life movement needed to follow the example of the civil rights
movement and adopt tactics of nonviolent civil disobedience, not only as
a way to stop abortions but, more important, to bring attention to the nation's moral decline. Terry had been inspired in part by Francis Schaeffer's
1981 book, *A Christian Manifesto*, which called on evangelicals to use
civil disobedience as a way to return the United States to "its religious
roots in matters like public prayer and religious education" and more
generally to "traditional Christian values." For Randall Terry, evangelicals
had been complicit in the "holocaust" against the unborn by not responding to abortion as murder. "For so many years, those in the pro-life
movement had been saying abortion is murder and then writing a letter
or carrying a sign once a year at a march," Terry later wrote in his memoir. "If you were about to be murdered, I'm sure you would want me to do
more than write your congressman!" The time had come, he said, to act
like those in St. Louis, on the basis that breaking one law was necessary
to stop a greater crime. "The logical response to murder," he admonished, "is to physically intervene on behalf of the victim." While Terry
was serving his thirty-day sentence for that first action in Binghamton,
he concluded that the pro-life movement had failed to create the "tension
and upheaval necessary to produce political and social change." In order
to build a real movement, with the ability to draw more and more activists and win the public's admiration, pro-lifers needed to follow the example of the civil rights movement and carry out a campaign of highly
disciplined, nonviolent direct actions that would call America home to
its time-honored values. Terry quickly parlayed his notoriety for the Binghamton action into making the case for a series of "rescues" (blockades)
at "abortuaries" across the nation. "A 'rescue mission,'" Terry explained,
"is a group of God-fearing people saying 'No! We're not going to let you
kill innocent children.'" Although the organization he founded, Operation Rescue, sounded like a paramilitary organization that might use violent means to prevent the killing of "innocent children," Terry conceived
of it as a model of nonviolence.[20]

After more than a year of organizing, Terry held his Operation Rescue
dress rehearsal on November 28, 1987—seven months after ACT UP first

came to national attention for its dramatic direct action tactics—at the Cherry Hill Women's Center in Cherry Hill, New Jersey. Terry had hoped to carry out his "rescue" at a clinic in Philadelphia, but the city's police, who had grown used to combating local clinic blockades and who knew that Operation Rescue was in town, basically cordoned off all of the clinics in the city. Following a predawn rally in Philadelphia, Terry therefore changed the group's plans at the last minute and led somewhere between three and four hundred people across the Delaware River to Cherry Hill. The blockade caught local police completely off guard; it took nearly all day to arrest those who would not clear away from the clinic's entrance, while the crowd sang and prayed and, according to Terry, "basically had a church service on the doorstep of hell for nearly eleven hours!" Eventually, 211 "mothers, fathers, grandmothers, grandfathers, and singles" were charged with trespassing and let go. Terry sounded triumphant afterward. "We stopped the killing for an entire day!" he exclaimed. "We choked the legal system!" Most important, Terry said, "no babies died" and "it was glorious, peaceful, and prayerful." Thanks to Terry's success in keeping the protests from getting violent, he now had the ear of more and more ministers across the country. And from ministers came more foot soldiers and money for Operation Rescue.[21]

By the summer of 1988, Operation Rescue had become a household name. In a dramatic leap in both scale and ambition, Terry led four days of blockades outside clinics in Manhattan, in Queens, and in Hicksville, Long Island, that saw sixteen hundred activists arrested. More than that, in getting unprecedented news coverage for the cause, Operation Rescue soon had to hire paid staff to manage the donations coming in through the mail. Over the course of the next year, the organization had turned into a moneymaking machine, taking in more than $1 million in contributions and sales of its pamphlets and videos. And much of that came in response to the "siege of Atlanta."[22]

Operation Rescue went to Dr. Martin Luther King Jr.'s hometown in the summer of 1988 in part because Atlanta was playing host to the Democratic National Convention, but also because Randall Terry wanted to cement in the public's mind what he saw as the similarities between the pro-life movement and the civil rights movement. Beginning on July 19, 1988, Atlanta police, who were committed to keeping the clinics open, arrested 134 Operation Rescue members at the Atlanta SurgiCenter. All of the arrestees left their ID at home and gave only "Baby

Doe" as a name to police. As a result, the courts could not easily process them for arraignment, and they were held for forty days, missing the Democratic Convention but in the meantime gathering support from national pro-life evangelicals like Jerry Falwell and Pat Robertson. In an effort to emulate the civil rights organizations that brought wave after wave of Freedom Riders south to take the place of those arrested, Operation Rescue's allies in Christian broadcasting essentially put out a call to which hundreds of activists responded. By the end of August, Atlanta police had arrested 753 people. In the meantime, Terry and others decided that the "Baby Doe" strategy did not work because it meant that too many people who might otherwise be participating in one blockade after another ended up sitting, instead, behind bars. Consequently, Operation Rescue geared up for a new wave of blockades in late September and early October, and the police prepared for more aggressive arrests.[23]

Of course, no matter how much Terry tried to make Operation Rescue look like a civil rights organization, most Americans could see that the analogy did not fit. For one thing, unlike so many civil rights activists who could speak of the evils of segregation from their own experience, Operation Rescue members were acting on behalf of people not yet born and, more abstractly, of American families. Second, unlike the civil rights organizations—such as the Congress of Racial Equality, the Student Nonviolent Coordinating Committee, or the Southern Christian Leadership Conference—that raised funds not for any wider agenda but only to support activists trying to eradicate segregation, Operation Rescue clearly counted on evangelical Christian organizations whose very identity was based on a much grander objective: bringing sinners to accept Jesus Christ as their savior. In that way, Operation Rescue's Atlanta campaign looked a lot more like Howard Jarvis's Proposition 13 campaign, relying on major investments of funding and infrastructure from deep-pocketed organizations with more ambitious goals. Unlike the tax revolt, however, Operation Rescue proved far more successful at mobilizing activists.

The confrontations over the next weeks brought the abortion wars to America's living rooms. The Atlanta police, tired of dealing with these pesky demonstrators, committed themselves to using "pain compliance" methods to "force demonstrators to get up and follow police orders when they tried to go limp." When, on October 4, 1988, hundreds of pro-life demonstrators took rapid transit into Atlanta's downtown, fanning out toward three of the clinics, they ran into massive police blockades. The protesters dropped to their knees, as they had in their nonviolence walk-throughs in the lead-up to the action, and started crawling between po-lice officers' legs. Some said the protesters looked like "zombies straight out of *Night of the Living Dead*," but it infuriated the police, who started "twisting wrists, bending back arms, and applying pressure from the thumb and forefinger on both sides of the neck." Operation Rescue failed in its efforts to block the clinic entrances, but it won the day in the press, as much of the news coverage focused on the police's forcible arrest of demonstrators. Although all the Operation Rescue blockaders amounted to what one observer called "a tiny fraction of the right-to-life volun-teers" across the country, "the media loved them." Both ABC's *20/20* and CBS's *48 Hours* newsmagazines produced extended segments on the At-lanta battles, and CNN, based in Atlanta, covered it like a foreign war.[24]

For a variety of reasons, Atlanta marked a turning point in the abor-tion wars. For one, it made Operation Rescue a national organization and, as a result, brought it not only grassroots credibility among the reli-gious right, but loads of cash and volunteers. The National Day of Rescue followed the Atlanta campaign and resulted in twenty-two hundred ar-rests in twenty-seven cities. Although major actions like those in Atlanta got a lot of attention, Operation Rescue remained focused on local bat-tles. "We are *not* asking *you* to send *us* money so that *we* can fight and win the war," one fundraising appeal admonished. The idea was to ob-tain money, of course, but also to organize blockades in a great many communities. By pro-choice group estimates, Operation Rescue groups carried out at least one blockade every weekend over the next year.[25]

But Atlanta also marked a surge in organizing against the blockades. Most clinics just learned to live with them by having employees take home all the phone numbers for the next day's scheduled patients so that they could be called in the event of a blockade; or, if a clinic received ad-vance word of a coming blockade, staff would come in to work early to try to both reschedule patients and keep the place open. In other cities, though, pro-choice activists took more direct defensive measures. In Chicago, for example, the Emergency Clinic Defense Coalition (ECDC) grew out of Women Organized for Reproductive Choice and responded to Operation Rescue by building a rapid-response capacity that could quickly mobilize counterdemonstrations when necessary. Such steps were taken very seriously, but also cautiously, because organizers recog-nized that with groups of passionate people trying to both blockade and defend a clinic, violence could erupt at any second. "Pickets and so forth are one thing," said Cathy Christeller of ECDC, "but the problem with clinic defense is that it's scary to the very people we're trying to defend—the women trying to use the clinics." Ultimately, clinic defense groups decided that they had no choice because if they did not show up, Operation Rescue would win and the clinics would close. Soon other cities mounted aggressive challenges to the clinic blockades. The Bay Area Coalition for Our Reproductive Rights, for example, sent spies south to Operation Rescue meetings in Los Angeles to gather intelligence on when, where, and how the group was planning actions. More than that, the Los Angeles police, which arrested more than a thousand blockaders, including 750 on a single day over Holy Week in March 1989, went further than their Atlanta counterparts in using pain compliance (including, as some reported, the use of "nunchaku—martial arts sticks—to grab and drag the protesters . . . at least one protester's arm was broken"). Later, Brookline, Massachusetts, saw battles so fierce that the cost of paying police overtime to keep the peace at the clinics rose to $17,000 a day. The city therefore sued Operation Rescue under the Racketeer Influenced and Corrupt Organizations (RICO) Act to try to recover $75,000 in overtime costs. The point was not to actually get the money but to curb future protests. The thousands of Americans galvanized by Randall Terry and Operation Rescue to confront the "holocaust" of abortion in their communities tapered off dramatically as the legal consequences escalated.[26]

This is another way in which Atlanta marked a turning point—Operation Rescue began to feel the full weight of state power. Most immediately, when Randall Terry refused to pay his $1,000 fine for his role in an Atlanta blockade, he wound up in prison for four months (saved only by an anonymous benefactor who paid his bail). Around the same time, a federal appeals court ruled that although it is constitutional to protest at a clinic, and even to try to speak with patients, "blocking access to public and private buildings had never been upheld as a proper method of communication in an orderly society," and the court fined Operation Rescue $50,000. When Terry shut down the organization's Binghamton headquarters in what most observers thought was an effort to dodge the fines, a federal judge fined ten individuals as well. The warning was not hard to decipher: Operation Rescue members and anyone else who blocked a clinic entrance could be held "*personally* liable."[27]

Meanwhile, in 1989 and 1990, both sides of the abortion wars continued to show their ability to mobilize large numbers of activists. More than three hundred thousand Americans took part in a massive abortion rights march in Washington on April 9, 1989, and then held another major march in November. Operation Rescue, meanwhile, claimed that by 1990 more than thirty-five thousand rescuers had been arrested and another sixteen thousand had risked arrest. As the scholar Faye Ginsburg has noted, even if these figures include a lot of people arrested multiple times, the numbers are staggering.[28]

In court, pro-lifers claimed victory when restrictions on abortion were upheld, while pro-choice activists warily breathed sighs of relief that *Roe v. Wade* was not overturned. Most significantly, in *Webster v. Reproductive Health Services* (1989), the Supreme Court upheld a Missouri law that declared life begins at conception and that prohibited the use of public facilities or public employees, including doctors, in performing abortions except to save the life of the mother. At the same time, the Court did not strike down *Roe*, but pro-choice organizers worried that it might overturn the decision before long. Randall Terry understood the limits of *Webster* and started holding "political training camps" for potential rescuers, to learn not only about the tactics of clinic blockades but also about how to put more pro-lifers in office so that they might one day change the composition of the Court to one that would strike down *Roe*.[29]

The climactic battle in the abortion wars came in Wichita, Kansas, where spectacle finally succumbed to the rule of law. Over forty-six days in the summer of 1991, Operation Rescue dominated the national news from outside the clinic of George Tiller, a physician known not only for specializing in abortion but also for his willingness to terminate a pregnancy through the second trimester. Tiller's father was a physician who, it turned out, started providing abortions in 1940 after a woman he had turned away died at the hands of a back-alley hack. His son, George, took over his father's practice and devoted himself to providing abortion services, and he was an outspoken defender of a woman's right to choose. By the 1980s, the more violently inclined in pro-life circles were talking about taking him out; in 1986, few were surprised when a bomb exploded at Tiller's clinic, causing $100,000 in damage. Tiller posted a sign that said HELL NO, WE WON'T GO![30]

Most public officials in Wichita—including the mayor, the police chief, and the city manager—were, like Kansas governor Joan Finney, ardently pro-life, and, as in St. Louis in the 1970s, that gave antiabortion activists the early upper hand. George Tiller and other abortion providers could see this, too, so when Operation Rescue announced it would soon descend on Wichita, they decided to just close their clinics for a week, rescheduling their patients. They hoped Operation Rescue would come for a week, declare victory, and leave. But it was a tactical blunder. Randall Terry promptly declared Wichita an abortion-free zone and invited evangelicals from all over the country to join an indefinite vigil there in the nation's heartland. As Risen and Thomas later wrote, "American fundamentalists came to see the shutdown of Wichita's clinics as a miracle, a sign from God, and a blessing" on their work. After a week, however, the police arrived on horseback and drove through the protesters, reopening the clinic.

Later in the day, a battle for the street outside Tiller's clinic erupted as rescuers blocked it and the police tried to clear them away. Mayor Bob Knight, sympathetic to Operation Rescue, ordered the police to ease up on the protesters, and henceforth it took all day—day after day—for them to remove the protesters. Tiller's lawyers then succeeded in getting a restraining order in federal court that should have stopped the blockades. The judge, Patrick Kelly, was not joking around; his restraining order mandated fines for individuals of $25,000 a day for the first violation and $50,000 a day after the first day. Terry and Operation Rescue simply ignored the court order. Police racked up 672 arrests in three days, but the violators were processed so quickly that they kept coming back for more. As a result, they continued to make it difficult for anyone to get into or out of the clinic, closing it at one point for twenty-six hours straight. When Judge Kelly realized that the police, concerned about disobeying the mayor, were not effectively enforcing the court order, he sent in U.S. marshals to keep the clinic open. It was a move reminiscent of the civil rights era, but not in the way Randall Terry would have liked. Governor Joan Finney then went to Wichita and, in light of the court orders, effectively encouraged lawlessness. "My hope and prayer is that Wichita's expression of support for the right to life of unborn babies will be peaceful, prayerful, and united in purpose," she said. "I commend you for the orderly manner in which you have conducted the demonstration"—a demonstration the court order was meant to end. In time, Operation Rescue brought its "Summer of Mercy" to an end because, ultimately, there was no escaping that court order. The organization struck a note of defiance as it left town, filling twenty-five thousand seats at Wichita State University's football stadium with pro-life supporters rallying to hear Pat Robertson, the founder of the new Christian Coalition.[31]

Within a year or two, a combination of factors had for the most part put an end to the rescue movement. First, the Supreme Court ruled in *Planned Parenthood of Southern Pennsylvania v. Casey* (1992) that although Pennsylvania could introduce a host of regulations making it more difficult to get an abortion, the right to an abortion, as articulated in *Roe*, remained safe. Led by Justices Sandra Day O'Connor, Anthony Kennedy, and David Souter, the majority recognized "the right of the woman to choose to have an abortion before viability and to obtain it without undue interference from the State." The "essential holding of *Roe v. Wade*," they wrote, "should be retained and once again reaffirmed." No amount of clinic blockades could shift this legal thinking. Second, with all of the fines, prison sentences, and threat of RICO prosecutions, the allure of civil-rights-style sit-ins on behalf of the unborn had faded. Third, the clinic defenses organized by pro-choice activists proved remarkably effective and were, in 1994, validated by Congress when it passed the Freedom of Access to Clinic Entrances (FACE) Act, which made it a federal crime to block someone from entering a clinic. Finally, the increased violence against abortion providers and their staff did a lot to discredit the movement in the public's eyes. George Tiller suffered an assassination attempt in 1993 and was ultimately murdered by an anti-abortion zealot in 2009. To most outsiders, it was hard not to associate the assassinations and other violence with Operation Rescue's mantra, "If you think that abortion is murder, act like it." By 1995, the organization was effectively wiped out by lawsuits and stiff jail sentences.[32]

In a relatively short time—from 1986 to 1991—Operation Rescue succeeded in taking pro-life politics to new heights. "If you were to track the whole abortion controversy, you'd find that in 1984 it almost went away," Randall Terry later said. "It was the rescues that brought it back." Terry's approach personalized abortion politics by focusing on communities and by holding his own constituency—evangelical Christians—responsible for not doing more to stop the holocaust. Furthermore, like other pro-life leaders, Terry suggested that this issue of what would later be called "family values" reflected larger value issues in American society. To save the family unit meant saving the nation, and one of the best ways to save it was to eliminate the obscene and indecent, including abortion, in American life.[33]

In mobilizing large numbers of people for clinic blockades primarily by appealing to a particular religious view of the family and the world, Operation Rescue straddled the divide between front porch politics and today's politics of more hardened worldviews set in opposition to one another. The grassroots protest attracted the media's and public's attention, but the message resonated mostly with those who shared the same religiously informed mind-set. Since the 1990s, aside from occasional demonstrations and marches marking the anniversary of *Roe v. Wade*, battles over abortion have mostly been fought by articulate pundit surrogates and lawyers. As the "culture wars" of the 1990s came to dominate political discourse, such became the dominant paradigm of the American political experience. The heyday of front porch politics was over.

Conclusion: The Passing of Front Porch Politics

●

The abortion wars were both the epitome of the culture wars and an exception to them. As in the wider culture wars, activists on both sides mobilized on behalf of their worldviews, pitting visions of immorality and national decline against the defense of constitutional rights and the belief that reproductive freedom was essential to women's true emancipation. In contrast to other culture wars, however, the contest over abortion drove many Americans into the streets.

In any number of well-publicized battles over "decency," proponents of protecting children, family, and "values" squared off against proponents of individual liberty or consumer choice. But a funny thing happened on the way to the culture war barricades: not many Americans showed up, at least not in person. In contrast to the abortion battles, which mobilized large numbers of pro-choice and pro-life activists to turn out at clinics and rallies, most of the so-called culture war battles were fought by elite talking heads and in the media chatter surrounding pop culture "events," such as the TV character Murphy Brown having a child out of wedlock. Perhaps these elites and pundits represented the views of millions of others, but those millions mostly stayed home; and when they did turn out in their communities, over such issues as sex education or "obscene" art exhibits, the campaigns tended to be much smaller than the movements chronicled in this book.

The low enlistment in grassroots culture war armies reveals the boundaries of front porch politics. The absence of significant grassroots activism on these issues suggests that sometimes the cultural issues at stake were not, in fact, core concerns—the kind that prompted a deep emotional response and a leap into action.

There were exceptions, of course. Battles over decency and popular culture often originated in a local context and were initiated by community activists. In 1974–75, a battle over school textbooks in West Virginia, for example, started locally and fueled national organizing around similar issues; that organizing, in turn, flowed back to fuel local campaigns in other communities. Alice Moore, a Christian fundamentalist member of the Kanawha County Board of Education, opposed new language arts textbooks because, as the historian Carol Mason has noted, the books allegedly "advocated unprincipled relativism, promoted antagonistic behavior, contained obscene material, put down Jesus Christ, and upheld communism." Critics like Moore charged that outside forces— for example, the Department of Health, Education and Welfare, with its promotion of multiculturalism—were imposing upon the community's self-understanding and how it instilled identity in its children. And although the local press consistently portrayed Moore as a courageous mother fighting an impersonal education system, hers was no solitary or spontaneous protest; in fact, she had preexisting ties to the Christian Crusade, a national evangelical and anticommunist organization based in Tulsa; to Norma and Mel Gabler, two nationally known textbook monitors based in Texas; and to the fledgling Heritage Foundation. Supporters of the new textbooks, on the other hand, rallied to their defense because they saw them as appropriate means—supplied by major American publishers such as Houghton Mifflin and Macmillan—for teaching "reading and writing as artful communication in multiethnic social contexts." Many citizens of Kanawha County saw a battle for "our children's minds," "control over our children," and, as Mason writes, "what it meant to be a concerned parent [and] a loyal American."[1]

By the late 1980s, however, it was uncommon for a culture wars battle to be fought most strenuously at the grass roots. In battles over pornography, "porn rock," or "obscene" art exhibitions, national leaders and organizations often led the charge, assisted by government prosecutors and police; local organizing certainly occurred, but the scale of such activism was much smaller.[2] Moreover, the terms of debate that circulated at the local level were often laid out by national organizers. As a result, the common mode of engaging a political issue involving values or the culture wars was through reading a national organization's newsletter and sending the group a check.

In retrospect, it is easier to see this movement away from grassroots organizing toward passive advocacy, checkbook activism, and spectator-ial political engagement, but at the time the change occurred so gradu-ally that few noticed. Today, whether we lament the loss of front porch politics or not, it is worth examining the reasons for its passing and fur-ther considering what replaced it.

Front porch politics faded as a dominant mode of political experience and mobilization after the 1980s for a variety of related reasons. For starters, as we have seen, mobilizing sufficient numbers and power at the grass roots is difficult and especially hard to sustain for a significant length of time. As the economist Juliet Schor famously documented in the early 1990s, most Americans were already "overworked" and "overspent." Working 320 more hours each year than workers in West Germany and France, Americans who might otherwise have organized around key is-sues were simply too weary. Relying on accidental activists instead of professional politicos may be an advantage when it comes to moral au-thority and credibility, but it is a disadvantage for organizing. Moreover, front porch politics did not always work, and its failures turned off some who might have seen it as a model. With the 1960s models of protest and resistance receding deeper into the past, would-be activists in the 1990s and 2000s looked back on the preceding decades and saw a great deal of frustration and ineffectiveness, and, at best, partial victories.[3]

In addition, the rise of a new (mostly cultural) politics, dominated by a language of moral values and driven by political operatives, eclipsed the front porch model. As think tanks and lobbying groups such as those dedicated to lowering taxes or promoting Christian values gained influ-ence and learned to frame their positions in front porch language, the impulse of would-be organizers at the local level to take to the streets ebbed. Most remained engaged in the political issues that interested them, but increasingly as spectators.

Politics as spectatorship was itself facilitated by advances in technology—principally cable and satellite television, and later the Internet. As new engines of entertainment, consumption, and largely private, indi-vidualized desire, these offered immediate distraction and escape from political engagement. At the same time, the advent of twenty-four-hour news and right-wing talk radio, the emergence of whole television net-works organized around highly partisan positions, and the proliferation of politically oriented websites further enabled a passive experience of politics. Increasingly, passion resided simply in adherence to a particular worldview (and hatred of its opposite), with political identity defined by the news media one consumed. To be sure, populist surges still occur, whether the Tea Party in its founding moment or Occupy Wall Street, both of which were facilitated by social media and Web-based organizing. But their grassroots energy is prone to quickly dissipate, or to be commandeered by party professionals, ultimately providing grist for politicians' talking points and tenuous claims of a "mandate."[4]

Just as important, tectonic shifts in the nation's economy proved too overwhelming to overcome via grassroots organizing focused mostly on local crises. The culture wars were fought concurrently with a rising national faith in the dynamic power (and, in the view of many, the inherent rationality and fairness) of the market. Using such big ideological frames to promote growth and the virtue of market forces emboldened those opposed to certain front porch causes—protecting tenants and the homeless, saving the family farm, stopping factory shutdowns, disciplining corporate polluters—to feel as though history was on their side and that they should therefore be uncompromising. More generally, it led a critical mass of Americans, in concert with powerful corporate interests, to favor deregulation, to all but sanction corporate malfeasance (particularly in the exploitation of workers and the environment), and, in a twisted version of the front porch ethos, to see taxes per se as the fundamental threat to individual thriving. A fraying liberalism, which might have woven widespread concern for the environment and economic fairness into a coherent ideological fabric, proved little match.

Rigid ideological support of the market is easy to maintain when the crisis in question is happening to someone else. As the historian Tony Judt wrote in *Ill Fares the Land* (2011), the last book he published in his lifetime, "These days, we take pride in being tough enough to inflict pain on others." Using a "misleadingly 'ethical' vocabulary," Americans have become increasingly comfortable deploying a "self-satisfied gloss" to distinguish themselves from those who suffer injuries brought on by the capriciousness of the market.[5] Market fundamentalism was present even in the heyday of front porch politics, but over time it has proliferated, becoming more hardened and hard-hearted, even in the face of growing inequality.

In the wake of the economic crisis of 2008, millions of Americans are again feeling "screwed" and less able to distinguish themselves from those "others" who are suffering. But, in a tragic twist, many citizens no longer have faith in *any* mechanism to reenergize a fading American dream and restore the fortunes even of the middle class. With the further discrediting of government and intense ideological polarization—especially the intransigence of the right—the prospect of successful political action in the service of shared goals seems almost laughable. Hope for solutions that work seems in meager supply. In such a climate, it is perhaps easiest to sit back and watch the political combat unfold on cable TV while stewing in anger and feelings of impotence.

In contrast, the American political experience of the 1970s and 1980s was defined by a comparatively robust civic life as Americans tried to articulate through action an understanding of the public good and tried to prevent others from experiencing the injuries and hardships they did. In mobilizing so many Americans to become directly involved in various political struggles in those decades, the front porch political ethos demonstrated that Americans were not fractured, disengaged, and self-seeking. And although they may have first leaped into the political breach out of personal anxiety or injury, they almost always acted collectively to seek justice, for themselves and for others. Even as those front porch campaigns, defined by an ethic of self-reliance, were powered by any number of emotions—including despair, anger, betrayal, and compassion—their common quest was for solutions, for what actually worked.

The great shame of American political life today is that even as we live in a historical moment similarly teeming with perceived threats, we have chosen to retain two of front porch politics' least useful elements: rage and a thoroughgoing distrust of government. Indeed, for many Americans, the primary rage is *at* the government, for always being *the* problem. Rage dominates what we see and hear in the newspapers, on television and radio. It's true that Barack Obama, the first man to reach the White House with community organizing on his résumé, recently won reelection in an apparent repudiation of those who rail against government. But even his rhetorical commitment to citizen action may be fleeting. Though Obama's 2012 victory speech waxed lyrical about the "folks" who worked on the presidential election campaign—the "young field organizer," the "volunteer" who went door-to-door—this is hardly evidence of a revival of the front porch political ethos in which Americans, on a grand scale, commit themselves to a political process that goes far beyond elections. Indeed, the health of the republic depends less on the national conversation that goes on at election time than on the absence or presence of Americans organizing at the grass roots. Some short-lived exceptions aside, we seem to have lost our belief that we can come up with solutions, that we can make a difference. We have lost our willingness to step off the front porch and participate in the political life of the nation, at the grass roots, in a fashion that goes beyond partisanship. We have, in short, lost an important part of our democratic soul. And so we mourn, perhaps without knowing it, the passing of a political culture in which experience and reason informed action and in which Americans worked, really worked, at politics.

Notes

Introduction: The Rise of Front Porch Politics in America

1. The profession's engagement with the history of conservatism was jump-started by a special issue of *American Historical Review* (1994) that included Brinkley, "The Problem of American Conservatism"; Ribuffo, "Why Is There So Much Conservatism in the United States and Why Do So Few Historians Know Anything About It?"; Yohn, "Will the Real Conservatives Please Stand Up? Or, the Pitfalls Involved in Examining Ideological Sympathies: A Comment on Alan Brinkley's 'Problem of American Conservatism.'" Another early essay is Kazin, "The Grass-Roots Right." A recent *Journal of American History* (2011) roundtable that considers the flurry of scholarship on conservatism includes Phillips-Fein, "Conservatism: A State of the Field"; McClay, "Less Boilerplate, More Symmetry"; Brinkley, "Conservatism as a Growing Field of Scholarship"; Critchlow, "Rethinking American Conservatism"; Durham, "On American Conservatism and Kim Phillips-Fein's Survey of the Field"; Lassiter, "Political History Beyond the Red-Blue Divide"; McGirr, "Now That Historians Know So Much About the Right, How Should We Best Approach the Study of Conservatism?"; and Phillips-Fein, "A Response."

    Titles that seek to explain the rise of the right in the 1970s and 1980s include Schulman, *The Seventies*; Schulman and Zelizer, *Rightward Bound*; Hodgson, *More Equal Than Others*; Perlstein, *Nixonland*; Wilentz, *The Age of Reagan*; Patterson, *Restless Giant*; Stein, *Pivotal Decade*; Schaller, *Right Turn*; Troy, *Morning in America*; Berkowitz, *Something Happened*; Jenkins, *Decade of Nightmares*; Sandbrook, *Mad as Hell*.

2. This argument was most famously made in the late 1990s by Robert Putnam in a series of articles and later a book, *Bowling Alone*. Others had made a similar case, including Robert Bellah et al., *Habits of the Heart* (1985).

3. A few scholars have argued that the Sixties effectively lived on through the 1970s and 1980s; see, for example, Gosse and Moser, *The World the Sixties Made*; Gosse, *Rethinking the New Left*; Berger, *The Hidden 1970s*; Tuck, editor of a special issue on the 1970s in *Journal of Contemporary History*; Surbrug, *Beyond Vietnam*. Scholars who have argued against the civic disengagement thesis include Freeman and Johnson,

Waves of Protest; Hall, *American Patriotism, American Protest*; and B. Martin, *The Other Eighties.*

4. See the preface to the 1996 edition of Bellah et al., *Habits of the Heart,* xxi. Such interpretations have been widely accepted even by scholars of the "new political history," which, when it addresses the 1970s and 1980s, focuses so tightly on policy, electoral politics, and political institutions that grassroots challenges are almost totally absent. On the new political history, see, for example, Zelizer, *Governing America.*

5. Kelley, *Race Rebels,* 9–10.

6. For example, Miller and Hoffmann find that "attitudinal differences among various groups" on key issues like abortion, homosexuality, and school prayer "have remained fairly stable over the past 25 years." Miller and Hoffmann, "The Growing Divisiveness," 721–52. See also Fiorina, *Culture War?*

7. All of these examples reinforce the political scientist Ronald Inglehart's argument that value systems and ideologies do not mobilize people to act; value systems may motivate a person to adapt an ideology (pp. 371–72), but people act only when they want to achieve a goal or solve a problem. According to Inglehart, the post-1960s United States witnessed more mobilization in part due to a rising political skill level among "mass publics," as education became more widespread and "political information more pervasive." But most citizens still needed a catalyst of some kind to propel them to activism. Inglehart, *Culture Shift in Advanced Industrial Society,* 371–72. And again, while Americans, especially those who identify with one or another religious tradition, were more likely to categorize themselves as "liberal" or "conservative" in the 1970s and 1980s, that did not mean they were more likely to become activists.

8. Here my work is informed by the relatively recent trend in social movement studies that emphasizes emotion as an essential mobilizing factor among activists. See, for example, Jasper, "The Emotions of Protest"; Goodwin, Jasper, and Polletta, *Passionate Politics*; Goodwin, Jasper, and Polletta, "Emotional Dimensions of Social Movements"; Gould, *Moving Politics.* According to Piven and Cloward, a change in consciousness must precipitate a change in behavior. In what I call "front porch politics," sensing a threat leads to one's consciousness being raised, which in turn leads to the impulse to act. "The movement must become defiant, violating the social expectations and even the laws the members of the movement deem unjust. The defiance must become collective to maximize its effect." Piven and Cloward, *Poor People's Movements,* 3–4.

9. I am grateful to Jeremy Varon for some of the language used here.

10. Theda Skocpol reminds us that dating from the nineteenth century, Americans have a long history of state and civil society working together "to support families and communities." That history veered off course after the 1960s, she argues, though in my view, the 1970s and 1980s were a time when Americans improvised to keep that spirit alive. As Skocpol concludes, "Family and Security for All" would make a good slogan on which to base a "new sense of national unity," because it has worked in the past. Skocpol, "Social Provision and Civic Community."

11. Kuttner, *Revolt of the Haves,* 25.

12. And although front porch politics is a type of grassroots politics, it does not include

all grassroots politics. Grassroots strategies and tactics can also be essential to campaigns that do not have a front porch perspective—such as human rights campaigns.

13. Goodwyn, *The Populist Moment*, 296. In addition, Piven and Cloward suggest that "economic and social dislocations that disrupt the structures and routines of daily life are a necessary condition for the rise of protest movements"; Piven and Cloward, *Poor People's Movements*, 11.

14. See Boyte, *Backyard Revolution*; Fisher, *Let the People Decide*; Delgado, *Organizing the Movement*; Boyte, Booth, and Max, *Citizen Action and the New American Populism*; and Bratt, Hartman, and Meyerson, *Critical Perspectives on Housing*.

15. Bellah et al., *Habits of the Heart*, 196, 199, 204.

16. Ibid., 207.

17. Only Matthew Lassiter seems to have picked up on this point. See his comment on Phillips-Fein's "Conservatism: A State of the Field": Lassiter, "Political History Beyond the Red-Blue Divide," 760–64.

18. Daniel Rodgers's excellent account of American intellectual history in the last quarter of the twentieth century reveals the developing infrastructure of neoliberal institutions—think tanks, law schools, economics and other social science faculties— that shaped economic discourse and policy, facilitated deindustrialization and globalization, and generally provided the rhetorical foundation for overcoming front porch challenges. Rodgers, *The Age of Fracture*.

19. In 2012, the Pew Research Center released polling data that showed Democrats and Republicans to be more divided than ever on values. Dan Balz, "Politics Is the Great Divider in the United States," *Washington Post*, June 5, 2012.

1: This Is the Dawning of the Age of Self-Reliance

1. Nixon, *RN*, 410; Schell, *The Time of Illusion*, 66; Wells, *The War Within*, 383; Small, *The Presidency of Richard Nixon*, 75.

2. Schell, *Time of Illusion*, 97–98; Wells, *War Within*, 424.

3. Wells, *War Within*, 500–503; Small, *Antiwarriors*, 144–45.

4. DeBenedetti and Chatfield, *An American Ordeal*, 310.

5. Rudenstine, *The Day the Presses Stopped*, 341–42; Nixon, *RN*, 513–14.

6. Kutler, *The Wars of Watergate*, 607.

7. Goldstein, *Political Repression in Modern America*, 478; Wise, *The American Police State*, 194, 399–400; Olmsted, *Challenging the Secret Government*, 81–144; MacKenzie, *Secrets*, 26–30; Schell, *Time of Illusion*, 59–60.

8. A. Theoharis, *Spying on Americans*, 194. COINTELPRO was first revealed when a group calling itself the Citizen's Committee to Investigate the FBI broke into a Bureau office in Media, Pennsylvania, in 1971 and shared with the press stolen COINTELPRO files. Most of the public, however, did not catch on until the Church and Pike committees later took testimony on the FBI.

9. Varon, *Bringing the War Home*, 154–55; Goldstein, *Political Repression in Modern America*, 528; Churchill and Vander Wall, *The COINTELPRO*, 140.

10. Goldstein, *Political Repression in Modern America*, 504–6; Donner, *Protectors of Privilege*, 92, 266; Cowan, Egleson, and Hentoff, *State Secrets*, 262.

11. Small, *Presidency of Richard Nixon*, 207.

12. Matusow, *The Unraveling of America*, 231–32; Small, *Presidency of Richard Nixon*, 212–13.

13. Yergin, *The Prize*, 615, 610; Vogel, *Fluctuating Fortunes*, 125–26.

14. Matusow, *Unraveling of America*, 6, 304–5; Small, *Presidency of Richard Nixon*, 213.

15. Greene, *The Presidency of Gerald R. Ford*, 73–77; Carroll, *It Seemed Like Nothing Happened*, 173, 175.

16. J. Martin, *Nader*, 112–13, 45.

17. Ibid., 125, 128–29.

18. Boyte, *Backyard Revolution*, 122.

19. Matusow, *Unraveling of America*, 229; Carroll, *It Seemed Like Nothing Happened*, 130; Small, *Presidency of Richard Nixon*, 212.

20. Cohen, *A Consumers' Republic*, 365–69.

21. Vogel, *Fluctuating Fortunes*, 108, 111.

22. Boyte, *Backyard Revolution*, xii–xiii, 2–3.

23. Boyte came out of the New Left and traced the citizen movement back to Sixties organizing traditions, particularly the geographically based community organizing associated with Saul Alinsky. Most of his writing on the "backyard revolution" placed it within a longer progressive tradition and focused on economics, with citizens confronting government and corporate power. See Boyte, *Backyard Revolution*.

24. Boyte, *Backyard Revolution*, 7–8.

25. Martin Scorsese, director, *Taxi Driver* (1976).

26. Fisher, *Let the People Decide*, 124.

27. Ibid., 124; Delgado, *Organizing the Movement*, 4–9.

28. Freeman, *Working-Class New York*, 259–70; Greene, *Presidency of Gerald R. Ford*, 90–94.

29. Susser, *Norman Street*, 6.

30. Freeman, *Working-Class New York*, 274–75.

31. Susser, *Norman Street*, 104, 111.

32. Ibid., 161–77.

33. Fisher, *Let the People Decide*, 142–43.

34. Ibid., 143–47.

35. See Guida West, *The National Welfare Rights Movement*; Schulman, *Seventies*, 264, n34; Delgado, *Organizing the Movement*, 23–25; Kornbluh, *The Battle for Welfare Rights*, 92–93.

36. Delgado, *Organizing the Movement*, 47, 107, 112; Atlas, *Seeds of Change*, 24–25; Fisher, *Let the People Decide*, 133–34, 138.

37. Delgado, *Organizing the Movement*, 47; Boyte, *Backyard Revolution*, 95.

38. Boyte, *Backyard Revolution*, 2–3, 109–10.

39. Ibid., 98–100.

40. Ibid., 63–65, 164–66.

41. Ibid., 65–68.

42. Wellstone, *How the Rural Poor Got Power*, xiii–xiv, 3–4, 8–10.

43. Ibid., 12–18.
44. Ibid., 33–44, 67.
45. Ibid., 95–96.
46. Ibid., 219.

2: The Long Shadow of Segregation

1. Quoted in Lassiter, *The Silent Majority*, p. 2.
2. Anderson, *The Pursuit of Fairness*, 127–29.
3. Self, *American Babylon*, 1–2, 42, 97, 104; Lassiter, *Silent Majority*, 1–3; Kirp, Dwyer, and Rosenthal, *Our Town*, 7.
4. On the attempt to distinguish de jure from de facto segregation, see Lassiter, "De Jure/De Facto Segregation"; on the development of federal housing policy, see Freund, *Colored Property*; see also Self, *American Babylon*, 104.
5. Self, *American Babylon*, 3; Lassiter, *Silent Majority*, 1–5.
6. Lassiter, *Silent Majority*, 1–2.
7. Kirp, Dwyer, and Rosenthal, *Our Town*, 2.
8. Ibid., 69.
9. Ibid., 72–75.
10. Ibid., 76–77.
11. Ibid., 86–87.
12. Ibid., 101–2, 120–21, 136.
13. Ibid., 125–35, 147, 154.
14. Carroll, *It Seemed Like Nothing Happened*, 42–43; Kotlowski, *Nixon's Civil Rights*, 36–37; Lassiter, *Silent Majority*, 5.
15. Lassiter, *Silent Majority*, 132–35.
16. Ibid., 136.
17. Ibid., 140, 141.
18. Ibid., 144, 145.
19. Ibid., 152.
20. Ibid., 161–65.
21. Ibid., 166–68.
22. Ibid., 186–89, 193–96.
23. Ibid., 202–6.
24. As Lassiter notes, the story was somewhat different twenty years later. Thanks to a dramatic rise in population (mostly from in-migrants) and a growing divide between rich and poor, there were renewed calls for neighborhood schools and school choice. *Silent Majority*, 217–21.
25. Mirel, *The Rise and Fall of an Urban School System*, 295–96.
26. Ibid., 314.
27. Ibid, 327–35.
28. Ibid., 335–45.
29. Ibid., 345–49; Formisano, *Boston Against Busing*, 12, 229.
30. Formisano, *Boston Against Busing*, 13.

31. Ibid., 17.
32. Ibid., 16.
33. Lukas, *Common Ground*, 116, 135–36.
34. J. Theoharis, "'They Told Us Our Kids Were Stupid,'" 29–31; Eaton, *The Other Boston Busing Story*, 23–24.
35. Lukas, *Common Ground*, 238.
36. Formisano, *Boston Against Busing*, 177; civil rights leader Julian Bond, speaking at a 1974 demonstration, identified what he saw as the main source of antibusing anger: "It's not the bus. It's us."
37. Formisano, *Boston Against Busing*, 75.
38. "Kennedy Jeered, Hit at Antibusing Rally," *Boston Globe*, September 10, 1974; Formisano, 76–77; Jane DuWors, interview in Hampton et al., *Voices of Freedom*, 597–98.
39. Formisano, *Boston Against Busing*, 77; J. Theoharis, "'They Told Us Our Kids Were Stupid,'" 34.
40. Formisano, *Boston Against Busing*, 79.
41. Mark Feeney, "Louise Day Hicks, Icon of Tumult, Dies," *Boston Globe*, October 22, 2003.
42. Formisano, *Boston Against Busing*, 124.
43. Ibid., 90.
44. Lukas, *Common Ground*, 327; J. Theoharis, "'I'd Rather Go to School in the South,'" 135.
45. Formisano, 203; Lukas, 642–50.
46. On Milwaukee, see Dougherty, *More Than One Struggle*; on Baltimore, see Durr, *Behind the Backlash*; on Los Angeles, see Sides, *L.A. City Limits*, and M. Davis, *City of Quartz*, 183–85.

3: Sexual Politics, Family Politics

1. *Playboy* interviews with both Vice President Nelson Rockefeller (October 1975) and California governor Jerry Brown (April 1976), the latter of whom had run against Carter in the Democratic primaries, fit in with a general editorial interest in politics in the mid-1970s. The magazine also featured articles on President Ford and the Patty Hearst trial, serialized excerpts from the Watergate exposé *All the President's Men*, and interviews with the likes of radicals Abbie Hoffman and Tom Hayden.
2. Robert Kerwin, "Women's Lib and Me," *Playboy*, May 1978, 100–104.
3. Lienesch, *Redeeming America*, 1–2.
4. On evangelicals taking up political causes, see Self, *All in the Family*, 339–42.
5. Lienesch, *Redeeming America*, 11–12.
6. Self, *All in the Family*, 305, 342.
7. All of the foregoing, see F. Davis, *Moving the Mountain*, 70–88; Evans, "Beyond Declension," 52–59; Evans, *Tidal Wave*, 158–60; R. Rosen, *The World Split Open*, 87.
8. Farrell, *Yours in Sisterhood*, 15, 31–32; Carroll, *It Seemed Like Nothing Happened*, 35; R. Rosen, *World Split Open*, 210.
9. F. Davis, *Moving the Mountain*, 215; Roberts, *A Necessary Spectacle*, 156–64.

10. Mary Mazzio, dir., *A Hero for Daisy*, 1999 (DVD).

11. Brownmiller, *In Our Time*, 180–85.

12. F. Davis, *Moving the Mountain*, 239–41.

13. Statistics are from ibid., 308, 311; see also Self, *All in the Family*, 210; Carroll, *It Seemed Like Nothing Happened*, 114.

14. R. Rosen, *World Split Open*, 182; F. Davis, *Moving the Mountain*, 314; Brownmiller, *In Our Time*, 199–201; Carroll, *It Seemed Like Nothing Happened*, 274.

15. In 1977, Oregon made headlines as the first state to criminalize marital rape, but a year later, a jury there freed John Rideout even though his wife, Greta, testified that he forced her to have sex two to three times a day, and violent sex at least once a week. She went to the police after he beat and raped her when she at first refused to submit. Even so, the jury acquitted him. A couple of months after the trial, the Rideouts separated and cops later busted John for breaking into Greta's new home. Eventually, he went to jail for harassing her. Although it seemed justice was not served in the case, historians credit the publicity it generated with galvanizing a legal reform movement. By 1997, all fifty states called marital rape a crime. With the Rideout verdict, it became clear that the jury—and the larger public it represented—did not understand why any woman would stay with an abusive husband like John Rideout. Greta Rideout had left her husband three times but always came back. Many wondered how bad life with her husband could have been if she kept coming back. R. Rosen, *World Split Open*, 183–84; F. Davis, *Moving the Mountain*, 316–17.

16. Flora Davis notes that "wife-beating is typically accompanied by psychological abuse that destroys the individual's self-confidence." F. Davis, *Moving the Mountain*, 320.

17. Brownmiller, *In Our Time*, 263–65; R. Rosen, *World Split Open*, 186; F. Davis, *Moving the Mountain*, 321–22; Enke, "Taking Over Domestic Space," 162–84.

18. F. Davis, *Moving the Mountain*, 163–64; Hodgson, *More Equal Than Others*, 146.

19. F. Davis, *Moving the Mountain*, 167–68; Brownmiller, *In Our Time*, 123–25.

20. The constitutional grounds on which the lawyers based their case sprang mostly from two more cautious approaches. First, they argued that the justices had already signaled their view that earlier constitutional amendments were based on an implicit guarantee of an individual's right to privacy. The freedom to practice one's religion and the freedom from unreasonable searches and seizures, for example, seemed to promise a right to privacy. Weddington and Hames therefore argued that decisions about one's medical condition fell under the protected right to privacy, and the state did not have the right to interfere with such decisions. Second, they argued that when the states compelled medical professionals to deny women certain types of medical care, it violated the Fourteenth Amendment's prohibitions against denying a citizen's liberty without due process.

21. Hodgson, *More Equal Than Others*, 148; F. Davis, *Moving the Mountain*, 172–79; Brownmiller, *In our Time*, 121–35; Carroll, *It Seemed Like Nothing Happened*, 179.

22. Self, *All in the Family*, 137. That their family ideal may have depended upon men having power over women, and religious authority over women's autonomy, did not matter. Only the midcentury male-led nuclear family ideal mattered.

23. Robert Self shows how the New Frontier and Great Society liberal establishment invested in "the white middle-class nuclear family headed by a patriotic and hetero-sexual male"—which he calls "breadwinner liberalism," though it "is best thought of as a national mythology." By the 1970s and 1980s, pro-family activists spoke of the nuclear family as if it had been the one constant model for family and national health since Christ's time—even though, as Self remarks, before the 1920s, "multigenerational families and multiple strategies of organizing family economy were far more common than male breadwinner nuclear families." Self, *All in the Family*, 4, 332.

24. Wandersee, *On the Move*, 183–84.

25. It's worth noting that the women's movement experienced the internal divisions that often occur in any social movement as well as official repression (most notably through infiltration by FBI agent provocateurs). Evans, *Tidal Wave*, 99, 100–102; Carroll, *It Seemed Like Nothing Happened*, 115; R. Rosen, *World Split Open*, 239–46.

26. Hodgson, *More Equal Than Others*, 144.

27. Wandersee, *On the Move*, 178.

28. Klatch, *Women of the New Right*, 4–5; F. Davis, quoting from an interview with Jane Mansbridge, *Moving the Mountain*, 387–88; see also Self, *All in the Family*.

29. Critchlow, *Phyllis Schlafly and Grassroots Conservatism*, 23.

30. Wandersee, *On the Move*, 178.

31. Critchlow, *Phyllis Schlafly and Grassroots Conservatism*, 217–18.

32. Ibid., 221.

33. There were other acronym-rich anti-ERA groups, too—Women Who Want to Be Women (WWWW), Happiness of Womanhood (HOW), American Women Are Richly Endowed (AWARE), Family Liberty and God (FLAG)—but STOP ERA was the most prominent.

34. Critchlow, *Phyllis Schlafly and Grassroots Conservatism*, 224–25.

35. Klatch, *Women of the New Right*, 136–37; Lienesch, *Redeeming America*, 70; Carroll, *It Seemed Like Nothing Happened*, 113.

36. Klatch, *Women of the New Right*, 47.

37. Mansbridge, *Why We Lost the ERA*, 3, 60–89.

38. Critchlow, *Phyllis Schlafly and Grassroots Conservatism*, 227–34; Mathews and DeHart, *Sex, Gender, and the Politics of ERA*, 57; Mansbridge, *Why We Lost the ERA*, 36–44.

39. Mansbridge, *Why We Lost the ERA*, 66, 165–72; F. Davis, *Moving the Mountain*, 394.

40. Escoffier, "Fabulous Politics," 192, 193.

41. Clendinen and Nagourney, *Out for Good*, 29–30.

42. D'Emilio, *Sexual Politics, Sexual Communities*, 234; Clendinen and Nagourney, *Out for Good*, 39.

43. Clendinen and Nagourney, *Out for Good*, 51–54.

44. D'Emilio, *Sexual Politics, Sexual Communities*, 237–38.

45. Clendinen and Nagourney, *Out for Good*, 188–98; Escoffier, "Fabulous Politics," 198–99.

46. Escoffier, *American Homo*, 58–60; Eskridge, *Gaylaw*, 7; Escoffier, "Fabulous Politics," 198; D'Emilio, *Sexual Politics, Sexual Communities*, 235–36.

47. Clendinen and Nagourney, *Out for Good*, 199–200; Alix Spiegel, "81 Words," *This*

American Life, Chicago Public Media, NPR, broadcast January 18, 2002, www.this americanlife.org/radio-archives/episode/204/transcript.

48. Spiegel, "81 Words"; Clendinen and Nagourney, *Out for Good*, 200–202.

49. Spiegel, "81 Words"; Clendinen and Nagourney, *Out for Good*, 208–9.

50. Clendinen and Nagourney, *Out for Good*, 210–11; Spiegel, "81 Words."

51. Bayer, *Homosexuality and American Psychiatry*, 176–77; Clendinen and Nagourney, *Out for Good*, 212–17; Spiegel, "81 Words."

52. Clendinen and Nagourney, *Out for Good*, 231.

53. Diamond, *Roads to Dominion*, 162–63.

54. Escoffier, "Fabulous Politics," 199.

55. Bryant, *The Anita Bryant Story*, 14, 16–17, 25–29; Clendinen and Nagourney, *Out for Good*, 291–96.

56. Bryant, *Anita Bryant Story*, 41–44, 50–52.

57. Ibid., 62.

58. Ibid., 87–91; the San Francisco journalist Randy Shilts observed that whenever Bryant found that the baiting had gone too far, "she did marvelously telegenic things like break into the chorus of 'Battle Hymn of the Republic.'" Shilts, *The Mayor of Castro Street*, 156; Clendinen and Nagourney, *Out for Good*, 307.

59. Bryant, *Anita Bryant Story*, 95, 102, 122–23.

60. Bryant, *Anita Bryant Story*, 125, 127, 135; Shilts, *Mayor of Castro Street*, 157; Clendinen and Nagourney, *Out for Good*, 308–9.

61. Bryant, *Anita Bryant Story*, 135; Shilts, *Mayor of Castro Street*, 213.

62. Shilts, *Mayor of Castro Street*, 159.

63. Ibid., 33.

64. Clendinen and Nagourney, *Out for Good*, 378–79; Shilts, *Mayor of Castro Street*, 240.

65. Clendinen and Nagourney, *Out for Good*, 381; McGirr, *Suburban Warriors*, 258; Mixner, *Stranger Among Friends*, 144; Shilts, *Mayor of Castro Street*, 215.

66. Shilts, *Mayor of Castro Street*, 225.

67. Ibid., 245–46.

68. Ibid., 231.

69. Rob Epstein, dir., *The Times of Harvey Milk* (1984; 20th Anniversary DVD, 2004); Shilts, *Mayor of Castro Street*, 230–31.

70. Mixner, *Stranger Among Friends*, 147–48.

71. Ibid., 149.

72. Mixner, *Stranger Among Friends*, 149; Clendinen and Nagourney, *Out for Good*, 387; Shilts, *Mayor of Castro Street*, 243.

73. Epstein, *Times of Harvey Milk*.

74. Shilts, *Stranger Among Friends*, 278, 315, 325, 328; Carroll, *It Seemed Like Nothing Happened*, 293; Epstein, *Times of Harvey Milk*.

75. Critchlow, *Phyllis Schlafly and Grassroots Conservatism*, 267.

76. W. B. Turner, "Mirror Images," 16.

Part II: The Environment

1. Vogel, *Fluctuating Fortunes*, 60–61.

4: Energy, Health, and Safety

1. Shabecoff, *A Fierce Green Fire*, 65–76.
2. Sale, *The Green Revolution*, 7. In his use of "future shock," Sale was riffing on the term introduced by Alvin Toffler in 1970.
3. Hays, *Beauty, Health, and Permanence*, 143.
4. Ibid., 5.
5. Shabecoff, *Fierce Green Fire*, 79.
6. Ibid., 97.
7. Sale, *Green Revolution*, 3; Shabecoff, *Fierce Green Fire*, 107; Steinberg, *Down to Earth*, 247.
8. Gottlieb, *Forcing the Spring*, 123–24, 127; *New York Times* obituary, April 15, 1964.
9. Shabecoff, *Fierce Green Fire*, 106.
10. Caldwell, Hayes, and MacWhirter, *Citizens and the Environment*, 131–33.
11. Shabecoff, *Fierce Green Fire*, 112.
12. Ibid., 115; Gottlieb, *Forcing the Spring*, 149.
13. Shabecoff, *Fierce Green Fire*, 113; Gottlieb, *Forcing the Spring*, 150, 155.
14. Shabecoff, *Fierce Green Fire*, 117–18.
15. Vogel, *Fluctuating Fortunes*, 110; Gottlieb, *Forcing the Spring*, 181; Sale, *Green Revolution*, 37; Shabecoff, *Fierce Green Fire*, 131.
16. Gottlieb, *Forcing the Spring*, 177.
17. Shabecoff, *Fierce Green Fire*, 133.
18. Gottlieb, *Forcing the Spring*, 186.
19. "Energy Blues," *Schoolhouse Rock! Special 30th Anniversary Edition*, DVD (Buena Vista Home Entertainment, 2002).
20. Caldwell, Hayes, and MacWhirter, *Citizens and the Environment*, 228–29; Vogel, *Fluctuating Fortunes*, 130; Mark J. Davis, dir., *The American Experience: The Alaska Pipeline*, DVD (PBS, 2006).
21. Carroll, *It Seemed Like Nothing Happened*, 122; Jacobs, "The Conservative Struggle and the Energy Crisis," 198–99, 204–7; Vogel, *Fluctuating Fortunes*, 133.
22. Updike quoted in Jacobs, "Conservative Struggle and the Energy Crisis," 193; Hodgson, *More Equal Than Others*, 13.
23. D. H. Davis, *Energy Politics*, 109.
24. Hays, *Beauty, Health, and Permanence*, 232–33; Berkowitz, *Something Happened*, 127–28.
25. As one expert noted at the time, a truly visionary energy program would have required several key components, all of which were unlikely to come to pass: "1) establishing mass transit systems and reducing the dependence on heavy, energy inefficient private automobiles . . . 2) improving architecture to eliminate energy wasted for heating, excessive lighting, and air conditioning; 3) freighting by train rather than road; 4) creating innovative community plans that would increase land-use efficiency; and 5) increasing reliance on communications technology to reduce travel." This kind of planning required a long view and the kind of political muscle that neither front porch grassroots organizers nor the post-Sixties federal government could muster. Caldwell, Hayes, and MacWhirter, *Citizens and the Environment*, 94.

26. Patterson, *Restless Giant*, 119–20; Gottlieb, *Forcing the Spring*, 184; Hays, *Beauty, Health, and Permanence*, 372, 240, 323.

27. Berkowitz, *Something Happened*, 128; Barrow, "An Age of Limits," 169.

28. Berkowitz, *Something Happened*, 130–31; Carroll, *It Seemed Like Nothing Happened*, 219–20; Hodgson, *More Equal Than Others*, 254; Barrow, "Age of Limits," 171; Carroll, *It Seemed Like Nothing Happened*, 220–21.

29. Barrow, "Age of Limits," 172, 174, 176.

30. Zaretsky, *No Direction Home*, 233; Carroll, *It Seemed Like Nothing Happened*, 216.

31. Montrie, *To Save the Land and People*, 3.

32. Ibid., 74.

33. Ibid., 104–5, 202–3.

34. Ibid., 156, 177–78.

35. Boyte, Booth, and Max, *Citizen Action and the New American Populism*, 105–8; Battista, "Labor and Liberalism," 311.

36. Boyte, Booth, and Max, *Citizen Action and the New American Populism*, 111; Battista, "Labor and Liberalism," 309.

37. Boyte, Booth, and Max, *Citizen Action and the New American Populism*, 105, 113–17; Battista, "Labor and Liberalism," 316–17.

38. Wasserman, *Energy War*, 140; Wellstone and Casper, *Powerline*, 241–42; D. H. Davis, *Energy Politics*, 200; Gyorgy, *No Nukes*, 432.

39. Wellstone and Casper, *Powerline*, 135–37, 140.

40. Ibid., 142–46.

41. Ibid., 165–67, 171–76.

42. Ibid., 206–7.

43. Ibid., 216–18; Carroll, *It Seemed Like Nothing Happened*, 320.

44. Wellstone and Casper, *Powerline*, 218, 220–21.

45. Ibid., 248–51.

46. Ibid., 274–87; Wasserman, *Energy War*, 138.

47. In 2002, the National Institute of Environmental Health Sciences acknowledged that link but called it weak; it recommended "continued education on practical ways of reducing exposure," though it is not clear if "practical ways" would include selling one's farm and moving to where there was no power line; http://www.niehs.nih.gov/health/topics/agents/emf/.

5: No Nukes!

1. Carroll, *It Seemed Like Nothing Happened*, 120–21; Hertsgaard, *Nuclear Inc.*, 61.

2. D. H. Davis, *Energy Politics*, 225; Gyorgy, *No Nukes*, 85; Hays, *Beauty, Health, and Permanence*, 178; Wasserman, *Energy War*, 13–14, 17.

3. D. H. Davis, *Energy Politics*, 225. Data gathered across thirty-seven years, from 1968 to 2005, showed, for example, that thermal pollution from the Calvert Cliffs nuclear power plant in Maryland caused male blue crabs—the ones that wind up on your plate—to steadily decline in size. George Abbe, "Blue Crab and Oyster Studies at the Estuarine Research Center," *Morgan State University—Estuarine Research Center Newsletter*, February 2005, 3.

4. D. H. Davis, *Energy Politics*, 228, 232; Gofman in MUSE album booklet.

5. Gyorgy, *No Nukes*, 381; D. H. Davis, *Energy Politics*, 217–18; Bedford, *Seabrook Station*, 129.

6. D. H. Davis, *Energy Politics*, 219; Wasserman, *Energy War*, 6; Walker, *Three Mile Island*, 65–67.

7. Caldwell, Hayes, and MacWhirter, *Citizens and the Environment*, 196–203.

8. Ibid., 204–10, 322–26.

9. Walker, *Three Mile Island*, 13, 27; Hertsgaard, *Nuclear Inc.*, 70; J. Martin, *Nader*, 172–78.

10. Hertsgaard, *Nuclear Inc.*, 71, 73.

11. Stauber and Rampton, *Toxic Sludge Is Good for You*, 38.

12. Walker, *Three Mile Island*, 18–19, 20; Gyorgy, *No Nukes*, 285.

13. Walker, *Three Mile Island*, 22, 38–40; Hays, *Beauty, Health, and Permanence*, 180, 243.

14. Walker, *Three Mile Island*, 11.

15. Gyorgy, *No Nukes*, 392; Wasserman, *Energy War*, 29, 33–38.

16. Epstein, *Political Protest and Cultural Revolution*, 8.

17. Gyorgy, *No Nukes*, 388; Wasserman, *Energy War*, 29–30.

18. Bedford, *Seabrook Station*, 5–6.

19. Epstein, *Political Protest and Cultural Revolution*, 10, 84.

20. Zunes, "Seabrook," 30; Kidder, "The Nonviolent War Against Nuclear Power," 70, 74.

21. Wasserman, *Energy War*, 53–54, 5.

22. Bedford, *Seabrook Station*, 82–84, 32.

23. Wasserman, *Energy War*, 62–63.

24. This included the towns of Hampton, Hampton Falls, North Hampton, Exeter, Kensington, Durham, and Rye; Wasserman, *Energy War*, 83.

25. Although it originated with Spanish anarchists, the concept of affinity groups—first imported to the New Left by Murray Bookchin—soon came to define direct action efforts in the environmental and No Nukes movements, even as both included plenty—probably majorities—of activists who did not identify themselves as either anarchists or New Leftists.

26. Epstein, *Political Protest and Cultural Revolution*, 65–66.

27. Kidder, "Nonviolent War Against Nuclear Power," 70.

28. Wasserman, *Energy War*, 69.

29. Epstein, *Political Protest and Cultural Revolution*, 65–66; Gyorgy, *No Nukes*, 398; Wasserman, *Energy War*, 69–72.

30. Epstein, *Political Protest and Cultural Revolution*, 68; Wasserman, *Energy War*, 69–75; Bedford, *Seabrook Station*, 78.

31. Wasserman, *Energy War*, 87–89.

32. Ibid., 103–4.

33. Gyorgy, *No Nukes*, 450–52; Solomon, *Made Love, Got War*, 88–89; Wasserman, *Energy War*, 106. Ultimately, the Trojan plant continued to operate until 1992, despite several ballot initiatives to try to shut it down. PG&E ended up closing it for safety reasons after inspectors found cracks in steam tubes that could, if overlooked, cause a crack in the main steam line, which could then overheat the core and lead to a meltdown. Although the steam tubes were projected to last thirty-five years, the

cracks were found after only sixteen years. The utility decommissioned the plant, passed the cost on to the ratepayers, and buried the reactor at Hanford. Later, it imploded the plant's soaring cooling tower.

34. Wasserman, *Energy War*, 108–14; Kidder, "Nonviolent War Against Nuclear Power," 72; Zunes, "Seabrook," 28.

35. Wasserman, *Energy War*, 114–20; Kidder, "Nonviolent War Against Nuclear Power," 74–76; Zunes, "Seabrook," 29.

36. Zunes, "Seabrook," 30; Epstein, *Political Protest and Cultural Revolution*, 80–81.

37. Epstein, *Political Protest and Cultural Revolution*, 59; Kidder, "Nonviolent War Against Nuclear Power," 76.

38. Gyorgy, *No Nukes*, 422, 424–25.

39. Wills, *Conservation Fallout*, 66, 77.

40. Ibid., 69–75; Wasserman, *Energy War*, 135; Gyorgy, *No Nukes*, 458.

41. Wills, *Conservation Fallout*, 76–77, 82–84.

42. Wills, *Conservation Fallout*, 88–91; Epstein, *Political Protest and Cultural Revolution*, 99.

43. Walker, *Three Mile Island*, 71–80.

44. Ibid., 86–101.

45. Ibid., 103, 44–46, 48–49.

46. Ibid., 137; Stauber and Rampton, *Toxic Sludge Is Good for You*, 39.

47. Walker, *Three Mile Island*, 148–50.

48. Ibid., 182–83, 229–30.

49. Wasserman, *Energy War*, x; Hertsgaard, *Nuclear Inc.*, 96; Walker, *Three Mile Island*, 241.

50. Hays, *Beauty, Health, and Permanence*, 182; D. H. Davis, *Energy Politics*, 221–22.

51. Walker, *Three Mile Island*, 215; Wasserman, *Energy War*, 67; Hertsgaard, *Nuclear Inc.*, 87–88.

52. Hertsgaard, *Nuclear Inc.*, 170; Stauber and Rampton, *Toxic Sludge Is Good For You*, 40.

53. Carroll, *It Seemed Like Nothing Happened*, 322.

54. J. Rosen, "Music and the Movement," 22; Robert Palmer, "Pop Music: Antinuclear Marathon at Garden," *New York Times*, September 21, 1979, C4; Robin Herman, "Nearly 200,000 Rally to Protest Nuclear Energy," *New York Times*, September 24, 1979, B1.

55. Hays, *Beauty, Health, and Permanence*, 179.

56. Wasserman, *Energy War*, 137; Wills, *Conservation Fallout*, 103; Hertsgaard, *Nuclear Inc.*, 200–202.

57. Wills, *Conservation Fallout*, 104–10, 115; Epstein, *Political Protest and Cultural Revolution*, 111, 102–4.

58. Epstein, *Political Protest and Cultural Revolution*, 105. Epstein is on firmer ground when she argues that Abalone came closer than the Clamshell or other alliances to building a utopian community "because it created a much more explicitly defined movement culture linking nonviolence and revolutionary aspirations through commitment to feminism and prefigurative politics." Epstein, *Political Protest and Cultural Revolution*, 95.

59. Bedford, *Seabrook Station*, 134–35.

60. Ibid., 154–56.
61. Ibid., 156, 183; Hertsgaard, *Nuclear Inc.*, 216, 210.
62. Bedford, *Seabrook Station*, 183.
63. Hertsgaard, *Nuclear Inc.*, 153; D. H. Davis, *Energy Politics*, 241; Bedford, *Seabrook Station*, 124; Walker, *Three Mile Island*, 224.
64. Hertsgaard, *Nuclear Inc.*, 63–64; Walker, *Three Mile Island*, 5, 8.
65. Bedford, *Seabrook Station*, ix.
66. And before the 2011 Fukushima disaster in Japan, it seemed to be working, as President Obama approved $8 billion in federal loan guarantees to promote the building of dozens of new nuclear power plants in the United States.

6: Toxic Waste in the Basement

1. Steinberg, *Down to Earth*, 239, 248.
2. Gottlieb, *Forcing the Spring*, 318–23; Caldwell, Hayes, and MacWhirter, *Citizens and the Environment*, 125–27.
3. Hays, *Beauty, Health, and Permanence*, 194; Vogel, *Fluctuating Fortunes*, 135.
4. Layzer, *The Environmental Case*, 53; Gibbs, *Love Canal*, 6. "Where the national groups are prone to settle their differences with polluters through compromise," Philip Shabecoff later wrote, "the grass-roots groups usually will settle for nothing less than complete victory because the health of their children as well as their own and the habitability of their homes are on the line." Shabecoff, *Fierce Green Fire*, 233–34.
5. Blum, *Love Canal Revisited*, 24.
6. Ibid., 20–24; Newman, "From Love's Canal to Love Canal," 125.
7. Blum, *Love Canal Revisited*, 22; Newman, "From Love's Canal to Love Canal," 125–26.
8. Newman, "From Love's Canal to Love Canal," 129.
9. Shabecoff, *Fierce Green Fire*, 234; Blum, *Love Canal Revisited*, 26.
10. Layzer, *Environmental Case*, 54–60; Gibbs, *Love Canal*, 20.
11. Gibbs, *Love Canal*, 35–36.
12. Layzer, *Environmental Case*, 61; Blum, *Love Canal Revisited*, 26–27.
13. Blum, *Love Canal Revisited*, 36–37.
14. Newman, "From Love's Canal to Love Canal," 128.
15. Blum, *Love Canal Revisited*, 66–68, 71–72.
16. Ibid., 33, 47, 51.
17. Krauss, "Challenging Power," 130.
18. Layzer, *Environmental Case*, 63; Blum, *Love Canal Revisited*, 54, 59.
19. Blum, *Love Canal Revisited*, 116; Newman, "From Love's Canal to Love Canal," 133; Gibbs, *Love Canal*, 65, 81, 88; Krauss, "Challenging Power," 136.
20. Layzer, *Environmental Case*, 60; Gibbs, *Love Canal*, 89.
21. Hays, *Beauty, Health, and Permanence*, 201; Blum, *Love Canal Revisited*, 98, 86–90, 94, 119.
22. Gibbs, *Love Canal*, 150; Layzer, *Environmental Case*, 63; Blum, *Love Canal Revisited*, 58–59.
23. Gibbs, *Love Canal*, 153.
24. Ibid., 161.

25. Blum, *Love Canal Revisited*, 106–8.

26. On movements to stop Appalachian strip mining, see Montrie, *To Save the Land and People*.

27. Schwab, *Deeper Shades of Green*, xviii; Gibbs, *Love Canal*, 3–4, 5; Cynthia Hamilton quoted in Newman, "From Love's Canal to Love Canal," 132.

28. Gottlieb, *Forcing the Spring*, 247; Carroll, *It Seemed Like Nothing Happened*, 304; McGurty, *Transforming Environmentalism*, 42; Stine, "Environmental Policy During the Carter Presidency," 184.

29. Boyte, Booth, and Max, *Citizen Action and the New American Populism*, 123.

30. Shabecoff, *Fierce Green Fire*, 207.

31. McGurty, *Transforming Environmentalism*, 44.

32. Patterson, *Restless Giant*, 176; Shabecoff, *Fierce Green Fire*, 208–9; Vogel, *Fluctuating Fortunes*, 262, 268.

33. Vogel, *Fluctuating Fortunes*, 266–67; McGurty, *Transforming Environmentalism*, 46–47; "Anne Gorsuch Burford, 62, Dies; Reagan EPA Director," obituary, *Washington Post*, July 22, 2004, B06.

34. Vogel, *Fluctuating Fortunes*, 262.

35. Shabecoff, *Fierce Green Fire*, 236.

36. Boyte, Booth, and Max, *Citizen Action and the New American Populism*, 123, 4, 128–29.

37. Ibid., 5, 128–31.

38. Vogel, *Fluctuating Fortunes*, 262; Gottlieb, *Forcing the Spring*, 277; Boyte, Booth, and Max, *Citizen Action and the New American Populism*, 124.

39. The mostly Mexican American United Farm Workers led an antipesticides campaign from 1965 to 1971; in Gary, Indiana, Community Action to Reverse Pollution (CARP) mobilized the city's black population, including gang members, to force the city council to curb U.S. Steel's coke oven carbon emissions in the 1970s; and then there were those poor whites in West Virginia and Kentucky who took on the surface miners for destroying their environment. See Pulido, *Environmentalism and Economic Justice*, and Hurley, *Environmental Inequalities*.

40. McGurty, *Transforming Environmentalism*, 12–13.

41. Ibid., 25, 29–30.

42. Gottlieb, *Forcing the Spring*, 339; McGurty, *Transforming Environmentalism*, 50.

43. McGurty, *Transforming Environmentalism*, 55, 58–65.

44. Ibid., 4.

45. Ibid., 104.

46. Ibid., 81–110.

47. "In Arkansas Toxic Waste Cleanup, Highlights of New Environmental Debate," *New York Times*, November 2, 1992; this especially became a NIMBY issue where the incineration of toxic waste—if companies could not dump it, they wanted to burn it— was concerned. In some places, like Jacksonville, Arkansas, officials could not agree which was more dangerous: an existing dump or cleaning up the dump site and burning the waste. The Vertac Chemical Company left its pesticide plant site in Jacksonville littered with thousands of rotting barrels of poisonous chemicals (including

DDT and Agent Orange), most of which sat there for decades. It took thirteen years—from 1979 to 1992—for the proposed incineration of the chemicals to be approved (by then Governor Bill Clinton), but a federal judge stopped it because incineration seemed more dangerous to public health than the original problem.

48. Gottlieb, *Forcing the Spring*, 249; McGurty, *Transforming Environmentalism*, 52; William Glaberson, "Coping in the Age of 'Nimby,'" *New York Times*, June 19, 1988; Stauber and Rampton, *Toxic Sludge Is Good for You*, 89; Layzer, *Environmental Case*, 53; McGurty, *Transforming Environmentalism*, x; Shabecoff, *Fierce Green Fire*, 237.

49. McGurty, *Transforming Environmentalism*, 5–6, Shabecoff, *Fierce Green Fire*, 241; Hurley, *Environmental Inequalities*, 179; Lee, "Beyond Toxic Wastes and Race," 49. Cole and Foster see the environmental justice movement "as separate from and as transcending the environmental movement—as a movement based on environmental issues but situated within the history of movements for social justice." Cole and Foster, *From the Ground Up*, 31.

50. Cole and Foster, *From the Ground Up*, 3; Bullard, "Anatomy of Environmental Racism and the Environmental Justice Movement," 18; Shabecoff, *Fierce Green Fire*, 244.

51. Wasserman, *Energy War*, 190–91; Steinberg, *Down to Earth*, 256; Schwab, *Deeper Shades of Green*, 326; Rosier, "Fond Memories and Bitter Struggles," 42–43.

52. Schwab, *Deeper Shades of Green*, 217–22.

53. Ibid., 223–30.

54. Ibid., 53–54.

55. Cole and Foster, *From the Ground Up*, 2–9.

56. Ibid., 134–35.

57. McGurty, *Transforming Environmentalism*, 137; Bullard, "Anatomy of Environmental Racism and the Environmental Justice Movement," 38.

58. As this book was going to press, New York State restarted its efforts to regulate fracking, apparently in response to a grassroots antifracking campaign; this, in a state where pro-fracking landowners in struggling upstate counties claimed to number seventy-seven thousand. See "Shift by Cuomo on Gas Drilling Prompts Both Anger and Praise," *New York Times*, October 1, 2012, A1; "Mixed Reactions on NY Fracking Decision," Politics and Policy Blog, NYTimes.com, http://green.blogs.nytimes.com/2012/09/21/mixed-reactions-on-n-y-fracking-decision/, accessed October 17, 2012.

Part III: Resisting the Dismantling of America

1. "Georgia Farm Despair Stokes Anger at GOP," *New York Times*, September 26, 1986.

2. One reviewer of the 1974 book *Screwing of the Average Man* noted that "when you list in one place all the ways in which citizens are taken to the cleaners, it is indeed depressing." David Sanford, review of David Hapgood, *Screwing of the Average Man* (New York: Doubleday, 1974), in *Washington Post*, December 10, 1974, B6; Johnson, *Sleepwalking Through History*, 427. Meanwhile, Jonathan Rieder's seminal study of racial backlash in a Brooklyn neighborhood cataloged the various, interchangeable phrases residents used suggesting emasculation and impotence under liberal policies that helped others (read: minorities) at their expense: "Others said they were being 'raped,' 'fucked up the ass,' or 'screwed' by utility rates, the tax system, or busing. Men

sometimes described a vague, malevolent force that was breaking their balls." Rieder, *Canarsie*, 98.

7: Fighting for Factory Jobs and Factory Towns

1. Stein, *Pivotal Decade*; Cowie, *Stayin' Alive*.
2. Lichtenstein, *State of the Union*, 14–17.
3. Ibid., 274.
4. Vogel, *Fluctuating Fortunes*, 170.
5. Ibid., 171–73.
6. Uchitelle, *The Disposable American*, 6–7; Phillips-Fein, *Invisible Hands*, 199; Lichtenstein, *State of the Union*, 236.
7. Joseph McCartin, "Turnabout Years," 222; Lichtenstein, *State of the Union*, 232.
8. Lichtenstein, *State of the Union*, 233–34.
9. Schulman, *Seventies*, 233; Patterson, *Restless Giant*, 158; Dallek, *Ronald Reagan*, 91–92; Troy, *Morning in America*, 78.
10. McCartin, *Collision Course*, 344; McCartin, "Turnabout Years," 225; Minchin, "Labor's Empty Gun," 22; Getman, *The Betrayal of Local 14*, 224–25.
11. Joseph A. Blum, "Unionism Divided Against Itself," *The Nation*, October 22, 1983, 363–65; "Struck Mine Opens Under Tight Guard," *New York Times*, August 21, 1983.
12. Rosenblum, *Copper Crucible*, 3–8.
13. Lichtenstein, *State of the Union*, 250; Schulman, *Seventies*, 234; "Hormel Plant Shut as Troops Arrive and Strikers Thin Ranks," *New York Times*, January 22, 1986, A12; Peter Rachleff, "They Say Give Back, We Say Fight Back," *Dollars and Sense: Real World Economics*, September/October 2000, available online at http://www .dollarsandsense.org/archives/2000/0900rachleff.html.
14. Minchin, "Labor's Empty Gun."
15. Minchin, " 'It Tears the Heart Right Out of You,' " 7.
16. Getman, *Betrayal of Local 14*, 218–19.
17. Minchin, "Labor's Empty Gun," 27; Minchin, " 'It Tears the Heart Right Out of You,' " 12.
18. See Franklin, *Three Strikes*.
19. Getman, *Betrayal of Local 14*, 211.
20. Brisbin, *A Strike Like No Other Strike*, 142–89; "Miners Cheered by Contract's Terms," *New York Times*, February 17, 1990, 10; "Coal Accord in Doubt as Fines Stand," *New York Times*, February 13, 1990, A18; "Coal Strike Ends, but Dispute About Eastern Clouds Labor's Mood," *New York Times*, February 21, 1990, A14.
21. Minchin, *Forging a Common Bond*; Draper, "No Retreat, No Surrender"; Juravich and Bronfenbrenner, *Ravenswood*, ix–xi, 1–3; "How a Union Won an Appalachian Struggle," *New York Times*, May 8, 1992, A12, A14; "Agreement at Ravenswood," editorial, *New York Times*, May 28, 1992, D18; "Different Tactics in Labor's Battles," *New York Times*, September 6, 1992, F23; "How a Union Won an Appalachian Struggle," *New York Times*, May 8, 1992, A12; Juravich and Bronfenbrenner, 193–94.
22. For a classic study of migrating manufacturing operations, see Cowie, *Capital Moves*; see also Uchitelle, *Disposable American*, ix.

23. Uchitelle, *Disposable American*, 5.

24. As Staughton Lynd, the historian and labor lawyer, noted in a season of steel mill closings, the U.S. Steel contracts with its unions included representative language: "The Company retains the exclusive rights to manage the business and plants and to direct the working forces . . . The right to manage the business and plants and to direct the working forces include the right to hire, suspend or discharge for proper cause, or transfer, and the right to relieve employees from duty because of lack of work or for other legitimate reasons." Lynd, "What Happened in Youngstown," 37–38.

25. Battista, *The Revival of Labor Liberalism*, 85, 91–92.

26. Bluestone and Harrison, *The Deindustrialization of America*, 14–16.

27. Ibid., 145–47, 188.

28. Lynd, "The Genesis of the Idea of a Community Right to Industrial Property," 931; Lynd, *The Fight Against Shutdowns*, 21; Lynd, "Genesis of the Idea of a Community Right to Industrial Property," n2, 926–27.

29. Lynd, "Genesis of the Idea of a Community Right to Industrial Property," 933.

30. Ibid., 927.

31. Lynd, "What Happened in Youngstown," 38.

32. Lynd, *Fight Against Shutdowns*, 21, 27, 33, 36.

33. Ibid., 28, 30, 41.

34. Ibid., 154–56; Lynd, "What Happened in Youngstown," 38, 43.

35. Lynd, "Genesis of the Idea of a Community Right to Industrial Property," 928–29, 939–40. Lynd notes that the mayor first asked U.S. Steel to donate its mill site to the city and then threatened to use eminent domain to seize it.

36. Ibid., 940.

37. Lieber, *Friendly Takeover*, 6. It was gratuitous because the blast furnaces were already useless. A blast furnace has to run twenty-four hours a day, otherwise it will cool, "causing the cracking of interior fire bricks that contain the magma of molten iron. It would cost many hundreds of thousands of dollars to rebuild . . . Once the heat is gone from a steel mill, it is like a dead body. Nothing short of divine intervention can bring it back." Maharidge, *Journey to Nowhere*, 22.

38. Maharidge, *Journey to Nowhere*, 20; Lynd, "Genesis of the Idea of a Community Right to Industrial Property," 928–29.

39. Maharidge, *Journey to Nowhere*, 35.

40. Ibid., 49.

41. At the same time, the Denominational Ministry Strategy, led by Protestant ministers, campaigned against investing in U.S. Steel or Mellon Bank and attacked churches that "harbor corporate executives on Sundays and make them feel like good Christians." DMS also used "highly unorthodox strategies" to get publicity, such as putting dead fish in safe deposit boxes and spilling skunk oil at businesses and churches with ties to U.S. Steel. David Morse, "The Campaign to Save Dorothy Six," *The Nation*, September 7, 1985, 174; "Clerics Split in Battles over Steel Jobs," *New York Times*, January 18, 1985, A10.

42. David Morse, "Campaign to Save Dorothy Six," *The Nation*, September 7, 1985, 174;

"Rally Presses Revival of Steel Plant," *New York Times*, May 19, 1985, 24; Lynd, "Genesis of the Idea of a Community Right to Industrial Property," 952.

43. Lieber, *Friendly Takeover*, 44–45.
44. William Serrin, "Town Backs Workers in Plan to Buy Steel Mill," *New York Times*, June 8, 1982, A16.
45. "Struggling to Save the Local Mill," *New York Times*, February 13, 1983.
46. Portz, *The Politics of Plant Closings*, 81–82.
47. Lieber, *Friendly Takeover*, 7.
48. Ibid., 207–10, 216, 218; "When Labor Owns the Mill," editorial, *New York Times*, January 16, 1984, A14.
49. Lieber, *Friendly Takeover*, 232–42; "Steel Industry Uncertain in Ohio Valley," *Intelligencer/Wheeling News Register*, February 21, 2011.
50. Portz, *Politics of Plant Closings*, 166–67.

8: The Heartland Uprising

1. Thomas Jefferson, letter to John Jay, August 23, 1785, in Boyd et al., *The Papers of Thomas Jefferson*, vol. 8, 426; Schlosser, introduction to George-Warren, ed., *FarmAid*, xiii.
2. Mooney and Majka, *Farmers' and Farm Workers' Movements*, xxiii–xxiv, 163–64; Shaw, 1; Ferriss and Sandoval, *The Fight in the Fields*, 67, 78–79, 89.
3. Cowie, *Stayin' Alive*, 51; Mooney and Majka, *Farmers' and Farm Workers' Movements*, 170–71.
4. Mooney and Majka, *Farmers' and Farm Workers' Movements*, xxv, 173, 176, 179.
5. Ibid., 185–86, 188, 191, 193; Ferriss and Sandoval, *Fight in the Fields*, 233–44.
6. Mooney and Majka, *Farmers' and Farm Workers' Movements*, 200–202.
7. Barger and Reza, *The Farm Labor Movement in the Midwest*, 29–30, 57.
8. Mooney and Majka, *Farmers' and Farm Workers' Movements*, 201–2; Barger and Reza, *Farm Labor Movement in the Midwest*, 73–75.
9. Barger and Reza, *Farm Labor Movement in the Midwest*, 58–59; Mooney and Majka, *Farmers' and Farm Workers' Movements*, 202.
10. Barger and Reza, *Farm Labor Movement in the Midwest*, 54–59.
11. Ibid., 60–67; Mooney and Majka, *Farmers' and Farm Workers' Movements*, 203; Valdes, "From Following the Crops to Chasing the Corporations," 54–55.
12. Valdes, "From Following the Crops to Chasing the Corporations," 56–57; Barger and Reza, *Farm Labor Movement in the Midwest*, 65.
13. Barger and Reza, *Farm Labor Movement in the Midwest*, 67–68. Libby's was initially included in the boycott, but Nestlé, its parent company, closed up Libby's processing operations in Ohio, leaving Campbell Soup as FLOC's main target.
14. Valdes, "From Following the Crops to Chasing the Corporations," 60–61, 69; Barger and Reza, *Farm Labor Movement in the Midwest*, 151–53.
15. Barger and Reza, *Farm Labor Movement in the Midwest*, 79–81; Mooney and Majka, *Farmers' and Farm Workers' Movements*, 203–4, 206–7, 209; "The Power of Organizing: Securing Farmworkers' Rights," *Multinational Monitor* 14:5 (May 1993).

16. Barnett, "The U.S. Farm Financial Crisis of the 1980s," 162–64; Ramirez-Ferrero, *Troubled Fields*, 8.

17. Barnett, "U.S. Farm Financial Crisis of the 1980s," 165, 170; Dudley, *Debt and Dispossession*, 2.

18. Barnett, "U.S. Farm Financial Crisis of the 1980s," 165–66.

19. Boyte, Booth, and Max, *Citizen Action and the New American Populism*, 134; Ramirez-Ferrero, *Troubled Fields*, 9.

20. Dudley, *Debt and Dispossession*, 35.

21. Barnett, "U.S. Farm Financial Crisis of the 1980s," 166.

22. Dudley, *Debt and Dispossession*, 122.

23. "Farm Wife Speaks Out on Personal Farm Crisis," *Carroll Daily Times Herald*, January 30, 1985, 5.

24. Dudley, *Debt and Dispossession*, 126–27.

25. Ramirez-Ferrero, *Troubled Fields*, 141.

26. "Farm Belt Suicides Reflect Greater Hardship and Deepening Despondency," *New York Times*, January 14, 1986.

27. Dudley, *Debt and Dispossession*, 14–15.

28. Ramirez-Ferrero, *Troubled Fields*, 2; "Rash of Suicides in Oklahoma Shows That the Crisis on the Farm Goes On," *New York Times*, August 17, 1987; "Farm Belt Suicides Reflect Greater Hardship and Deepening Despondency," *New York Times*, January 14, 1986; John McCormick, "Uprooting a Way of Life," *Newsweek*, February 18, 1985, 54.

29. "Farm Belt Suicides Reflect Greater Hardship and Deepening Despondency," *New York Times*, January 14, 1986; Barnett, "U.S. Farm Financial Crisis of the 1980s," 169; Allison et al., "Hope in the Heartland," 93–94.

30. Adams, *Fighting for the Farm*, 4; Dudley in Adams, *Fighting for the Farm*, 186–87, 177; Dudley, *Debt and Dispossession*, 18.

31. Dudley and others cite the "disincentives to political involvement, at social as well as psychological levels": failing farmers were alienated from their communities, "ostracized by their friends and neighbors." For every story of activist farmers protesting a foreclosure, "tens of thousands of farm families avoided the spotlight, settled out of court, or suffered for years in silence behind closed doors." Dudley, *Debt and Dispossession*, 5; see also Peggy Barlett, another anthropologist, who studied Dodge County, Georgia, and concluded that although falling prices, drought, soaring interest rates, and other factors played a role in driving farms out of business, an ambitious "risk-oriented farm management style" was most often responsible. In sum, these interpretations suggest that individuals had the power to determine how they fared in the farm crisis. How one experienced the farm crisis, then, came down to individual responsibility. Like Dudley, Barlett relies primarily on farmers who survived the crisis, who generally credit their own fortitude and frugality for seeing them through. Such understandings generally set the terms of analysis accepted by these scholars. Had it been possible to track down an equal number of farm families who had been forced off their land, the terms of debate would undoubtedly have

been different. Barlett, *American Dreams, Rural Realities*. On the other hand, sociologists such as Linda Lobao found that farmers with "higher gross sales, no off-farm work, and a larger percentage of income from farming" had "more confidence about their ability" to keep farming and belonged to the greater number of political organizations. In contrast, farmers with poorer financial conditions were more likely to withdraw "from organizational, community, and political activism." Lobao, "Organizational, Community, and Political Involvement as Responses to Rural Restructuring," 194, 198, 201.

32. Mooney and Majka, *Farmers' and Farm Workers' Movements*, 94, 98–100.

33. According to Browne, coffee shop conversations "are as much an enduring tradition of farm-town America as spring planting and fall harvest. Following the demise of those thousands of once socially active local farm groups, coffee klatches of farmers and businesspeople remain a forum for cussing and discussing agricultural policy and its effects on farm economics and rural communities." Browne, *Private Interests, Public Policy, and American Agriculture*, 64; "Strike Talk Began in Small Colorado Town," *Nevada Daily Mail*, December 23, 1977, 1.

34. "Farm Strikers Give Bergland Five-Point Plan," *New York Times*, January 7, 1978, 8; Dudley, *Debt and Dispossession*, 150–53.

35. Ramirez-Ferrero, *Troubled Fields*, 124.

36. Browne and Lundgren, "Farmers Helping Farmers," 14–15.

37. "Farms, Food and Fair Play," *New York Times*, January 8, 1978, NES8; "City in Texas Encircled in a Parade of Tractors," *New York Times*, January 4, 1978, A14; "Farm Strikers Give Bergland a Five-Point Plan," January 7, 1978, 8; Ramirez-Ferrero, *Troubled Fields*, 132; Browne, *Private Interests, Public Policy, and American Agriculture*, 68.

38. Mooney and Majka, *Farmers' and Farm Workers' Movements*, 102; "Strength of the Farmer Is Not Limited to the Land," *New York Times*, March 26, 1978, E5.

39. Mooney and Majka, *Farmers' and Farm Workers' Movements*, 103; "Strength of the Farmer Is Not Limited to the Land," *New York Times*, March 26, 1978, E5; "Wage-Price Council Attacks Farm Bill as Spur to Inflation," *New York Times*, March 23, 1978, D1; "The Rush to Buy Off Farmers," editorial, *New York Times*, March 26, 1978, E16; "Commodities: Farmer's Strike and Rising Prices," *New York Times*, May 1, 1978, D3.

40. "A Harvest of Ill Will," *Newsweek*, February 19, 1979, 61; "When Farmers Tied Up Washington," *U.S. News & World Report*, February 19, 1979, 7; "Farmers Raising Cain," *Time*, February 19, 1979; "Farmers Stage a Protest over Newspaper Reports," *New York Times*, February 17, 1979, 19; "Mass Protest Has Simply Gone Out of Style," *New York Times*, March 18, 1979, E5.

41. Browne, *Private Interests, Public Policy, and American Agriculture*, 70–72.

42. Ramirez-Ferrero, *Troubled Fields*, 134–35; Susan Dentzer, "Bitter Harvest," *Newsweek*, February 18, 1985, 52; "Reagan Says Minority of Farmers Are in Severe Financial Distress," *New York Times*, February 24, 1985, 27.

43. Barnett, "U.S. Farm Financial Crisis of the 1980s," 65; Ramirez-Ferrero, *Troubled Fields*, 146.

44. David Kline, "Embattled Independent Farmer," *New York Times Sunday Magazine*, November 29, 1981, SM35; on the rise of industrial farming and implications for American food quality, see also Eric Schlosser, *Fast Food Nation*.

45. Dudley, *Debt and Dispossession*, 86–87.

46. Summers, "From the Heartland to Seattle," 306, 314–16; Dudley, *Debt and Dispossession*, 88; Hunter, *Breaking Hard Ground*, 93–94; "Farmers March in Protest in Chicago and St. Paul," *New York Times*, January 22, 1985, A6; "Rally in Ames Dramatizes Farmers' Plight," *Carroll Daily Times Herald*, February 27, 1985, 1; "Farmers Wait to See Rally's Effect on Policies," *Carroll Daily Times Herald*, February 28, 1985, 1; "Farmers at Ames Rally Vow, 'We Will Win,'" *Carroll Daily Times Herald*, February 28, 1985, 1; "Farmers at Iowa Rally Sound Call for Federal Aid," *New York Times*, February 28, 1985, B7.

47. "Throwing Money at Farmers," editorial, *New York Times*, March 1, 1985, A26; "Reagan Kills Farm Aid as Battle Opens on Spending," *New York Times*, March 10, 1985, E1; "When Nothing Happens and They Call It News," *New York Times*, March 22, 1985, A14. In a later editorial, *The New York Times* agreed with Reagan that farm subsidies should be eliminated because they only served to keep a "floor under farm income," thus "artificially" raising crop prices, which, in turn, resulted in a "windfall to foreign producers." What farmers really needed was extended loan repayment periods to help them "weather the crisis" and at little cost to taxpayers. "The Aid Some Farmers Need," editorial, *New York Times*, September 30, 1985.

48. Schwab, *Raising Less Corn and More Hell*, 197–202; Boyte, Booth, and Max, *Citizen Action and the New American Populism*, 141.

49. "Farm Sale Protested," *Carroll Daily Times Herald*, January 10, 1985, 12.

50. Schwab, *Raising Less Corn and More Hell*, 159–64; "Jackson Leads Peaceful Protest of Farm Foreclosure," *New York Times*, April 9, 1985, A12.

51. Schwab, *Raising Less Corn and More Hell*, 221–23.

52. $10 million was far more than, say, the $750,000 raised by the MUSE shows, but far less than the $50 million hoped for by Nelson and the organizers. "14-Hour Concert in Illinois Sept. 22 Will Seek $50 Million to Help Farmers," *New York Times*, September 15, 1985, 26; "Next: We Are the Farm," *Newsweek*, September 23, 1985, 33; "Concert: A Daylong Mix of Country with Rock," *New York Times*, September 23, 1985, A16; "Musicians Give Concert to Aid Nation's Farmers," *New York Times*, September 23, 1985, A16; "Farm Aid Benefit Concert Hailed as Arousing Public," *New York Times*, September 24, 1985, A18.

53. "Concert: A Daylong Mix of Country with Rock," *New York Times*, September 23, 1985, A16; "Harvest Song: Willie Nelson Plans a Benefit," *Time*, September 23, 1985; "Farm Aid Benefit Concert Hailed as Arousing Public," *New York Times*, September 24, 1985, A18; "What Farm Aid Can't Deliver," editorial, *New York Times*, September 25, 1985, A18; Dudley, *Debt and Dispossession*, 102; George-Warren, *Farm Aid*, 3, 26. Farm Aid carries on to this day—still under the guidance of Nelson, Neil Young, John Cougar Mellencamp, and Dave Matthews—though its focus is less on helping farmers with their debt troubles as on promoting community-supported agriculture over agribusiness's "factory farms."

54. Kopkind, "A Populist Message Hits Home," 432–33.

55. Mooney and Majka, *Farmers' and Farm Workers' Movements*, 100, 111; Browne, *Private Interests, Public Policy, and American Agriculture*, 73–75, 77, 83; Browne and Lundgren, "Farmers Helping Farmers," 18.

56. Hunter, *Breaking Hard Ground*, 50–53; Schwab, 135–39, 141; the Minnesota Farm Advocates continues its work to this day, with eleven full-time advocates (see http://www.mda.state.mn.us/about/commissionersoffice/farmadvocates.aspx).

57. Hunter, *Breaking Hard Ground*, 93–98; Boyte, Booth, and Max, *Citizen Action and the New American Populism*, 135; Barrett, *Mending a Broken Heartland*, 68–69.

58. Schwab, *Raising Less Corn and More Hell*, 150–53.

59. Ibid., 145, 147. On diffusion, see Givan, Roberts, and Soule, *The Diffusion of Social Movements*.

60. Allison et al., "Hope in the Heartland," 93, 97–98; Schwab, *Raising Less Corn and More Hell*, 252–55, 257, 262.

61. Browne and Lundgren, "Farmers Helping Farmers," 21; "Washington Loosens Grip on Indebted Farms," *New York Times*, March 6, 1988, E5; "80,000 Farms Face Foreclosure Peril," *New York Times*, November 12, 1988, 1.

62. Summers, "From the Heartland to Seattle," 324; Barnett, "U.S. Farm Financial Crisis of the 1980s," 169; Frank, *What's the Matter with Kansas?*, 64–66; Hodgson, *More Equal Than Others*, 205–9.

63. Hodgson, *More Equal Than Others*, 207. The anthropologist and activist Laura DeLind cautions that the rise of community-supported agriculture (CSAs may serve more than 100,000 Americans) and the parallel rise of the organic food consumer and "locavore" movement are a mixed blessing. The way that farmers and consumers "negotiate their positions across a more personable market divide" where the "'community' in community-supported agriculture exists more as metaphor than as fact" actually makes it less likely that we will see "ecological accountability and a deep social and economic challenge to the food system." DeLind, "Considerably More Than Vegetables, a Lot Less Than Community," 203.

64. Jackson had been attending antiforeclosure rallies since 1984 and finished second in the 1988 Iowa caucuses, behind cross-border favorite son Illinois senator Paul Simon. As Jackson's Iowa coordinator told a reporter, "You'll never see a big, burly old farmer come up and hug Dick Gephardt and start crying. You will see that with Jesse Jackson." "New Jackson Finding Dividends in Iowa," *New York Times*, February 4, 1988. In the 1988 campaign, Lyndon LaRouche claimed to favor parity pricing and an end to farm foreclosures. Unlike Jackson, he also favored a rollback of environmental regulations, including those prohibiting the use of pesticides like DDT. The AAM and various farm service organizations such as Groundswell and the Iowa Farm Unity Coalition were aware of LaRouche's efforts to win the support of farmers and publicized his antigovernment, anti-Semitic views from the start. By the end of the 1980s, with the notion of government betrayal more prevalent, more farmers became receptive not only to LaRouche's arguments but to those put forward by the militia movement, including the Posse Comitatus. "As the local store fronts are being boarded up, as rural institutions such as schools, hospitals,

churches and banks are being closed, whole communities develop the same symptoms as a depressed individual," said Mona Lee Brock, a rural counselor, in 1990. "They become angry, withdrawn communities [with] the need for someone to blame. They have paranoid feelings toward money lenders, and the county, state, and federal government." Dyer, *Harvest of Rage*, 62. See also Jim Corcoran, *Bitter Harvest*.

9: Revolts at Home

1. I. W. Martin, *The Permanent Tax Revolt*, 98, 126. Soon scholars were calling the tax revolt "a major turning point in American politics," and even twenty years later, "a political earthquake . . . a rebellion against government itself." D. A. Smith, *Tax Crusaders*, 57; Hodgson, *More Equal Than Others*, 43.
2. D. A. Smith, *Tax Crusaders*, 10, 14.
3. Self, "Prelude to the Tax Revolt," 147–49; I. W. Martin, *Permanent Tax Revolt*, 4–5.
4. I. W. Martin, *Permanent Tax Revolt*, 62–66, 69–70.
5. Schrag, *Paradise Lost*, 135.
6. Ibid., 133–34, 138, 141; Kuttner, *Revolt of the Haves*, 51.
7. I. W. Martin, *Permanent Tax Revolt*, 54–55; Schrag, *Paradise Lost*, 144–45.
8. Taft quoted in D. A. Smith, *Tax Crusaders*, 157.
9. Kuttner, *Revolt of the Haves*, 39–41; D. A. Smith, *Tax Crusaders*, 28–29; Schrag, *Paradise Lost*, 131.
10. I. W. Martin, *Permanent Tax Revolt*, 102.
11. Kuttner, *Revolt of the Haves*, 65–66.
12. D. A. Smith, *Tax Crusaders*, 29; Self, "Prelude to the Tax Revolt," 159.
13. I. W. Martin, *Permanent Tax Revolt*, 104.
14. D. A. Smith, *Tax Crusaders*, 73, 77, 81; Kuttner, *Revolt of the Haves*, 73; Schrag, *Paradise Lost*, 147; I. W. Martin, *Permanent Tax Revolt*, 105.
15. Kuttner, *Revolt of the Haves*, 75–76; Schrag, *Paradise Lost*, 148–50; I. W. Martin, *Permanent Tax Revolt*, 105.
16. D. A. Smith, *Tax Crusaders*, 17; Kuttner, *Revolt of the Haves*, 94. Some have suggested that the tax revolt was driven by racism, with the overwhelming number of white Californians who supported Proposition 13 (67 percent) doing so because they were fed up with other people getting all of the benefits from government while they poured in all the money. Thomas and Mary Edsall, for example, point to polls that show that only 29 percent of black Californians supported Proposition 13 and that 73 percent of Californians favored welfare cuts, while majorities opposed cuts to police, schools, and transportation. Reading these polls as evidence of a divided electorate "along lines of taxpayers versus tax recipients," however, is misleading because there is no indication that race or even antiwelfare sentiment drove support for Prop 13. It is more likely that California voters, feeling the acute pain of paying higher property taxes, simply wanted the taxes reduced and, knowing it would cost the state revenue, prioritized public safety, education, and transportation over welfare. No doubt there were some (including some racists) who resented the public assistance that went to minorities and the poor, but there is no evidence

to suggest that this sentiment was representative of those who voted for Prop 13. Edsall and Edsall, *Chain Reaction*, 130–31.

17. Kuttner, *Revolt of the Haves*, 94; I. W. Martin, *Permanent Tax Revolt*, 105, 107. Martin notes that the most antigovernment component of Proposition 13 was the requirement for a two-thirds majority of any legislative body to raise *any* tax, but that provision got the least attention at the time. I. W. Martin, *Permanent Tax Revolt*, 101–2.

18. Kuttner, *Revolt of the Haves*, 85, 87, 89; Schrag, *Paradise Lost*, 8, 151–53.

19. Zisk, *Money, Media, and the Grass Roots*, 90–137; Schrag, *Paradise Lost*, 11, 18.

20. I. W. Martin, *Permanent Tax Revolt*, 120; Kuttner, *Revolt of the Haves*, 148–51.

21. Kuttner, *Revolt of the Haves*, 163, D. A. Smith, *Tax Crusaders*, 96.

22. Kuttner, *Revolt of the Haves*, 313, 318; D. A. Smith, *Tax Crusaders*, 109.

23. D. A. Smith, *Tax Crusaders*, 90, 92, 111, 123. In Ohio, by contrast, the Ohio Public Interest Campaign succeeded in qualifying a Fair Tax initiative for the ballot (it had three parts: a circuit breaker to reimburse any tax over 2.5 percent of income in households earning under $30,000 a year; repeals of various business tax exemptions and abatements; and an income tax increase on those earning more than $30,000), only to see it defeated by a business lobby that poured money into the campaign, predicting the death of industry and a hemorrhaging of jobs in a state already reeling from the onset of the steel collapse. See Kuttner, *Revolt of the Haves*, 319–24.

24. Atlas and Dreier, "The Tenants' Movement and American Politics," 378–79; Lowe, "Rent Control Surge May Be Just a Start," 175. A 1979 GAO report on the housing crisis said that in the latest data on "the percentage of renters paying 25 percent or more of income for rent, 42 percent (1975 data) of Atlanta renters, 50 percent (1974 data) of Minneapolis–St. Paul renters, and 44 percent (1976 data) of Seattle renters fall into this category." General Accounting Office, "Rental Housing," 26–28.

25. Public housing accounted for only 2 percent of housing in the United States. It was funded by the federal government but administered by local housing authorities.

26. R. Williams, *The Politics of Public Housing*, 175, 222–28.

27. Corr, *No Trespassing*, 140–41; Lawson, *The Tenant Movement in New York City*, 229.

28. Atlas and Dreier, "Tenants' Movement and American Politics," 383–84, 388.

29. Navarro, "Rent Control in Cambridge, Mass.," 85–88; Dreier, "The Politics of Rent Control," 165; McAfee, "Socialism and the Housing Movement," 406–11. The Cambridge Tenants Organizing Committee papers are deposited at the University of Massachusetts–Boston library.

30. Atlas and Dreier, "Tenants' Movement and American Politics," 386–87; Heskin, "Is a Tenant a Second Class Citizen?," 99.

31. Lowe, "Rent Control Surge May Be Just a Start," 174; Heskin, "Is a Tenant a Second Class Citizen?," 101; Dreier, "Politics of Rent Control," 168.

32. Heskin, *Tenants and the American Dream*, 56–57; Heskin, "Is a Tenant a Second Class Citizen?," 102.

33. Heskin, *Tenants and the American Dream*, 57–58, 61–63; Heskin, "Is a Tenant a

Second Class Citizen?," 102; Jacob, "How Rent Control Passed in Santa Monica," 178–79.

34. Atlas and Dreier, "Tenants' Movement and American Politics," 396; Dreier, "Politics of Rent Control," 169; Hartman, "Landlord Money Defeats Rent Control in San Francisco," 198–99. The next year, the San Francisco hard-core punk band Dead Kennedys released its most seminal album, *Fresh Fruit for Rotting Vegetables*. The fourth track on the record is "Let's Lynch the Landlord."

35. N. Smith, "New City, New Frontier," 91; von Hassel, *Homesteading in New York City*, 117.

36. "Feeble" because mostly middle-income residents benefited from the HUD scheme, and in any case fewer than a thousand homes were transferred to homesteaders each year, so it solved neither the abandonment issue nor the low-income housing problem. Borgos, "Low-Income Homeownership and the ACORN Squatters Campaign," 430–31.

37. Lawson, *Tenant Movement in New York City*, 235–36.

38. Feffer, "The Land Belongs to the People," 68–69, 71, 73, 76; Atlas, *Seeds of Change*, 75.

39. Borgos, "Low-Income Homeownership and the ACORN Squatters Campaign," 433; Atlas, *Seeds of Change*, 75; Feffer, "Land Belongs to the People," 83, 90.

40. Atlas, *Seeds of Change*, 75–76; Borgos, "Low-Income Homeownership and the ACORN Squatters Campaign," 434–35.

41. Borgos, "Low-Income Homeownership and the ACORN Squatters Campaign," 429, 436, 438; Atlas, *Seeds of Change*, 76.

42. Atlas, *Seeds of Change*, 77; Borgos, "Low-Income Homeownership and the ACORN Squatters Campaign," 440.

43. Van Kleunen, "The Squatters," 288–89; von Hassel, *Homesteading in New York City*, 4–5, 81. The tension between the homesteaders and the squatters, who often felt that they were competing for properties, came to a head in the early 1990s. To set the record straight, squatters issued the LES Squatter Community Statement, in which they affirmed that they were no different from other homesteaders—diverse in their racial and ethnic backgrounds, low-income, and committed to using their "resources and creativity" to rebuild structures "left abandoned by the city for years." "We've proven through squatting that we can provide immediate, safe housing for people who live in the buildings while working on them . . ." Van Kleunen, "Squatters," 285–86.

44. N. Smith, "New City, New Frontier," 75.

45. Ibid., 80–81, 85–86; van Hassel, *Homesteading in New York City*, 55.

46. Abu-Lughod, "The Battle for Tompkins Square Park," 239–42, 244–45; N. Smith, "New City, New Frontier," 61–62.

47. Abu-Lughod, "Battle for Tompkins Square Park," 252–53.

48. Ibid., 255, 257. According to the *Village Voice* reporter Sarah Ferguson, the city's failure to provide any alternative housing solution for the people in the park made Tompkins Square a symbol of the city's failure "to cope with its homeless population." Quoted in N. Smith, "New City, New Frontier," 63; von Hassel, *Homesteading in New York City*, 17.

Part IV: Resisting Nightfall

1. Paul Theroux, "Subway Odyssey," *New York Times*, January 31, 1982, 237–38.
2. Katz, *The Undeserving Poor*, 196.
3. Ibid., 193.

10: The Politics of Homelessness

1. Hopper, "Homelessness Old and New," 770–71.
2. Jonathan Alter, "Homeless in America," *Newsweek*, January 2, 1984.
3. O'Malley, "Homelessness: New England and Beyond," 13–14. By comparison, 27 percent of British housing was public. The figure was 43 percent for Holland, 20 percent for West Germany, 16 percent for France, and 35 percent for Sweden. Hopper, "Homelessness Old and New," 771.
4. Hopper, *Reckoning with Homelessness*, 176; Hopper, "Homelessness Old and New," 758.
5. A 1991 report commissioned by the U.S. Conference of Mayors came up with a demographic profile of the homeless from a survey of twenty-eight major cities: 50% were single men; 35% were families with children; 12% were single women; 3% were unemployed youth. Children were 24% of homeless, African Americans 48%, whites 34%, Hispanics 15%, Native Americans 3%, and Asians less than 1%. Only 18% were employed in full- or part-time jobs; one-third of the homeless population were veterans ("a figure that is an appalling indictment of an entire array of Veterans Administration services"); homeless vets were better educated than the rest of the homeless population (80% had high school diplomas and one-third had been to college, if not graduated). Of homeless vets, 40–60% were Vietnam vets. O'Malley, "Homelessness: New England and Beyond," 10–11. In Ropers's summary, a survey of the homeless in L.A. in 1984 found that "it appears that the contemporary urban homeless are younger, more nonwhite, and more recently homeless than previous generations of the chronically homeless, who were traditionally older white males. The data also suggest that Los Angeles homeless are not newcomers to Los Angeles, that they are socially isolated, and that in large proportion that they are part of the labor force. A large number of the men interviewed were veterans." Ropers, *The Invisible Homeless*, 35–65. According to Hopper, children constituted "a larger proportion of the sheltered population than [did] unattached men, a fact replicated in poverty statistics." Hopper, "Homelessness Old and New," 768.
6. Bogard, *Seasons Such as These*, 103–9, 197. In 1987, the *Los Angeles Times* did a systematic survey and found that approximately 200,000 residents of Los Angeles County—mostly refugees from Mexico and Central American war zones—lived in 42,000 car garages. Ropers, *Invisible Homeless*, 27.
7. By 1991, during the Bush recession, those numbers had become more constant, as the city housed 8,700 to 9,000 individuals and 4,200 families a night. Hopper, "Homelessness Old and New," 767.
8. Weinreb and Rossi, "The American Homeless Family Shelter 'System,'" 87, 102.
9. All of these quotes are originally cited in Hopper, "Homelessness Old and New," n72, 794.

10. Contrasting views are present in the writing of George F. Will and Kim Hopper; Will quoted in Mitchell, "The End of Public Space," 118; Hopper, "Homelessness Old and New," 784; Ropers, *Invisible Homeless*, 28; O'Malley, "Homelessness: New England and Beyond," 14.

11. O'Malley, "Homelessness: New England and Beyond," 15.

12. B. G. Link et al., "Public Attitudes and Beliefs about Homeless People," 143–48.

13. Hopper, *Reckoning with Homelessness*, 176.

14. Hopper, "Homelessness Old and New," 787.

15. Snow, Soule, and Cress, "Identifying the Precipitants of Homeless Protest Across 17 U.S. Cities, 1980–90," 1184, 1189, 1192; Cress and Snow, "The Outcomes of Homeless Mobilization," 1073.

16. Hopper, *Reckoning with Homelessness*, 179–80. Wagner and Cohen also blame this image of the homeless as passive victims on the "tendency of researchers to study the poor at the point of maximum disempowerment. It is not surprising to find that studies conducted exclusively at soup kitchens, shelters, or hospital emergency rooms document a higher degree of stress, disorganization, and depression." Wagner and Cohen, "The Power of the People," 544.

17. Hopper, *Reckoning with Homelessness*, 178.

18. Bogard, *Seasons Such as These*, xi–xii; O'Malley, "Homelessness: New England and Beyond," 15.

19. Bogard, *Seasons Such as These*, 10–12; Rader, *Signal Through the Flames*, 58.

20. Rader, *Signal Through the Flames*, 7, 43–46.

21. "In that proximity [to one's neighbors]," Snyder said, "lies the basic message of every world religion; reach out, turn to your neighbor, share what you have and what you are, because we can only cause needless, constant pain to those who are strangers to us." Rader, *Signal Through the Flames*, 107.

22. Bogard, *Seasons Such as These*, 13–14, 21–25; Rader, *Signal Through the Flames*, 106–7.

23. Rader, *Signal Through the Flames*, 112–22; Bogard, *Seasons Such as These*, 15–18.

24. Rader, *Signal Through the Flames*, 134; Bogard, *Seasons Such as These*, 35.

25. Bogard, *Seasons Such as These*, 76, 80, 81, 189, 127; Rader, *Signal Through the Flames*, 183.

26. Hopper, *Reckoning with Homelessness*, 181; Bogard, *Seasons Such as These*, 31–33, 37–38, 99; "New Program in Shelters Stresses Work Ethic," *New York Times*, September 7, 1983, B1; Hopper, *Reckoning with Homelessness*, 177; Campbell and McCarthy, "Conveying Mission Through Outcome Measurement," 341; Simon, "Municipal Regulation of the Homeless in Public Spaces," 157–58.

27. Simon, "Municipal Regulation of the Homeless in Public Spaces," 150.

28. Ibid., 150.

29. Ibid., 152.

30. Ropers, *Invisible Homeless*, 190–93.

31. Ibid., 198–99, 201, 203.

32. Ibid., 194–95, 197, 205–6.

33. "Atlanta's Effort to Cope with Cut in Federal Aid," *New York Times*, March 19, 1985, A21; "Atlanta Homeless Find Place in Public Eye," *New York Times*, December 9,

1986, A18; "Atlanta's Vagrant-Free Zone Stirs a Protest," *New York Times*, December 26, 1986, A22; Hopper, *Reckoning with Homelessness*, 179; "Raising the Roof to Help the Homeless," *New York Times*, March 15, 1988, A16.

34. Cress and Snow, "Outcomes of Homeless Mobilization," 1085, 1089.

35. Simon, "Municipal Regulation of the Homeless in Public Spaces," 154–56.

36. "Miami Ordered to Create Homeless Zones," *New York Times*, November 18, 1992.

37. S. Turner, "Recognition of the Voting Rights of the Homeless," 104, 120–22.

38. Bogard, *Seasons Such as These*, 165, 177, 196–97; Hopper, *Reckoning with Homelessness*, 179, 181–82, 183–84, 189, 193; Foscarinis, "The Federal Response," 161, 171.

11: AIDS Politics

1. Chambre, *Fighting for Our Lives*, 1–2; "Rare Cancer Seen in 41 Homosexuals," *New York Times*, July 3, 1981, 20; Brier, *Infectious Ideas*, 21; Clendinen and Nagourney, *Out for Good*, 477; Gould, *Moving Politics*, 59; Armstrong, *Forging Gay Identities*, 168; Sides, *Erotic City*, 181.

2. Clendinen and Nagourney, *Out for Good*, 478; Brier, *Infectious Ideas*, 23; Armstrong, *Forging Gay Identities*, 159; Gould, *Moving Politics*, 73.

3. Clendinen and Nagourney, *Out for Good*, 484–85, 488, 529; D'Emilio and Freeman, *Intimate Matters*, 354; Chambre, *Fighting for Our Lives*, 30; Gould, *Moving Politics*, 118; "11,000 Boycott Start of Classes in AIDS Protest," *New York Times*, September 10, 1985, B1; "Ryan White Dies of AIDS at 18; His Struggle Helped Pierce Myths," *New York Times*, April 9, 1990, D10. In California, in July 1986, Lyndon LaRouche gathered 683,000 signatures (twice the number required) to get Proposition 64 on the ballot. It called AIDS an "infectious, contagious and communicable disease," and if passed it would have empowered the state to contain AIDS by making those infected with HIV or AIDS "subject to quarantine and isolation statutes." But times had changed since the Briggs Initiative. The gay community in California was able to fight back using an existing political infrastructure. David Mixner, MECLA, and others raised money, put together a vigorous media campaign, and defeated the initiative 71 to 29 percent. Californians, it turned out, valued civil liberties more than LaRouche and his allies thought. Clendinen and Nagourney, *Out for Good*, 540–41.

4. Chambre, *Fighting for Our Lives*, 5; Gould, *Moving Politics*, 51.

5. Chambre, *Fighting for Our Lives*, 16–17; Clendinen and Nagourney, *Out for Good*, 460, 462.

6. Chambre, *Fighting for Our Lives*, 13, 16–19; D'Emilio and Freeman, *Intimate Matters*, 256.

7. In a case of what might be called front porch paranoia, the board of a cooperative apartment building tried to get Dr. Joseph Sonnabend evicted from his office in the building out of fear that his AIDS patients passing through the lobby would decrease the value of their apartments. The Lambda Legal Defense Fund succeeded in defending Sonnabend. Chambre, *Fighting for Our Lives*, 20–22.

8. Gould, *Moving Politics*, 85, 88, 89, 100.

9. Chambre, *Fighting for Our Lives*, 33–34.

10. Armstrong, *Forging Gay Identities*, 161–64.

11. Sides, *Erotic City*, 178; Brier, *Infectious Ideas*, 45–46. According to Armstrong, public health officials described this success as the "greatest behavior change ever seen in public health" and as a "dazzling success." Armstrong, *Forging Gay Identities*, 165.

12. Sides, *Erotic City*, 178–80.

13. Stoller, *Lessons from the Damned*, 1–2.

14. Ibid., 81, 83, 86–87; Sides, *Erotic City*, 182–83, 199–203. In New York, Dr. Joyce Wallace was the first to work with prostitutes on HIV/AIDS. For related San Francisco background, see Vicky Funari and Julie Query, dirs., *Live Nude Girls Unite!*, DVD (2000).

15. Stoller, *Lessons from the Damned*, 64–65, 98, 102–3, 105.

16. Clendinen and Nagourney, *Out for Good*, 480–81; Brier, *Infectious Ideas*, 11.

17. In one exception, in October 1985, San Francisco AIDS activists chained themselves to the doors of the federal building and demanded that the government increase its AIDS research budget by $500 million. In time, close to a hundred people, most of them people with AIDS and many of them homeless, built a tent city outside the building in United Nations Plaza and expanded their demands to include FDA approval of AIDS drugs that were in use in other countries, and Social Security benefits. As the historian Josh Sides has argued, the vigil did not have "any significant impact on federal AIDS policy," but it did play an educational role. For scores of federal employees who could not avoid the tent city as they went to and from work, the realities of AIDS struck home for the first time. Sides reports that employees "began bringing coffee, doughnuts, casseroles, barbecue grills, and other immediate necessities" to the tent city occupants. In short, he writes, "the vigil brought the disease out of the places where AIDS victims congregated—clinics, hospices, and house gatherings in the Castro—into the visible public space." Sides, *Erotic City*, 192.

18. Gould, *Moving Politics*, 50, 104; Armstrong, *Forging Gay Identities*, 157. On Reagan not saying "AIDS" in public, Brier claims he did not utter the term in public until 1986, but Gould says he first mentioned the term in response to a reporter's question in September 1985. Brier, *Infectious Ideas*, 80; Gould, *Moving Politics*, 49.

19. Brier, *Infectious Ideas*, 79–80.

20. Ibid., 79, 89–92.

21. Ibid., 92, 96.

22. W. A. Link, *Righteous Warrior*, 348–49; Clendinen and Nagourney, *Out for Good*, 534–38, 548; Gould, *Moving Politics*, 132, 137, 141.

23. Clendinen and Nagourney, *Out for Good*, 542–44.

24. Gould, *Moving Politics*, 147; Halcli, "AIDS, Anger, and Activism," 139; Brier, *Infectious Ideas*, 157; Chambre, *Fighting for Our Lives*, 124.

25. Brier, *Infectious Ideas*, 159–60; Clendinen and Nagourney, *Out for Good*, 554, 558; Gould, *Moving Politics*, 4, 8, 9; Stoller, *Lessons from the Damned*, 125.

26. Brier, *Infectious Ideas*, 160; Chambre, *Fighting for Our Lives*, 122; Halcli, "AIDS, Anger, and Activism," 143.

27. Gould, *Moving Politics*, 154–55.

28. Brier, *Infectious Ideas*, 161–63, 169, 172; Martin, *Other Eighties*, 175.

29. See also Felicia Kornbluh's "Disability Rights, Antiprofessionalism, and Civil Rights" for an account of how blind people organized for a "maximum feasible participation" mandate in social services.

30. Brier, *Infectious Ideas*, 165–66; B. Martin, *Other Eighties*, 175; Gould, *Moving Politics*, 401–2.

31. Capozzola, "A Very American Epidemic," 220–23; Gould, *Moving Politics*, 225–26, 228.

32. Gould, *Moving Politics*, 402–3.

33. Ibid., 402.

34. B. Martin, *Other Eighties*, 178; Chambre, *Fighting for Our Lives*, 126, 128; "Cuomo Defuses Protest and Still Makes a Point," *New York Times*, January 4, 1990, B5; W. A. Link, *Religious Warrior*, 351.

35. Sides, *Erotic City*, 194; Gould, *Moving Politics*, 275; Halcli, "AIDS, Anger, and Activism," 145.

36. Gould, *Moving Politics*, 230, 276.

37. Ibid., 230, 232.

38. Brier, *Infectious Ideas*, 183, 187; Chambre, *Fighting for Our Lives*, 130; Gould, *Moving Politics*, 294–95.

12: Abortion Wars

1. Mason, *Killing for Life*, 115; Ginsburg, "Rescuing the Nation," 230, 231; Risen and Thomas, *Wrath of Angels*, 240–47, 253; Gorney, *Articles of Faith*, 462.

2. Hunter, *Culture Wars*, 186; Luker, *Abortion and the Politics of Motherhood*, 113, 118.

3. Luker, *Abortion and the Politics of Motherhood*, 7–8, 160, 176.

4. Solinger, *Pregnancy and Power*, 200, 202.

5. Staggenborg, *The Pro-Choice Movement*, 88, 93–95, 100, 116–17.

6. Ibid., 82, 127.

7. O'Keefe's Norwich action was not the first clinic blockade. An earlier one at Sigma Reproductive Health Services in Rockland, Maryland, was led by six women who sat down in front of the doors leading from the waiting room to the procedure rooms. Police pleaded with them to leave for three hours before finally arresting them. The event garnered no media attention to speak of, but it inspired others, including John O'Keefe. Risen and Thomas, *Wrath of Angels*, 59–62, 65.

8. Risen and Thomas, *Wrath of Angels*, 132–33, 141, 143.

9. Ibid., 156, 170–71, 180.

10. Ginsburg, *Contested Lives*, 89–95.

11. Ibid., 153–54, 162–63, 170.

12. Ibid., 188, 182.

13. Ibid., 178, 177.

14. Ibid., 193–94, 185.

15. Solinger, *Pregnancy and Power*, 226; Staggenborg, *Pro-Choice Movement*, 129.

16. Risen and Thomas, *Wrath of Angels*, 74, 75, 114, 197–99; Solinger, *Pregnancy and*

Power, 207; Hall, *American Patriotism, American Protest*, 120; Wilder, "The Rule of Law, the Rise of Violence, and the Role of Morality," 82.

17. Mason, *Killing for Life*, 2–4, 9–11, 14; Risen and Thomas, *Wrath of Angels*, 106–7.

18. Ginsburg, *Contested Lives*, 115–16, 120.

19. Risen and Thomas, *Wrath of Angels*, 91–93, 114–15.

20. Ginsburg, "Rescuing the Nation," 229, 231; Wilder, "Rule of Law, the Rise of Violence, and the Role of Morality," 81; Gorney, *Articles of Faith*, 462.

21. Risen and Thomas, *Wrath of Angels*, 262–63; Ginsburg, "Rescuing the Nation," 277.

22. Risen and Thomas, *Wrath of Angels*, 268–69, 294; Hall, *American Patriotism, American Protest*, 124.

23. Hall, *American Patriotism, American Protest*, 125; Risen and Thomas, *Wrath of Angels*, 273–76; Ginsburg, "Rescuing the Nation," 232.

24. Risen and Thomas, *Wrath of Angels*, 282–84, 285; Gorney, *Articles of Faith*, 463.

25. Hall, *American Patriotism, American Protest*, 129; Ginsburg, "Rescuing the Nation," 232.

26. Kahl, *Controversy and Courage*, 64–65; Staggenborg, *Pro-Choice Movement*, 133; Risen and Thomas, *Wrath of Angels*, 286–88; Sharp, "Culture Wars and City Politics," 748; Hertz, *Caught in the Crossfire*, 227.

27. Ginsburg, "Rescuing the Nation," 235.

28. Ibid., 228, 233.

29. Staggenborg, *Pro-Choice Movement*, 206, n1; Ginsburg, "Rescuing the Nation," 233.

30. Risen and Thomas, *Wrath of Angels*, 321.

31. Risen and Thomas, *Wrath of Angels*, 326–28, 329, 333.

32. Ginsburg, "Rescuing the Nation," 228–29.

33. Ibid., 227.

Conclusion: The Passing of Front Porch Politics

1. On the West Virginia textbook wars, see Mason, "An American Conflict," 352, 353; Mason, *Reading Appalachia from Left to Right*, 3, 7, 8, 20–25; Hunter, *Culture Wars*, 21–24; Heins, *Not in Front of the Children*, 138–42. On battles over sex education, see Irvine, *Talk About Sex*, 126, 128; Zimmerman, *Whose America?*, 203, 204, 206, 207, 210.

2. On pornography, see Strub, *Perversion for Profit*; Strub, "Lavender, Menaced Lesbianism, Obscenity Law, and the Feminist Antipornography Movement"; Downs, *The New Politics of Pornography*. On battles over music and television, see Chastagner, "The Parents' Music Resource Center"; Gore, *Raising PG Kids in an X-Rated Society*; Gray, "Rate the Records"; Nuzum, *Parental Advisory*; Heins, *Sex, Sin, and Blasphemy*; Heins, *Not in Front of the Children*; D. Kennedy, "Frankenchrist Versus the State"; Shank, "Fears of the White Unconscious"; Zappa, *The Real Frank Zappa Book*. On obscenity and decency, see Hunter, *Culture Wars*; Lane, *The Decency Wars*.

3. Schor, *The Overworked American*; Schor, *The Overspent American*; Putnam, *Bowling Alone*.

4. Some scholars see online political advocacy as a promising democratic develop-

ment, particularly as such operations—from MoveOn to Daily KOS—have a greater flexibility to take up a range of issues and reach a greater number of like-minded people than the advocacy groups of the late twentieth century (the ones that relied primarily on check writing) ever did. Still, it is hard not to see such advocacy as a substitute for front porch political engagement, enabling a relatively passive form of political engagement more often than active mobilization. See Karpf, *The MoveOn Effect*.

5. Judt, *Ill Fares the Land*, 36.

Bibliography

Abu-Lughod, Janet. "The Battle for Tompkins Square Park." In Janet Abu-Lughod, ed., *From Urban Village to East Village: The Battle for New York's Lower East Side*. Malden, MA: Blackwell, 1994.

Adams, Jane, ed. *Fighting for the Farm: Rural America Transformed*. Philadelphia: University of Pennsylvania Press, 2003.

Allison, Roger, et al. "Hope in the Heartland: The Missouri Rural Crisis Center." In Terry Pugh, ed., *Fighting the Farm Crisis*. Saskatoon: Fifth House, 1987.

Anderson, Terry H. *The Pursuit of Fairness: The History of Affirmative Action*. Oxford: Oxford University Press, 2004.

Armstrong, Elizabeth A. *Forging Gay Identities: Organizing Sexuality in San Francisco, 1950–94*. Chicago: University of Chicago Press, 2002.

Atlas, John. *Seeds of Change: The Story of ACORN, America's Most Controversial Antipoverty Community Organizing Group*. Nashville: Vanderbilt University Press, 2010.

Atlas, John, and Peter Dreier. "The Tenants' Movement and American Politics." In Rachel G. Bratt, Chester Hartman, and Ann Meyerson, eds., *Critical Perspectives on Housing*. Philadelphia: Temple University Press, 1986.

Bailey, Beth. "She 'Can Bring Home the Bacon': Negotiating Gender in Seventies America." In Beth Bailey and David Farber, eds., *America in the Seventies*. Lawrence: University Press of Kansas, 2004.

Barger, W. K., and Ernesto M. Reza. *The Farm Labor Movement in the Midwest: Social Change and Adaptation Among Migrant Farmworkers*. Austin: University of Texas Press, 1994.

Barlett, Peggy F. *American Dreams, Rural Realities: Family Farms in Crisis*. Chapel Hill: University of North Carolina Press, 1993.

Barnett, Barry J. "The U.S. Farm Financial Crisis of the 1980s." In Jane Adams, ed., *Fighting for the Farm: Rural America Transformed*. Philadelphia: University of Pennsylvania Press, 2003.

Barrett, Joyce. *Mending a Broken Heartland: Community Response to the Farm Crisis*. Alexandria, VA: Synergy Publishing, 1987.

Barrow, John C. "An Age of Limits: Jimmy Carter and the Quest for a National Energy

Policy." In Gary M. Fink and Hugh Davis Graham, eds., *The Carter Presidency: Policy Choices in the Post–New Deal Era*. Lawrence: University Press of Kansas, 1998.

Battista, Andrew. "Labor and Liberalism: The Citizen Labor Energy Coalition." *Labor History*, 40:3 (August 1999): 301–21.

———. *The Revival of Labor Liberalism*. Urbana: University of Illinois Press, 2008.

Baumohl, Jim, ed.. *Homelessness in America*. Phoenix: Oryx Press, 1996.

Bayer, Ronald. *Homosexuality and American Psychiatry: The Politics of Diagnosis*. Princeton: Princeton University Press, 1987.

Beckwith, Karen. "Collective Identities of Class and Gender: Working-Class Women in the Pittston Coal Strike." *Political Psychology* 19:1 (March 1998): 147–67.

Beder, Sharon. *Global Spin: The Corporate Assault on Environmentalism*. Rev. ed. Foxhole, UK: Green Books, 2002.

Bedford, Henry F. *Seabrook Station: Citizen Politics and Nuclear Power*. Amherst: University of Massachusetts Press, 1990.

Bellah, Robert, et al. *Habits of the Heart: Individualism and Commitment in American Life*. 3rd ed. Berkeley: University of California Press, 2007.

Berger, Dan. *The Hidden 1970s: Histories of Radicalism*. New Brunswick: Rutgers University Press, 2010.

Berkowitz, Edward D. *Something Happened: A Political and Cultural Overview of the Seventies*. New York: Columbia University Press, 2006.

Bluestone, Barry, and Bennett Harrison. *The Deindustrialization of America: Plant Closings, Community Abandonment, and the Dismantling of Basic Industry*. New York: Basic Books, 1982.

Blum, Elizabeth D. *Love Canal Revisited: Race, Class, and Gender in Environmental Activism*. Lawrence: University Press of Kansas, 2008.

Bogard, Cynthia. *Seasons Such as These: How Homelessness Took Shape in America*. New York: Aldine de Gruyter, 2003.

Borgos, Seth. "Low-Income Homeownership and the ACORN Squatters Campaign." In Rachel G. Bratt, Chester Hartman, and Ann Meyerson, eds., *Critical Perspectives on Housing*. Philadelphia: Temple University Press, 1986.

Boyd, Julian P., et al. *The Papers of Thomas Jefferson*. Princeton: Princeton University Press, 1950.

Boyte, Harry. *Backyard Revolution: Understanding the New Citizen Movement*. Philadelphia: Temple University Press, 1980.

Boyte, Harry, Heather Booth, and Steve Max. *Citizen Action and the New American Populism*. Philadelphia: Temple University Press, 1986.

Bratt, Rachel G., Chester Hartman, and Ann Meyerson, eds., *Critical Perspectives on Housing*. Philadelphia: Temple University Press, 1986.

Brier, Jennifer. *Infectious Ideas: U.S. Political Responses to the AIDS Crisis*. Chapel Hill: University of North Carolina Press, 2009.

Brinkley, Alan. "Conservatism as a Growing Field of Scholarship." *Journal of American History* (December 2011): 748–51.

———. "The Problem of American Conservatism," *American Historical Review* 99 (April 1994): 409–29.

Brisbin, Richard A., Jr. *A Strike Like No Other Strike: Law and Resistance During the Pittston Coal Strike of 1989–90.* Baltimore: Johns Hopkins University Press, 2002.

Browne, William P. *Private Interests, Public Policy, and American Agriculture.* Lawrence: University Press of Kansas, 1988.

Browne, William P., and Mark H. Lundgren. "Farmers Helping Farmers: Constituent Services and the Development of a Grassroots Farm Lobby." *Agriculture and Human Values* (Spring/Summer 1987): 11–28.

Brownmiller, Susan. *In Our Time: Memoir of a Revolution.* New York: Dial Press, 1999.

Bryant, Anita. *The Anita Bryant Story: The Survival of Our Nation's Families and the Threat of Militant Homosexuality.* Old Tappan, NJ: Fleming H. Revell, 1977.

Bullard, Robert D. "Anatomy of Environmental Racism and the Environmental Justice Movement." In Robert D. Bullard, ed., *Confronting Environmental Racism: Voices from the Grassroots.* Boston: South End Press, 1993.

Caldwell, Lynton K., Lynton R. Hayes, and Isabel M. MacWhirter. *Citizens and the Environment: Case Studies in Popular Action.* Bloomington: Indiana University Press, 1976.

Campbell, Gordon J., and Elizabeth McCarthy. "Conveying Mission Through Outcome Measurement: Services to the Homeless in New York City." *Policy Studies Journal* 28:2 (2000): 338–52.

Capozzola, Christopher. "A Very American Epidemic: Memory Politics and Identity Politics in the AIDS Memorial Quilt, 1985–93." In Van Gosse and Richard Moser, eds., *The World the Sixties Made: Politics and Culture in Recent America.* Philadelphia: Temple University Press, 2003.

Carroll, Peter. *It Seemed Like Nothing Happened: America in the 1970s.* New York: Holt, Rinehart and Winston, 1982.

Carter, David. *Stonewall: The Riots That Sparked the Gay Revolution.* New York: St. Martin's Press, 2004.

Chambre, Susan M. *Fighting for Our Lives: New York's AIDS Community and the Politics of Disease.* New Brunswick: Rutgers University Press, 2006.

Chastagner, Claude. "The Parents' Music Resource Center: From Information to Censorship." *Popular Music* 18:2 (May 1999): 179–92.

Churchill, Ward, and Jim Vander Wall. *The COINTELPRO Papers: Documents from the FBI's Secret War Against Dissent in the United States.* Boston: South End Press, 1990.

Clarke, Susan E. "Ideas, Interests, and Institutions Shaping Abortion Politics in Denver." In Elaine B. Sharp, ed., *Culture Wars and Local Politics.* Lawrence: University Press of Kansas, 1999.

Clendinen, Dudley, and Adam Nagourney. *Out for Good: The Struggle to Build a Gay Rights Movement in America.* New York: Touchstone, 1999.

Cohen, Lizabeth. *A Consumers' Republic: The Politics of Mass Consumption in Postwar America.* New York: Vintage, 2003.

Cole, Luke W., and Sheila R. Foster. *From the Ground Up: Environmental Racism and the Rise of the Environmental Justice Movement.* New York: New York University Press, 2001.

Corr, Anders. *No Trespassing: Squatting, Rent Strikes and Land Struggles Worldwide.* Boston: South End Press, 1999.

Cowan, Paul, Nick Egleson, and Nat Hentoff. *State Secrets: Police Surveillance in America*. (New York: Holt, Rinehart and Winston, 1974.

Cowie, Jefferson. *Capital Moves: RCA's 70 Year Quest for Cheap Labor*. New York: New Press, 2001.

———. "Nixon's Class Struggle: Romancing the New Right Worker, 1969–73." *Labor History* 43 (August 2002): 257–83.

———. *Stayin' Alive: The 1970s and the Last Days of the Working Class*. New York: New Press, 2010.

———. "'Vigorously Left, Right, and Center at the Same Time.'" In Beth Bailey and David Farber, eds., *America in the Seventies*. Lawrence: University Press of Kansas, 2004.

Cress, Daniel M., and David A. Snow. "The Outcomes of Homeless Mobilization: The Influence of Organization, Disruption, Political Mediation, and Framing." *American Journal of Sociology* 105:4 (January 2000): 1063–1104.

Critchlow, Donald T. *Phyllis Schlafly and Grassroots Conservatism: A Woman's Crusade*. Princeton: Princeton University Press, 2005.

———. "Rethinking American Conservatism: Toward a New Narrative." *Journal of American History* (December 2011): 752–55.

Dallek, Robert. *Ronald Reagan: The Politics of Symbolism*. Cambridge, MA: Harvard University Press, 1999.

Davis, David Howard. *Energy Politics*. 4th ed. New York: St. Martin's Press, 1993.

Davis, Flora. *Moving the Mountain: The Women's Movement in America Since 1960*. New York: Touchstone, 1992.

Davis, Mike. *City of Quartz: Excavating the Future in Los Angeles*. New York: Vintage, 1992.

DeBenedetti, Charles, and Charles Chatfield. *An American Ordeal: The Antiwar Movement of the Vietnam Era*. Syracuse, NY: Syracuse University Press, 1990.

Delgado, Gary. *Organizing the Movement: The Roots and Growth of ACORN*. Philadelphia: Temple University Press, 1987.

DeLind, Laura B. "Considerably More Than Vegetables, a Lot Less Than Community." In Jane Adams, ed., *Fighting for the Farm: Rural America Transformed*. Philadelphia: University of Pennsylvania Press, 2003.

D'Emilio, John. *Sexual Politics, Sexual Communities: The Making of a Homosexual Minority in the United States, 1940–70*. 2nd ed. Chicago: University of Chicago Press, 1998.

D'Emilio, John, and Estelle B. Freedman. *Intimate Matters: A History of Sexuality in America*. 2nd ed. Chicago: University of Chicago Press, 1997.

Diamond, Sara. *Roads to Dominion: Right-Wing Movements and Political Power in the United States*. New York: Guilford Press, 1995.

Donner, Frank. *Protectors of Privilege: Red Squads and Police Repression in Urban America*. Berkeley: University of California Press, 1990.

Dougherty, Jack. *More Than One Struggle: The Evolution of Black School Reform in Milwaukee*. Chapel Hill: University of North Carolina Press, 2004.

Downs, Donald Alexander. *The New Politics of Pornography*. Chicago: University of Chicago Press, 1989.

Draper, Alan. "No Retreat, No Surrender: Concessions, Resistance and the End of the Postwar Settlement." *Labour/Le Travail* 51 (Spring 2003).

Dreier, Peter. "The Politics of Rent Control." In John Gilderbloom et al., *Rent Control: A Source Book*. 3rd ed. Santa Barbara: Foundation for National Progress, 1981.

Duberman, Martin. *Stonewall*. New York: Dutton, 1993.

Dudley, Kathryn Marie. *Debt and Dispossession: Farm Loss in America's Heartland*. Chicago: University of Chicago Press, 2000.

Durham, Martin. "On American Conservatism and Kim Phillips-Fein's Survey of the Field." *Journal of American History* (December 2011): 756–59.

Durr, Kenneth D. *Behind the Backlash: White Working-Class Politics in Baltimore, 1940–80*. Chapel Hill: University of North Carolina Press, 2003.

Eaton, Susan. *The Other Boston Busing Story: What's Won and Lost Across the Boundary Line*. New Haven: Yale University Press, 2001.

Edelstein, Andrew J., and Kevin McDonough. *The Seventies: From Hot Pants to Hot Tubs*. New York: Dutton, 1990.

Edsall, Thomas Byrne, with Mary D. Edsall. *Chain Reaction: The Impact of Race, Rights, and Taxes on American Politics*. New York: Norton, 1991.

Eisenbach, David. *Gay Power: An American Revolution*. New York: Carroll and Graf, 2006.

Enke, Anne. "Taking Over Domestic Space: The Battered Women's Movement and Public Protest." In Van Gosse and Richard Moser, eds., *The World the Sixties Made: Politics and Culture in Recent America*. Philadelphia: Temple University Press, 2003.

Epstein, Barbara. *Political Protest and Cultural Revolution: Nonviolent Direct Action in the 1970s and 1980s*. Berkeley: University of California Press, 1991.

Escoffier, Jeffrey. *American Homo: Community and Perversity*. Berkeley: University of California Press, 1998.

———. "Fabulous Politics: Gay, Lesbian, and Queer Movements, 1969–99." In Van Gosse and Richard Moser, eds., *The World the Sixties Made: Politics and Culture in Recent America*. Philadelphia: Temple University Press, 2003.

Eskridge, William N., Jr. *Gaylaw: Challenging the Apartheid of the Closet*. Cambridge, MA: Harvard University Press, 1999.

Evans, Sara M. "Beyond Declension: Feminist Radicalism in the 1970s and 1980s." In Van Gosse and Richard Moser, eds., *The World the Sixties Made: Politics and Culture in Recent America*. Philadelphia: Temple University Press, 2003.

———. *Personal Politics: The Roots of Women's Liberation in the Civil Rights Movement and the New Left*. New York: Knopf, 1979.

———. *Tidal Wave: How Women Changed America at Century's End*. New York: Free Press, 2004.

Farrell, Amy Erdman. *Yours in Sisterhood: Ms. Magazine and the Promise of Popular Feminism*. Chapel Hill: University of North Carolina Press, 1998.

Feffer, Andrew. "The Land Belongs to the People: Reframing Urban Protest in Post-Sixties Philadelphia." In Van Gosse and Richard Moser, eds., *The World the Sixties Made: Politics and Culture in Recent America*. Philadelphia: Temple University Press, 2003.

Forriss, Susan, and Ricardo Sandoval. *The Fight in the Fields: Cesar Chavez and the Farmworkers Movement*. New York: Harcourt Brace, 1997.

Fiorina, Morris. *Culture War? The Myth of a Polarized America*. New York: Longman, 2005.

Fisher, Robert. *Let the People Decide: Neighborhood Organizing in America*. Boston: Twayne, 1984.

Fleming, Cynthia Griggs. *In the Shadow of Selma: The Continuing Struggle for Civil Rights in the Rural South*. Lanham, MD: Rowman and Littlefield, 2004.

Formisano, Ronald. *Boston Against Busing: Race, Class, and Ethnicity in the 1960s and 1970s*. Chapel Hill: University of North Carolina Press, 1991.

Foscarinis, Maria. "The Federal Response: The Stewart B. McKinney Homeless Assistance Act." In Jim Baumohl, ed., *Homelessness in America*. Phoenix: Oryx Press, 1996, 160–71.

Frank, Thomas. *What's the Matter with Kansas?: How Conservatives Won the Heart of America*. New York: Metropolitan Books, 2004.

Franklin, Stephen. *Three Strikes: Labor's Heartland Losses and What They Mean for Working Americans*. New York: Guilford Press, 2002.

Freeman, Jo, and Victoria Johnson. *Waves of Protest: Social Movements Since the Sixties*. Lanham, MD: Rowman and Littlefield, 1999.

Freeman, Joshua. *Working-Class New York: Life and Labor Since World War II*. New York: New Press, 2000.

Freund, David. *Colored Property: State Policy and White Racial Politics in Suburban America*. Chicago: University of Chicago Press, 2010.

Ganz, Marshall. *Why David Sometimes Wins: Leadership, Organization, and Strategy in the California Farm Worker Movement*. New York: Oxford University Press, 2009.

General Accounting Office. "Rental Housing: A National Problem that Needs Immediate Attention." In John Gilderbloom et al, *Rent Control: A Source Book*. 3rd ed. Santa Barbara: Foundation for National Progress, 1981.

George-Warren, Holly, ed. *Farm Aid: A Song for America*. Emmaus, PA: Rodale Press, 2005.

Getman, Julius. *The Betrayal of Local 14: Paperworkers, Politics, and Permanent Replacements*. Ithaca, NY: Cornell University Press, 1998.

Gibbs, Lois. "Citizen Activism for Environmental Health: The Growth of a Powerful New Grassroots Health Movement." In Sylvia Hood Washington, Paul C. Rosier, and Heather Goodall, eds., *Echoes from the Poisoned Well: Global Memories of Environmental Injustice*. Lanham, MD: Lexington Books, 2006.

———. *Love Canal: The Story Continues*. Rev. ed. Gabriola Island, BC: New Society Publishers, 1998.

Gilderbloom, John I., and Stella M. Capek. "Santa Monica a Decade Later: Urban Progressives in Office." *National Civic Review* (Spring/Summer 1992): 115–31.

Ginsburg, Faye D. *Contested Lives: The Abortion Debate in an American Community*. Updated ed. Berkeley: University of California Press, 1998.

———. "Rescuing the Nation: Operation Rescue and the Rise of Anti-Abortion Militance." In Rickie Solinger, *Abortion War: A Half Century of Struggle, 1950–2000*. Berkeley: University of California Press, 1998.

Givan, Rebecca Kolins, Kenneth M. Roberts, and Sarah A. Soule. *The Diffusion of Social Movements: Actors, Mechanisms, and Political Effects*. Cambridge: Cambridge University Press, 2010.

Goldstein, Robert Justin. *Political Repression in Modern America: From 1870 to the Present*. Boston: G. K. Hall, 1978.

Goodwin, Jeff, James M. Jasper, and Francesca Polletta. "Emotional Dimensions of Social Movements." In David Snow, Sarah Soule, and Hanspieter Kriesi, eds., *Blackwell Companion to Social Movements*. Malden, MA: Blackwell, 2007.

——. *Passionate Politics: Emotions and Social Movements*. Chicago: University of Chicago Press, 2001.

Goodwyn, Lawrence. *The Populist Moment: A Short History of the Agrarian Revolt in America*. New York: Oxford University Press, 1978.

Gore, Tipper. *Raising PG Kids in an X-Rated Society*. Nashville: Abingdon Press, 1987.

Gorney, Cynthia. *Articles of Faith: A Frontline History of the Abortion Wars*. New York: Touchstone, 1998.

Gosse, Van. *Rethinking the New Left: An Interpretive History*. New York: Palgrave, 2005.

Gosse, Van, and Richard Moser. *The World the Sixties Made: Politics and Culture in Recent America*. Philadelphia: Temple University Press, 2003.

Gottlieb, Robert. *Forcing the Spring: The Transformation of the American Environmental Movement*. Rev. ed. Washington, DC: Island Press, 2005.

Gould, Deborah B. *Moving Politics: Emotion and ACT UP's Fight Against AIDS*. Chicago: University of Chicago Press, 2009.

Gray, Herman. "Rate the Records: Symbolic Conflict, Popular Music, and Social Problems." *Popular Music and Society* 13:3 (1989): 5–16.

Greene, John Robert. *The Presidency of Gerald R. Ford*. Lawrence: University Press of Kansas, 1995.

Gyorgy, Anna. *No Nukes: Everyone's Guide to Nuclear Power*. Boston: South End Press, 1979.

Hage, David, and Paul Klauda. *No Retreat, No Surrender: Labor's War at Hormel*. New York: Morrow, 1989.

Halcli, Abigail. "AIDS, Anger, and Activism: ACT UP as a Social Movement Organization." In Jo Freeman and Victoria Johnson, *Waves of Protest: Social Movements Since the Sixties*. Lanham, MD: Rowman and Littlefield, 1999.

Hall, Simon. *American Patriotism, American Protest: Social Movements Since the Sixties*. Philadelphia: University of Pennsylvania Press, 2011.

Hampton, Henry, et al., eds. *Voices of Freedom: An Oral History of the Civil Rights Movement from the 1950s Through the 1980s*. New York: Bantam, 1990.

Hartman, Chester. "Landlord Money Defeats Rent Control in San Francisco." In John Gilderbloom et al., *Rent Control: A Source Book*. 3rd ed. Santa Barbara: Foundation for National Progress, 1981.

Harvey, David. "Rent Control and a Fair Return." In John Gilderbloom et al., *Rent Control: A Source Book* (3rd ed.). Santa Barbara: Foundation for National Progress, 1981, 80–82.

Hays, Samuel P. *Beauty, Health, and Permanence: Environmental Politics in the United States, 1955–85*. Cambridge: Cambridge University Press, 1987.

Heins, Marjorie. *Not in Front of the Children: "Indecency," Censorship, and the Innocence of Youth*. New York: Hill and Wang, 2001.

——. *Sex, Sin, and Blasphemy: A Guide to America's Censorship Wars*. 2nd ed. New York: New Press, 1998.

Hertsgaard, Mark. *Nuclear Inc.: The Men and Money Behind Nuclear Energy*. New York: Pantheon, 1983.

Hertz, Sue. *Caught in the Crossfire: A Year on Abortion's Front Line*. New York: Prentice Hall, 1991.

Heskin, Allan David. "Is a Tenant a Second Class Citizen?" In John Gilderbloom et al., *Rent Control: A Source Book*. 3rd ed. Santa Barbara: Foundation for National Progress, 1981.

———. *Tenants and the American Dream: Ideology and the Tenant Movement*. New York: Praeger, 1983.

Hodgson, Godfrey. *More Equal Than Others: America from Nixon to the New Century*. Princeton: Princeton University Press, 2004.

Hopper, Kim. "Homelessness Old and New: The Matter of Definition." *Housing Policy Debate* 2:3 (1991): 757–813.

———. *Reckoning with Homelessness*. Ithaca, NY: Cornell University Press, 2003.

Hunter, Dianna. *Breaking Hard Ground: Stories of the Minnesota Farm Advocates*. Duluth: Holy Cow Press, 1990.

Hurley, Andrew. *Environmental Inequalities: Class, Race, and Industrial Pollution in Gary, Indiana, 1945–80*. Chapel Hill: University of North Carolina Press, 1995.

Inglehart, Ronald. *Culture Shift in Advanced Industrial Society*. Princeton: Princeton University Press, 1989.

Jacob, Mike. "How Rent Control Passed in Santa Monica." In John Gilderbloom et al., *Rent Control: A Source Book*. 3rd ed. Santa Barbara: Foundation for National Progress, 1981.

Jacobs, Meg. "The Conservative Struggle and the Energy Crisis." In Julian Zelizer and Bruce Schulman, eds., *Rightward Bound: Making America Conservative in the 1970s*. Cambridge, MA: Harvard University Press, 2008.

Jasper, James M. "The Emotions of Protest: Affective and Reactive Emotions in and Around Social Movements." *Sociological Forum* 13, 397–424.

Jenkins, Philip. *Decade of Nightmares: The End of the Sixties and the Making of Eighties America*. New York: Oxford University Press, 2006.

Johnson, Haynes. *Sleepwalking Through History: America in the Reagan Years*. New York: Anchor Books, 1991.

Judt, Tony. *Ill Fares the Land*. New York: Penguin, 2010.

Juravich, Tom, and Kate Bronfenbrenner. *Ravenswood: The Steelworkers' Victory and the Revival of American Labor*. Ithaca, NY: Cornell University Press, 1999.

Kahl, Mary C. *Controversy and Courage: Upper Hudson Planned Parenthood from 1934 to 2004*. New York: iUniverse, 2004.

Karpf, David. *The MoveOn Effect: The Unexpected Transformation of American Political Advocacy*. New York: Oxford University Press, 2012.

Katz, Michael. *The Undeserving Poor: From the War on Poverty to the War on Welfare*. New York: Pantheon, 1989.

Kazin, Michael. "The Grass-Roots Right: New Histories of U.S. Conservatism in the Twentieth Century." *American Historical Review* 97 (February 1992): 136–55.

———. *The Populist Persuasion: An American History*. New York: Basic Books, 1995.

Kelley, Robin D. G. *Race Rebels: Culture, Politics, and the Black Working Class*. New York: Free Press, 1994.

Kennedy, David. "Frankenchrist Versus the State: The New Right, Rock Music and the Case of Jello Biafra." *Journal of Popular Culture* 24:1 (1990): 131–48.

Kennedy, Sheila Rauch. "The Grassroots Home: How Local Communities Are Fighting Homelessness." In Padraig O'Malley, ed., "Homelessness: New England and Beyond." Special issue of *New England Journal of Public Policy* (May 1992): 583–98.

Kidder, Tracy. "The Nonviolent War Against Nuclear Power." *Atlantic Monthly* (September 1978): 70–76.

Killen, Andreas. *1973 Nervous Breakdown: Watergate, Warhol, and the Birth of Post-Sixties America.* New York: Bloomsbury, 2006.

Kingsolver, Barbara. *Holding the Line: Women in the Great Arizona Mine Strike of 1983.* Rev. ed. Ithaca, NY: Cornell University Press, 1996.

Kirp, David, John P. Dwyer, and Larry A. Rosenthal. *Our Town: Race, Housing and the Soul of Suburbia.* New Brunswick: Rutgers University Press, 1995.

Klatch, Rebecca E. *Women of the New Right.* Philadelphia: Temple University Press, 1987.

Kleinknecht, William. *The Man Who Sold the World: Ronald Reagan and the Betrayal of Main Street America.* New York: Nation Books, 2009.

Kolodny, Robert. "The Emergence of Self-Help as a Housing Strategy for the Urban Poor." In Rachel G. Bratt, Chester Hartman, and Ann Meyerson, eds., *Critical Perspectives on Housing.* Philadelphia: Temple University Press, 1986.

Kopkind, Andrew. "A Populist Message Hits Home." *The Nation,* July 18, 1987, reprinted in Kopkind, *The Thirty Years' War: Dispatches and Diversions of a Radical Journalist, 1965–94.* London: Verso, 1995.

Kornbluh, Felicia. *The Battle for Welfare Rights: Politics and Poverty in Modern America.* Philadelphia: University of Pennsylvania Press, 2007.

———. "Disability Rights, Antiprofessionalism, and Civil Rights: The National Federation of the Blind and 'the Right to Organize' in the 1950s." *Journal of American History* 97:4 (March 2011): 1023–47.

Kotlowski, Dean J. *Nixon's Civil Rights: Politics, Principle, and Policy.* Cambridge, MA: Harvard University Press, 2001.

Krauss, Celene. "Challenging Power: Toxic Waste Protests and the Politicization of White, Working-Class Women." In Nancy Naples, ed., *Community Activism and Feminist Politics: Organizing Across Race, Class, and Gender.* New York: Routledge, 1998.

Kutler, Stanley. *The Wars of Watergate: The Last Crisis of Richard Nixon.* New York: Knopf, 1990.

Kuttner, Robert. *Revolt of the Haves: Tax Rebellions and Hard Times.* New York: Simon and Schuster, 1980.

Lane, Frederick S. *The Decency Wars: The Campaign to Cleanse American Culture.* Amherst, NY: Prometheus Books, 2006.

Lassiter, Matthew. "De Jure/De Facto Segregation: The Long Shadow of a National Myth." In Matthew Lassiter and Joseph Crespino, eds., *The Myth of Southern Exceptionalism.* New York: Oxford University Press, 2010.

———. "Political History Beyond the Red-Blue Divide." *Journal of American History* (December 2011): 760–64.

———. *The Silent Majority: Suburban Politics in the Sunbelt South.* Princeton: Princeton University Press, 2005.

Lawson, Ronald, ed. *The Tenant Movement in New York City, 1904–84.* New Brunswick: Rutgers University Press, 1986.

Layzer, Judith A. *The Environmental Case: Translating Values into Policy.* Washington, DC: CQ Press, 2002.

Lee, Charles. "Beyond Toxic Wastes and Race." In Robert D. Bullard, ed., *Confronting Environmental Racism: Voices from the Grassroots.* Boston: South End Press, 1993.

Leight, Claudia, Elliot Lieberman, Jerry Kurtz, and Dean Pappas. "Rent Control Wins in Baltimore." In John Gilderbloom et al., *Rent Control: A Source Book.* 3rd ed. Santa Barbara: Foundation for National Progress, 1981.

Lichtenstein, Nelson. *State of the Union: A Century of American Labor.* Princeton: Princeton University Press, 2002.

Lieber, James B. *Friendly Takeover: How an Employee Buyout Saved a Steel Town.* New York: Penguin, 1996.

Lienesch, Michael. *Redeeming America: Piety and Politics in the New Christian Right.* Chapel Hill: University of North Carolina Press, 1993.

Link, Bruce G., et al. "Public Attitudes and Beliefs About Homeless People." In Jim Baumohl, *Homelessness in America.* Phoenix: Oryx Press, 1996.

Link, William A. *Righteous Warrior: Jesse Helms and the Rise of Modern Conservatism.* New York: St. Martin's Press, 2008.

Lobao, Linda M. "Organizational, Community, and Political Involvement as Responses to Rural Restructuring." In Paul Lasley, F. Larry Leistritz, Linda M. Lobao, and Katherine Meyer, *Beyond the Amber Waves of Grain: An Examination of Social and Economic Restructuring in the Heartland.* Boulder: Westview Press, 1995.

Lowe, Cary. "Rent Control Surge May Be Just a Start." In John Gilderbloom et al., *Rent Control: A Source Book.* 3rd ed. Santa Barbara: Foundation for National Progress, 1981.

Lukas, J. Anthony. *Common Ground: A Turbulent Decade in the Lives of Three American Families.* New York: Knopf, 1985.

Luker, Kristen. *Abortion and the Politics of Motherhood.* Berkeley: University of California Press, 1984.

Lynd, Staughton. *The Fight Against Shutdowns: Youngstown's Steel Mill Closings.* San Pedro, CA: Singlejack Books, 1983.

———. "The Genesis of the Idea of a Community Right to Industrial Property in Youngstown and Pittsburgh, 1977–87." *Journal of American History* 74:3 (December 1987): 926–58.

———. "What Happened in Youngstown: An Outline." *Radical America* 15:4 (July–August 1981): 37–48.

MacKenzie, Angus. *Secrets: The CIA's War at Home.* Berkeley: University of California Press, 1997.

Maharidge, Dale. *Journey to Nowhere: The Saga of the New Underclass.* New York: Hyperion, 1996.

Mansbridge, Jane J. *Why We Lost the ERA*. Chicago: University of Chicago Press, 1986.

Martin, Bradford. "Cultural Politics and the Singer/Songwriters of the 1970s." In Julian Zelizer and Bruce Schulman, eds., *Rightward Bound: Making America Conservative in the 1970s*. Cambridge, MA: Harvard University Press, 2008.

———. *The Other Eighties: A Secret History of America in the Age of Reagan*. New York: Hill and Wang, 2011.

Martin, Isaac William. *The Permanent Tax Revolt: How the Property Tax Transformed American Politics*. Stanford: Stanford University Press, 2008.

Martin, Justin. *Nader: Crusader, Spoiler, Icon*. New York: Perseus, 2002.

Mason, Carol. "An American Conflict: Representing the 1974 Kanawha County Textbook Controversy." *Appalachian Journal* 32:3 (Spring 2005): 352–78.

———. *Killing for Life: The Apocalyptic Narrative of Pro-Life Politics*. Ithaca, NY: Cornell University Press, 2002.

———. *Reading Appalachia from Left to Right: Conservatives and the 1974 Kanawha County Textbook Controversy*. Ithaca, NY: Cornell University Press, 2009.

Mathews, Donald, and Jane Sherron DeHart. *Sex, Gender, and the Politics of ERA: A State and the Nation*. New York: Oxford University Press, 1990.

Matusow, Allen. *The Unraveling of America: A History of Liberalism in the 1960s*. New York: Harper and Row, 1984.

McAfee, Kathy. "Socialism and the Housing Movement: Lessons from Boston." In Rachel G. Bratt, Chester Hartman, and Ann Meyerson, eds., *Critical Perspectives on Housing*. Philadelphia: Temple University Press, 1986.

McCartin, Joseph A. *Collision Course: Ronald Reagan, the Air Traffic Controllers, and the Strike That Changed America*. New York: Oxford University Press, 2011.

———. "Turnabout Years: Public Sector Unionism and the Fiscal Crisis." In Bruce Schulman and Julian Zelizer, eds., *Rightward Bound: Making America Conservative in the 1970s*. Cambridge, MA: Harvard University Press, 2008.

McClay, Wilfred M. "Less Boilerplate, More Symmetry." *Journal of American History* (December 2011): 744–47.

McGirr, Lisa. "Now That Historians Know So Much About the Right, How Should We Best Approach the Study of Conservatism?" *Journal of American History* (December 2011): 765–70.

———. *Suburban Warriors: The Origins of the New American Right*. Princeton: Princeton University Press, 2001.

McGurty, Eileen. *Transforming Environmentalism: Warren County, PCBs, and the Origins of Environmental Justice*. New Brunswick: Rutgers University Press, 2008.

Mezies, Ian. "Homelessness in Boston: The Media Wake Up." In Padraig O'Malley, ed., "Homelessness: New England and Beyond." Special issue of *New England Journal of Public Policy* (May 1992).

Miller, Alan S., and John P. Hoffmann. "The Growing Divisiveness: Culture War or a War of Words?" *Social Forces* 78:2 (December 1999): 721–52.

Miller, Mike. *The People Fight Back: Building a Tenant Union*. San Francisco: Organize Training Center, 1979.

Minchin, Timothy J. *Forging a Common Bond: Labor and Environmental Activism During the BASF Lockout*. Gainesville: University Press of Florida, 2003.

———. "'It Tears the Heart Right Out of You': Memories of Striker Replacement at International Paper Company in De Pere, Wisconsin, 1987–88." *Oral History Review* 31:2 (Summer/Autumn 2004): 1–27.

———."'Labor's Empty Gun': Permanent Replacements and the International Paper Company Strike of 1987–88," *Labor History* 47:1 (February 2006): 21–42.

Mirel, Jeffrey. *The Rise and Fall of an Urban School System: Detroit, 1907–81*. 2nd ed. Ann Arbor: University of Michigan Press, 1999.

Mitchell, Don. "The End of Public Space? People's Park, Definitions of the Public, and Democracy." *Annals of the Association of American Geographers* 85:1 (March 1995): 108–33.

Mixner, David. *Stranger Among Friends*. New York: Bantam, 1996.

Montrie, Chad. *To Save the Land and People: A History of Opposition to Surface Coal Mining in Appalachia*. Chapel Hill: University of North Carolina Press, 2003.

Mooney, Patrick H., and Theo J. Majka. *Farmers' and Farm Workers' Movements: Social Protest in American Agriculture*. New York: Twayne, 1995.

Navarro, Peter. "Rent Control in Cambridge, Mass." *Public Interest* 78 (Winter 1985): 83–100.

Newman, Richard. "From Love's Canal to Love Canal: Reckoning with the Environmental Legacy of an Industrial Dream." In Jefferson Cowie and Joseph Heathcott, eds., *Beyond the Ruins: The Meanings of Deindustrialization*. Ithaca, NY: Cornell University Press, 2003.

Niebanck, Paul L. "Toward a Fuller Understanding of Rent Control." In Paul L. Niebanck, ed., *The Rent Control Debate*. Chapel Hill: University of North Carolina Press, 1985.

Nixon, Richard. *RN: The Memoirs of Richard Nixon*. New York: Touchstone, 1990.

Nord, Mark. "Homeless Children and Their Families in New Hampshire: A Rural Perspective." *Social Service Review* 69:3 (September 1995): 461–78.

Olmsted, Kathryn. *Challenging the Secret Government: The Post-Watergate Investigations of the CIA and FBI*. Chapel Hill: University of North Carolina Press, 1996.

O'Malley, Padraig, ed. "Homelessness: New England and Beyond." Special issue of *New England Journal of Public Policy* (May 1992).

Patterson, James T. *Restless Giant: The United States from Watergate to Bush v. Gore*. New York: Oxford University Press, 2005.

Pawel, Miriam. *The Union of Their Dreams: Power, Hope, and Struggle in Cesar Chavez's Farm Worker Movement*. New York: Bloomsbury, 2009.

Perlstein, Rick. *Nixonland: The Rise of a President and the Fracturing of a Nation*. New York: Scribner, 2008.

Phillips-Fein, Kim. "Conservatism: A State of the Field." *Journal of American History* (December 2011): 723–43.

———. *Invisible Hands: The Making of the Conservative Movement from the New Deal to Reagan*. New York: Norton, 2009.

———. "A Response." *Journal of American History* (December 2011): 771–73.

Piven, Frances Fox, and Richard Cloward. *Poor People's Movements: Why They Succeed, How They Fail.* New York: Vintage, 1978.

Portz, John. *The Politics of Plant Closings.* Lawrence: University Press of Kansas, 1990.

Pulido, Laura. *Environmentalism and Economic Justice: Two Chicano Struggles in the Southwest.* Tucson: University of Arizona Press, 1996.

Putnam, Robert. *Bowling Alone: The Collapse and Revival of American Community.* New York: Simon and Schuster, 2000.

Rachleff, Peter. *Hard-Pressed in the Heartland: The Hormel Strike and the Future of the Labor Movement.* Boston: South End Press, 1993.

Rader, Victoria. *Signal Through the Flames: Mitch Snyder and America's Homeless.* Kansas City, MO: Sheed and Ward, 1986.

Ramirez-Ferrero, Eric. *Troubled Fields: Men, Emotions, and the Crisis in American Farming.* New York: Columbia University Press, 2005.

Reed, T. V. *The Art of Protest: Culture and Activism from the Civil Rights Movement to the Streets of Seattle.* Minneapolis: University of Minnesota Press, 2005.

Ribuffo, Leo P. "Why Is There So Much Conservatism in the United States and Why Do So Few Historians Know Anything About It?" *American Historical Review* 99 (April 1994): 438–49.

Rieder, Jonathan. *Canarsie: The Jews and Italians of Brooklyn Against Liberalism.* Cambridge, MA: Harvard University Press, 1985.

Risen, James, and Judy L. Thomas. *Wrath of Angels: The American Abortion War.* New York: Basic Books, 1998.

Roberts, Selena. *A Necessary Spectacle: Billie Jean King, Bobby Riggs, and the Tennis Match That Leveled the Game.* New York: Crown, 2005.

Rodgers, Daniel T. *The Age of Fracture.* Cambridge, MA: Harvard University Press, 2011.

Rome, Adam. *The Bulldozer in the Countryside: Suburban Sprawl and the Rise of American Environmentalism.* Cambridge: Cambridge University Press, 2001.

Ropers, Richard H. *The Invisible Homeless: A New Urban Ecology.* New York: Human Sciences Press, 1988.

Rosen, Jay. "Music and the Movement: MUSE Represents a Happy Match Between Rock 'n Roll and Resistance to Nuclear Power." *The Progressive* (January 1980): 22–23.

Rosen, Ruth. *The World Split Open: How the Modern Women's Movement Changed America.* New York: Penguin, 2000.

Rosenblatt, Paul C. *Farming Is in Our Blood: Farm Families in Economic Crisis.* Ames: Iowa State University Press, 1990.

Rosenblum, Jonathan D. *Copper Crucible: How the Arizona Miners Strike of 1983 Recast Labor-Management Relations in America.* 2nd ed. Ithaca, NY: Cornell University Press, 1998.

Rosier, Paul C. "Fond Memories and Bitter Struggles: Concerted Resistance to Environmental Injustices in Postwar Native America." In Sylvia Hood Washington, Paul C. Rosier, and Heather Goodall, eds., *Echoes from the Poisoned Well: Global Memories of Environmental Injustice.* Lanham, MD: Lexington Books, 2006.

Rudenstine, David. *The Day the Presses Stopped: A History of the Pentagon Papers Case.* Berkeley: University of California Press, 1996.

Russo, Vito. *The Celluloid Closet: Homosexuality in the Movies.* New York: Harper and Row, 1987.

Sale, Kirkpatrick. *The Green Revolution: The American Environmental Movement, 1962–92.* New York: Hill and Wang, 1993.

Sandbrook, Dominic. *Mad as Hell: The Crisis of the 1970s and the Rise of the Populist Right.* New York: Knopf, 2011.

Schaller, Michael. *Right Turn: American Life in the Reagan-Bush Era, 1980–92.* New York: Oxford University Press, 2006.

Schell, Jonathan. *The Time of Illusion.* New York: Knopf, 2006.

Schlosser, Eric. *Fast Food Nation: The Dark Side of the All-American Meal.* Boston: Houghton Mifflin, 2001.

Schor, Juliet. *The Overspent American: Why We Want What We Don't Need.* New York: Basic Books, 1998.

———. *The Overworked American: The Unexpected Decline of Leisure.* New York: Basic Books, 1991.

Schrag, Peter. *Paradise Lost: California's Experience, America's Future.* Berkeley: University of California Press, 1999.

Schulman, Bruce. *The Seventies: The Great Shift in American Culture, Society, and Politics.* New York: Da Capo, 2001.

Schulman, Bruce, and Julian Zelizer, eds. *Rightward Bound: Making America Conservative in the 1970s.* Cambridge, MA: Harvard University Press, 2008.

Schwab, Jim. *Deeper Shades of Green: The Rise of Blue-Collar and Minority Environmentalism in America.* San Francisco: Sierra Club, 1994.

———. *Raising Less Corn and More Hell: Midwestern Farmers Speak Out.* Bloomington: University of Illinois Press, 1988.

Self, Robert O. *All in the Family: The Realignment of American Democracy Since the 1960s.* New York: Hill and Wang, 2012.

———. *American Babylon: Race and the Struggle for Postwar Oakland.* Princeton: Princeton University Press, 2003.

———. "Prelude to the Tax Revolt: The Politics of the 'Tax Dollar' in Postwar California." In Kevin M. Kruse and Thomas J. Sugrue, *The New Suburban History.* Chicago: University of Chicago Press, 2006.

Shabecoff, Philip. *A Fierce Green Fire: The American Environmental Movement.* New York: Hill and Wang, 1993.

Shank, Barry. "Fears of the White Unconscious: Music, Race, and Identification in the Censorship of 'Cop Killer.'" *Radical History Review* 66 (1996): 124–45.

Sharp, Elaine B. "Culture Wars and City Politics: Local Government's Role in Social Conflict." *Urban Affairs Review* 31:6 (July 1996): 738–58.

Shaw, Randy. *Beyond the Fields: Cesar Chavez, the UFW, and the Struggle for Justice in the 21st Century.* Berkeley: University of California Press, 2010.

Shawcross, William. *Sideshow: Kissinger, Nixon, and the Destruction of Cambodia.* New York: Simon and Schuster, 1979.

Shilts, Randy. *And the Band Played On: Politics, People and the AIDS Epidemic.* New York: St. Martin's Press, 1987.

———. *The Mayor of Castro Street: The Life and Times of Harvey Milk*. New York: St. Martin's Press, 1982.

Sides, Josh. *Erotic City: Sexual Revolutions and the Making of Modern San Francisco*. New York: Oxford University Press, 2009.

———. *L.A. City Limits: African American Los Angeles from the Great Depression to the Present*. Berkeley: University of California Press, 2003.

Simon, Harry. "Municipal Regulation of the Homeless in Public Spaces." In Jim Baumohl, ed., *Homelessness in America*. Phoenix: Oryx Press, 1996.

Skocpol, Theda. "Social Provision and Civic Community: Beyond Fragmentation." In Jonathan Rieder, ed., *The Fractious Nation? Unity and Division in Contemporary American Life*. Berkeley: University of California Press, 2003.

Small, Melvin. *Antiwarriors: The Vietnam War and the Battle for America's Hearts and Minds*. Wilmington, DE: SR Books, 2002.

———. *The Presidency of Richard Nixon*. Lawrence: University Press of Kansas, 1999.

Smith, Daniel A. *Tax Crusaders and the Politics of Direct Democracy*. New York: Routledge, 1998.

Smith, Neil. "New City, New Frontier: The Lower East Side as Wild, Wild West." In Michael Sorkin, ed., *Variations on a Theme Park: The New American City and the End of Public Space*. New York: Hill and Wang, 1992.

Snow, David A., Sarah A. Soule, and Daniel M. Cress. "Identifying the Precipitants of Homeless Protest Across 17 US Cities, 1980–90." *Social Forces* 83:3 (March 2005): 1183–1210.

Solinger, Rickie. *Abortion Wars: A Half Century of Struggle, 1950–2000*. Berkeley: University of California Press, 1998.

———. *Pregnancy and Power: A Short History of Reproductive Politics in America*. New York: New York University Press, 2005.

Solomon, Norman. *Made Love, Got War: Close Encounters with America's Warfare State*. Sausalito: PoliPoint, 2007.

Staggenborg, Suzanne. *The Pro-Choice Movement: Organization and Activism in the Abortion Conflict*. New York: Oxford University Press, 1991.

Stauber, John, and Sheldon Rampton. *Toxic Sludge Is Good for You: Lies, Damn Lies and the Public Relations Industry*. Monroe, ME: Common Courage, 1995.

Stein, Judith. *Pivotal Decade: How the United States Traded Factories for Finance in the Seventies*. New Haven: Yale University Press, 2011.

Steinberg, Ted. *Down to Earth: Nature's Role in American History*. New York: Oxford University Press, 2002.

Stine, Jeffrey K. "Environmental Policy During the Carter Presidency." In Gary M. Fink and Hugh Davis Graham, eds., *The Carter Presidency: Policy Choices in the Post–New Deal Era*. Lawrence: University Press of Kansas, 1998.

Stoller, Nancy E. *Lessons from the Damned: Queers, Whores, and Junkies Respond to AIDS*. New York: Routledge, 1998.

Strub, Whitney. "Lavender, Menaced Lesbianism, Obscenity Law, and the Feminist Antipornography Movement." *Journal of Women's History* 22:2 (Summer 2010): 83–107.

———. *Perversion for Profit: The Politics of Pornography and the Rise of the New Right*. New York: Columbia University Press, 2011.

Summers, Mary. "From the Heartland to Seattle: The Family Farm Movement of the 1980s and the Legacy of Agrarian State Building." In Catherine McNicol Stock and Robert D. Johnston, *The Countryside in the Age of the Modern State: Political Histories of Rural America*. Ithaca, NY: Cornell University Press, 2001.

Surbrug, Robert. *Beyond Vietnam: The Politics of Protest in Massachusetts, 1974–90*. Amherst: University of Massachusetts Press, 2009.

Susser, Ida. *Norman Street: Poverty and Politics in an Urban Neighborhood*. New York: Oxford University Press, 1982.

Switzer, Jacqueline Vaughn. *Green Backlash: The History and Politics of Environmental Opposition in the U.S.* Boulder: Lynne Rienner, 1997.

Theoharis, Athan. *Spying on Americans: Political Surveillance from Hoover to the Huston Plan*. Philadelphia: Temple University Press, 1978.

Theoharis, Jeanne. "'I'd Rather Go to School in the South': How Boston's School Desegregation Complicates the Civil Rights Paradigm." In Jeanne Theoharis and Komozi Woodard, eds., *Freedom North: Black Freedom Struggles Outside the South, 1940–80*. New York: Palgrave, 2003.

———. "'They Told Us Our Kids Were Stupid': Ruth Batson and the Educational Movement in Boston." In Jeanne Theoharis and Komozi Woodard, eds., *Groundwork: Local Black Freedom Movements in America*. New York: New York University Press, 2005.

Troy, Gil. *Morning in America: How Ronald Reagan Invented the 1980s*. Princeton: Princeton University Press, 2005.

Tuck, Stephen, ed. "Introduction: Reconsidering the 1970s: The 1960s to a Disco Beat?" *Journal of Contemporary History* 43 (2008): 617–88.

Turner, Suzie. "Recognition of the Voting Rights of the Homeless." *Journal of Law and Politics* 3:1 (Winter 1986): 103–26.

Turner, William B. "Mirror Images: Lesbian/Gay Civil Rights in the Carter and Reagan Administrations." In John D'Emilio, William B. Turner, and Urvashi Vaid, eds., *Creating Change: Sexuality, Public Policy and Civil Rights*. New York: St. Martin's Press, 2000.

Uchitelle, Louis. *The Disposable American: Layoffs and Their Consequences*. New York: Vintage, 2007.

Valdes, Denis Nodin. "From Following the Crops to Chasing the Corporations: The Farm Labor Organizing Committee, 1967–83." In National Association for Chicano Studies, *The Chicano Struggle: Analyses of Past and Present Efforts*. Binghamton, NY: Bilingual Press, 1984.

Van Kleunen, Andrew. "The Squatters: A Chorus of Voices . . . but Is Anyone Listening?" In Janet Abu-Lughod, ed., *From Urban Village to East Village: The Battle for New York's Lower East Side*. Malden, MA: Blackwell, 1994.

Varon, Jeremy. *Bringing the War Home: The Weather Underground, the Red Army Faction, and Revolutionary Violence in the Sixties and Seventies*. Berkeley: University of California Press, 2004.

Vogel, David. *Fluctuating Fortunes: The Political Power of Business in America.* New York: Basic Books, 1989.

von Hassell, Malve. *Homesteading in New York City, 1978–93: The Divided Heart of Loisaida.* Westport, CT: Bergin and Garvey, 1996.

Wagner, David. *Checkerboard Square: Culture and Resistance in a Homeless Community.* Boulder: Westview Press, 1993.

Wagner, David, and Marcia B. Cohen. "The Power of the People: Homeless Protesters in the Aftermath of Social Movement Participation." *Social Problems* 38:4 (November 1991): 543–61.

Walker, J. Samuel. *Three Mile Island: A Nuclear Crisis in Historical Perspective.* Berkeley: University of California Press, 2004.

Wandersee, Winifred D. *On the Move: American Women in the 1970s.* Boston: Twayne, 1988.

Wasserman, Harvey. *Energy War: Reports from the Front.* Westport, CT: Lawrence Hill, 1979.

Weinreb, Linda, and Peter H. Rossi. "The American Homeless Family Shelter 'System.'" *Social Service Review* 69:1 (March 1995): 86–107.

Wells, Tom. *The War Within: America's Battle over Vietnam.* Berkeley: University of California Press, 1994.

Wellstone, Paul. *How the Rural Poor Got Power: Narrative of a Grass-Roots Organizer.* Minneapolis: University of Minnesota Press, 2003.

Wellstone, Paul, and Barry M. Casper. *Powerline: The First Battle of America's Energy War.* Minneapolis: University of Minnesota Press, 2003.

West, Guida. *The National Welfare Rights Movement: The Social Protest of Poor Women.* New York: Praeger, 1981.

Wilder, Marcy J. "The Rule of Law, the Rise of Violence, and the Role of Morality: Reframing America's Abortion Debate." In Rickie Solinger, *Abortion Wars: A Half Century of Struggle, 1950–2000.* Berkeley: University of California Press, 1998, 73–94.

Wilentz, Sean. *The Age of Reagan: A History, 1974–2008.* New York: HarperCollins, 2008.

Williams, Jean Calterone. "The Politics of Homelessness: Shelter Now and Political Protest." *Political Research Quarterly* 58:3 (September 2005): 497–509.

Williams, Rhonda Y. *The Politics of Public Housing: Black Women's Struggles Against Urban Inequality.* New York: Oxford University Press, 2004.

Wills, John. *Conservation Fallout: Nuclear Protest at Diablo Canyon.* Reno: University of Nevada Press, 2006.

Wise, David. *The American Police State: The Government Against the People.* New York: Random House, 1976.

Wright, Talmadge. *Out of Place: Homeless Mobilizations, Subcities, and Contested Landscapes.* Albany: State University of New York Press, 1997.

Yergin, Daniel. *The Prize: The Epic Quest for Oil, Money, and Power.* New York: Simon and Schuster, 1991.

Yohn, Susan. "Will the Real Conservatives Please Stand Up? Or, the Pitfalls Involved in Examining Ideological Sympathies: A Comment on Alan Brinkley's 'Problem of American Conservatism.'" *American Historical Review* 99 (April 1994): 430–37.

Zappa, Frank. *The Real Frank Zappa Book*. New York: Touchstone, 1990.

Zaretsky, Natasha. *No Direction Home: The American Family and the Fear of National Decline, 1968–80*. Chapel Hill: University of North Carolina Press, 2007.

Zelizer, Julian. *Governing America: The Revival of Political History*. Princeton: Princeton University Press, 2012.

Zisk, Betty. *Money, Media, and the Grass Roots: State Ballot Issues and the Electoral Process*. Newbury Park, CA: Sage, 1987.

Zunes, Stephen. "Seabrook: A Turning Point." *The Progressive*, September 1978, 28–31.

Acknowledgments

This may seem strange, but of the many people I need to thank for their help and inspiration—for informing this project over its long life—I'd like to start with dozens whom I mostly knew only slightly. These are the citizens of Londonderry, New Hampshire, who, in the late 1970s, gathered once a year for town and school district meetings in an elementary school gymnasium. My father, as school district moderator and assistant town moderator, pulled strings to get me a job as "mic boy" at the meetings. In the interests of democracy, the town had outfitted the gymnasium with a portable microphone system; when the moderator called on a citizen to speak, either I or the town moderator's son—this was nepotism, let's face it—would carry a handheld mic over to the speaker.

Looking back now, those town meetings seem quaint. But I learned a lot in that gymnasium that I did not appreciate at the time. I learned how moderators could deftly move a discussion along by calling on citizens they could rely on to call for a vote; I learned how tedious democracy can be; and I learned, too, that democracy can be pretty entertaining. Sometimes an audience member would challenge my father's tabulation of a hand vote and he would bet them a six-pack that he was right (I do not recall his ever losing those bets).

Of course, in southern New Hampshire at the time, most folks were Republicans, but I can recall few instances in which party affiliation mattered in those town meetings. Rather, what mattered most was how people felt personally about an issue before the town. In the late 1970s, with confrontations over the Seabrook nuclear power plant occurring to our east and the Massachusetts "tax revolt" raging to our south, citizens most often stood to ask fundamental and existential questions: How will this proposal affect me? How will it affect my children? How will it affect the future I imagine for my family, for this community?

In the early 1980s, my parents, Bill and Judy Foley, were recognized for their work on behalf of the town by being named Citizens of the Year. Only much later, after my father died and I had occasion to think about the ways, formal and informal, in which he educated me about politics, did I come to see the important influence the New England institution of the town meeting had on me.

In addition, as this book's endnotes and bibliography make clear, I am deeply indebted, too, to all of the scholars, journalists, and activists whose work has made mine possible. I stand on their broad shoulders and can only hope that this book spurs further historical research on the many less-well-known campaigns featured here.

This book is also the product of many long conversations with fellow academics and organizers, as well as with friends and family members. I am grateful especially to Jonathan Rosen, Ian Lekus, Felicia Kornbluh, Matt Daloisio, Frida Berrigan, Kurt Foley, Tony Foley, Dave McBride, Kevin Vickery, Brendan O'Malley, Tim McCarthy, John McMillian, Marc Favreau, Anthony Giacchino, Natasha Zaretsky, Erik Goldner, Michael Ferber, Harvard Sitkoff, Sandi Cooper, François Ngolet, Alice Varon, and Jeremy Varon for helping me to think about American politics in new ways. David Lichtenstein deserves thanks for getting me to think differently about pretty much everything.

Matthew Lassiter, Meg Jacobs, and Robert Self graciously shared some of their own work before it was published.

And I have been fortunate in the opportunities I have had, particularly after moving to England, to present portions of my work at uncommonly stimulating conferences and symposia where I received valuable comments and challenges, including the German Historical Institute's Accidental Armageddons conference in Washington, D.C.; the Centre for Democratic Culture's History of Political Engagement International Workshop at the University of Sheffield; the symposium on post-1960s political mobilization held at the Centre d'Études Nord-Américaines of the École des Hautes Études en Sciences Sociales in Paris; and research seminars at the New School for Social Research and the University of Cambridge.

In both New York and Sheffield, I have been lucky, too, to be surrounded by scholars with a similar interest in political engagement. At

Sheffield, I am especially grateful to Gary Rivett for his hard work in getting the Stories of Activism oral history and archive project off the ground; the meetings and workshops we have held with Sheffield activists, past and present, have influenced my thinking on this book project as well.

In the meantime, I have learned more about activism from fellow organizers with Witness Against Torture than from anyone else. Endless meetings and intense direct action confrontations will do that to you, but I am especially appreciative of the type of citizenship and humanity modeled by Matt Daloisio, Frida Berrigan, Carmen Trotta, and Jeremy Varon. I cannot imagine my life, or this project, without them.

I received generous funding in the form of research grants from the City University of New York's College of Staten Island, PSC-CUNY, and the University of Sheffield's Faculty of Arts and Humanities. And I am extremely grateful for the research fellowship from the U.K. Arts and Humanities Research Council. All of these were essential to helping me make progress on the project.

I write best in total isolation and have been incredibly fortunate to have friends and family who afforded me the quiet and space where much of this book was written: Jimmy and Carolyn Walkin, Matt and Amanda Daloisio, Pat and John Dale, and Mike Eastwood.

Many years ago, even before I finished my doctoral dissertation, Harvard Sitkoff showed me the publishing ropes and introduced me to editors. He gets all the credit for bringing me together with Thomas LeBien, Hill and Wang's former publisher, who not only signed up this book but encouraged and prodded me all the way through the writing of the first complete draft. Thomas was equal parts critic, sounding board, cheerleader, and editor, and as a result he has had as much to do with the intellectual development of this book as anyone. Most of all, in editing the unwieldy first draft, he helped me to see more clearly the significance of my own argument and evidence. I was lucky to have the project picked up by Dan Gerstle, who offered tremendously helpful advice on a subsequent draft, and Alex Star, who, over multiple drafts, pressed me to sharpen my ideas and smooth the rough edges. Alex challenged me where I needed challenging, edited the final draft with surgical precision, and got me to the finish line. Thanks to his hard work, it is a much better book. Chris Richards and Dan Gerstle helped with every other publishing task, large and small, and copy editor Emily DeHuff saved me from numerous stylistic blunders.

Along the way, the press enlisted referees Felicia Kornbluh and Jeremy Varon, both of whom provided clear-eyed, detailed, and immensely helpful feedback on the manuscript. I do not know what I would have done without their cogent, forceful critiques, though any errors of fact or interpretation that remain are mine alone.

Then there is Kathy. It seems such a feeble gesture to dedicate *Front Porch Politics* to Kathy Dale, who has lived with this project almost as long as she has lived with me. She deserves so much more. Her steady support through the thick and thin of writing this book, changing jobs, moving to another continent, and raising a family is impossible to match. And my daughters: I suppose it is possible that Emma will read this book in the next few years, though she would no doubt enjoy it more if it had a higher rock-and-roll quotient. Hattie and Ophelia, meanwhile, came into this world to find me always at work on a book on a subject they are still too young to think much about. That said, I hope this book contributes to their political education just as my father's example influenced me. Theirs will be a world that will need more, not less, political engagement.

Index

A Note About the Author

Michael Stewart Foley is the author of *Confronting the War Machine: Draft Resistance During the Vietnam War*, winner of the Scott Bills Memorial Prize from the Peace History Society. He has edited or coedited three other books and is a founding editor of *The Sixties: A Journal of History, Politics, and Culture*. A native New Englander, he has taught American history at the City University of New York and, in England, at the University of Sheffield. He is now a professor of American political culture at the University of Groningen in the Netherlands.